...ERS LIFE

MARTIAL VIRTUES
AND
MANLY ROMANITAS
IN THE EARLY
BYZANTINE EMPIRE

MICHAEL
EDWARD
STEWART

KISMET PRESS
MMXVI

ROMANITAS I

THE SOLDIER'S LIFE

Martial Virtues and Manly *Romanitas* in the
Early Byzantine Empire

Michael Edward Stewart

kısmet·press

Libera Scientia | Free Knowledge

The Soldier's Life
Martial Virtues and Manly Romanitas in the Early Byzantine Empire
by Michael Edward Stewart

Romanitas, 1
Series Editors: Tim Barnwell & N. Kıvılcım Yavuz

Published in 2016
by Kismet Press LLP
15 Queen Square, Leeds, LS2 8AJ, UK
kismet.press
kismet@kismet.press

Printed and bound by IngramSpark with acid-free paper, using a print-on-
demand model with printers in the US, EU, and Australia.

A catalogue record for this book is available from the British Library.

ISBN 978-0-9956717-0-6 (pbk)
ISBN 978-0-9956717-2-0 (hbk)
ISBN 978-0-9956717-1-3 (ebk)

For John-David, Annabelle, Sophia, and
Charlotte
Πάντα σέθεν φιλέω.

CONTENTS

PREFACE

THE TWO HUNDRED AND FIFTY YEARS FROM 380 TO 630 CE WAS a time of dramatic social and political upheaval for the Roman Empire. It is during this era that classical Rome fades away and a recognisable early medieval Christian state takes its place. By investigating the connections between images of the soldier's life and conceptions of idealised Roman masculinity found in the literature and iconography of this period, this book considers an aspect of this transformation. It seeks to answer three primary questions. First, to what degree did the supposed demilitarisation of the late Roman upper classes influence traditional codes of manly *Romanitas* that had long been related intimately to the idealisation of the soldier's life? Second, how valid are the claims made by several recent studies on late Roman/early Byzantine masculinity that suggest that social developments and the Empire's military defeats in the fourth century led to the growth of a "Christian" ideology of masculinity based partly on a rejection of the militarism and the ideals of the soldier's life? Finally, how influential and revolutionary were these theological and spiritual codes of manly conduct, and how did they adopt, as well as challenge, time-honoured notions of manly *Romanitas* based heavily on military virtues?

As is the case with most historians, my environment has influenced me. Indeed, events surrounding September 11, 2001 and the ensuing wars in Afghanistan and Iraq provided me with the original impetus for attempting to understand how a demilitarised segment of a population could embrace militarism and men's martial virtues as a type of hyper-manliness. Living in the United States in this period, I found myself bombarded on a daily basis by a myriad of visual and literary images promoting the soldier's life as the epitome of the manly life. Even more interesting, were the various ways non-soldiers both publicly admired and sought to connect themselves with the state's martial legacy and the manly identity of its soldiers. The image of a president, who had avoided fighting in Vietnam as a youth, draping himself in manly martial imagery made me ponder the ways similarly non-martial emperors from the later Roman and early Byzantine Empire, may have promoted their own martial and masculine ideology. In the highly patriotic world of post-9/11 America, the field of battle seemed to provide a realm where soldiers—who hailed largely from the less privileged classes—could establish a raw manliness superior to that of powerful executives, politicians, musicians, famous actors, and professional athletes. While appreciating the dangers of making anachronistic comparisons between a modern state like the United States and an ancient one such as the early Byzantine, it made me consider the ways and some of the reasons civilian members of a population could, not just admire, but appear to share in a "group" masculinity shaped by the exploits of a relatively small percentage of men.

List of Abbreviations

AABS	Australian Association for Byzantine Studies (*Byzantina Australiensia*)
ANCL	Ante-Nicene Christian Library
BAR	British Archaeological Reports
BCE	Before the Common Era (or BC)
BH	*Basileia Historia*
BMGS	Byzantine and Modern Greek Studies
BS	*Byzantinoslavica*
Byzantion	*Byzantion. Revue Internationale des Éstudes Byzantines*
BZ	*Byzantinische Zeitschrift*
CAH	Cambridge Ancient History
CCAA	*The Cambridge Companion to the Age of Attila*
CCAJ	*The Cambridge Companion to the Age of Justinian*
CE	Common Era (or AD)
CM	*Chronicon Minora*
CSHB	Corpus Scriptorum Historiae Byzantinae
Chron	*Chronicon*
CIC	Corpus Iuris Civilis
CSCO	Corpus Scriptorium Christianorum Orientalium
Scr. Arab.	Scriptores Arabici
Scr. Syr.	Scriptores Syri
CSEL	Corpus Scriptorum Ecclesiasticorum Latinorum
CTh	*Codex Theodosianus*
DOML	Dumbarton Oaks Medieval Library

EHR	*English Historical Review*
Epist.	*Epistulae*
Frag.	*Fragmenta*
GRBS	*Journal of Greek, Roman, and Byzantine Studies*
HA	*Historia Augusta*
HE	*Historia Ecclesiastica*
JRS	*Journal of Roman Studies*
JHS	*Journal of the History of Sexuality*
JLA	*Journal of Late Antiquity*
JTS	*Journal of Theological Studies*
JWH	*Journal of Women's History*
LCL	Loeb Classical Library
MGH	Monumenta Germaniae Historica
MGH AA	Auctores Antiquissimi
MGH SRL	Scriptores rerum Langobardicarum et Italicarum
PG	*Patrologia Cursus Completus, Series Graecea*
PL	*Patrologiae Cursus Completus, Series Latina*
PLRE	*The Prosopography of the Later Roman Empire*
SC	Sources chrétiennes
TTH	Translated Texts for Historians

LIST OF PLATES

Justinian, though Zeno and Anastasius I are possibilities as well. The horse rears over the female personification of earth, whilst Winged Victory crowns the emperor. Beneath the rider, barbarians cower. On the side panels, soldiers carry miniature victories. (p. 246)

11. The David Plates, ca. 613–30. Nine silver pieces depicting Old Testament scenes from the life of the Hebrew King David. Metropolitan Museum of Art, New York City, New York. (p. 314–315)

Acknowledgements

WHEN ONE'S PURSUIT OF ONE'S ACADEMIC DREAMS SPANS three decades and two continents, there are many people who need to be thanked when a goal is achieved. This book has truly been a collaborative effort. Similar to how reclusive Albert's Lyrebirds from my local rainforest in Mudgeeraba borrow from an eclectic array of natural and man-made sounds to hone their own unique songs, I have depended on a wealth of intellectual mentors to create my own voice. The genesis for this current project sparked from a meeting over fifteen years ago in a coffee shop in San Diego, where the chair for my prospective master's thesis, Mathew Kuefler, probed to see if I understood the rigorous road ahead. I am grateful that he accepted my rather naive "yes." Without his diligent efforts in my formative years, this book would never have been possible. A second debt is to John Moorhead, who kindly met with a freshly arrived immigrant with hopes of pursuing a dissertation in sunny south-east Queensland, Australia. His positive spirit and sharp wit kept me going during the difficult days, and his diligent perseverance and faith allowed me to find my topic.

I also owe much to Elizabeth Cobbs-Hoffman, David Christian, Michael Whitby, Lynda Garland, and Shaun Tougher for their thoughts, criticisms, and encouragement on various aspects and forms of this project during its fifteen-year genesis from MA to PhD to monograph. Conor Whately, in particular, has read more versions of this work than should ever be expected. After ten years of living in a similar textual community, I was happy to "shout" the long promised stout(s) at IMC Leeds 2015. Next, I must thank the journals who have helped hone the arguments found in this current study. Parts of chapter 2 appeared in *Masculinities: A Journal of Culture and Identity*. A version of chapter 3 appeared in *Byzantina Symmeikta* 26. A portion of chapter 7 appeared in *Porphyra* 22. Lastly, chapter 8 is based on a paper published in *Parekbolai* 4. It also contains a section found in *Cerae* 2. I appreciate the comments and criticisms of the editors and anonymous referees of these journals, which contributed to the reworked versions of these papers found in this monograph. Not to be omitted, are the editors and the two anonymous readers for Kısmet, whose constructive criticisms and suggestions led to a better final product. Stubbornly sticking to my guns in some instances, I am, of course, responsible for any errors of fact or interpretation.

On a more personal note, special tribute must be paid to my mother, Anne Marie, who always shared her love of learning and academia with a son more interested in playing with his baseball cards. Your efforts were worth it. My sisters Jodi, Stephanie, and Heidii, my father Ted and his wife Pam were always there for moral support as well. Gratitude to my eldest sister Jenny, thank you for all of your kindness over the years, gifts of precious books, and for all the unpaid editing.

But above all, none of this research would have been feasible without the love of my wife Gina and children John-David, Annabelle, Sophie, and Charlotte, who put up with numerous days and nights of a distracted daddy typing away surrounded by a mountain of texts and a sea of hastily scribbled notes. I dedicate this work to you.

I

INTRODUCTION

Rome's Masculine *Imperium*

AT THE DAWN OF THE FIFTH CENTURY, ANYONE SPENDING TIME in one of the many major or minor cities scattered throughout the Western and Eastern halves of the Roman Empire would have quite literally found themselves surrounded by visual reminders of what one modern scholar describes as Rome's masculine *imperium*.[1] Across its vast expanse, a remarkable homogeneity of material culture bound the state's disparate cities.[2] A zealous militarism certainly represented a common theme in any community's expression of its *Romanitas* (loosely defined in English as "Roman-ness").[3] Strolling along the colonnaded streets, or wandering through any of the many public areas that defined these population centres, one would have been constantly confronted by the Romans' adulation of their military

---

1 Williams, *Roman Homosexuality*, 135.
2 Jones, *Later Roman Empire*, 1015; Cameron, *Christianity and the Rhetoric of Empire*, 77–78.
3 For the centrality of military success to the ideology of the fifth-century Christian Roman Empire, see Millar, *Greek Roman Empire*, 41–42.

Plate 1. Emperor Constantine, head from a colossal statue (ca. 313–15), Palazzo dei Conservatori, Rome, Italy.

legacy and their admiration of their soldiers' martial virtues.[4] One sixth-century source tells us that the city of Rome alone had 3,785 bronze statues of emperors and famous military commanders.[5] If only on a subconscious level, the marble and bronze statuary of bellicose-looking Roman emperors and other famous military heroes—living and dead—would have communicated clearly to literates and illiterates about the integral relationship between the local community's well-being and the central leadership's militarism.[6]

In the Empire's larger cities, this militant message took on even more blatant forms. Funded by the substantial wealth of the imperial family and the upper-crust of the aristocracy, magnificent state monuments touted past and current ideologies.[7] A variety of artistic mediums expressed the idea found in one mid-sixth century Eastern Roman historian that for Rome "to triumph forever over our enemies is our birthright and ancestral privilege."[8] Intricately carved marble reliefs on exterior walls, columns, and other memorials spoke to this faith by providing the onlooker with a continuous pictorial narrative of Roman victories over "barbarian" enemies.[9] A visitor to Constantinople in the

4　At the close of the fourth century Roman monuments remained primarily pagan, see Testa, *Senatori, popolo, papi*, 105–25.

5　Pseudo-Zachariah, *HE* 10.16, ed. and trans. Brooks; ed. Greatrex and trans. Phenix and Horn.

6　For a recent study on the use and meaning of sculpture in the city of Rome, see Geiger, *The First Hall of Fame*. On the prevalence of imperial statues promoting the emperor's military function, Elsner, *Art and the Roman Viewer*, 54–57. For the illiteracy of the majority of the late Roman population, see Treadgold, *The Early Byzantine Historians*, 351.

7　Heather, *The Fall of the Roman Empire*, 38–39.

8　Agathias, *Histories* 2.12.2, ed. Keydell; trans. Frendo: συγγενὲς γὰρ ἡμῖν καὶ πάτριον κρατεῖν ἀεὶ τῶν πολεμίων.

9　Davies, "Greek and Roman Sculpture," 651–52. On the close connection in the Roman world between representational art and the written text, see Stock, *Implications of Literacy*, 81.

first two decades of the fifth century would have witnessed the construction of the magnificent column featuring the Emperor Arcadius (r. 395–408). Modelled on the Emperor Trajan's (r. 98–117) column, in thirteen windings, the monument depicted naval and terrestrial military scenes that showed the decidedly non-martial emperor "leading" his army to victory over the *magister militum* Gaïnas and his Goths.[10]

Mosaics and paintings complemented these sculpted forms, as the one in Milan described to us by the fifth-century Eastern Roman historian Priscus, featuring Roman emperors "sitting upon golden thrones surrounded by dead barbarians at their feet."[11] Victorious generals also featured in these displays of Roman military might.[12] In the middle of the sixth century, the historian Procopius described a magnificent mosaic from Justinian's palace in Constantinople commemorating the Empire's victories over the Vandals in North Africa and in Italy against the Goths:

> On either side is war and battle, and many cities being captured, some in Italy, some in Libya; and the Emperor Justinian is winning victories through his General Belisarius, and the General is returning to the Emperor, with his whole army intact, and he gives him spoils, both kings and kingdoms and all things that are most prized among men. In the centre stand the Emperor and the Empress Theodora, both seeming to rejoice and to celebrate

10 *Chron. Paschale*, 579.15–18, trans. Whitby and Whitby. For an excellent account of these columns from the second to the fifth centuries, see Beckmann, *Column of Marcus Aurelius*.

11 Priscus, *frag.* 22.3, ed. and trans. Blockley: τοὺς μὲν Ῥωμαίων βασιλεῖς ἐπὶ χρυσῶν θρόνων καθημένους Σκύθας δὲ ἀνηρημένους.

12 In the West, for example, the Roman senate dedicated a bronze statue to the Roman general Aëtius (ca. 391–454) for his military victories, describing the general as the "guarantor of [senatorial] liberties," quoted and trans. in Sivan, *Galla Placidia*, 146.

victories over both the King of the Vandals and the King of the Goths, who approach them as prisoners of war to be led into bondage.[13]

Commissioning these visual monuments for public consumption represented one of the first steps an emperor took after a military triumph.[14] Such pictorial visions of Rome's martial prowess served a calculated purpose. Foreign embassies headed for an audience with the emperor in Constantinople followed a path dominated by such martial iconography.[15] Dining in the imperial palace would have offered these foreign diplomats little respite from these militarised visuals; the imperial dishware could be decorated with vivid scenes depicting an emperor's triumphs over the Empire's cowering enemies,[16] imagery that none too subtly highlighted to the foreign envoys the early Byzantine's cultural, martial, and, indeed, masculine supremacy.[17]

Even the coins that one carried on their person to perform the simplest of transactions spoke to the Romans' sense of

13 Procopius, *Buildings* 1.10.16–20, ed. Haury; trans. Dewing: ἐφ'ἑκάτερα μὲν πόλεμός τέ ἐστι καὶ μάχη, καὶ ἀλίσκονται πόλεις παμπληθεῖς, πῇ μὲν Ἰταλίας, πῇ δὲ Λιβύης· καὶ νικᾷ μὲν βασιλεὺς Ἰουστινιανὸς ὑπὸ στρατηγοῦντι Βελισαρίῳ, ἐπάνεισι δὲ παρὰ τὸν βασιλέα, τὸ στράτευμα ἔχων ἀκραιφνὲς ὅλον ὁ στρατηγός, καὶ δίδωσιν αὐτῷ λάφυρα βασιλεῖςτε καὶ βασιλείας, καὶ πάντα τὰ ἐν ἀνθρώποις ἐξαίσια. Κατὰ δὲ τὸ μέσον ἑστᾶσιν ὅ τε βασιλεὺς καὶ ἡ βασιλὶς Θεοδώρα, ἐοικότες ἄμφω γεγηθόσι τε καὶ νικητήρια ἑορτάζουσιν ἐπί τε τῷ Βανδίλων καὶ Γότθων βασιλεῖ, δορυαλώτοις τε καὶ ἀγωγίμοις παρ' αὐτοὺς ἥκουσι.

14 Herodian, *BH* 3.9.12, trans. Whittaker: τούτων δὲ αυτῷ δεξιῶς καὶ ὑπὲρ πᾶσαν εχὴν προχωρησάντων ἐπέστειλε τῇ τε συγκλήτῳ καὶ τῷ δήμῳ, τὰς τε πράξεις μεγαληγορῶν, τὰς μάχας τε καὶ τὰς νίκας δημοσίαις ἀνέθηκε γραφαῖς.

15 On these visual power displays by the Romans and Sasanian Persians as an essential aspect of the two states' power relationship, Canepa, *Two Eyes*, 130–41.

16 Corippus, *In laudem Iustini Augusti minoris* 3.110–25, ed. and trans. Cameron.

17 Canepa, *Two Eyes*, 185.

superiority over their foes, and correspondingly offered a means to demonstrate the integral link between the manly valour of the emperor and his soldiers in the establishment and maintenance of this dominion. On the obverse of a coin a fearsome headshot of the emperor regularly in military garb served as a customary design, while on the reverse, a favourite motif in the later Empire was the representation of the emperor or his soldiers armed to the hilt standing over recoiling barbarian captives with captions like: "The glory of the Romans" (Gloria Romanorum), or "The return of happy times" (Fel Temp Reparatio).[18] Behind all of this imagery, one observes a long-held Graeco-Roman conviction that history represented a process whereby the manly conquered the unmanly (plates 3, 4, and 10).[19]

Such assertions represent more than just the anachronistic whims of modern scholars striving to uncover ancient masculinities. Another Eastern Roman historian, writing in the early years of the fifth century, informs us that imperial image-makers created these art forms with the express intent of impressing upon their visual audience "the *andreia* [manliness, courage] of the emperor and the might of his soldiers."[20]

Christian iconography was not immune to these militant themes. In early fifth-century Rome, a mural depicted the hand of God smiting the Empire's enemies.[21] The basilicas sprouting up on Rome's outskirts advertised the militant Christianity of their

18 An excellent introduction and catalogue of imperial coinage issued from 27 BCE to 498 CE is found in Van Meter, *Handbook of Roman Imperial Coins*.

19 Kuefler, *Manly Eunuch*, 49.

20 Eunapius, *frag.* 68, ed and trans. Blockley. I have changed Blockley's "courage" for ἀνδρείον to "manliness": ἀνδρείαν μὲν γὰρ βασιλέως ἢ ῥώμην στρατιωτῶν.

21 Eunapius, *frag.* 68. Despite disapproving of this Christian message, Eunapius recorded the inscriptions on the mural: θεοῦ χεὶρ ἐλαύνουσα τοὺς βαρβάρους [...] βάρβαροι τὸν θεὸν φεύγοντες. The *dextera Dei* (hand of God) appearing from a cloud to drive off the barbarians iconography also appeared around the same time on coins of the Eastern empress Aelia Eudoxia (r. 395–404).

founder, the Emperor Constantine I (r. 306–37), functioning as much as memorials to the first Christian emperor's family and his triumphs over his pagan rivals as places of worship. Consecrated in 324, Constantine had symbolically constructed the Lateran basilica "over the barracks of the crack troops of Maxentius, the rival Constantine had defeated in 312."[22] In the heart of the city, the emperor erected a colossal statue of himself clasping "his Christian war standard emblazoned with a Christian monogram,"[23] while an inscription on its base, declared: "by this salutary sign, the true proof of bravery, I saved and delivered your city from the yoke of the tyrant; and moreover I freed and restored to their ancient fame and splendour both the senate and the people of the Romans" (plate 1).[24]

In a centralised governmental system like that found in the Later Roman/early Byzantine Empire, such imperial propaganda provided the emperors and their backers with a powerful tool to publicise their authority and manipulate popular opinion across the expanse of their territories.[25] The classically educated elites, who represented an essential audience for these media campaigns, would have understood the social significance of the ideology, and in particular, the militaristic symbolism intrinsic to these art forms. Though living in increasingly independent halves of the Empire, these men, to borrow the words of one modern

For a discussion of the Jewish and Christian influences on this motif, see MacIsaac, "The Hand of God," 322–28.

22 Brown, *Through the Eye of a Needle*, 242–44.

23 Odahl, "The Christian Basilicas of Constantinian Rome," 3–5.

24 This is a Greek translation of the original Latin inscription, Eusebius, *HE* 9.9.11, trans. Lake and Oulton: τούτῳ τῷ σωτηριώδει σημείῳ, τῷ ἀληθεῖ ἐλέγχῳ τῆς ἀνδρείας τὴν πόλιν ὑμῶν ἀπὸ ζυγοῦ τοῦ τυράννου διασωθεῖσαν ἠλευθέρωσα, ἔτι μὴν καὶ τὴν σύγκλητον καὶ τὸν δῆμον Ῥωμαίων τῇ ἀρχαίᾳ ἐπιφανείᾳ καὶ λαμπρότητι ἐλευθερώσας ἀποκατέστησα. For the controversy surrounding the accuracy of Eusebius' highlighting of the Christian-martial iconography, see Barnes, *Constantine and Eusebius*, 46, n. 18.

25 Heather and Moncur, *Philosophy and Empire*, 35–37.

scholar, identified "with the name of Rome and Roman traditions completely."[26] Raised in educational systems based on a steady diet of classical Latin authors, such as Sallust, Seneca the younger, and Vergil in the West and Greek authors like Homer, Herodotus, and Thucydides in the East, the literate classes in both halves of the Empire remained intimately aware of the time-honoured idealisation of the military ethic as an essential aspect of both manly *Romanitas* and Rome's right to *imperium*.[27]

This book explores this androcentric and bellicose world. It contends that in many of the visual and literary sources from the fourth to the seventh centuries, conceptualisations of the soldier's life and the ideal manly life were often the same. By taking this stance, the book questions the view found in recent approaches on late Roman and early Byzantine masculinity that suggest a Christian ideal of manliness based on extreme ascetic virtues and pacifism had superseded militarism and courage as the dominant component of hegemonic masculine ideology. Although the study does not reject the relevance of Christian non-martial constructions of masculinity for helping one understand early Byzantine society and its diverse representations of manly *Romanitas*, it seeks to balance these present studies' heavy emphasis on Christian "rigorist" writers with the more customary attitudes we find in the secular and more moderate religious texts, praising military virtues as an essential aspect of Byzantine manliness. To be sure, in a world where the religious and the secular intermingled, Byzantines could be both religious-spiritual and militaristic, sometimes simultaneously. Far from rejecting classical martial values, Christian masculine ideology regularly

26 Long, *Claudian's In Eutropium*, 217.

27 For the Byzantine elites' familiarity with these classical sources, see Treadgold, *Early Byzantine Historians*, 1–2, 368–69, 372–75. As Treadgold points out, we have more surviving Byzantine manuscripts of Thucydides' history (97)—a good guide to ancient popularity—than the most popular early Byzantine classicising historian, Procopius' *Wars* (54), or Greek versions of Eusebius' *Ecclesiastical History* (24).

embraced the secular-military ideal. Certainly, the connection between martial virtues and "true" manliness remained a potent cultural force in the early Byzantine Empire. Indeed, the reader of this work will find that the "manliness of war" is on display in much of the surviving early Byzantine literature, secular and religious.

The period examined in this study extends roughly from the close of the fourth century to the opening of the seventh century; these two termini, however, are only approximate. Though it relies primarily on Greek writers from the Eastern Empire, at times it has been essential to consult Latin sources from the Western half of the Empire. To understand fully larger social and political trends in the early Byzantine Empire it is necessary to explore developments and writers from both earlier periods of Roman history, and Eastern and Western perspectives.

A larger topic such as mine that consults a variety of authors across a wide range of literary genres creates certain challenges. Any historian attempting to understand the "larger" picture recognises that there will be gaps in their scholarship, and places for further research. Nevertheless, as I argue in this study, the narrower genre-based approach favoured by many gender historians has proven flawed. The tendency by some to focus on a limited number of genres and/or a smaller sample of writers has led to an inchoate vision of early Byzantine masculinity. By balancing diachronic discussions on larger societal shifts and continuities with more intimate vignettes from individual ancient writers from the close of the fourth century to the rise of militant Islam in the seventh century, I strive to provide both a macro and a micro outlook of early Byzantine masculinity.

Chapter 2 investigates how current historians formulate and use masculinity as a tool of historical inquiry. Offering a brief summary of the growth of gender studies in the past forty years, it delves into some of the ongoing debates surrounding masculinity as a legitimate means for understanding ancient cultures such as Rome and Byzantium. Chapter 3 focuses on the persistent relevance of martial virtues in late Roman conceptualisations and representations of heroic manliness. The chapter explores the close association between the soldier's life and Roman concepts of manliness from the Republic to the later Empire across a range of literary and visual sources. Chapter 4 switches the attention to the seeming paradox between the images of ideal martial manliness disseminated by the fifth-century Roman emperors and their supporters, and the reality of the increasing demilitarisation of a segment of the Roman leadership. The chapter looks to understand how the declining military role of the emperor after Theodosius I's death in 395 influenced literary representations of exemplary leadership that had long depended on the intimate connections between an emperor's manly military qualities and the Empire's prosperity. I pay particular attention to late fourth- and early fifth-century portrayals of the Emperor Julian's (r. 361–63) life and short reign. Chapter 5's purpose is twofold. First, it examines the development and rise of Christian heroes, the martyr, the holy man, and the bishop that both challenged and adopted traditional codes of Roman masculinity. Second, it explores the innate paradox of a religion that readily paired irenic and militaristic ideologies. It shows how and why a religion that the older scholarly consensus considered pacifist and peaceful could simultaneously embrace violence and war. Chapter 6 uses the reign of Theodosius II as a framework in order to challenge the dominant modern view that supposes that the fifth century had witnessed a major shift away from martial virtues as a critical component of imperial propaganda and self-definition. The chapter pays particular attention to the nuanced ways martial and non-martial ideology shaped codes of leadership in the Western and Eastern imperial regimes. It suggests that one finds an imperial ideology increasingly interweaving classical and Christian ideologies. So where secular sources continued to portray military victories as largely the result of good planning and Roman soldiers' manly virtues, more theological and spiritual Christian texts naturally emphasised the religious aspects of warfare, and drawing heavily on Old Testament ideas and language, sought to establish the emperor as a military leader chosen by God.

By moving into the second half of the fifth century and considering the reigns of two soldier-emperors, Leo I and Anthemius, chapter 7 builds on the arguments from the previous chapter. Using these two regimes as a pivot, I seek to uncover how these two soldier-emperors in East and West Rome shaped and defined their martial *Romanitas* as a means of highlighting their right to rule and as a way to overcome their non-Roman rivals, Aspar and Ricimer. Chapter 8 concentrates on one early Byzantine historian, Procopius, and discusses the ways he utilised the field of battle to not only relate Justinian's military campaigns, but to comment on the role that courage, manliness, and men's virtues played in determining events. Chapter 9 concludes the study, by looking at how the increasing focus on religious ideology as an aspect of imperial propaganda during the reign of the Emperor Heraclius (r. 610–41) influenced seventh-century ideals of masculinity. It delves into these messages for hints of continuity and change in cultural codes of masculinity and self-identity during this transformative era of Byzantine history.

Terminology

First, some comments on the terminology used in this monograph. I employ the terms "Eastern Roman Empire" and "early Byzantine Empire" interchangeably to describe what the early Byzantines thought of still as simply the "Roman Empire."[28] The majority of early Byzantines certainly saw themselves as "Romans" living in their own God-protected Roman state.[29] In the period covered in this study, the early Byzantine Empire could be described, though not exclusively, in Latin as *res publica Romana*,

---

28 Although scholars continue to debate the specifics, few dispute the early Byzantine's Roman identity. Anthony Kaldellis (*Hellenism in Byzantium*, 45–47) has argued forcefully that the Byzantines should be considered the nation state of the Romans. Some have advocated for the superficiality of this Roman identity, see e.g., Pohl, "Introduction," 1–23.

29 Dagron, *Empereur et prêtre*, 142.

imperium Romanum, regnum Romanum, and in Greek as γῆν τὴν Ῥωμαίων, τὰ Ῥωμαϊκά, Ῥωμαϊκή ἀρχῆς, and Ῥωμαίων πολιτεία. At times, I use "later Roman Empire" to describe events in the Western and Eastern halves of the Empire in the third, fourth, and the early part of the fifth centuries, before division created what has recently been described as "twin" Empires.[30] Indeed, by the second half of the fifth century, intellectuals such as the Eastern Roman diplomat and historian Priscus increasingly differentiated "the Eastern Romans" (οἱ ἑῷοι Ῥωμαῖοι) from the "the Western Romans" (οἱ ἑσπέριοι Ῥωμαῖοι).[31] Nonetheless, despite their Roman self-identification, the label "Byzantine" remains useful for the modern historian wanting to differentiate the largely Greek-speaking Christian Roman Empire ruled from Constantinople from its Latin-speaking pagan predecessor based in Rome.[32]

"Early Byzantine historians" is used as the preferred expression to describe the secular and the ecclesiastical historians as a group, rather than the "late antique" or "late classical" for secular writers like Ammianus, Priscus, Procopius, and Agathias preferred by some recent publications.[33] I made this choice out of a desire for better precision, since "late antiquity" can now extend from the third to the ninth centuries and encompass lands and cultures outside the Roman Empire. The expression "early Byzantine" also reflects the Eastern origins of the majority of the literary sources

---

30 Millar, *Greek Roman Empire*, 3.

31 E.g., Priscus, *frag.* 39.

32 For some lucid discussions of the current scholarly controversies surrounding the use of the terms "Byzantium" and "empire," see Cameron, *Byzantine Matters*, 26–45; Kaldellis, *Byzantine Republic*, 19–31. To simplify their views, while both scholars accept the modern use of the term "Byzantium," Kaldellis argues that we should see it as primarily Roman and a republic, not an empire, while Cameron contends that it is better seen as an empire (albeit one that changed immensely over its thousand-year history), which amalgamated Christian, Hellenistic, and Roman themes.

33 For the use of the category "late classical historians" see, e.g., Rohrbacher, *Historians of Late Antiquity*.

consulted, as well as the growing influence of Christianity on these intellectuals, Christian and non-Christian. The study avoids "late classical" because of its links with an older historiographical tradition discussed later in this chapter. "Secular history" is a term also used at times. Secular history, a subcategory of the classicising model, was a by-product of the Empire's fourth-century Christianisation, and I use this expression as a means to differentiate this literary genre from church history and other Christian literary forms;[34] the writers in this genre could be either Christian or non-Christian.[35]

Romanitas, the concept used in the title of this book, has been described aptly as not the shared biological traits of "a specific group," but the fluid characteristics "that made a man Roman, made him an appropriate husband, father, general, and politician, and which distinguished him from a woman, child, barbarian or slave."[36] Moreover, different ethnic groups and regional identities could appropriate and shape "the form in which *Romanitas* was expressed in different places and in different circumstances."[37] In other words, *Romanitas* represents a flexible concept that over time meant distinct things to diverse peoples.[38]

Admittedly, as Guy Halsall notes, ancient references to *Romanitas* are not common. It appears more frequently in the works of current academics than in the body of Roman sources

34 On the expression "secular history," see Evans, *Procopius*, 40.

35 Ammianus, Eunapius, Olympiodorus, and Zosimus were non-Christians, while Candidus, Malchus, Eustathius, Procopius, Agathias, and Theophylact were likely Christians. Priscus' religious affiliation is unclear. Against this current consensus, Kaldellis argues that Procopius and Agathias were both non-Christians, see Kaldellis, "Things Are Not What They Are," 295–300; Kaldellis, *Procopius of Caesarea*.

36 Merrills and Miles, *Vandals*, 88.

37 Merrills and Miles, *Vandals*, 88–89.

38 Ioannis Stouraitis ("Roman Identity in Byzantium," 55–57) chooses to believe that Roman identity represented primarily an ideal of the ruling elite.

that survive.[39] The first surviving evidence of its use comes from an early third-century harangue, where the Christian writer Tertullian ridiculed the men of Carthage for aping Roman culture.[40] Yet, in spite of its rarity, *Romanitas* captures usefully the ancient Romans' sense of "us" versus "them" and, consequently, provides a valuable tool for one hoping to recover the nuanced ways individuals regarded themselves and others as Romans/non-Romans and manly/unmanly men. It also captures the Romans' androcentrism. Following recent scholarship's lead, I use the further expression "manly *Romanitas*" as a means to convey the intimate relationship between *Romanitas* and existing codes of idealised masculinity.[41]

Although there is no precise counterpart in ancient Greek to *Romanitas*, the adverb Ῥωμαϊκῶς, with its meaning "in the Roman fashion," captures the Latin concept's essence.[42] Moreover, although constantly evolving, vital facets of Byzantine self-identity remained linked to the meanings captured by *Romanitas*. As Ionnas Smarnakis comments:

> The traditional Byzantine concept of the term "Roman," which defined their own God-protected empire and emphasized the Roman and Christian roots of the imperial ideology, underwent several changes through the centuries. Besides its strong political content, *romanitas* eventually came to encompass a vast body of different, changing, and

39 Halsall, "Barbarian Invasions," 40.
40 Tertullian, *De pallio* 4.1, quoted and trans in McKechnie, "Tertullian's *De Pallio* and Life in Roman Carthage," 57–58: "Why at this time, if Romanness is salvation for everything, are you still not taking honourable attitudes towards the Greeks?" (quid nunc, si est Romanitas omni salus, nec honestis tamen modis ad Graios estis?).
41 Merrills and Miles, *The Vandals*, 88–90.
42 For the early Byzantines' emphasis on the religious and political aspects of *Romanitas*, see Rapp, "Hellenic Identity," 127–47.

often overlapping meanings: it stressed the contrast between "civilized" Romans and "uncivilized" barbarians; it declared a political identification with the Roman state; and finally, it referred to an ethnic group of people who believed that they had a common origin, spoke the same Greek language and followed the Christian Orthodox religion.[43]

When speaking of a "Christian or classical ideology" of masculinity, I do not suggest that the Christian, non-Christian, and/or secular writers analysed in this study held unitary views of these two categories or represented homogenous groups; this study distinguishes between the opinions and ideas of individual writers. For instance, on an issue like Christian attitudes towards military service, several voices coexisted; strict theologians who preached a stringently pacifist approach must be balanced with other Christian theologians who believed in the compatibility of religious piety and military duty. I therefore avoid using expressions such as "the church and/or Christians believed" or "non-Christians or pagans believed." With that said, one might speak reasonably of a classical notion of masculinity, which arose from the interlinked literary and cultural customs of Greece and Rome, and of a Christian ideology of masculinity, that was gradually articulated from the first to the sixth centuries.[44] This is not to reject overlap between the two systems. Indeed, the commonalities between the two ideologies far outnumber the diversities. This close association should not surprise since Christianity emerged within the shadows of the pagan Empire. When formulating their multifaceted discourses on masculinity, New Testament authors had frequently tapped into existing pagan Graeco-Roman masculine traditions.[45] As we shall discover, this symbiotic relationship between the two ideologies only grew

43 Smarnakis, "Rethinking Roman Identity after the Fall (1453)," 212–13.
44 Kuefler, *Manly Eunuch*, 10.
45 Conway, *Behold the Man*, 177–86.

more pronounced after the Emperor Constantine's conversion to Christianity in 312.

As I use them, the terms "pagan" and "non-Christian," like many religious terms, are somewhat problematic. Few individuals labelled in the ancient and the modern literature as pagans would have identified with this description. To attack their opponents, Christian writers used "pagan" (paganus) largely as a pejorative term. As a category for religious identification, in Latin and in contemporary English, it remains somewhat vague. Ancient Christians used this term, in fact, to describe those who practised one of the myriad of ancient religions found in the late antique Eastern Mediterranean region, someone with little or no religious beliefs, or even in some situations, Christians whom they perceived to be marginal or unorthodox. The Greek equivalent to pagan, "Hellene" (Ἕλληνες), is equally imprecise, in that it could describe one's religion, adherence to Greek philosophy, language, or culture, or someone from the geographical region of mainland Greece.[46] Non-Christian represents a much less loaded term than pagan, but I use it when the exact religion of the individual is unknown. When we know a great deal about the type of non-Christian religion that is being practised, I provide a more precise identity.[47]

"Manliness" and "courage" can be difficult values to distinguish from one another in ancient Greek. Because my goal is to reproduce faithfully early Byzantine masculine ideology, I try to take care when rendering the meaning of the various Greek words that are translated commonly into English simply as "bravery" and "courage." When possible, terms like ἀλκή, θάρσος, μένος, προθῡμία, and τόλμα are given their more precise meanings. This precision is important because a word such as θάρσος or θράσος, which scholars translate commonly as "courage" or "bravery," is sometimes better translated into English as "rashness." Such

---

46 Kaldellis, *Hellenism in Byzantium*, 184.

47 For the problematic nature of the recently fashionable term "polytheist," see Cameron, *Last Pagans of Rome*, 25–32.

exactness is particularly important for this investigation since "rashness" could be perceived by Greek and early Byzantine writers as a quality of an "unmanly" man. Moreover, one of the primary terms for Graeco-Roman conceptualisations of manhood, ἀνδρεία, can mean either "manliness" or "courage," depending on the context used by the ancient author.

In Latin, *virtus*, linked etymologically to the Latin term for man, *vir*, could also be understood as "manliness." Craig Williams posits that *virtus*, which "can be often translated as 'valour' or even 'virtue' [...] is always implicitly gendered," concluding, "*Virtus* is the ideal of masculine behaviour that all men ought to embody, that some women have the good fortune of attaining, and that men derided as effeminate conspicuously fail to achieve." When providing or amending a translation, I will always try to adhere to the more specific meaning, though, at times, my choice must remain a personal preference.[48] It is important, however, that even when "courage" seems the preferred translation for ἀνδρεία that one keeps the conceptualisation of "manliness" in mind.[49]

When evaluating early Byzantine writers' masculine language I stick primarily to terminology linked to the Greek root for "man" (ἀνήρ) in the sense of adult male, rather than human being or for words with accepted gendered meanings.[50] For example, I look for terms or their cognates that in ancient Greek describe typical masculine traits, such as "manliness and courage" (ἀνδρεία), "masculine, manly, strong" (ἄρρην), "manly virtue" (ἀνδραγαθία), "strength or steadfastness" (ἀνδρικός). Adding an alpha prefix (α), meaning "not," to ἀνήρ creates "negative" terminology, such as "cowardice or unmanliness" (ἀνανδρία). Of course, I recognise that these terms are not always linked specifically to one's anatomical sex. My account contains "manly women" and "effeminate men." Yet, I will argue that when an early Byzantine

48 Full discussion in Williams, *Roman Homosexuality*, 127; Williams, *Roman Homosexuality*, 2nd ed., 139.
49 For this necessity, see Cohen, "High Cost of *andreia* at Athens," 145.
50 The same method applies for "feminine" terminology.

described a man as "womanish" it served to point out a defect in his character; on the other hand, when a woman was portrayed as "manly," or she put on the "masculine temper," it functioned commonly as a compliment.[51]

As noted above, Greek vocabulary describing manliness and unmanliness was not limited to words linked to the ἀνήρ root. An entire cache of terms displays the gendered relationship between ideal and non-ideal behaviour. Some words clearly have gendered functions. The positive connotations of the "toughness" (ἀσφαλής) or "steadfastness" (βέβαιος) of men may be contrasted with the negative associations given to the terms describing the "softness" (μᾰλᾰκία), and the "delicateness" (τρῠφή) of women. When men displayed μᾰλᾰκία, τρῠφή, or their cognates, these words became terms to describe weak or effeminate men. A lack of firmness or steadfastness also created unmanly men. Similar contrasts occur in Latin where masculine men display *fortitudo* (strength) whereas effeminate men and women display *mollitia* (softness).[52]

Translations and Transliteration

This study relies on a combination of my own and existing translations. References to the edition and translator are provided in the footnote when a translation is used for the first time, but not in subsequent references unless a different edition or translation is used. I will always note when either I alter certain vocabulary within a translation or when the rendition of passages or words from Latin or Greek into English is my own. However, when I modernise English words or idioms found in some of the older translations, no notation will be made. It is always problematic to utilise Greek words within English translations that regularly

51 See, e.g., Procopius, *Wars* 5.2.3–4: τῆς δὲ φύσεως ἐς ἄγαν τὸ ἀρρενωπὸν ἐνδεικνυμένη.

52 For a discussion on these gendered associations in Latin, see Kuefler, *Manly Eunuch*, 21–22.

rely on providing their readers with "sense" rather than following the original syntax. A number of times in the study, I altered translations to reflect more accurately the Greek syntax. It was a personal choice to largely leave terms in their original cases within the translations, rather than provide the nominatives.

Finally, even with the gradual move towards Greek name-spellings in recent scholarship, I have adopted the Latin name-spellings familiar to a more general reading audience. This means, for example, that I have used "Belisarius" instead of "Belisarios" and "Priscus," and not "Priskos."

II
The Study of Men as a Gender

I HAVE CHOSEN MASCULINITY AS A MEANS TO EXPLORE SOCIAL changes in the early Byzantine world purposely. In the historiographical tradition, one's gender remained firmly rooted in biology; "one was born man or woman."[1] Scholars long regarded the borders between man and woman as secure and impenetrable. In the past forty years, this paradigm has changed, however. Scholarship has shown the susceptibility of notions like gender to various interpretations and instability.[2] Hence, the cultural environment that one grows up in plays a fundamental role in shaping one's perception of concepts such as masculinity.[3]

The study of men as a gender developed in the wake of advances made in women's studies in the past fifty years. Linked indelibly with the social upheaval of this time, few topics in recent academia have gained as much focus or generated as much enmity. Gender studies emerged from the women's movement of the 1960s–80s. Reacting to the dominance of men in historical writing, these works aimed initially to provide women a place in the evaluation

1 Pohl, "Gender and Ethnicity in the Early Middle Ages," 23.
2 Searle, *Construction of Social Reality*, 41–45.
3 Ruse, *Homosexuality*; Stein, *The Mismeasure of Desire*.

of the past.[4] Scholarship in this area suggested that the degraded social role that women played in much of history remained intimately connected with the idealisation of the "universalised masculine." Where the masculine was considered essential and perfect, the feminine was perceived to be insignificant and flawed.[5]

Somewhat ironically, building on the methods of these feminist scholars, researchers began exploring conceptualisations of masculinity throughout history. Several of these studies noted that women represent only one of many groups that have been marginalised in the historical record. Ethnic minorities, slaves, and members of the lower classes have habitually been treated as the "equivalent to women because they were subordinated men."[6] Even though modern academics such as the philosopher Judith Butler appreciate that men and women seldom make up homogeneous social groups, she submits that "the feminine is always the outside and the outside is always feminine."[7]

Despite critiques of his work by some feminist scholars and classicists, Michel Foucault's innovative research remains fundamental for studies considering masculinity in the ancient Greek and Roman world.[8] Foucault's proposition that concepts such as sexuality both change over time and remain intimately connected with the symbiotic power relationships amongst all members of a society has influenced a generation of scholars.[9] Additionally, his work showed that the old contrast of the sexually promiscuous pagan versus the chaste and "repressed" Christian was deeply flawed.[10] He also pointed out that Greek and Roman

4 Smith, "Introduction," 1–5.
5 Kuefler, *Manly Eunuch*, 2–3.
6 Williams, *Roman Homosexuality*, 135.
7 Butler, *Bodies That Matter*, 48. For the example of African-American men, see Harris, "Honor: Emasculation and Empowerment."
8 An excellent discussion on the continuing influence of Foucault's paradigms on modern scholarship is found in Behr, *Asceticism*, 4–15.
9 Foucault, *Use of Pleasure*, 25–32.
10 Foucault, *Use of Pleasure*, 32.

forms of sexuality differed from current concepts; Foucault argued that sexual orientation was an invention of nineteenth-century Western Europeans.[11] In a viewpoint particularly embraced by this study, for Foucault, masculine ideology formed the core of Greek and Roman morality. These systems, he explained, represented "an elaboration of masculine conduct carried out from the viewpoint of men in order to give form to *their* behaviour."[12]

Rhetoric and Reality

Feminist scholars who continue to criticise the methodology of Foucault and/or the study of masculinity in general seem uncomfortable embracing a field that once more places men at the forefront of historical inquiry.[13] Accounts of aristocratic men certainly dominate the historical record. So then how and, perhaps more importantly, why study men as a gender? Unlike the obstacles that stand in the way of scholars trying to find a "historical voice" for marginalised groups like women or the lower classes, the sources for the analysis of masculine ideologies are readily available. This very abundance makes finding "real" men in history problematic. When one looks at the literary portraits of men found in Roman and early Byzantine periods, quite often only stylised images emerge. This point is particularly relevant when examining the iconography and historiography of the Eastern Roman Empire. Similar to present-day celluloid action heroes and villains, the men depicted in these accounts frequently display rhetorical notions of ideal and non-ideal masculine conduct, producing men who often seem more like cartoon characters than genuine human beings. Nonetheless, heroism itself functions as a hyper-masculinity. Unquestionably,

---

11 Foucault, *An Introduction*, 43. For Foucault's ideas on the modern construction of homosexuality and the reaction of recent gender scholars to his work, see Kuefler, *The Boswell Thesis*, 9–11.

12 Foucault, *Use of Pleasure*, 22–23.

13 Conway, *Behold the Man*, 9

much of what one finds in the texts explored in this study provides primarily a "public" view of codes of ideal manly conduct. Yet, just as the 1980s' action hero Rambo tells one about American notions of masculinity, foreigners, and the Reagan era's political environment itself, the heroes, villains, and barbarians found in the early Byzantine literature divulge significant aspects of the Byzantine value system. This popularity does not mean that everyone in the Eastern Roman Empire adhered to the models of manliness and unmanliness found in these works. Still, similar to the themes of hyper-masculinity and unmanliness seen in modern movies, these writings appealed to a diverse audience, and therefore reflect the values—of not only the Empire's hierarchy, but also large segments of its population. Moreover, although classicising histories were published in relatively small quantities for a select audience, it was customary to have sections of these writings recited in front of live audiences, suggesting that even illiterates may have been familiar with these works.[14]

Of course, dissonances existed between men's expected social roles and the actual personalities of early Byzantine men. In the real world, men consistently failed to live up to the stringent masculine ideal articulated in the literary and visual sources of the day. The nature of the source material means that the private world of early Byzantine men remains mostly hidden. In other words, the social category of "man" differed from the personal identities of many Eastern Roman men. Much like the case of their female counterparts, the cultural construction of "man" was often insufficient to contain individual "men."[15]

Several other challenges confront the researcher attempting to separate the "real man" from the "constructed" one. Perhaps the most critical question is how does one define or study a topic as seemingly ambiguous as masculinity? By masculinity, scholars

---

14 Blockley, *Classicising Historians*, 92–94; Evans, *Procopius*, 37. Cf. the more pessimistic views found in Rapp, "Hellenic Identity," 129.

15 Kuefler, *Manly Eunuch*, 2. For an excellent example of this methodology in women's history, see Schulenburg, *Forgetful of Their Sex*.

do not refer generally to the anatomical or biological features of the male body, which remain relatively constant among a range of societies and over time, but to the variety of meanings that these cultures place or have placed on persons with a male body. Therefore, a man may display "feminine" traits, yet remain biologically male. The "feminine" trait itself, however, may be transient and open to a wide range of interpretations. Behaviours that one culture, group, or era labels as "masculine" might be called "womanly," "unmanly," or "effeminate" (all three of these expressions mean essentially the same thing) in another society, group, or period.[16] For instance, excessive sexual encounters with women, which may be regarded as a sign of manliness in modern-day Western culture, commonly indicated "unmanliness" in the Roman world.[17]

Scholars describe this process as the social construction of gender. Defined simply, social construction means that one's knowledge of objects or ideas develops by interacting with the surrounding social order. Consequently, the cultural environment in which one grows up plays a fundamental role in shaping one's perception of a flexible notion such as masculinity. As John Searle argues, a twenty-dollar note is by its nature a worthless piece of paper; it holds no intrinsic value except the worth a culture places upon it. It obtains value (cultural meaning) because people communally experience money as having worth, and so come to attach value to it.[18] Researchers apply this same argument to subjective constructions like masculinity and ethnicity. This does not mean that all human characteristics are socially constructed. This point is particularly true of sexual orientation, which may be non-voluntary and biologically orientated; nonetheless, how

16 Montserrat, "Reading Gender," 153–58.
17 Williams, *Roman Homosexuality*, 143–44.
18 Searle, *Construction of Social Reality*, 41–45.

a culture understands and defines sexual orientation is socially constructed.[19]

As mentioned above, it is more challenging to ascertain the value systems of individuals who act outside the established boundaries of conventional society. Masculine ideology is not always defined by a dominant paradigm, but can also be shaped by an individual's will and choice, which may be created through the effect of subcultures or other social groupings. Modern academics label these competing ideologies as subordinate masculinities.[20] The fact that this study relies primarily on ancient literature and imperial iconography for its analysis of manly *Romanitas* limits its scope somewhat. Since the majority of these writers or artists owed their position to either the church hierarchy or the emperor, how cutting edge or subversive could their writings be? For this reason, this study deals primarily with "hegemonic" masculine ideologies originating from the political elite and imposed upon the population. Hegemonic masculinity is the changeable yet dominant masculine paradigm by which "femininities and rival masculinities are marginalised or subordinated."[21] It is difficult to know whether holy men's lives or classicising historians' manly heroes and unmanly villains represented widespread notions of masculinity or even the views of other members of the upper class who did not leave a written record. In spite of their limitations, however, one may use the classicising and ecclesiastical historians to find traces of individuals or subcultures that did not follow the mainstream masculine ideologies. Indeed, the very need for writers to praise or attack certain individuals for their ideal or non-ideal conduct might imply that segments of the population did not follow such stringent codes.

It is also vital to differentiate between present-day and early Byzantine notions of masculinity. One should avoid seeing a

19 A critique of social construction is found in Partner, "No Sex, No Gender," 419–43.
20 Mazzo-Karras, *From Boys to Men*, 17–22.
21 Connell, *Masculinities*.

world with numerous and rapidly changing masculinities like our own. Byzantine civilisation had far more stable and restricted views about masculinity, or indeed, about society in general, than is typically found in our modern world, where rapidly changing cultures and technologies have created far more adaptable and varied understandings of these concepts.[22] This point is particularly relevant in early Byzantine historiography. Without a doubt, the classicising historians emulated the Greek prose and techniques of their classical models Herodotus, Thucydides, and Polybius.[23] Hagiographers and ecclesiastical historians borrowed heavily from the Old and the New Testament and their predecessors such as Tertullian (ca. 160–ca. 225), Clement of Alexandria (ca. 160–ca. 215), and Origen (184–253). As one scholar reminds us, late Roman and early Byzantine writers "knew the ideas of, borrowed from, responded to, or distanced themselves from earlier writers (orthodox or heretical)."[24] They also remained well aware of classical and contemporary secular writings. Therefore, to better comprehend late Roman and early Byzantine writers and their constructions of masculinity, it is imperative to familiarise one's self with these earlier works.

Intertextuality

The past twenty years has undeniably witnessed an upsurge of scholars highlighting the intertextuality of many forms of early Byzantine literature. This trend is of particular interest for this study since several early Byzantine historians, who play a vital role in this investigation, depended heavily on their classical models for essential elements, allusions, and themes in their writings. For instance, the writings of the mid-sixth century Byzantine historian Procopius that serve as a focal point for chapter 8 of this book have received extensive attention lately from classical scholars

---

22 Discussed in McDonnell, "McDonnell on Kaster."

23 Kaldellis, *Procopius of Caesarea*, 35; Greatrex, "Classical Past," 40–56.

24 Kuefler, *Manly Eunuch*, 8–10.

interested in examining the influence of earlier historians on his work. Homer, Aristophanes, Thucydides, Herodotus, Polybius, Plato, and Xenophon have all been shown to greater and lesser degrees to influence his writings.[25]

Exploring the text beneath the text has shed needed light on formerly underappreciated paradigms and possibilities. A greater appreciation of early Byzantine authors' sophistication represents one welcome by-product of these innovative approaches. Rather than merely garnishing their works with an artificial veneer of classical references, recent intertextual studies have shown how some early Byzantine intellectuals shrewdly wielded direct and indirect classical allusions as literary tools—and oft-times potent weapons—to delve into sensitive topics and/or political issues. Operating in a shared thought world of symbol and allegory the author and select members of his audience were privy to details in the text that the less educated reader might miss. In this way, for instance, Procopius could skilfully manipulate classical mimesis as a means to criticise the Emperor Justinian and, in particular, aspects of his foreign policy.[26]

Unquestionably, a thorough understanding of their classical models is essential for comprehending these early Byzantine writers' and their contemporary audience's views on concepts such as identity, virtue, courage, and masculine ideology. Yet, we should not underestimate the extent that these early Byzantine writers were products of their own times. We must keep in mind that Homer and Thucydides lived in far different worlds than early Byzantine writers such as Procopius and Priscus, and that abstract concepts like barbarians, courage, heroism, and masculinity had

---

25 Full discussion of the influence of these sources on Procopius in Whately, *Battles and Generals*, 45–56.

26 Three examples of this approach are found in Pazdernik, "Procopius and Thucydides on the Labors of War," 149–87; Kruse, "The Speech of the Armenians in Procopius," 868–93; Kaldellis, *Procopius of Caesarea*, 18–36.

not remained static over the intervening centuries.[27] There is also a danger of overemphasising early Byzantine intellectuals' indebtedness to earlier authors or propensity to transmit clandestine agendas, by overstating concealed allusions or marginalising the aspects of these early Byzantine histories that differ from their earlier models. This approach has led to some thought provoking, yet I believe, faulty conclusions concerning Procopius' religious beliefs, the enduring viability of an organised pagan movement in sixth-century Constantinople, and the historian's "true" attitudes towards Belisarius and the Emperor Justinian's military campaigns.[28] What is more, some of the world described in Procopius and other early Byzantine classicising writings would have bewildered Herodotus and Thucydides. Foremost of these novelties was the Christian influence on these works.[29]

Still, just because Procopius, or another early Byzantine historian, uses a "Thucydidean concept" or narrative strategy does not necessarily mean the subsequent thoughts or descriptions do not reflect "sixth-century values." Indeed, imagine if we rejected early Byzantine writers' use of passages and concepts found in the Old and New Testament, and/or early Christian theologians, as "products of an earlier age," and hence not representative of early Byzantine values. Early Byzantium was not a monolithically Christian world. Raised in a culture that educated many young elites on the writings of Thucydides and other classical authors,

---

27 For the reshaping of Homer's ἀνὴρ ἀγαθὸς in fifth-century Periclean Athens and the gradual shift in an important post-Homeric word for courage and manliness, ἀνδρεία, in the classical Greek world, see Bassi, "Semantics of Manliness," 25–58.

28 See, e.g., Kaldellis' controversial proposal that Procopius was not a Christian, but that he was at the centre of a pagan neoplatonic revival in sixth-century Constantinople. For a critique of Kaldellis' methodological approach to Procopius and other early Byzantine intellectuals, see Whitby, "Religious Views of Procopius and Agathias," 73–93.

29 Full discussion in Cameron, *Procopius and the Sixth Century*, 64–65.

it is little wonder that some long-established views on manliness and unmanliness also survived.

So, while it is vital to look back into the classical past and forward into the Middle Ages in an attempt to achieve a better understanding of the early Byzantine mindset, just as imperative is looking at this era as a unique historical epoch.[30]

Genre

Recent scholarship has also emphasised the importance of placing works within their proper genre. This approach is particularly relevant for a study like mine that relies so heavily on the ecclesiastical and classicising historians for its conclusions. Scholars have shown the difficulty and dangers of differentiating writers' actual convictions from the constraints of their genre.[31] It is certainly important to appreciate that the ecclesiastical and classicising historians frequently conformed to strict styles of Graeco-Roman rhetoric. For example, without careful analysis, Procopius' three works—the *Buildings*, the *Secret History*, and the *Wars*—may appear either to have different authors, or to be the work of one severely schizophrenic individual. In *Buildings*, Procopius extolled Justinian as God's messenger on earth, leading the Empire back to glory. In contrast, in the *Secret History* Justinian appeared as the "Lord of the Demons" (δαιμόνων ἄρχων) driving Byzantium to disaster.[32] The *Wars* took the middle ground, mixing negative and positive descriptions of the emperor. These discrepancies, however, partly reflect the nature and the limitations of the historical models that Procopius followed. The *Wars* was a work of secular history that focused on great men and great battles. The *Secret History* followed the literary genre of invective and satire, while the *Buildings* adhered to the restrictions

---

30 Cameron, *Procopius and the Sixth Century*, 32.

31 Brubaker, "Sex, Lies, and Textuality," 83–101.

32 Procopius, *Buildings* 1.1.16; Procopius, *Secret History* 30.34.

of "the most artificial of all classical genres to modern taste, that of panegyric."[33]

Once again, we find ourselves asking if writers such as Ammianus, Priscus, or Procopius tell us much about "real" Byzantine men and women. As Leslie Brubaker has argued, a writer like Procopius' construction of feminine and masculine virtues closely followed classical Roman and Christian precepts. Particularly in the *Secret History*, Theodora represents "everything a late Roman should not be."[34] Brubaker questions whether Procopius tells us anything about the "real" Theodora and Justinian, declaring that the *Secret History* "is useless as a source of history about what really happened."[35] Peter Heather too has warned that Procopius' portrait of the individuals in the *Secret History* may not expose the historian's true beliefs. Heather goes so far as to posit that Procopius in this work aimed primarily

---

33   Averil Cameron stresses (*Procopius*, 25, 60) that seeing *Secret History* simply as an exaggerated satire does not give "justice to its complexity and its earnestness, and should not be used to obscure the substantial portion of the work that is devoted to detailed political accusation." Geoffrey Greatrex goes further ("Dates of Procopius' Works"), maintaining that the *Secret History* is not a separate genre from *Wars*, but was made up of material that Procopius hoped to insert into *Wars* if the emperor predeceased him. Opposing these views, in a sharp revision, Henning Börm ("Procopius, His Predecessors, and the Genesis of the *Anecdota*") submits that the hasty composition of the *Secret History* indicates that it was produced because Procopius feared a coup was inevitable, and he needed to disassociate himself from Belisarius and Justinian's inner circle. Therefore, the views portrayed in this work are merely an attempt by Procopius to ingratiate himself to the "new" regime, and therefore not reflective of his "true" views at all. I see the points of view expressed by Procopius in the *Secret History* as exaggerated, yet sincere, suggesting that it is representative of the historian's more pessimistic mindset towards Justinian's floundering Gothic campaign around 550–52, when he probably composed the diatribe.

34 Brubaker, "Sex, Lies, and Textuality," 87, 100–01.

35 Brubaker, "Age of Justinian," 432.

to create a comical view of Theodora, Justinian, Belisarius, and Antonina. The ancient audience was not supposed to be shocked by these characterizations, but amused.[36] Though I doubt aspects of both assertions above, they serve as further timely reminders of the difficulties facing the modern interpreter attempting to uncover the "truths" about actual Byzantine men and women.

Unquestionably, challenges confront the researcher attempting to separate the "real" man and woman from the "constructed" one. Kate Cooper has commented perceptively that Roman writers habitually created literary descriptions of women as a means to describe men's characters. She posits, for instance, that in Plutarch's works, men's inability to control their passion for women frequently threatened social stability. The clash between "the public man and his rival for power, the legitimate wife and the adulterous temptress"[37] represented a common theme in Roman and Byzantine literature. Moreover, Cooper submits that the influence of the Enlightenment and the current "conception of individual autonomy"[38] has hindered scholars' attempts to comprehend the experience of Roman men and women. She stresses that "the notion of a private sphere divested of public significance would have seemed impossible (and undesirable) to the ancient mind. The *domus* [household], along with its aspect of family and dynasty, was the primary unit of cultural identity, political significance, and economic production."[39]

This conflict presents challenges for anyone hoping to interpret our ancient authors. I agree, however, with Cooper's further contention that an understanding of these rhetorical constructions helps to provide a more detailed "picture of how ancient women (and men) understood themselves."[40] Despite our authors frequently designing cartoon-like images of Byzantine men, even

36 Heather, *Restoration of Rome*, 111–16.
37 Cooper, *Virgin and the Bride*, 10.
38 Cooper, *Virgin and the Bride*, 14.
39 Cooper, *Virgin and the Bride*, 11–14.
40 Cooper, *Virgin and the Bride*, 11–13.

these exaggerated portraits can provide the modern reader with insight on these individuals who helped to shape ideals of manly *Romanitas*.

Moreover, the Byzantine sources used in this study do not cut across any neat rubrics we might wish to impose on them. Without question, the boundaries between genres are not as steadfast or impermeable as some have contended. We find historians such as Procopius and Theophylact retelling miracles, and relating the deeds of saints and church leaders. As we will see, ecclesiastical historians readily combined hagiography and panegyric with more traditional historical methods based on the deeds of men in battle. Accounts of the martyrs relied regularly upon literary precedents found in classical biography. So too did descriptions of battles and secular events find their way into saints' lives. Sometimes it is difficult to categorise a particular genre for our sources. Works like John Malalas' sixth-century history, for instance, defy easy categorising into any precise genre.[41]

There is of course no such thing as a truly objective or representative reporter, and this study is somewhat limited by the perceptions and prejudices of its sources. It is difficult to know how deeply Byzantines believed the rhetoric we find in the literary and visual record.[42] Yet, like the examples of over-the-top gendered martial rhetoric found in the present-day United States of America, we should not underestimate the impact of such bombast in the shaping of larger societal values and public opinion.

Besides, whether these writers provide accurate portraits of events or individuals is not as important as the depictions of masculinity themselves. A false depiction based on misconceptions or bias reveals as much about how these authors constructed a concept such as gender as a "truthful" account. For example, Procopius' scathing portrayal of the general Belisarius in *Secret History* may or may not be factual or even reflective of the historian's

---

41 For the problems with categorising Malalas' history as purely a chronicle, see Burgess and Kulikowski, "The Historiographical Position of John Malalas."

42 Kaldellis, *Byzantine Republic*, 196–97.

actual views; however, the negative traits he attributes to the general adds insight into early Byzantine attitudes towards gender and masculinity.[43] In sum, one must read a work carefully—and as a whole—to grasp the author's major themes and views on *Romanitas* and masculinity. If one takes this care, one may delve beneath the surface of the literary categories to uncover their "beliefs" about what kind of actions and manners made one "manly" or "unmanly."

Recent Historiographical Disputes

Investigations of masculinity often serve a political purpose. Some researchers delve into a topic such as "homosexuality" or "homosociality" as a means of exploring how particular societies such as Greece and Rome had greater tolerance towards same-partner sex and/or same-sex desire between men than their present-day counterparts.[44] By showing that cultural views on masculinity are constantly evolving, some of these scholars hope to uncover how and why Christianity established a "hostile" ideology that condemned sexual relations between men, banned women in the clergy, and in the West prohibited the marriage of priests.[45] By using historical texts against the Catholic Church, these activists therefore hope to influence the church's future platform towards these issues. They contend that the church instituted these policies in reaction to the social concerns of late antiquity and the Middle Ages, and for that reason, its stance on these matters should be adapted to reflect a more inclusive and more progressive modern world.[46] For these academics, the study of history provides the opportunity not only to see the "way things were," but also a chance for glimpsing "the way things might be."[47]

---

43 A point made by Brubaker, "Sex, Lies, and Textuality," 100–01.

44 On the neologism, "homosociality," which describes broader social relations between men, see Masterson, *Man to Man*, 5–6.

45 Although recent scholarship has rejected many of his ideas, an influential work in this field remains Boswell, *Christianity, Social Tolerance, and Homosexuality*.

46 Smith, "Introduction," 3–4.

47 I am indebted to Mathew Kuefler for this quotation.

This agenda helps to explain why many studies on late antique masculinity focus on men as sexual beings. It might also account for the reluctance by some academics to accept social history as a legitimate historical tool. Some of the criticism is scathing. Warren Treadgold's view is typical of these sceptics. He writes: "Byzantine thinking had little in common with today's Postmodernism, which looks for truth in panegyrics and saints' lives, for bias in historiography, everywhere for sexuality, and nowhere for religious faith."[48] Even Peter Brown's masterful *Body and Society* has been accused of portraying bodies as predominantly sexual vessels.[49] John Behr maintains that our current preoccupation with sexuality has caused researchers like Brown to overstate the importance of this issue for our late antique writers.[50] Yet, we should also not neglect Byzantines as sexual beings. I agree with Anthony Kaldellis that we should not think of the Byzantines as "prudes" who had no interest in sexual matters.[51]

Other critics of social history accuse its practitioners of using anachronistic methods in their research. In the field of ancient sexualities and masculinity, the debate between those labelled as Essentialists and Social Constructionists has been particularly venomous. Sceptics claim that most investigations on sexual difference in the Graeco-Roman world are flawed because they project prevailing perceptions of sexuality and gender onto Greek and Roman societies where these concepts held greatly different meanings. Likewise, many classicists have frowned on the "gendered" approach to understanding ancient Rome and Greece. These detractors submit that much of the work by social historians has misunderstood, mistranslated, or stretched the meanings of important Greek and Latin terminology to support their theories. They also maintain that many of these studies by social historians have focused too heavily on rhetorical sources and too narrowly on

48 Treadgold, *Early Byzantine Historians*, 14.
49 See, e.g. Louth, "Review of Peter Brown's *The Body and Society*."
50 Behr, *Asceticism*, 11–15.
51 Kaldellis, *Byzantine Republic*, 185.

private aspects of masculinity, particularly sexuality.[52] In response, some social historians have reversed the charges by accusing their detractors of misinterpreting their work, and of using outdated and anachronistic methods themselves. One finds an illustration of this counter-attack in Bruce O'Brian's contention that historians have always looked to the past to both illuminate contemporary concerns and to find "themselves"; suggesting that no historian can achieve complete detachment.[53] He and other social historians submit that at least they are aware of the dangers of interpreting the past through modern eyes.

Regardless of the acrimony at times between the two schools of thought, scholars in the past fifteen years have taken steps to reconcile the disparate methods preferred by classicists and social historians. Political events in the first decade of the twenty-first century led to an increased awareness that concepts such as heroism and manliness mean different things in different societies and change over time. The aftermath of the attacks on the twin towers in New York City on September 11, 2001, in particular, saw an increased interest by academics on how ancient thinkers formulated the abstract concepts of manliness and courage.[54] These studies have provided me with crucial insights and inspiration for this study. These investigations have combined traditional historical, philological, and archaeological analysis with gender and socio-linguistics studies to explore Roman masculinity by examining the semantic range and gendered meanings of terms and concepts like *virtus* and ἀρετή. Using a methodology particularly embraced by this study, in *Andreia: Studies in Manliness and Courage in Classical Antiquity*, a group of classical

---

52 For a sample of the debate concerning the labelling of John Boswell and his disciples as "essentialists" see Halperin, "One Hundred Years of Homosexuality"; Hexter, "John Boswell's Gay Science."

53 O'Brian, "R. W. Southern, John Boswell and the Sexuality of Anselm," 172–74.

54 For the influence of the events of 9/11 on the study of Greek and Roman masculinity, see Rabieh, *Plato and the Virtue of Courage*, 2–4; Rosen and Sluiter, "General Introduction," 1–2.

scholars explore "what the word *andreios* means, what it means to be *andreios* to an ancient Greek." This study and others practising a similar methodology have provided me with keen insights. Most importantly, they have shown me the fluidity of these concepts by revealing how "gendered" vocabulary like *virtus*, ἀνδρεία, and ἀρετή have shifted meanings over time and, at times, meant different things to different people according to the context they were used.[55]

Other researchers based in classics have adopted some of the techniques developed in gender history to investigate how masculine ideologies of the Republic and early and later Empire governed the public speech and behaviour of Roman men.[56] The focus by several of these studies on the importance of martial virtues in helping to define notions of "true" manliness throughout Roman history has proven particularly helpful for my own work. In *Roman Manliness: Virtus and the Roman Republic*, McDonnell examines the changing usage of the term *virtus* from the early to the late Roman Republic. Though outside the period examined in this monograph, this study offers some intriguing insights on how terminology and abstract values like manliness shift over time. For McDonnell, the public notion of manliness as represented by the concept of *virtus* embodied the most important aspect of Republican Roman masculinity. Of special interest for this study is McDonnell's contention that the military framework of *virtus* reflected the intimate link between masculinity and militarism in the Republic. He stresses that in Republican Rome the "bond between the form of the state and the status of being a man was closer and more essential in Rome than in" other ancient cultures "because [...] serving the Republic was the only way many Roman males could lay claim to being a man."[57] McDonnell proposes that

---

55 Rosen and Sluiter, "General Introduction," 4.

56 See, e.g., Edwards, *The Politics of Immorality*; Gleason, *Making Men*; Williams, *Roman Homosexuality*; Foxhall and Salmon, *When Men Were Men*; Hobbs, *Plato and the Hero*.

57 McDonnell, *Roman Manliness*, 11.

in the first century BCE social and political change caused a change in Roman masculine ideology away from martial courage. In a view that this book partly challenges, McDonnell argues that the introduction of full-time soldiers who fought their wars primarily on the frontiers of the Roman Empire meant that men no longer needed to prove their *virtus* on the battlefield. This development created a gulf "between the civilian and military sides of Roman society."[58] Consequently, he declares that during the Principate the emperors monopolised "military glory and martial *virtus*" while an increasingly "emasculated Roman nobility was left to cultivate a private, Hellenic type of *virtus*."[59]

In *The Manly Eunuch: Masculinity, Gender Ambiguity and Christian Ideology in Late Antiquity*, Mathew Kuefler amalgamates established historical methods with gendered approaches. He posits that a Christian ideology of masculinity had risen to dominance in the fourth and fifth centuries. Martial virtues, in a metaphorical and actual sense, play an important role in Kuefler's view of what he describes as the rise to dominance of a "new" Christian masculine ideal in the fourth and the fifth centuries. His study provided me with a springboard for my own topic. Though this study challenges some of Kuefler's suggestions, it seeks to emulate his careful textual analysis as a means to understand how political and social change influenced masculine ideology in the early Byzantine Empire. This book, indeed, is partly my attempt to take up Kuefler's challenge to see if his conclusions, which largely focused on the Western half of the Empire, might be applied to the early Byzantine Empire.[60]

To close, if critics of scholarship examining ancient masculinities have been correct in pointing out the dangers of letting current obsessions with sexuality "cloud" our view of the past, it is just as vital to point out the androcentric nature of Rome and Byzantium in comparison to many modern Western cultures. Living in a

---

58 McDonnell, *Roman Manliness*, 388.

59 McDonnell, *Roman Manliness*, 384–89.

60 Kuefler, *Manly Eunuch*, 9.

world of increasing gender equality can hinder our understanding of the Romans and the early Byzantines. Unquestionably many Roman and Byzantine men from the governing classes valued "true" manliness as a cultural ideal. As we will see in the chapters to come, discussions of masculinity and femininity permeate the ancient literature. Moreover, existing notions of manly martial *Romanitas* shaped both Roman and non-Roman identity across the period covered in this book. Militarism, with its continued links to existing codes of masculinity, remained central to this discourse. Although the past must always remain a "foreign country," familiarising ourselves with these ancient masculinities provides us not only with a better knowledge of Rome and Byzantium, but also offers essential insights into our own era.

Plate 2. The third-century Grande Ludovisi sarcophagus (251/52) in Rome's
Museo Nazionale Romano, Palazzo Altemps.

Comrades, this is the way the glory of the Roman Empire has grown, the way our state, as long as it crushed rebel nations and their wars, has won the rule of the entire world. The Roman soldier has no fear of nations that take up arms, nor did he ever turn his back in fear of an enemy force, however great its number. No, he was loyal to his fellows, watchful and cunning, strong to endure the toils of war valiantly.

Corippus, *Iohannis* 4.405–16

III

VITA MILITARIS:
THE SOLDIER'S LIFE

IN ANCIENT ROME, MARTIAL VIRTUES AND IDEALISED masculinity went hand in hand. Throughout its long history, Rome's expansion and survival had depended on its men's ability to dominate the multiplicity of ethnic groups that lived along its borders. Not surprisingly then, the hyper-masculine qualities of the Roman soldier became the standard by which many Roman men measured their own worth. Indeed, similar to many cultures that ascended to prominence primarily through military aggression, images of the soldier's life and the ideal man's life were regularly the same in Roman society.

For Roman intellectuals, like the Augustan poet Vergil (70–19 BCE), Rome's rise had depended upon its men's superior military *virtus*.[1] We find this militaristic ideology expressed in a famous passage from the poet's *Aeneid*: "Remember Rome, these are your skills: to rule over peoples, to impose morality, to spare

---

1   Vergil: *Aeneid*, trans. Harrison, 10, introduction, 22.

your subjects and to war against the proud."² During the era of the Roman Republic, legendary generals such as Gaius Marius (157–86 BCE) and Julius Caesar (100–44 BCE) had faced and defeated large forces of foreign peoples. In the first and second centuries, the Roman emperors had consolidated these earlier military victories. The late Roman historian, Ammianus Marcellinus, described this era as a time when the state had entered its "manhood" and "won laurels of victory in every part of the globe."³ The third and fourth centuries had witnessed an upsurge of attacks along the Empire's boundaries; yet Roman military might had overcome even these threats.⁴ As many earlier Roman intellectuals, Ammianus and his peers seemed convinced that these numerous victories over enemy forces had occurred, not only because they had better equipment and tactics, but also because the Romans were better men.⁵

As we will see in this chapter and the ones that follow, the majority of Romans in the late Roman and Byzantine era followed these convictions. Christians and non-Christians admired the attributes that they felt distinguished the typical Roman soldier

2 Vergil, *Aeneid* 6.851–53 (my trans.): "Romane, memento (hae tibi erunt artes), pacique imponere morem, parcere subiectis et debellare superbos." McDonnell (*Roman Manliness*, 152–53) and Williams (*Roman Homosexuality*, 135) discuss the martial and gendered aspects of this passage.

3 Ammianus, *Res gestae* 14.6.3, trans. Rolfe: "in iuvenem erectus et virum, ex omni plaga quam orbis ambit immensus, reportavit laureas et triumphos." Relying on literary precedents, in this passage (14.6.3–5) Ammianus compares the history of the city of me to a human life, infancy, childhood, adulthood, and old age.

4 Ammianus, *Res gestae* 31.5.11–17.

5 McDonnell (*Roman Manliness*, 3), commenting on the intimate relationship between masculinity and *virtus* in Republican Rome, concludes, "*Virtus* is the special inheritance of the Roman people, and it was by this *virtus*, this 'manliness', that Roman supremacy had been built." See too Williams (*Roman Homosexuality*, 127) on the etymological connection between *virtus* and manliness.

from his civilian and foreign counterparts—physical and spiritual strength, bodily perfection, courage, prudence, discipline, self-mastery, unselfishness, and camaraderie. Certainly, many intellectuals in the later Empire agreed with the time-honoured consensus that Roman pre-eminence had been achieved because its early citizens had avoided the "life of effeminacy" (vita mollitia)[6] brought on by wealth and the sedentary life and "fought in fierce wars" which allowed them to "overcome all obstacles by their manliness [*virtute*]."[7] This linking of Roman greatness with the special martial virtues of its men is not surprising, considering that few other cultures have ever sent such a large percentage of their citizens to war.[8] Yet, the Roman/Byzantine state of the fifth and sixth centuries had developed into an entity far different to that of the Late Republican hero, Publius Cornelius Scipio Africanus (235–183 BCE), or the Principate of Augustus (r. BCE 27–14 CE). One area of change had been a notable decline in the Roman upper classes' participation in warfare, as well as an

6 Ammianus, *Res gestae* 31.5.14: "Verum mox post calamitosa dispendia res in integrum sunt restitutae, hac gratia, quod nondum solutioris vitae mollitie sobria vetustas infecta nec ambitiosis mensis nec flagitiosis quaestibus inhiabat, sed unanimanti ardore, summi et infimi inter se congruentes, ad speciosam pro re publica mortem tamquam ad portum aliquem tranquillum properabant et placidum" (my trans.). For the close association of *mollitia* with effeminacy see Williams, "The Meanings of Softness."

7 Ammianus, *Res gestae* 14.6.10: "ita magnitudo Romana porrigitur, non divitiis eluxisse, sed per bella saevissima, nec opibus nec victu nec indumentorum vilitate gregariis militibus discrepantes, opposita cuncta superasse virtute." I have added a "their" and replaced the translator Rolfe's "valour" for *virtute* with "manliness." Cf. Herodian, *BH* 2.2.4–6; Ambrose, *Epist.* 73.7; Theophylact Simocatta, *History* 2.14.6, ed. de Boor and rev. Wirth; trans. Whitby and Whitby.

8 On this connection as a common theme in Roman literature, see Williams, *Roman Homosexuality*, 135–37. For the large percentage of Roman citizens serving within the armies of the Republic and the early Empire, see Hopkins, *Conquerors and Slaves*, 31–35.

increased reliance upon non-Roman soldiers within the ranks and in the highest echelons of military command.[9]

The Manliness of War

In the era of the Republic, the ruling elite of Roman society had served as both political and military leaders. To be considered as "real" men, even the aristocracy's most affluent members had needed to prove their virility on the battlefield. Provincial governors until the third century CE were typically men from the aristocracy who functioned as both civilian administrators and garrison commanders.[10] It is no coincidence then that in this era a Roman man's identity was entwined tightly with the notion that "precarious manhood" was best demonstrated and won on the battlefield. As one recent study on Roman masculinity avers, serving the state as a soldier "was the only way many Roman males could lay claim to being a man."[11] According to one Roman historian, this egalitarian martial ethic represented the determining factor in their defeat of rivals more dependent on mercenaries such as the Carthaginians.[12] In many of the ancient sources, the lives of warrior-aristocrats like Scipio stood as exemplars of righteous and manly Roman behaviour at its

---

9 For the importance of non-Romans as both enlisted men and officers in the later Roman army: Southern and Dixon, *Late Roman Army*, 48–50, 67–73; Liebeschuetz, *Barbarians and Bishops*, 20–21. We do find, however, in the sixth-century Eastern Roman army a shift back to a force made up of predominantly citizen soldiers. For this development, see Jones, *Later Roman Empire*, 670; Teale, "Barbarians in Justinian's Armies."

10 Goffart, *Barbarian Tides*, 190.

11 McDonnell, *Roman Manliness*, 10–11.

12 Polybius, *Histories* 6.52, ed and trans. Paton: αἴτιον δὲ τούτων ἐστὶν ὅτι ξενικαῖς καὶ μισθοφόροις χρῶνται δυνάμεσι, Ῥωμαῖοι δ' ἐγχωρίοις καὶ πολιτικαῖς.

apex.[13] This association of the manliness of its elites with the establishment and maintenance of Rome's *imperium* helps us to appreciate why Roman intellectuals, such as the Stoic Seneca (ca. 4 BCE–65 CE), argued that there was no virtue or manliness if an enemy were lacking.[14]

In the second and the third centuries, however, Roman men's military roles were being redefined. What modern scholars describe as the crisis of the third century played a part in this change. The twofold threats of external invasions and crippling civil wars ignited by rival claimants to the purple challenged the Empire's military capabilities and created the necessity for reform.[15] Establishing control over the frequently rebellious Roman forces throughout the Empire represented a key step in quashing this chaos. Those in power entrusted the defence of the state to a professional army of mixed descent that fought its battles mostly on the Empire's outer fringes.[16] The imperial authorities also sought to curtail the danger presented by mutinous regional military commanders. The Emperor Diocletian (r. 284–305), carved the provinces into smaller, more manageable administrative units and increased the number of imperial leaders, first to two then to four. In a further effort to curb the threat of usurpation and create a more effective fighting force, the "senatorial amateurs," who had regularly used their military commissions merely as an obligatory step in their political careers, were no longer required to fulfil their military duties.[17] Sometime probably in Diocletian's

---

13 See, e.g., Polybius, *Histories* 31.25; Cicero, *De officiis* 3.1.4, trans. Millar. For Scipio as a prime example of aristocratic excellence and martial manliness, see Eckstein, *Moral Vision*, 28–30, 79–82.

14 Seneca, *De providentia* 2.4, 2.7, 4.16, trans. Basore.

15 On the combined military threat presented in the third century by a resurgent Persia in the East and the multiplicity of ethnic groupings along the Rhine and the Danube, see Williams, *Diocletian and the Roman Recovery*, 25–35.

16 See Devijver, "Les milices équestres et la hiérarchie militaire"; Eich, "Militarisierungs- und Demilitarisierungstendezen," 511–15.

17 Williams and Friel, *Theodosius*, 81, 100.

reign, serving in the army became hereditary, and the sons of soldiers and veterans were obligated to follow their fathers' example.[18] Although not strictly enforced, another law created in 364 restricted Roman civilians' use of weapons.[19]

Even though men from the upper classes continued to serve as officers and provide a vital reserve of civil and military leadership upon whom the government could call in times of crisis, many wealthy aristocrats chose instead to pursue comfortable lives in one of the Empire's major cities or on their provincial estates.[20] In the fourth century, the roles of "elite" citizens in the military decreased even further, and to meet its recruitment needs the army, at times, depended on the enrolment of foreign troops.[21]

The imperial army's shifting demographics clearly upset some Romans.[22] In his *Roman History*, Dio Cassius (ca. 150–235), a Greek-speaking Roman senator and provincial governor, harshly criticised the Emperor Septimius Severus (r. 193–211) for the make-up of his army:

> There were many things Severus did that were not to our liking, and he was blamed for making the city turbulent through the presence of so many troops and for burdening the State by his excessive expenditures of money, and most of all, for placing his hope of safety in the strength of his army rather than in the good will of his associates in the government. But some found fault with him particularly because he abolished the practice of

18 Southern and Dixon, *Late Roman Army*, 67.

19 CTh 15.15, ed Mommsen and Meyer: "Quodarmorum usus interdictus est."

20 Williams and Friel, *Theodosius*, 25.

21 Liebeschuetz, *Barbarians and Bishops,* 7, 248. For the difficulty of determining whether these "barbarian" soldiers had been granted Roman citizenship, see Mathisen, "*Peregrini, Barbari*, and *Cives Romani*."

22 E.g., Tacitus' (*Annals* 1.16–49, trans. Moore and Jackson) disdain for mutinous soldiers from the lower ranks.

selecting the body-guard exclusively from Italy, Spain, Macedonia and Noricum, — a plan that furnished men of more respectable appearance and of simpler habits, — and ordered that any vacancies should be filled from all the legions alike. Now he did this with the idea that he should thus have guards with a better knowledge of the soldier's duties, and should also be offering a kind of prize for those who proved brave in war; but, as a matter of fact, it became only too apparent that he had incidentally ruined the youth of Italy, who turned to brigandage and gladiatorial fighting in place of their former service in the army, and in filling the city with a throng of motley soldiers most savage in appearance, most terrifying in speech, and most boorish in conversation.[23]

Contrary to some recent interpretations, we should not see in this episode an elite Roman male's rejection of the manliness of Roman soldiers.[24] Some context is needed. Firstly, Dio's primary target was Severus, so we should be on the lookout for exaggeration and tropes. Secondly, some of Dio's irritation stemmed from his belief that the young men of Italy had not been granted the chance to become manly soldiers and therefore had been forced to take up the unmanly lives of thieves and gladiators.[25] Dio certainly did not dismiss the value of the soldier's life; in fact, he seems to hint that if

23 Dio Cassius, *Roman History* 75.2, trans. Cary.
24 See, e.g., Wilson, *Unmanly Men*, 64.
25 Many Roman intellectuals categorised gladiators as unmanly, because—like many public performers—they had given up dominion over their own bodies. Williams argues (*Roman Homosexuality*, 140–41) that Roman masculinity was centred on the notion of control. By "subjugating himself to others for the sake of pleasuring or entertaining them," the gladiator opened himself up to gendered prejudice because he was deemed to have relinquished this essential command over his own body.

they had been "allowed" to join Severus's army, these Italian boys would have been moulded into manly Roman men. Thirdly, we should never forget that non-Roman mercenaries and provincials had long played an important part in the Roman armies. So seeing non-Roman mercenaries or Roman soldiers from the Empire's fringes on the streets of Rome was probably not as shocking as the historian suggests.[26]

We should definitely not take the concepts of the "demilitarisation" of the Roman citizenry or the "barbarisation" of the late Roman army too far. Though it is notoriously difficult to determine with any certainty either the size of the late Roman/ early Byzantine army or the percentage of Romans serving compared to non-Romans—particularly within the non-officer corps—the foreign component was never as high as some historians imply. The majority of soldiers throughout the period covered in this study remained Roman.[27] It is also worth remembering that units such as the eighth Squadron of Vandals, that in the early part of the fourth century had originally comprised almost entirely of "Vandals," by the fifth century consisted primarily of Roman provincials.[28] One must also be aware of the changing nature of the *foederati* (φοιδερᾶτο) in the period covered in this study. In the fourth century, *foederati* consisted primarily of non-Roman groups who had agreed to fight on Rome's behalf.[29]

---

26 A thorough description of the recruitment of both Roman and non-Roman soldiers in the late Roman army from the fourth to the sixth centuries is found in Southern and Dixon, *Late Roman Army*, 67–75. Some of these more traditional views on recruitment have been recently challenged. See, e.g., Whitby, "Emperors and Armies," 166–73; Lee, *War in Late Antiquity*, 79–85.

27 Whitby, "Emperors and Armies," 166–67.

28 Lee, *War in Late Antiquity*, 84–85.

29 For an in-depth discussion about the changing nature of *foederati* in the fifth and sixth centuries, see McMahon, "The *Foederati*, the *Phoideratoi*, and the *Symmachoi*."

Yet, as Procopius explained, by the sixth century the φοιδεράτοι consisted of Romans and non-Romans.[30]

Clearly, the native element represented the majority in the early Byzantine army. The most recent statistical analysis proposes that the number of non-Romans in the Eastern Roman army in positions of command held steady at "less than a third" during the fourth and the fifth centuries. After the fifth century, the Byzantine army's foreign component declined to perhaps a fifth of the overall total. This shift was due to a combination of legislative efforts to monitor recruitment and financial reforms undertaken during the reign of Anastasius I, which appear to have made military service much more attractive. Indeed, conscription, which had been prevalent in the fourth century, by the close of the fifth century had been largely abandoned.[31] To be sure, many of these Roman soldiers hailed from the Empire's fringes. For example, the majority of commanders and subordinate officers in Belisarius' mid-sixth century armies in Africa and Italy hailed from the Balkans and Armenia.[32]

While it is notoriously difficult to come up with the precise numbers of soldiers serving in the late Roman and early Byzantine periods, recent suggestions for approximately 500,000 to 645,000 as the total for the combined forces of the fourth-century army and 300,000 for the sixth-century Eastern Roman forces—including frontier troops, fleet, and the field army—seem reasonable.[33] Making an educated estimate, Warren Treadgold submits that

30 Procopius, Wars 3.11.3–5.

31 CJ, 12.35.17, ed. Kruger, 470–71; Jones, Later Roman Empire, 669–70; Treadgold, Byzantium and Its Army, 14–15; Southern and Dixon, Late Roman Army, 65. Cf., however, the insightful caveats concerning the difficulty in differentiating between conscription and volunteerism in the sixth century found in Whitby, "Recruitment in Roman Armies," 64–74.

32 Conant, Staying Roman, 205–09.

33 Whitby, "Emperors and Armies," 167; Treadgold, Byzantium and Its Army, 43–86, 158; Haldon, Warfare, Society and State, 99–101; Lee, War in Late Antiquity, 78–79.

around the year 395, soldiers—not including veterans—comprised around 2% of the East Roman population. During Justinian's reign, this percentage had dipped to around 1.4 %.[34] While these percentages may appear low, they are higher than the current ratio of civilians to soldiers in the United States armed forces, where in 2013 only .5 % of the population were serving.[35] Whatever the exact tallies, the army was by far the largest "employer in the empire."[36]

The older assumption that military service had become progressively more unpopular amongst fourth-century Roman men from all classes has also been challenged.[37] Revisionist scholars propose that desertion by Roman soldiers in the fourth and fifth centuries was no greater than that of earlier periods.[38] As a recent study on the Roman army explains, despite the strict discipline and physical punishments men in the lower ranks could experience, "Military service was regarded as an honourable profession and [...] soldiers expected to be treated with respect."[39]

Moreover, the reigning emperors' relatives in this period frequently served as high-ranking military commanders. These positions were not just symbolic. For instance, the future Emperor Basiliscus (r. 475/76), the Empress Aelia Verina's brother, led

---

34 Treadgold, *Byzantium and Its Army*, 159–65. The decline under Justinian was largely a result of the additional peoples gained during the emperor's Western reconquests.

35 Eikenberry and Kennedy, "Americans and Their Military." Despite these shrinking numbers, the majority of Americans continue to hold an idealised image of the manliness of the soldier's life, see Kusz, "From NASCAR Nation to Pat Tillman."

36 Treadgold, *Byzantium and Its Army*, 158. In comparison, the entire government bureaucracy only had around 30,000 members.

37 For the "problem" of desertion in the late Roman army, see MacMullen, *Corruption and the Decline of Rome*, 52–55.

38 See, e.g., Williams and Friell, *Theodosius*, 211; Lee, *War in Late Antiquity*, 82–83.

39 Rankov, "Military Forces," 65.

the failed campaign against the Vandals in 468. Three of the Emperor Anastasius' (r. 491–518) nephews—Hypatius, Pompey, and Probus—held important military commands during the first quarter of the sixth century. No less than seven of Justinian's relatives served in the Byzantine high command during and after his reign. The emperor's cousins Marcian and Germanus were *magistri militum*, while the aristocrat and senator Areobindus, who was married to Justinian's niece Praejecta, served as *magister militum Africae* in 545. Little wonder, then, that potential rivals to an emperor from Constantinople's upper-crust seldom served as top-level commanders. The emperor and his inner circle regulated who received these commands, and naturally tended to prefer trustworthy individuals with close personal links. Those *magister militum* who were not related to the emperor generally had a record of faithfulness to the imperial regime.[40]

For example, Justinian's key commanders, Belisarius and Narses, were likely given top commands partly because of their proven fidelity. Narses had risen to prominence under Justinian. He had first attended Justinian and Theodora as a *cubicularius* (chamberlain), ultimately attaining the top post available to a court eunuch, the position of *praepositus sacri cubiculi* (grand chamberlain). He also acted as treasurer (a favourite position for Byzantine eunuchs) and later served as *spatharius* (bodyguard). So too had Narses performed coolly under pressure during an uprising in 532 known as the Nika revolt, which had seen the near overthrow of Justinian. The combination of Narses' quick-thinking during the revolt and his close relationship with Theodora— due in part to their shared Christological position—provide the probable rationale for the eunuch's appointment in 535 to lead a Byzantine army into Alexandria to reinstate the monophysite Theodosius as patriarch.[41]

---

40 Brown, *Gentlemen and Officers*, 64; Parnell, "The Origins of Justinian's Generals," 6; Whately, "Militarization," 1–16.
41 Stewart, "*Andreios* Eunuch-Commander Narses," 6–10.

Belisarius and another prominent general, Sittas, had served as bodyguards for the then general Justinian during Justin I's reign.[42] Belisarius had also proven his faithfulness during the Nika revolt. With Justinian's reign in deep peril, Belisarius had led the counterattack against the emperor's rioting subjects that had finally quashed the insurrection.[43]

Even though the emperor granted the *magister militum* and later the exarch the freedom to appoint their own subordinate commanders, he could and did interfere in the process.[44] We may attribute some of the emperor's interest in these military appointments to paranoia. As Henning Börm has usefully highlighted, the danger of usurpation within the capital from a blue-blood aristocrat posed a greater threat to fifth- and sixth-century Eastern Roman emperors than a potential revolt from a general in the field.[45] The menace of rebellion in Constantinople, then, helps to explain the emperor's reluctance to allow potential rivals from the Roman elite to hold important military commands.

Yet, nobles did not necessarily need close imperial links to strive for a military career. One finds, in fact, a growing number of men from elite Eastern Roman families serving in the armed forces.[46] These men could not always count on their pedigree to land top commands. Even members of the imperial family needed to serve and succeed as junior officers before taking on the highest ranks in the military.[47] This militarization of East Rome's ruling

42 Procopius, *Wars* 1.12.21.

43 *Chron. Paschale* s.a. 621.

44 Conant, *Staying Roman*, 227–29.

45 Börm, "Justinians Triumph," 81.

46 Whately, "Militarization."

47 Parnell, "The Origins of Justinian's Generals," 6; Whately, "Militarization," 53–54.

elites only accelerated in the latter half of the sixth century.[48] Examining the *Prosopography of the Later Roman Empire* for sixth-century entries, Conor Whately has found that out of the 953 possible entries 301 were elite soldiers.[49]

Of course, some of the military roles sought out by the nobility were largely ceremonial. For a price, the sons of East Rome's elite could obtain a place in the palace guard, the *Scholae*. The *Scholae*, formed originally in the early fourth century by Constantine I as an elite cavalry unit, by the reign of Justinian (r. 527–65) had largely taken on a ceremonial function.[50] Nevertheless, the need for these leading families to have their sons take on these symbolic military roles points to the allure of the values found in the soldier's life.

For its heavy fighting, the late Roman and early Byzantine armies relied heavily on conscripts from the customary recruiting grounds found in Empire's rural and upland areas.[51] The army continued to offer citizens from more humble origins attractive career opportunities.[52] Military service represented one of the few career paths that provided members of the lower classes some upward mobility. This was due to a combination of factors. A soldier's length of service usually assured a continual line of promotions and pay increases. Consequently, barring premature death or maiming, these men could expect a stable career of steady advancement.[53] So too could valorous deeds in battle earn one

---

48 On the "newly militaristic mentality" of Justinian's regime, see Conant, *Staying Roman*, 253–61. For the increasing influence of military elites in the reign of Maurice, see Barnish, Lee, and Whitby, "Government and Administration."

49 Whately "Militarization," 53.

50 Frank, "*Scholae Palatinae*."

51 Whitby, "Emperors and Armies," 166. As Whitby and Whitby point out, however (*Chron. Paschale*, 117–18, n. 351), well into the sixth century, the *Scholae* continued to play an important role in protecting the emperor during revolts.

52 Lee, *War in Late Antiquity*, 82.

53 Jones, *Later Roman Empire*, 663–64.

immediate recognition and promotion. Procopius, for instance, revealed how the courageous actions of one of Narses' soldiers in battle had led to the man's immediate elevation to the general's personal guard.[54]

To be sure, as we observed in the case of Dio Cassius, some urbanised elites perceived these citizen soldiers to be little better than barbarians, and saw them as potential threats to the "civilised" parts of the Empire. Late Roman and early Byzantine writers frequently criticised Roman soldiers for their troublesome behaviour, particularly when the military interacted with Roman civilians.[55] One fourth-century critic of the senatorial elites even tells us that some members of the nobility had rejected military service as "a squalid occupation unfitting for a free man."[56] This reluctance to serve, however, probably had more to do with practical reasons, such as a dislike of distant postings, dissatisfaction with the late Roman government, and some landowners' reluctance to give up tenants, than with "an extreme loathing or fear of military service on the part of the Roman citizenry."[57]

Of course, the majority of indigenous and non-Roman recruits probably did not join the imperial army out of any great sense of patriotism or because they felt particularly inspired by the ideals of Roman martial manliness espoused in the educated Roman elite's

---

54 Procopius, *Wars* 8.29.13–18.

55 Elton, "Off the Battlefield." As Elton points out (50), ancient writers tend to complain about a minority of soldiers' poor behaviour, rather than point out the majority of military men "who did their jobs." For the interaction between civilians and Roman soldiers during late antiquity, as well as a full discussion of the violence Roman soldiers inflicted on Roman civilians, see Lee, *War in Late Antiquity*, 163–75.

56 Claudius Mamertinus, *Gratiarum actio suo Juliano imperatori* (trans. Lieu) 20.1: "Militiae labor a nobilissimo quoque pro sordido et inliberali reiciebatur."

57 Southern and Dixon, *Late Roman Army*, 68. Cf. Jones, *Later Roman Empire*, 1062. Contra Kuefler, *Manly Eunuch*, 40.

writings. Most, as mentioned above, enlisted for financial reasons and saw a military career as the best way to climb the Roman social ladder. Moreover, some elite Romans—like their privileged modern American counterparts—might praise the virtues and manliness of the soldier's life, yet feel little compunction to serve themselves.

Nonetheless, as we will see throughout the remainder of this study, entering the imperial army did help to transform the manly identity of non-Romans and men from Roman society's lower strata. Nurtured in an environment where martial masculinity represented an integral element of their thought-world and discourse, civilian Roman ruling elites could not help but to admire the deeds and manly virtues of these Roman soldiers. The civilian educated elite's lingering respect for manly martial virtues, to some extent then, contributed to the swift rise of a number of these formerly obscure soldiers into the notoriously competitive Roman hierarchy.

Some of the most powerful fifth-century political players in the Eastern and the Western halves of the Empire had risen through the ranks. By the 430s, in both halves of the Empire, Roman generals and other members of the officer-corps had integrated themselves into Roman civil society.[58] This growing acceptance of non-Romans and low-born Romans in positions of political authority helps to explain the growing puissance of these elite soldiers. As will be explored more fully in chapter 6, the intrigues of militarised elites like Bonifatius, Aëtius, and Ricimer in the West, and Aspar and the two Theoderics in the East, dominated fifth-century politics.

Of course, it is also true, that from the reign of Arcadius (r. 395–408) emperors had ceased to lead the army into battle personally. In Walter Kaegi's words, "Some had made a gesture of departing to campaign, but they had not really led the armies in the field."[59]

58 Croke, "Dynasty and Ethnicity," 153.

59 Kaegi, *Heraclius*, 68–69. In 611, the emperor Heraclius (r. 610–42) broke with this precedent by leading the military campaign against the Persians.

One may contrast this reluctance with the third and fourth centuries when the majority of emperors campaigned frequently with their armies and used their martial prowess as a primary means of asserting their authority.[60] Nevertheless, emperors without military backgrounds represented the exception not the rule throughout the period covered in this study. In the West, Constantius III (r. 421) Avitus (r. 455–56), Majorian (r. 457–61), Anthemius (r. 467–71), Glycerius (r. 473–74), Julius Nepos (r. 474–75), and in the East, Marcian (r. 450–57), Leo I (r. 457–74), Zeno (r. 474–75, 476–91), Justin I (r. 518–27), Tiberius II (r. 574–82), Maurice (r. 582–602), and Phocas (r. 602–10) had all begun their careers as soldiers. So too had the famous non-campaigning Justinian I first served in the palace guards (*kandidatoi*) during the reign of the Emperor Anastasius I (r. 491–518), and commanded imperial troops in Constantinople (*magister militum praesentalis*) under Justin I.[61]

One may attribute this tendency to avoid combat to a number of interrelated factors, including these emperors' age when they attained the purple, internal politics, and the stark lessons learned in the wake of the deaths of the fourth-century emperors Julian and Valens in battle.[62] So too could a non-campaigning emperor avoid relying on the army's whims for his right to govern.[63] Moreover, the emperor could blame any military defeats on his generals, whilst basking in the glory of any of their victories, no matter how minor. He could also keep an eye on potential threats to his rule from within Constantinople's ruling elite.[64] For the reasons given above, we should not see the trend of emperors avoiding combat during their reign as evidence of a larger imperial and/or societal

---

60 Kaldellis, *Byzantine Republic*, 175.

61 Constantine Porphyrogennetos, *De cerimoniis* 1.93, ed. CSHB; trans. Moffatt and Tall: Εὑρεθεὶς δὲ ὁ εὐσεβέστατος δεσπότης Ἰουστινιανός, τηνικαῦτα κανδιδάτος ὤν.

62 Lee, *War in Late Antiquity*, 35.

63 Kaldellis, *Byzantine Republic*, 176.

64 Börm, *Prokop und die Perser*, 95.

rejection of the conventional reverence for the emperor as an ideal military man.

A number of men from the late Roman upper classes undoubtedly cultivated a more genteel lifestyle than their warlike ancestors from the Republic did. Some gender scholars submit that developments like these helped to transform the notion that Roman men, regardless of social status, needed to prove their heroic qualities by serving as idealised warrior-elites.[65] From at least the first century CE, public displays of martial courage as a primary means of attaining a masculine identity had been complemented by alternative strategies of manliness based on non-martial pursuits. During the early Principate, Stoic and Christian intellectuals had popularised codes of masculinity centred on self-control and a mastery over one's passions such as anger and lust.[66] To be seen as a "true" man, one did not necessarily need to prove his courage and manliness in times of war, but could earn a masculine identity through private and public displays of self-control, endurance, and courage by fighting internalised "battles" with his body and emotions.[67] As Catherine Edwards explains, "The Stoic wise man turned his body into a battlefield on which he might show his *virtus*, prove himself a *vir fortis*."[68]

Moreover, as the influential works of Maud Gleason have claimed, "the immense security of *Pax Romana*" had permitted men from the privileged classes the luxury to undertake more "civilised" modes of male self-fashioning based upon the rhetorical skills that they used in the political and legal rivalries

65 For the upward social mobility military service continued to offer late Roman men from the lower classes, Jones, *Later Roman Empire,* 550–51.

66 For the similarities and subtle, yet important, differences between Stoic and Christian ideals of renunciation and self-control, see Brown, *Body and Society,* 30–31, 178–80.

67 Conway, *Behold the Man,* 24–31. For Cicero's focus on his "ethical *virtus*" and continual battle, not against barbarians, but "vice itself," see McDonnell, *Roman Manliness,* 350–51.

68 Edwards, "Suffering Body," 262.

that filled their days. Public speaking and face-to-face verbal confrontations with political rivals provided an alternative means for privileged Roman men to display their verbal dexterity, and correspondingly their manliness.[69] As Gleason sees it, "Rhetoric was callisthenics of manhood." During these often tense verbal confrontations, a man would be constantly judged by his peers not just by his "mastery of words," but also on his ability to use the correct manly voice, contain his emotions, and thus maintain the proper facial expressions and gestures. She further suggests that from the second to the fifth century CE, "displays of *paideia* in public served to distinguish authentic members of the elite from other members of society, the gap between the educated and the uneducated came to be seen as no way arbitrary but the result of a nearly biological superiority."[70] More problematic is her proposal that the Roman upper nobility had rejected athletics and warfare as an essential component of hegemonic masculine ideology. In her own words:

> Perhaps physical strength once had been the definitive criterion of masculine excellence on the semi-legendary playing fields of Ilion and Latium, but by Hellenistic and Roman times the sedentary elite of the ancient city had turned away from warfare and gymnastics as definitive agnostic activities, firmly redrawing the defining lines of competitive space so as to exclude those without wealth, education, or leisure.[71]

69 Gleason, *Making Men*. For advocates of Gleason's thesis: Barton, *Sorrows of the Ancient Romans*; Burrus, *Begotten Not Made*; Connolly, "Like the Labors of Heracles"; Wilson, *Unmanly Men*.

70 Gleason, *Making Men*, 22–23.

71 Gleason, *Making Men*, 17.

It has been proposed that developments like these "could not help but have serious consequences for men's identity."[72] Yet, as even one advocate of Gleason's thesis acknowledges, this reshaping of masculine self-fashioning, and seeming rejection of martial virtues as a key component of Roman manliness, "may be less an indication of the luxury of the secure than an instance of making a virtue out of necessity."[73] The remainder of this chapter examines some of these shifts and reflects on how they influenced the customary Roman belief in the integral relationship between physical prowess in battle and standards of manliness. Arguing against the standard view in gender studies, however, it suggests that despite these changes, and the adoption of these alternative strategies of masculinity, many Roman writers in the early Byzantine period continued to link notions of heroic manliness with the established ideals of manly virtue found in both visual and textual representations of the soldier's life. Let us look more closely, then, to expressions of this view.

The Emperor as an Exemplar of Martial Manliness

The conception of the emperor as the embodiment of Roman martial prowess and idealised manliness in the later Empire was ubiquitous.[74] The links between masculinity, military virtues, and the emperors' divine right to rule were never far beneath the surface of this imagery (e.g., plates 1, 2, 6).[75] By concentrating notions of heroic masculinity into the figure of the emperor, imperial ideology created a portrait of the ideal emperor as a

---

72 Kuefler, *Manly Eunuch*, 39. Cf. Gleason, *Making Men*, 14; Burrus, *Begotten Not Made*, 19–22, 180; McDonnell, *Roman Manliness*, 384–89.

73 Burrus, *Begotten Not Made*, 21.

74 For the use of this iconography as an essential component of imperial propaganda in the later Empire, see McCormick, *Eternal Victory*, esp. ch. 1–3.

75 Kuefler, *Manly Eunuch*, 26.

Plate 3. Fourth-century silver plate (Hermitage, St. Petersburg, Russia) depicting the Emperor Constantius II. In the military scene, the emperor is mounted and wielding a lance. He is being crowned by Winged Victory.

Plate 4. CONSTA-NTINVS AVG, helmeted cuirassed bust
right. Reverse: VIRTVS-EXERCIT. Two captives seated
below vexillum inscribed VOT / XX.

model of hyper-manliness for all aspiring men to emulate.[76] This paradigm reflected the increasing domination of state ideology by the imperial family and its direct supporters, and it helps to illuminate the growing autocratic power of the later Roman emperors. Though far from a move towards the "Oriental despotism" argued for in the older historiographical tradition, the reigns of Diocletian and his successors certainly witnessed the growth of a more elaborate court ceremonial, along with an increased promotion of the emperor in literary and visual portrayals as an authority reliant predominantly upon divine assistance (at first that of pagan divinities, and then the Christian God) for his authority (e.g., plate 4).[77]

Emperors' lives represent the focal point in many of the literary texts that have survived from the later Roman Empire. A wide range of literary genres, including history, poetry, panegyric, biography, invective, and satire, utilised the lives of past and present emperors as didactic tools for their audiences.[78] "Good" emperors, such as Trajan (r. 97–117) and Marcus Aurelius (r. 161–80), served as exemplars of virtue and masculinity, while "bad" emperors like Nero (r. 54–68) and Domitian (r. 81–96), illustrated the Graeco-Roman belief in the connection between vice and unmanliness.[79] We observe in the texts at our disposal that the deeply rooted Hellenic virtues of courage in battle, justice in politics, and calm majesty in the face of defeat helped to define notions of ideal rulership.[80] For our Eastern authors, these qualities remained closely aligned to the four cardinal virtues: φρόνησις

---

76 Conway, *Behold the Man*, 39.

77 A thorough examination of the increased authority wielded by emperors in the fourth- and fifth- century empire may be found in MacCormack, "The World of the Panegyrists." Cf., however, Kaldellis (*Byzantine Republic*) for the restrictions placed on imperial authority in Byzantine civilisation.

78 On the role of these literary genres in the later Empire, see Hägg and Rousseau, *Greek Biography and Panegyric in Late Antiquity*.

79 Conway, *Behold the Man*, 24.

80 Kaldellis, *Procopius of Caesarea*, 221.

(prudence), δικαιοσύνη (justice), σωφροσύνη (temperance), and ἀνδρεία (manliness or courage), that served as vital components of the principle term for "goodness" and ideal manly behaviour in ancient Greek, ἀρετή.[81] Shadowing concepts found in Plato's descriptions of the ideal philosopher-king, a model late Roman emperor needed to be both a φιλόλογος (lover of reason) and a φιλοπόλεμος (lover of war).[82] Efficiently melding these expected political and military virtues allowed the emperor to become an exemplar of not only ideal rulership, but of supreme manly conduct as well.[83]

The flowery prose of the panegyrists, who flourished in this age, publicised the "excellence" of their targeted emperor by relating to their audience the leader's adherence to these dual themes. As one late Roman writer tells us, panegyrists sought to mould an image of the reigning emperor in a similar way to the artist who sculpted a beautiful statue.[84] As with sculpture, in this medium image was everything. Since these speeches' authors sought to present the reigning emperor as an exemplary figure,

---

81 See, e.g., Menander Rhetor, *Second Treatise* 373, ed. and trans. Russell and Wilson: ἀρεταὶ δὲ τέσσαρές εἰσιν, ἀνδρεία, δικαιοσύνη, σωφροσύνη, φρόνησις. For the adoption of this Hellenic model into Roman intellectual culture, see McDonnell, *Roman Manliness*, 149. Cicero translated these four principle virtues into Latin as *temperantia*, *prudentia*, *iustitia*, and *fortitudo*, Cicero, *De officiis* 1.5.15. Late antique examples for the continuity of this concept include Ammianus, *Res gestae* 22.4, and Ambrose, *De officiis* 1.24.115, ed. and trans. Davidson.

82 For these two traits as essential qualities for a model late Roman emperor to display, see Themistius, *Or.* 4.54a. On Plato's depiction in the *Republic* of the idealised philosopher-king: Plato, *Republic* 521d, 525b, 543a, trans. Lee. On the *Republic*'s influence on late Roman and early Byzantine intellectuals, see Kaldellis, *Procopius of Caesarea*, 106–17.

83 For the Roman emperors as the personification of Roman manliness, see Montserrat, "Reading Gender," 153–82; Kuefler, *Manly Eunuch*, 26–29; Conway, *Behold the Man*, 45–47.

84 Synesius, *De regno* 14.2.

concrete facts seldom got in the way. Like the variety of solid materials available to the sculptor, a long list of established virtues acted as the moral substance out of which an author moulded his portrait.[85] "Courage," in many of these representations, made up one of the foremost characteristics for an emperor to display, and according to one prominent fourth-century practitioner, the one virtue that served as a true "mark of royalty."[86] As an imperial virtue in the fourth and early fifth centuries, this "courage" (in Latin expressed as *fortitudo* or *virtus*, and in Greek usually as ἀνδρεία) usually refers to behaviour in battle.[87] Courage in war differed from the "courage of spirit" (animi fortitudo) displayed by Hellenic philosophers or the "soldiers of Christ" (militia Christi) who were being popularised by the Christian and non-Christian intellectuals of the age.[88] This promotion of physical courage typified the customary view that an emperor's bravery was less metaphorical, and thus needed to be applied in wartime to prove his ability to perform his primary role as the protector of the Roman realm.

Two early fourth-century panegyrics composed by anonymous authors in praise of the Emperor Constantine I provide us with vivid examples of these views. In the first, from 310, the author compliments Constantine for taking on the rigours of the soldier's life. He wrote:

---

85 Noreña, "Ethics of Autocracy," 273.

86 Themistius, *Or.* 1.5c (trans. Heather and Moncur). See too, Ambrose *De officiis* 1.33.175, where he wrote that "courage [*fortitudo*] belongs on a higher scale than the other virtues."

87 Noreña, "Ethics of Autocracy," 275.

88 Similar to the Stoics, many Christian theologians placed spiritual courage on a higher plane than physical bravery. Christian intellectuals such as Ambrose in *De officiis* 1.129 (trans. Davidson), however, found it important to point out in their writings the value of the physical courage (*fortitudo*) that led "people to protect the country in time of war." Ambrose (*De officiis* 1.34.193–96) detailed the contrasts between "physical courage" and "spiritual courage."

> Fortune has placed you above all checks to the acquisition of glory, you wished to advance by serving as a soldier, and by confronting the dangers of war and by engaging the enemy even in single combat you have made yourself more notable among the nations, since you cannot become more noble.[89]

"For it is a wonderful thing, beneficent gods, a heavenly miracle," the author continued,

> to have as Emperor a youth whose courage [*fortitudo*], which is even now very great, nonetheless is still increasing, and whose eyes flash and whose awe-inspiring yet agreeable majesty dazzles us at the same time as it invites our gaze.[90]

Another panegyric in 313 continued the personification of Constantine as an emblem of Roman victory and hyper-manliness, exalting, "Every kind of war, weapon, and enemy yields to you alone, the memorials of manliness [*virtutum*] preserved in writing from the memory of every age yield to you as well."[91] Even though these authors purposefully created cartoon-like descriptions of Constantine, they emphasise for us how standards of model leadership and manliness in the later Empire remained closely bound to conventional notions of martial prowess and a continued adulation of the soldier's life.

We uncover further examples of these militaristic themes in the imperial biographies that thrived in this period. Several of these ancient studies, which one modern critic has labelled μυθιστορία

---

89 *Panegyric of Constantine* 6, 3.3, ed. Mynors; trans. Nixon and Rodgers.

90 *Panegyric of Constantine* 6, 17.1–2.

91 *Panegyric of Constantine* 12, 24.3 (I have changed "valor" for *virtutum* to "manliness").

(*mythistoria*) have come down to us.[92] Though of minimal historical worth, these imperial portraits offer essential insight into the types of behaviours that the Roman authors of the period considered worthy of praise or condemnation. In works such as the *Historia Augusta*, probably composed by an anonymous author in the last quarter of the fourth century (while pretending to be six different authors writing in the late third and early fourth centuries), and the *Liber de caesaribus* written by the Roman aristocrat Sextus Aurelius Victor (ca. 320–ca. 390), the supreme virtues of particular rulers could be contrasted to the supreme vice of others.[93] Similar to the depictions of celebrities found in present-day gossip magazines, these commentaries on the emperors were less concerned with providing accurate accounts of these men's lives than with looking back on these rulers, and by way of an array of titillating anecdotes "making moral judgments on them."[94]

Military virtues in these sources represented a prerequisite for any "good" and manly emperor to demonstrate, whilst their authors perceived a disinclination to fight as a typical trait of "bad" and unmanly rulers.[95] This belief followed Menander Rhetor's view that military abilities represented the mark of a "true" emperor.[96] Praise of one's military prowess did not necessarily need to correspond to actual deeds on the battlefield. The *Historia Augusta*, for instance, described the mediocre Emperor Claudius II's (r. 268–70) rather tepid military record as comparable to the triumphant Roman generals of the past, lauding the emperor for displaying the "valour" (virtus) of Trajan,

92 Syme, "The Composition of the *Historia Augusta*," 123.

93 For the debate surrounding the date of the publication of the *Historia Augusta*, see Cameron, *Last Pagans of Rome*, 743–82.

94 Kuefler, *Manly Eunuch*, 27.

95 Kuefler, *Manly Eunuch*, 26–29.

96 Menander Rhetor, *Basiliskos Logos* 3.73.17–25.

the "righteousness" (pietas) of Antoninus, the "self-restraint" (moderatio) of Augustus.[97]

Although more constrained by the tenets of their genre to provide their readers with accurate accounts of both men's characters and events, the more sophisticated histories of this era also tended to concentrate on the emperors' deeds and the moral fibre.[98] The classicising historians assumed that "great" men made history, and that a leader's manly or unmanly conduct repeatedly determined the Empire's well-being.[99] It is hardly surprising to find that these writers, who focused on great wars and the personalities of a few major characters as the primary shapers of events, in their accounts paid so much attention to the emperor's moral and martial qualities. A passage from Eunapius' *Universal History* provides evidence of this tendency in the later Empire:

> It was clear to all that if the Roman state rejected luxury and embraced war, it would conquer and

97 HA, *Claudius II* 2.3, ed. and trans. Magie.

98 For an early Byzantine discussion of these restrictions, see Agathias, *Histories* preface, 1–21: Καλὸν μέν τι χρῆμα καὶ εὔδαιμον νῖκαι πολέμων καὶ τρόπαια πόλεών τε ἀνοικισμοὶ καὶ ἀγλαΐσματα καὶ ἄπαντα ὁπόσα μεγάλα τε καὶ ἀξιάγαστα ἔργα. ταῦτα δὲ καὶ τὰ τοιάδε δόξαν μέν τινα καὶ ἡδονὴν τοῖς κτησαμένοις ἐπάγει, ἀποβιοῦσι δὲ αὐτοῖς καὶ ἐκεῖσε οἰχομένοις οὔτι μάλα ἐθέλουσιν ἕπεσθαι, ἀλλὰ καὶ λήθη παρεμπεσοῦσα ἐπικαλύπτει καὶ παρατρέπει τὰς ἀληθεῖς τῶν πράξεων ἀποβάσεις· ἤδη δὲ καὶ τῶν ἐπισταμένων ἀποβιούντων οἴχεται καὶ διαδιδράσκει ἡ γνῶσις σὺν αὐτοῖς σβεννυμένη. οὕτως ἄρα μνήμη γυμνὴ ἀνόνητόν τι καὶ οὐ μόνιμον οὐδὲ τῷ μακρῷ συνεκτείνεσθαι πέφυκε χρόνῳ. καὶ οὐκ ἂν οἶμαι ἢ πατρίδος προκινδυνεύειν ἔνιοι ἔγνωσαν ἢ ἄλλους ἀναδέχεσθαι πόνους, εὖ εἰδότες, ὡς, εἰ καὶ σφόδρα μέγιστα δράσαιεν, συναπολεῖται τὸ κλέος αὐτοῖς καὶ διαρρυήσεται, μόνῳ τῷ βίῳ αὐτῶν ἐκμεμετρημένον, εἰ μή τις, ὡς ἔοικε, θεία προμήθεια τὸ ἀσθενὲς τῆς φύσεως ἀναρρωννῦσα τὰ ἐκ τῆς ἱστορίας ἐπεισήγαγεν ἀγαθὰ καὶ τὰς ἐνθένδε ἐλπίδας.

99 For this emphasis in the classicising historians: Sacks, "Meaning of Eunapius' History"; Rohrbacher, *Historians of Late Antiquity*, 70; Kaldellis, *Procopius of Caesarea*, 20; Treadgold, *Early Byzantine Historians*, 21.

enslave all the world. But God has set a deadly trait in human nature, like the poisonous gall in a lobster or thorns on a rose. For in high authority he has implanted love of pleasure and ease, with the result that, while they have all the means with which to unite mankind into one polity, our Emperors in their concern for the transient turn to pleasure while neither pursuing nor showing interest in the immortality which is brought by glory.[100]

As this quote shows, the conservative historian believed that "soft" and unmanly Roman emperors who had abandoned their martial role threatened the state's survival. This equation of the military life with idealised manliness and the state's well-being on the one hand, and civilised luxury with effeminacy and decline on the other hand, represented a standard theme in the Graeco-Roman literary tradition.[101]

For some recent critics, later Roman/early Byzantine writers' reliance on well-trodden virtues and vices hinders our ability to explore the "real" personalities of these men in any great depth.[102] To be sure, these ancient authors remained somewhat constrained by both the limitations of their genres and their intense focus on literary style. Their use of these stock behaviours to describe the emperor's character, however, represents more than just an

---

100 Eunapius, *frag.* 55.5–10: καὶ συμφανές γε ἅπασι κατέστη ὡς ἡ Ῥωμαίων βασιλεία, τρυφὴν μὲν ἀρνουμένη, πόλεμον δὲ αἱρουμένη, οὐδὲν ἀφίησι τῆς γῆς τὸ ἀνήκοον καὶ ἀδούλωτον. ἀλλὰ δεινόν γέ τι χρῆμα ταῖς τῶν ἀνθρώπων φύσεσιν ὁ θεὸς ἐγκατέμιξεν, ὥσπερ τοῖς ὀστακοῖς τὴν ἐπικίνδυνον χολὴν καὶ τοῖς ῥόδοις ἀκάνθας, οὕτω ταῖς ἐξουσίαις συγκατασπείρας τὴν ἡδονὴν καὶ ῥαθυμίαν, δι' ἥν, πάντα ἐξὸν εἰς μίαν μεταστῆσαι πολιτείαν καὶ συναρμόσαι τὸ ἀνθρώπινον, αἱ βασιλεῖαι τὸ θνητὸν σκοποῦσαι πρὸς τὸ ἡδὺ καταφέρονται, τὸ τῆς δόξης ἀθάνατον οὐκ ἐξετάζουσαι καὶ παρεκλέγουσαι.

101 Williams, *Roman Homosexuality*, 139.

102 This is a criticism made of Procopius by Cameron, *Procopius and the Sixth Century*, 148–49.

example of these authors blurring the lines between literature and history by relying on empty rhetoric procured haphazardly from their classical models. It is always vital to keep in mind that rhetoric frequently functioned for these early Byzantine historians as a way to comment on current events.[103] The notion of an emperor actively avoiding a life of luxury and taking on the rigours of the martial life held a particular appeal for those intellectuals writing during the reigns of Theodosius I's heirs, Arcadius and Honorius—emperors who had largely eschewed their expected roles in political and military affairs.[104]

Synesius of Cyrene

To support this contention, let us concentrate briefly on an Eastern writer from the late fourth and early fifth centuries, Synesius of Cyrene (ca. 370–ca. 414), whose personal and public writings centred on martial metaphors as a means to comment on contemporary events and rulers.[105] A brief survey of some of the themes found in his writings will give way to a more detailed analysis of the classicising and ecclesiastical historians' views on late Roman men's militarism as a crucial aspect of men's heroic conduct and masculine self-fashioning in the chapters to follow. As a Christian from the Eastern provincial elite who served both as a soldier and as a local bishop, Synesius provides an ideal focus for our discussion on the continued vibrancy of classical martial virtues as an essential component of the emperor's, and indeed every Roman man's, masculine identity. His life also serves as a reminder that not all Christian Roman aristocrats had abandoned their civilian and military roles within the late Roman administration.

103 Anthony Kaldellis, who criticises postmodernist attempts to see all Roman historical writing as "fundamentally a form of fiction," makes this point in Kaldellis, *Procopius of Caesarea*, 6–16.

104 Cameron, Long, and Sherry, *Barbarians and Politics*, 4.

105 On Synesius, see Roques, *Synésios de Cyrène*.

Though largely fictitious, a purported speech to the Emperor Arcadius, probably composed in 398 or 399, provides us with a poignant example of how depictions of virtuous and manly emperors remained tied to the military ethos.[106] Relying upon conventional imagery regarding the unmanliness of peoples from the Eastern Mediterranean, Synesius opened his discussion on ideal leadership with an episode describing a Persian embassy arriving at the military camp of the third-century Roman emperor Carinus (r. 283–85) to sue for peace.[107] Accustomed to the lavish and unmanly lifestyle "typical" in the Persian court, the ambassadors entered the emperor's camp expecting to find similar pomp and ceremony. Synesius painted, however, a scene of egalitarianism typical in conventional Roman literary depictions of manly military men.[108] The Emperor Carinus' purple tunic "was laying in the grass" while the emperor enjoyed a simple meal with his men. To the horror of the effete Persians, after warning the he was preparing to lay waste to their lands, the emperor invited the Persians to join him in his simple soldier's meal. They refused, but according to Synesius, once the Persian emperor and his soldiers heard the story, they were amazed to hear that the Roman emperor had deigned to share a simple meal with his men. While the Persian soldiers were impressed, according to Synesius, the braggart (Persian) king arrived back to his camp in terror and was "ready to yield in everything, he of the tiara and robes, to one in a simple woollen tunic and cap."[109]

It was likely no accident that in an address to an emperor he later denigrated for being unwarlike and living the hedonistic life

---

106 Cameron, Long, and Sherry (*Barbarians and Politics*, 103–42) reconstruct the date and political and social circumstances surrounding this address.

107 For the depiction of peoples from the Eastern Mediterranean as unmanly in the classical tradition, Harrell, "Marvellous *Andreia*," 47.

108 For the linking of the austere life of the soldier with codes of ideal Roman masculine conduct, see McDonnell, *Roman Manliness*, 4–50; Williams, *Roman Homosexuality*, 62–80; Kuefler, *Manly Eunuch*, 42–43.

109 Synesius, *De regno* 12.

of a jellyfish, Synesius espoused the conventional lifestyle of an archetypical Roman warrior-emperor shunning the luxurious life of the imperial court for the rigours of the soldier's life. Persian despotism and the unmanliness of Barham II appear to parallel the conditions Synesius found in the court of Arcadius.[110] Synesius' audience would have been immediately struck by the stark contrast of the ascetic manliness of Carinus with the current ruler's abandonment of the martial life for the "softer" and more unmanly lifestyle of the palace.

This spoken and unspoken criticism of the existing regime leads the reader to the most memorable part of the speech, where Synesius recommended the removal of all barbarians from high office and the army. Synesius relied heavily upon gendered metaphors tightly bound to time-honoured martial virtues to condemn the demilitarisation of the Romans from all levels of society. Echoing Plato,[111] Synesius declared:

> The same organization holds good for the State as in the family; the male element must defend and the female occupy itself with the care of the household

110 Synesius, *De regno* 14.3: "Philosophy demanded of the king that he should often mix with the military, and not keep to his palace, for it taught us that goodwill towards him, his only real safeguard, was fortified by this daily intercourse." For contemporary Roman perceptions of Arcadius, see Holum, *Theodosian Empresses*, 50.

111 Plato, *Meno* 17e, trans. Lamb, "Why, there is no difficulty, Socrates, in telling. First of all, if you take the virtue of a man, it is easily stated that a man's virtue is this—that he be competent to manage the affairs of his city, and to manage them so as to benefit his friends and harm his enemies, and to take care to avoid suffering harm himself. Or take a woman's virtue: there is no difficulty in describing it as the duty of ordering the house well, looking after the property indoors, and obeying her husband. And the child has another virtue—one for the female, and one for the male; and there is another for elderly men—one, if you like, for freemen."

within. How then can you endure that the male
element should be foreign?[112]

He continued with the lament that he and other "true" Romans
should be ashamed of allowing "foreigners" to win glory in war.
Instead, he insisted, the *politeia* must recover the "courage of the
Romans" ('Ρωμαίων φρονήματα) and, in order to achieve their
own victories, remove the barbarians not only from the army, but
just as importantly the magistracies.[113] One can sense Synesius'
conviction that Roman males' time-honoured role as soldiers had
led to Rome's dominion; therefore, by abandoning their role as
soldiers, Roman men threatened the Empire's existence. These
sentiments represented more than just conventional rhetoric
to Synesius. When his home town of Cyrene faced "barbarian"
attacks, he heeded his own advice by recruiting and leading his
own rag-tag soldiers into battle.[114]

In the next part of his address, Synesius depended upon Roman
rhetorical prejudice that expressed the view that—like other
marginalised groups—foreigners were best suited for submissive
roles in both the public and the private realms of Roman society:

For my part, I wonder at many other things, but not
least at this our absurd conduct. All this is in the face
that every house, however humble, has a Scythian
[Goths] for a slave. The butler, the cook, the water-
carrier, all are Scythians, and as to retinue, the slaves
who bend under the burden of the low couches on
their shoulders that their masters may recline in the
streets, these are all Scythians also; for it has been

112 Synesius, *De regno* 14.8 (Greek text according to Terzaghi): τέτακται γὰρ
ὥσπερ ἐν οἴκῳ καὶ πολιτείᾳ ὁμοίως τὸ μὲν ὑπερασπίζον κατὰ τὸ ἄρρεν, τὸ δὲ
εἰς τὴν ἐπιμέλειαν ἐστραμμένον τῶν εἴσω κατὰ τὸ θῆλυ. πῶς οὖν ἀνεκτὸν παρ'
ἡμῖν ἀλλότριον εἶναι τὸ ἄρρεν.
113 Synesius, *De regno* 14.9 (Greek text according to Terzaghi).
114 Synesius, *Epist.* 132 (trans. Fitzgerald).

proved of old that theirs is the most useful race, and the fittest to serve the Romans. But that these fair-haired men who arrange their locks like the Euboeans should be slaves in private to the same men whom they govern in public, this is strange, perhaps the most incredible of the spectacle, and I know not what sort of a thing the so-called riddle may be, if this is not one.[115]

In this passage, one finds the age-old Roman belief in the intimate connection between notions of proper masculine conduct and Roman men's right to dominion.[116] Like many within the predominantly conservative nobility of the day, Synesius indicated that Roman *imperium* depended upon its men's ability to assert their manly *Romanitas* on the field of battle. One sees further evidence of this conviction when Synesius concluded this part of his harangue by asserting that Roman men's "strong arm" and "their will" had earned them the right to "govern all men with whom they come in contact." It looks probable then that from Synesius' perspective, by treating these "barbarians" on near equal terms with the "god-like" Romans of the senatorial classes, Theodosius I and his heirs had upset the natural hierarchal order whereby women were inferior to men, slaves to freeborn, the low-born to the nobility, and non-Romans to Romans.[117]

115 Synesius, *De regno* 15.2. The comparison to the Euboeans is a reference to Synesius' literary model the second-century sophist Dio Chrysostom's (*The Euboean* 151–52, trans. Cohoon) condemnation of pederasty because it "humiliated future leaders."

116 In a similar manner to how they explained their "natural" ascendancy over women, Roman writers pointed to biological, environmental, and social factors to support their claims of supremacy over non-Romans, see e.g., Arian, *Anabasis of Alexander* 2.7.5; Herodian, *BH* 2.9.11; Julian, *Against the Galileans* 116A, 138B; Vegetius, *Epitome of Military Science* 1.2, trans. Milner.

117 For the prevalence of this anxiety amongst the nobility during the reigns of Theodosius I and his heirs, see Williams and Friell, *Theodosius*, 34–35.

As one specialist on the period has noted, Synesius' impractical recommendation to eliminate all barbarians from the army and political office probably represents more "emotive rhetoric" than a "serious political suggestion."[118] However, when read along with Synesius' personal letters that praise the courage and manliness of those Romans like himself who took up arms to defend their lands from barbarian raiders, while condemning those who refused to fight as cowardly and unmanly (including his own brother), it points to the continued relevance of martial virtues as a central component of heroic Roman manliness and, indeed, *Romanitas*.[119] More importantly for our purpose, Synesius' letters allow rare access into his private life, providing a vivid example of how the rhetoric of manly martial *Romanitas* could motivate one man to take up arms against those he viewed as inferior barbarians.[120]

Synesius' speech was provocative; he intended it to be so. While Synesius probably never delivered this exact address in front of Arcadius, it sums up neatly the attitudes of many elite Roman men frustrated with a political reality whereby select generalissimos and eunuch-advisors had increasingly monopolised access to the

---

118 Cameron, Long, and Sherry, *Barbarians and Politics*, 136.

119 See, e.g. Synesius, *Epist.* 94, 104, 113, 130, 132.

120 One should not underestimate how in times of crisis civilians in a martial culture can be motivated by patriotic martial ideals. Certainly, an upsurge of patriotism in the post 9/11 United States of America led a number of "elites" to abandon their civilian lives and volunteer for military service. The famous example of the professional athlete Pat Tillman, who continues to be adulated by the vast majority of the American public for abandoning a lucrative NFL career to serve and die in George Bush's Afghanistan campaign in 2004, shows how civilian elites can lionise the manly virtues of the soldier's life without feeling the need to serve themselves. Full discussion in Kusz, "From NASCAR Nation to Pat Tillman," 77–88.

imperial family and, for some, represented the true power behind Theodosius I's feeble and "effeminate" sons.[121]

As we will see in the chapters to come, this negative attitude towards "unwarlike" emperors and their closest advisors is common in the textual evidence from the later Roman and the early Byzantine Empire. Part of this disdain may reflect the upper classes' frustration at being cut off progressively from access to the emperor's confidence and political power. One recent study on Roman masculinity even claims that the "minor political role" that the men from the aristocracy had in the later Empire played an essential part in the reshaping of these men's masculine identity, and the creation of a "new" Christian masculine ideal.[122]

Though one should remain sceptical of such sweeping generalisations, without a doubt many late Roman authors, who largely hailed from the aristocracy and bureaucracy, appeared uncomfortable with the later Empire's growing autocracy.[123] This stance is not startling, considering that the classical texts that made up much of the foundation of these men's early education stressed the importance of free will for men seeking to achieve "true" manliness.[124] These established ideals preached that "manly freedom and nobility" depended upon a man's propensity to challenge and reject despotic rule.[125] The Eastern Roman historians in their works adhered to the customary Hellenistic

---

121 Contra Jones (*Later Roman Empire*, 1037), Cameron (Cameron, Long, and Sherry, *Barbarians and Politics*, 128) rejects the idea that Synesius gave this exact this speech in front of Arcadius, suggesting plausibly that Synesius probably recited a far less inflammatory piece, and only latter presented the speech in its current form to a group of his peers.

122 Kuefler, *Manly Eunuch*, 49–69.

123 Brown, *Power and Persuasion*, 137.

124 E.g., Herodotus, *Histories* 7.107, ed. Hude, trans. Godley; Plato, *Republic* 579a.

125 Kaldellis, *Procopius of Caesarea*, 142.

distrust of despotism, and tended to link servility to effeminacy.[126] With these thoughts in mind, let us conclude this chapter by examining how the growing dominance of the emperor and his supporters influenced the masculine identity of those within the ruling hierarchy, as well as the Roman nobility, who as previously mentioned were playing less significant roles within the military and administrative branches of the later Roman government.

Military Aristocracy

Scholars have long understood that the later Empire experienced the growing accumulation of political power into the hands of the imperial family and their allies, Roman and non-Roman.[127] This process, which one historian labels the "personalization of late Roman politics," led to the breakdown of the three-tiered system of Roman society that had allowed the leisured classes to coexist "with a professional class of officials and soldiers whose primary purpose was to maintain the smooth working and safety of the Empire."[128] The internal court politics discussed earlier played a part in these developments. Threatened by their rivals from within the Roman aristocracy, emperors in this period increased their independent authority and progressively insulated themselves from public view. Consequently, at the higher levels of public service, the emperor gathered a cadre of relatives, foreign mercenaries, and eunuchs who frequently owed their survival to the ruling regime.[129] As a reward for their loyalty, the emperor

---

126 For the use of these *topoi* in Eunapius: Sacks, "Meaning of Eunapius' History," 63; and for Procopius, see Kaldellis, *Procopius of Caesarea*, 145.

127 Goffart, *Barbarian Tides*, 194–95, 234–35.

128 Goffart, *Barbarian Tides*, 234.

129 Eunuchs and "barbarians" in positions of prominence were particularly vulnerable to execution during political crises or regime changes. For the expendability of eunuchs, see Hopkins, *Conquerors and Slaves*, 176–96, and for the vulnerability of senior non-Roman military commanders, Williams and Friell, *Theodosius*, 148.

regularly appointed many of these "new men" into the rapidly expanded senatorial orders in Rome and Constantinople.[130]

By accumulating such power into his hands, the emperor, along with members of his family and the Roman army under his control, tended to monopolise military glory and martial excellence, whereas demilitarised members of the landowning classes focused on more intellectual forms of men's self-fashioning.[131] As stressed earlier, however, the separation of the upper classes from the highest levels of military service and the corridors of political power was never complete.[132] Nevertheless, the rise of a long series of emperors in the fourth and fifth centuries who owed their elevation to military or dynastic connections, and not to their rapport with the aristocracy, helped to create an inner circle of ruling elites dependent upon their own interpersonal relationships for their positions of power.[133] The growing dominance of these alliances also contributed to the formation in this era of what some specialists call a "separate military aristocracy," based not so much on ethnicity or class, but on ties of loyalty and good old-fashioned martial virtues.[134] This new hierarchy welcomed successful non-Romans, who had commonly risen from within the ranks of the army.[135]

130 A thorough discussion of the expansion of the senatorial orders in the West and the East is found in Jones, *Later Roman Empire*, 523–62.

131 An excellent discussion on the Roman nobility of the late Roman era cultivating less martial pursuits is found in Barnish, "Transformation and Survival in the Western Senatorial Aristocracy."

132 On the continuing power wielded by the Eastern aristocracy, see Brown, *Power and Persuasion*, 3–34, and for the West: Matthews, *Western Aristocracies*, 1–3, 30, 50. Cf. the remarks of Kuefler, *Manly Eunuch*, 50.

133 For the connections between the imperial family and these military strongmen, see Matthews, *Western Aristocracies*, 32–55, 88–100, and O'Flynn, *Generalissimos*.

134 Goffart, *Barbarian Tides*, 191; Demandt, "The Osmosis of Late Roman and Germanic Aristocracies."

135 Amory, *People and Identity*, 27.

*Plate 5. An ivory diptych of Stilicho with
his wife Serena and son Eucherius.*

Like most "barbarians" in the later Empire, many of these men were far removed from the fur-clad wild marauders portrayed frequently in the ancient and modern historiographical tradition. Non-Roman elites serving in the late Roman army often dressed in contemporary Roman fashions and possessed magnificent villas decorated with the latest mosaic floors and furnishings. As a study on the late Roman army puts it, "the Germans who attained positions of authority in the army and the civilian office were more Roman than the Romans, attuned to Roman civilisation and attuned to Roman life."[136]

By the second half of the fourth century, non-Roman generals had largely bridged the divide that had traditionally separated them from the Roman civilian elite.[137] As Mary Harlow has shown, accommodation was a two-way street, by the year 400, the Roman ruling elite had increasingly embraced "Germanic" or "Eastern" styles of dress. The diptych of Stilicho (plate 5, ca. 400) reflects this "elision of civilian and military modes of presentation." The intricately woven gold-chalmys that Stilicho wears, that in the third century was not seen as appropriate dress for civic occasions or civilian officials, by the opening of the fifth century had become the accepted garment for imperial officials, civilian and military and Roman and non-Roman. So too had the formerly "barbarian fashions" of leggings and trousers "made it through the military into the mainstream of Roman dress."[138]

As we see in Stilicho's diptych, these men too could attain marriage alliances with the imperial family, and if they could not aspire to become emperors themselves, they might dream to have their sons become contenders for the purple.[139] By 399, in fact,

136 Southern and Dixon, *Late Roman Army*, 50.
137 For the ways traditional letter writing broke down some of the obstacles between the cultivated elite and non-Roman generals, see McLaughlin, "Bridging the Cultural Divide."
138 Harlow, "Clothes Maketh the Man," 54–65.
139 These alliances were also open to foreign leaders. For some examples from the later Empire, see Goffart, *Barbarian Tides*, 195–96.

all three Eastern *magistri militum* (top-level commanders) were Goths—Alaric, Gainas, and Fravitta—while in the West, the son of a Roman mother and a Vandal father, Stilicho, served as the commander-in-chief of the Western army, and as guardian and the true power behind the titular Western emperor, Honorius. Stilicho had married Theodosius I's niece Serena (plate 5), whilst Honorius' first wife, Thermantia, was Stilicho's daughter, and his co-emperor Arcadius' wife Eudoxia was the daughter of the Frankish general Bauto and his Roman wife.[140] In 414, Galla Placidia, the daughter of the Emperor Theodosius I, and Emperor Valentinian I's granddaughter, married the Gothic King Athaulf (r. 410–15).[141] Appealing to the Roman ruling-classes traditional snobbery, non-Romans like Athaulf depicted themselves as scions of a shared noble, if non-Roman lineage.[142] This development helps to explain why, despite the Roman elites' traditional disdain for mixed marriages with those considered as barbarians, the Theodosians could and did intermarry with formidable non-Romans boasting the correct pedigree.[143]

Even though, early in the fifth century, the ruling classes in the Eastern half of the Empire had taken steps to curb this dependence on these foreigners by curtailing the power of the military and reducing the size of the force, throughout the fifth century foreigners continued to hold important civil and military

140 Ambrose, *Epist.* 1.24.8; Zosimus, *New History* 4.53, trans. (French) Paschoud, trans. (English) Ridley. Bauto had served as Western *magister militum* under the Western emperors Gratian and Valentinian II. He had gained Theodosius' trust by supporting the Eastern emperor's military campaigns in Macedonia in 380 and then attacking Theodosius' rival the Western usurper Magnus Maximus in 383/84.

141 Orosius, *Against the Pagans* 7.40.1, 7.43.2, ed. Zangemeister, trans. Fear. Hydatius, *Chron.* 57, ed. Burgess.

142 Arnold, *Theoderic*, 159–61.

143 For these marriages amongst the imperial family and non-Roman elites, see Sivan, *Galla Placidia*, 9–11; Croke, "Dynasty and Aristocracy."

positions within both the Eastern and Western administrations.[144] Certainly, the Roman and non-Roman associates of this "military aristocracy" represent the primary players and representatives of ideal manly conduct in the secular texts that have survived from the early Byzantine period.

Though the sources from this era maintained a generally hostile attitude towards the foreigners in the imperial service,[145] it is worth bearing in mind that it usually only took a "barbarian" two generations to become "Roman."[146] Moreover, as David Parnell points out, "Non-Romans could in fact loyally serve the emperor and work in the Byzantine military without being Roman."[147] A "heroic man" (ἀνὴρ ἡρωϊκός) in this age could be either a "native" or a "barbarian" serving in the Western or Eastern Roman armies.[148] There seems to be a contradiction between the xenophobia we find in some of the late Roman sources, and the reality of increased accommodation. On this paradox, Walter Goffart comments:

---

144 On these reforms, see Liebeschuetz, *Barbarians and Bishops,* 248. Note, however, some convincing insights and criticisms made by Goffart (*Barbarian Tides,* 299, n. 72) rejecting Liebeschuetz's contention that the Eastern Empire survived because of these reforms and that the Western Empire declined because of its continued reliance on non-Roman military generalissimos. As Goffart points out, we must recognise that the Alanic general Aspar and his family played dominant roles during the reigns of Theodosius II, Marcian, and Leo I. So too did the fifth-century army in the West depend heavily on Roman military commanders such as Castinus, Felix, Bonifatius, and Aëtius.

145 For the general hostility of the majority of Romans towards the appointment of these non-Romans to positions of high command, see Cameron, *Claudian,* 371.

146 A point made in Kaldellis, *Hellenism in Byzantium,* 77.

147 Parnell, "Barbarians and Brothers-in-Arms," 812.

148 See, e.g., Olympiodorus, *frag.* 40, ed. and trans. Blockley.

> Hostility to barbarians was built into the language; almost by definition, barbarians stood for what imperial citizens shunned. But literature does not directly mirror everyday reality. Sheer aversion was not a practical attitude in an age of rapid social and cultural change. The admission of elite barbarians into the Roman military elite was an established fact in the third century and only increased as time went on.[149]

Such strict ethnic polarisation found in writers like Eunapius and Synesius appear to be in dissonance with the realities of the day. To be sure, the boundaries between Roman and foreigner had always been surmountable. In contrast to the Greeks, the Romans' multiracial empire, along with their tradition of inclusion, had contributed to a somewhat more nuanced notion of foreigners' "otherness." From the Republican era, Rome's growth had depended upon its soldier's ability to conquer foreign lands and make Romans out of barbarians.[150] The Roman Empire in this period, to borrow the words of Jonathan Conant, "was a remarkably flexible cultural system [...] unthreatened by the survival of distinctively local customs and conventions, and easily capable of assimilating foreigners."[151]

149 Goffart, *Barbarian Tides*, 192.

150 For a selection of essays on Greek attitudes towards barbarians, from the classical period to the later Middle Ages, see Harrison, *Greeks and Barbarians*. Romans, like the Augustan geographer, Strabo (63/64 BCE–ca. 24 CE), stressed that barbarism was an escapable condition. In his writings (e.g., *Geography*, 2.5.26, 3.38) he showed that by bringing good government and civilisation to barbarian peoples, Roman imperialism could overcome some of the environmental and social factors that had contributed to these non-Roman peoples' "savage" personalities. For these views in Strabo's writings, see Maas, "Strabo and Procopius," 71–75.

151 Conant, *Staying Roman*, 5

Although we should not discount all the negative attitudes towards "foreigners" in the Roman service, visions of a "pure" Roman state like those found in Synesius and Eunapius appear to be based on the customary prejudicial attitudes of the upper classes, particular political crises, and rhetorical practices, as much as a conviction that all of these foreigners needed to be eliminated from the armies. In reality, even a staunch critic of foreigners, like Eunapius, could praise a "barbarian" such as Fravitta for his martial virtues, "proper" religious views, and proven fidelity to the Empire.[152] Undeniably, in the aftermath of the disastrous military defeat at Adrianople in 378, that saw the Eastern Roman army's near annihilation and the Eastern emperor Valens' death, those in power realised that the state's security depended on the institution of a more conciliatory policy towards foreign peoples than former emperors had had the luxury to employ.[153]

One finds, as well, that even conservative intellectuals in the fourth and fifth centuries supported the separation of the civilian and military branches of the imperial administration.[154] In his famous debate with a "Greek" expatriate who had joined the Huns, the fifth-century diplomat and historian, Priscus of Panium, countered the former citizen's claim that the Roman state had fallen into decline because of its citizens' rejection of their martial legacy. The Greek explained that, because of his wealth, after his capture when the Huns sacked his *polis* he was allowed to prove his worth in combat, and, having established his "valour" (ἀριστεύσαντα), was granted his freedom. The Huns

---

152 Eunapius, *frag.* 69.2. Fravitta's support of Hellenic religious practices for Eunapius showed his manly *Romanitas*, whilst the dispatching of his fellow Goth, Gainas, proved his loyalty. Cf. a similar view of Fravitta by the largely anti-non-Roman ecclesiastical historian Socrates, *HE* 6.1, ed. Hansen, trans. Walford.

153 For the political reasoning behind Theodosius I's policy of "appeasement" towards the Goths and other foreign peoples after 378, see Williams and Friell, *Theodosius*, 23–35.

154 Ammianus, *Res gestae* 21.16.3.

accepted him as an "elite" person and permitted him to marry
and to have a family. The Greek then contrasts the choice he had
under the Huns with what he saw as the plight of many Roman
men within the late Empire. Like earlier Roman historians, the
Greek hinted that many Roman men had been enervated by their
inability to protect themselves and the Empire from both internal
and external threats. He blamed the Eastern Empire's current
troubles (early in the 440s) on the emperors' ban on men carrying
weapons and therefore allowing a professional army to fight for
the Romans' freedom:

> But amongst the Romans, since on account of
> their tyrants not all men carry weapons, they place
> their hope of safety in others and are thus easily
> destroyed in war. Moreover, those who do use arms
> are endangered still more by the cowardice [κακία]
> of their generals, who are unable to sustain a war.[155]

In response, Priscus supported the status quo by extolling the
benefits of a division of labour within the Empire. In his mind,
the "wise and good men" of the Roman polity had "ordained
that some should be guardians of the laws and that others should
attend to weaponry and undergo military training, with their sole
object that they be ready for battle and go out confidently to war
as if some familiar exercise." Stressing his primary point that not
all Roman men needed to prove their prowess on the battlefield,
Priscus surmised one should leave battles to those trained to fight.
Priscus, in fact, criticised the Huns for forcing an "inexperienced
man" to fight, claiming, "The Romans are wont to treat even
their household slaves better." The dialogue concludes with the
weeping Greek agreeing that "The laws were fair and the Roman

---

155 Full debate in Priscus, *frag.* 11.2.405–510.

polity was good, but that the authorities were ruining it by not taking the same thought for it as those of old."[156]

Though some scholars doubt this exchange's historicity, it provides us with further evidence that Romans from the educated classes had come to terms with having an army made up of Romans and non-Romans. This sentiment, however, does not mean that men such as Priscus rejected the importance of martial virtues for both the Empire's well-being and the shaping of heroic codes of manliness. The opposite seems true. Throughout the fragments that survive, Priscus expressed his admiration of the courage and manliness of soldiers who stood up to barbarians like the Huns. He goes to great lengths, in fact, to contrast those he considered effeminate appeasers with the courageous and manly conduct of those who faced the Huns in diplomacy and in battle with old-fashioned Roman élan.[157] The appreciation civilians like Priscus had for strong military leaders offers evidence that one need not serve in the military in order to appreciate the manly virtues it instilled in Roman soldiers and men.

We should also question the argument made by one recent study on late Roman masculinity that the barbarisation of the late Roman army led to its decreased efficiency and reliability.[158] The non-Romans who served within the late Roman armies did so, on the whole, with remarkable loyalty and reliability, even when fighting peoples from their own ethnic grouping. As Arnold H. M. Jones noted over half a century ago, this dependability is not

156 Priscus, *frag.* 11.2.405–53. In what remains of his reply, Priscus failed to dispute the Greek's accusations concerning the cowardice and unwarlike qualities of Theodosius II and his generals, suggesting he agreed that the current political turmoil was due to these men's poor military record, rather than an indication of larger failure of the Roman military and political system.

157 For the cowardice and the unmanliness of Theodosius II and his generals: Priscus, *frags* 1.3, 3.3.10–15. For the martial qualities of the Emperor Marcian, Eastern Roman soldiers, the Asimuntians, and Attila: Priscus, *frags* 5.18–20, 9.3. 40–80.

158 Kuefler, *Manly Eunuch*, 43–49.

surprising considering their high level of assimilation to Roman ideals, and the reality that the multiplicity of ethnic groups who served in the Roman forces shared little sense of tribal allegiance.[159]

Lastly, we must reject the idea that late Roman men saw the disasters of the fifth century as evidence that the barbarian enemies who threatened the Empire had become better soldiers, or as Mathew Kuefler claims, "manlier than the Romans."[160] Depictions of the later Empire such as the assertion above bring to mind the image of cowed, unmanly demilitarised Roman aristocrats handing over their lands to "magnificently armoured barbarians" that so angers scholars like Walter Goffart.[161] As Goffart rightfully reminds us, "The 'fall' of the West Roman Empire is not now (perhaps not ever) envisioned as a military defeat by brave barbarians of enervated troops that had lost the will to fight."[162] Even in the imperial West's final years, Roman generals like Aëtius continued to prove this dominance on the battlefield.[163]

Most scholarship on the late Roman army agrees with this assessment, contending that when properly led, the Eastern and the Western Roman armies continued to hold a distinct advantage in direct confrontations with their foes.[164] Ancient and modern

---

159 For these points: Jones, *Later Roman Empire*, 621–22; Southern and Dixon, *Late Roman Army*, 50, 69–71.

160 Kuefler, *Manly Eunuch*, 48.

161 The notorious view that Christianity brought about the Roman Empire's downfall by weakening the martial manliness of the Roman was popularised by Edward Gibbon in the eighteenth century. For echoes of this theme in recent works on late Roman masculinity, see Cooper, "Gender and the Fall of Rome."

162 Goffart, *Barbarian Tides*, 28.

163 For the Western army's continued effectiveness under Aëtius' command, see Elton, "Defence in Fifth-Century Gaul."

164 Wijnendaele, "Stilicho," 280; Southern and Dixon, *Late Roman Army*, 177; see also Heather, *Fall of the Roman Empire*, 446, who argues that the dual problems of the Hunnic invasions combined with political infighting in the fifth-century Western Empire led to a perfect storm of calamity, whereby

historians have observed that, with few notable exceptions, the supposed "martial spirit" and superior manliness of the foreign barbarians proved "no match for the disciplined military face of Rome."[165] The gradual decline of the Western army stemmed primarily from financial factors and internal political bickering rather than an inability to match non-Romans on the battlefield. The loss of North Africa to the Vandals in the 430s and 440s ultimately had disastrous consequences for the Western Empire and its army. A vital loss of tax revenues and corn from this region made it difficult for Valentinian III's regime to pay, clothe, and feed his troops.[166]

Laudatory accounts of military men pervade the pages of the secular texts that survive.[167] Much of this literature articulates long-honoured notions of heroism and masculinity, whereby Roman military men like the late fourth-century general Sebastianus and the sixth-century commander Belisarius offer true exemplars of Roman virtue and manliness. Therefore, while the Christianisation of the Roman Empire is perhaps the most important event in late antiquity, it is a mistake to conclude its establishment led to the immediate weakening of traditional notions of masculinity based, in part, on martial virtues and the xenophobic belief in the right for Roman masculine dominion over non-Romans.

Contrary to the arguments made by some historians, most Roman men in the early Byzantine Empire did not have the luxury or the desire to contemplate whether Christians fighting spiritual battles or aristocratic intellectuals were more courageous or "manlier" than actual Roman soldiers fighting in the "real"

"the barbarian peoples had just enough military might to carve out their enclaves."

165 Goffart, *Barbarian Tides*, 25.

166 McEvoy, *Child Emperor Rule*, 264–65.

167 The fifth-century historian Socrates (*HE* 5.25.11–12), for instance, expressed his belief in the superiority of the "native" Roman soldiers in Theodosius I's army in comparison to those Roman and enemy troops he considered barbarians.

world. In fact, in spite of the military challenges faced by the Eastern Roman army throughout the early Byzantine period, and the disappearance of the Western army in the fifth century, many Byzantines continued to trust in the superior manliness and courage of their soldiers.[168] We can therefore question one recent scholar's assertion that, along with the emperor, "the holy man and the bishop were the most powerful and evocative figures in late antiquity."[169] As Warren Treadgold suggests, sentiments like the one expressed in the preceding passage are not surprising considering that many recent studies on the period tend to rely heavily on Christian panegyrics and hagiographies for their conclusions, while largely ignoring ancient secular texts that offer a far more jaded view of monks, bishops, and holy men.[170]

While I do not reject the relevance of these Christian "heroes" for contributing to our understanding of early Byzantine society and its diverse constructions of masculinity, it is vital to balance these often hagiographical Christian accounts with the more customary attitudes we find in the secular, and indeed some Christian theological sources, praising military virtues as an essential aspect of Roman heroic manliness. It was, in fact, the Eastern Romans' ability to continue to communicate long-established martial ideals as a key barometer of men's heroic conduct that helped to maintain a continuing sense of *Romanitas* throughout the Byzantine era.

---

168 In doing so, I align myself with recent scholarship refuting Gleason's assertion that Roman elites had abandoned physical prowess centred on ἀνδρεία in battle as "a major source of masculine identity." See, e.g., Van Nijf, "Athletics, *Andreia*, and the *Askesis*-Culture."

169 Rapp, *Holy Bishops*, 3.

170 Treadgold, *Early Byzantine Historians*, 8–9. For similar opinions, see Kaldellis, *Procopius of Caesarea*, 1–60; Ward-Perkins, *The Fall of Rome*, 1–12.

Plate 6. Probus diptych (Acosta Cathedral, Italy) depicting
the Emperor Honorius in full military regalia. It probably
commemorates a Roman victory over the Goths in 406.

IV

THE MANLY EMPEROR: CONCEPTUALISATIONS OF MANLINESS, COURAGE, AND IDEAL LEADERSHIP AT THE OPENING OF THE FIFTH CENTURY

When you were born fierce *Germania* trembled along the
Rhine's full course, Caucasus shook his forests in fear, and
the people of Meroë, confessing your divinity, laid aside
their quivers and drew the useless arrows from their hair.
Claudian, *Panegyric on the Third Consulship of Honorius*

THE PROBUS DIPTYCH DEPICTS THE NOTORIOUSLY NON-
martial Emperor Honorius (r. 393–423) as an ideal Roman

military leader and man (Plate 6).[1] Decked out in ornate armour and holding a labarum in his right hand, which proclaims, "In the name of Christ, may you always be victorious" (IN NOMINE XRI VINCAS SEMPER), the young leader likely celebrates a Roman military victory in 406 over a Gothic band, led by the pagan Radagaisus.[2] Literary propaganda emanating from the Western court in Ravenna also focused on propagating the young emperor's martial reputation. The court's chief propagandist the poet Claudian (ca. 370–404 CE), a native Greek-speaker from Alexandria based in Italy, praised a juvenile Honorius for his hunger to enter "in the bloody storm of battle" and to trample "upon the slaughtered bodies of his foes."[3] Yet, despite the visual and literary representations of military valour found in the passages cited above, Honorius never fought in battle, and his forces faced frequent setbacks at the hands of external and internal enemies alike. Indeed, sixth-century Byzantine intellectuals attempting to explain the fifth-century disasters that had led to the loss of nearly two-thirds of Roman territory laid the blame squarely on the "negligence" of Honorius and what they describe as the "effeminate upbringing" of his Western imperial successors.[4]

This seeming paradox between the images of ideal martial manliness disseminated by the fifth-century Roman emperors and their supporters, and the reality of the increasing demilitarisation of the Roman leadership, serves as a focal point for this chapter.

1   For detailed analysis, see Cameron, "Probus Diptych."

2   For the melding of Christian and classical "triumphal" elements in late Roman imperial imagery, see Elsner, *Imperial Rome and Christian Triumph*, 84–87; Alchermes, "Art and Architecture," 343–45.

3   Claudian, "Panegyric on the Third Consulship of the Emperor Honorius (396 CE)," ed. and trans. Platnauer.

4   On the fifth-century Western emperors' "effeminate upbringing" (θῆλυς παιδεία) and "laziness" (ῥαθυμία) as a factor behind the Vandals' and Goths' fifth-century triumphs, see Procopius, *Wars* 3.3.9–16; Justinian, *Nov.* 30. 11; John Lydus, *On Powers* 2.11, ed. and trans. Bandy; Jordanes, *Romana* 332, ed. Mommsen; Cassiodorus, *Variae* 11.1.9–10.

Though it avoids entering into the centuries old debate of why, or even whether, "Rome" fell, the chapter seeks to understand how the declining military role of the emperor after Theodosius I's death in 395 influenced literary representations of idealised leadership that had long depended on the intimate connections between an emperor's courage, his manliness, and the well-being of the Empire. The chapter opens by examining how secular historians writing at the opening of the fifth century depicted the defeat at Adrianople in 378 as a symptom of a crisis of Roman manliness. It then assesses the ways these and other Roman intellectuals represented the Emperor Julian as a prototypical manly emperor draped in intellectual and martial virtues.

Adrianople and the Revival of Classical Historiography

On a sweltering August day in 378, a Roman army led by the Eastern emperor Valens (r. 364–78) found itself surrounded by a large force of Goths. Wearied after a long march out from the gates of the Thracian city of Adrianople in the blistering summer sun, and let down by the Roman cavalry's failure to break the Gothic lines, the fatigued Romans nevertheless pressed forward to meet the advance of a confident and well-rested enemy. The last great Roman historian writing in Latin, Ammianus, provides a vivid account of what happened next:

> The ground covered with streams of blood whirled their slippery foothold from under them, so they could only strain every nerve to sell their lives dearly; and they opposed the onrushing foe with such great resolution that some fell by the weapons of their own comrades. Finally, when the whole scene was discoloured with the hue of dark blood, and wherever men turned their eyes heaps of slain

met them, they trod upon the bodies of the dead without mercy.[5]

According to Ammianus, the Romans faced their deaths with typical Roman courage; yet, as the sun set, the triumphant Goths cut down Valens and the remainder of the Roman soldiers who had not fled. As a result, in a single afternoon, sixteen regiments constituting two-thirds of the core of the Eastern Roman army fell, including a large number of its elite officer corps.[6] Reflecting upon this defeat, Ammianus lamented, "The annals record no such massacre of a battle except the one at Cannae."[7]

Modern scholars too point to Adrianople as a key turning point in Roman history, claiming that it challenged the Romans' "assumption of ultimate military superiority over the barbarians."[8] Certainly, several early Byzantine historians agreed with their present-day counterparts concerning the importance of this battle, but their reasoning for the defeat, as well as their understanding of the realities it reflected differ somewhat from current academics. These ancient writers tended to depict the setback at Adrianople, as well as the other political and social challenges faced by the Empire around the turn of the year 400, as failures of Roman courage and manliness on the part of certain members of the late Roman imperial leadership and the aristocracy. Whereas the ecclesiastical historians of this era typically attributed the military misfortunes of the Western and Eastern halves of the Empire on the failure by some to follow "correct Christian belief," many of

5   Ammianus, *Res gestae* 31.13.6 (trans. Rolfe): "Et quia humus rivis operata sanguineis gressus labiles evertebat, conabantur modis omnibus vitam impendere non inultam: adeo magno animorum robore opposite incumbentibus, ut etiam telis quidam propriis interirent. Atra denique cruoris facie omnia conturbante, et quocumque se inflexerant oculi, acervis caesorum aggestis, exanimate cadavera sine parsimonia calcabantur."

6   Heather and Moncur, *Philosophy and Empire*, 205.

7   Ammianus, *Res gestae* 31.13.19 (trans. Rolfe).

8   Matthews, *Western Aristocracies*, 99.

the secular histories produced from the late fourth to the second half of the sixth centuries present these setbacks as an indication that certain members of the Roman populace had failed to live up to the stringent codes of masculine behaviour that had long defined ideal leaders and manly men. [9]

Eunapius and Ammianus

To illustrate the pervasiveness of this paradigm in the writings of the early Byzantine classicising historians, let us investigate how two important practitioners of this genre, Ammianus and Eunapius, depicted the events leading to Adrianople as a reflection of a crisis of Roman manliness.[10] Ammianus, a native of Antioch and a former soldier in the Eastern Roman army, composed in his adopted city of Rome a grand history in classical Latin depicting events from 96 CE to Valens' death at Adrianople. Eunapius was born to aristocratic parents in Sardis in Western Anatolia. By writing in Attic Greek a history of the Roman world from 270 to 404, Eunapius helped to revive a quiescent Greek classical historiographical tradition.[11] The two historians shared more than just a similar drive to revive classical historiography as a means of commenting on contemporary affairs. Each author first published

---

9   See, e.g., Theodoret, *HE* 6.40; ed. Parmentier and Hansen; Sozomen, *HE* 6.40, ed. Bidez and Hansen, trans. Walford; Socrates, *HE* 4.37; Rufinus, *HE* 2.13, ed. Mommsen, ed. Swartz and Mommsen, rev. by Winkleman. For a complete discussion of contemporary reactions, see Lenski, "*Intium mal Romano imperio.*"

10 Barnes (*Sources of the Historiae Augusta*, 117–20), Matthews (*Roman Empire of Ammianus*, 164–79), and Cameron (*Last Pagans of Rome*, 669–71) contend that Eunapius' history was published before Ammianus' work, and used by him as a source. Treadgold (*Early Byzantine Historians*, 77) and Paschoud (*Eunape, Olympiodore, Zosime*, 153–99) argue against both of these points.

11 The circumstances of their compositions and some of the current historiographical debates concerning these two histories are summarised in Treadgold, *Early Byzantine Historians*, 47–89.

his history in the tumultuous last decade of the fourth century, and their conservative perspective on late Roman society seems to have appealed to a similarly select reading audience, a group whose social influence far outweighed its relatively small numbers.[12] Though Eunapius' largely anti-Christian history has never been noted for its objectivity, originality, or attention to detail, for our purposes its emphasis on the qualities of a few leading men as the primary movers of events provides important material by which to observe the views of a segment of the population disillusioned with the direction the Empire had taken in the decades before and after Adrianople.[13]

Warning their privileged reading audiences from the senatorial and curial ranks about the dangers of abandoning the manly virtues that the historians thought had made Rome great appears to have served as an important aim for both writers. As one recent study argues, Ammianus had composed his history as a way to shame the men of the city of Rome to reform their unmanly ways.[14] One can go further. Although Ammianus reserved his harshest criticisms for individuals from the highest echelons of Roman society, the historian aimed this gendered warning at his

12 For the social background of the classicising historians' reading audiences, see Treadgold, *Early Byzantine Historians*, 71, 376. According to Jones ("Caste System of the Later Roman Empire") by the close of the fourth century, the entire Empire had around 2,000 senators and 250,000 *curiales*.

13 Most modern historians, e.g., Kaegi, *Byzantium and the Decline of the West*, 77–86, Blockley, *Classicising Historians I*, 18–20, Treadgold, *Early Byzantine Historians*, 89, believe that Eunapius' history took a strong stance against Christianity and the Christian emperors. Though cf. Sacks, "Meaning of Eunapius' History," who argues for a more even-handed approach towards Christians and non-Christians on the part of Eunapius in both editions of his history. Treadgold (*Early Byzantine Historians*, 83) points out that Eunapius eliminated much of the anti-Christian sentiment found in the first edition of the history in the second edition, published around 404, with the aim of "reaching a wider audience."

14 Treadgold, *Early Byzantine Historians*, 70.

cultivated readers throughout the Empire.[15] For such a purpose, the defeat at Adrianople made a fitting climax. Indeed, in the opening to his narrative of the battle, Ammianus cautions his audience about the dangers of the "effeminate life" (vitae mollitia), a licentious lifestyle, which the historian claimed had become typical of many of his contemporaries from the Roman upper classes.[16] This "debauched" way of life, according to Ammianus, made a Roman recovery from such defeat all the more difficult.[17] In the past, proclaimed the historian, Romans "high and low alike" had overcome "calamitous losses" as devastating as Adrianople through a combination of their "communal ardour" (unanimanti ardore), "valour" (virtus), and a willingness to die protecting the state.[18]

Contrasting this golden past with a gloomier present, the historian described what he saw as the increasingly unmanly makeup of the Roman upper-crust. In stark comparison to their "austere" and "warlike" ancestors, many men from the aristocracy observed by the historian in Rome had seemed more interested in attending extravagant feasts and parading around the city in ostentatious clothing while surrounded by throngs

---

15 Copies of Ammianus' history were available in the Eastern half of the Empire. In opposition to Treadgold (*Early Byzantine Historians*, 70), I take Ammianus' suggestion that his history might never find an audience as a ritualised gesture common in classicising histories, and in reality his assertion seems to be another dig at the Roman upper classes, whose libraries the historian claimed (*Res gestae* 14.6.18) were "shut up forever like tombs."

16 Ammianus, *Res gestae* 31.5.14 (my trans.).

17 Gavin Kelly (*Ammianus*, 27–28) proposes that this passage, and others in his history, reflect Ammianus' dissatisfaction with the military response by the imperial leadership in the decades after Adrianople. I agree with this assessment, but reject his further contention that Ammianus' castigation of the Roman nobility and the imperial leadership after Julian represents an attack on the Empire's rapid Christianisation.

18 Ammianus, *Res gestae* 31.5.14 (my trans.).

of grovelling servants. [19] The Romans had long perceived these types of behaviours as typical of women and unmanly men.[20] Ammianus lamented that whereas their forefathers had acted "as skilful directors of battles" leading their brave and manly soldiers, many of the nobility of his day instead spent their time arranging banquets and assembling bands of eunuchs, whom he disparaged as "troops of mutilated men" (mutilorum hominum agmina).[21] Having abandoned the political and military offices that had helped them to both hone and express their own manliness, these unmanly aristocrats could no longer be expected to lead real soldiers into battle, but merely command eunuchs, described by another Eastern émigré to Rome, Claudian, as an "Unhappy band [...] whom the male sex has discarded and the female will not adopt."[22] As Shaun Tougher explains, for Ammianus "The eunuchs had an emphatic part in the decline of Rome, and the destruction of its heroes."[23]

Such a negative and gendered attitude towards eunuchs permeates the late Roman literature. Similar to ancient women, much of the hostile rhetoric hurled at eunuchs served as literary devices whereby the authors could attack their main targets. To take just two examples of many, Claudian used Eutropius to attack Arcadius' Eastern Court,[24] whereas Ammianus set his

19 The Romans had no exact equivalent for the English term "aristocracy"; when describing these men from the upper-crust of Roman society, Ammianus used the more specific terms of *nobiles* (14.6.21, 14.6.24) and *nobilitas* (28.4.6). For the highly stratified social structure of the later Roman Empire in the West, see Cameron, *Last Pagans of Rome*, 11, 354.

20 Ammianus, *Res gestae* 16.6. 7–12. On the customary Roman connection of "lavish" dressing on the part of men with effeminacy, see Harlow, "Clothes Maketh the Man," 46–69.

21 Ammianus, *Res gestae* 14.6.17 (trans. Hamilton).

22 Claudian, *In Eutropium* 1.466–67 (trans. Platnauer): "Linquite femineas infelix turba latebras, alter quos pepulit sexus nec suscipit alter."

23 Tougher, "Ammianus and the Eunuchs," 63.

24 Long, *Claudian's In Eutropium*, 221–62.

sights on certain members of the upper stratum of the Roman aristocracy and those eunuchs who had served in the regime of the historian's bête noire—Constantius II (r. 337–61).[25] Similar to Claudian, Ammianus in this digression and other passages from his history seemed to be making a connection between the increasing prevalence of eunuchs and the growth of Roman decadence and unmanliness.[26] As Kathryn Ringrose explains, "The appearance and behaviour of eunuchs represented the antithesis of appropriate male behaviour. The eunuch was scorned as shameful, neither man nor woman, a monstrosity, an outsider, and pitifully womanlike."[27] The very ease by which a man could quite literally be severed from the "source" of his sexual identity troubled many late Roman writers. Claudian quipped that the knife made "males womanish."[28] It appeared a very simple process indeed for a man to become a non-man. As Peter Brown remarks, "The physical appearance and the reputed character of eunuchs acted as constant reminders that the male body was a fearsomely plastic thing."[29]

The sentiments discussed above help to explain some of the hostility towards eunuchs found in Ammianus and other authors of the time. Such views have also led some modern scholars to surmise that by the fifth century, eunuchs made up their own unique gender category. Modifying the older paradigm that proposed that eunuchs represented a "third sex" in Byzantine culture, Kathryn Ringrose contends it is better to see eunuchs as

25 Tougher, *The Eunuch in Byzantine History and Society*, 71.

26 See, e.g., Claudian, *In Eutropium* 112–41, 335–41, 409. For Ammianus' positive, negative, and neutral attitudes towards eunuchs, see Sidéris, "La comédie des castrats."

27 Ringrose, *Perfect Servant*, 12. On how the increased prevalence of eunuchs in both halves of the Empire during the fourth and fifth centuries provided writers with a means to comment on a perceived crisis of masculinity, see Kuefler, *Manly Eunuch*, 31–36.

28 Claudian, *In Eutropium* 1.48.

29 Brown, *Body and Society*, 10.

making up a third gender, "male in sex, but with a difference."[30] One historian has gone as far as saying that the indefinite gender status of eunuchs symbolised to some late Roman men the frailties and "instabilities of the Late Roman gender system."[31] Shaun Tougher is more hesitant to consider eunuchs as a third gender, maintaining, I believe correctly, that "there existed a multiplicity of concurrent gender identities for eunuchs: masculine, feminine, other (both positive and negative)."[32]

Therefore, it should not surprise that the late Roman literature expressed much of its hostility towards eunuchs in gendered terms.[33] A frequently gendered and hostile view of eunuchs appears particularly prevalent at the close of the fourth century, a time when relations between the regimes of Arcadius and his brother Honorius dramatically broke down. Claudian designed a famously hostile portrait of the Eastern eunuch-general and consul, Eutropius. The poet's gendered invective, *In Eutropium* (Against Eutropius), lambasted the Eastern Romans for allowing an "unmanly" eunuch to take on the hyper-masculine duties of a military commander and consul. When describing the shame of having a eunuch leading Roman armies, the poet lamented with double entendre, "Sister shall we ever have the power to cure the East of effeminacy. Will this corrupt age never stiffen up?"[34] To those in Constantinople who had "allowed" a eunuch to fight, he scolded "To leave arms to men."[35] It is probable then that Ammianus used the anecdote we discussed earlier, as well as other

30 Ringrose, *Perfect Servant*, 2–23.

31 Kuefler, *Manly Eunuch*, 36.

32 Tougher, "Social Transformation," 82.

33 One begins to see a more positive attitude towards eunuchs from the fifth century. For this shift in the early and middle Byzantine Empire, see Tougher, "Social Transformation," 70–82.

34 Claudian, *In Eutropium* 2.112–14: "Nedum mollitiia, nedum, germana, mederi possumus Eoae? numquam corrupta rigescent saecula?" (trans. Kuefler, *Manly Eunuch*).

35 Claudian, *In Eutropium* 1.281: "arma relinque viris" (trans. Platnauer).

episodes concerning eunuchs found in his history, as edifying tales to expose what he saw as the increasing emasculation of some members of the Roman nobility.

Of course the Romans' adulation of their past guaranteed that recent achievements would pale in comparison with the "heroic" deeds of their ancestors. In rebuking members of the landowning classes for failing to match the standards of their pugnacious ancestors, Ammianus followed a long line of Roman historians.[36] Prone to pessimism, Roman literature had a tradition of presenting Roman masculinity in a perpetual state of crisis.[37] As already mentioned, for the Romans the dichotomy between virtue and vice was often a gendered one. The traits and actions depicted in the *exempla* above certainly include many of the stock behaviours found in typical Roman literary depictions of "unmanly" (*muliebris, semivir, enervatus*) or "effeminate" (*effeminatus, femineo, mollis*) men (for the ancient Romans these two concepts were interchangeable).[38] Military metaphors imagining the ideal manly Roman man as a soldier, intellectual, or a public official, and the typical unmanly Roman man as a non-martial, uneducated, politically disengaged citizen basking in the lap of civilised luxury, had long served as stock elements in Roman invective.[39]

In fact, current scholarly consensus largely rejects Ammianus' depiction of the late Roman Western aristocracy in Rome as a lethargic group of men shut off from political power.[40] It is

36 See, e.g., Polybius, *Histories* 31.25; Herodian, *BH* 2.2. 3–6.

37 Burrus, *Begotten Not Made*, 19.

38 Kuefler, *Manly Eunuch*, 25.

39 Kuefler, *Manly Eunuch*, 3, 55–61. Cf. Sozomen (*HE* 9.6.5–6) attributing Alaric's sack of Rome in 410 to "divine anger that was retribution for their [Romans] great luxury and licentiousness."

40 John Mathew's *Western Aristocracies* is particularly instructive on the Western Roman aristocracy at the opening of the fifth century; though compare his work with some of the revisionist account found in Salzman, *Christian Aristocracy*.

probable then that some of this hostile attitude towards members of the Roman *nobilitas* reflects the conservative historian's reliance on such ritualised themes. Moreover, as mentioned above, Ammianus seemed to aim his primary criticisms at specific individuals within Rome. He certainly did not universally condemn the Roman elite or believe that the Roman Empire was not capable of great future achievements. His history unquestionably provides examples of men from the Roman upper classes leading soldiers, acting courageously, and displaying the political and military virtues that had long epitomised "true" manliness in a highly male-centric culture.[41] We also observe elsewhere in his history Ammianus praising the rigid separation of the civil and the military administration.[42]

Ammianus based many of his negative characterisations on his own experiences in his civilian and military life, and the majority of his descriptions were of men he knew and, as such, probably reveal observed behaviours and accurately relate the former soldier's uneasiness about the "frivolous" lifestyle of the elite in Rome. Ammianus throughout his history unquestionably reveals a deep inner resentment and hostility towards men from the highest levels of the Roman aristocracy.[43]

These sentiments, however, were not based on the Christian religion of these men, as proposed by one recent analysis of Ammianus' history, but on the conservative intellectual's equation of the virtues of the soldier's or the statesman's life with his traditional perception of an ideal Roman man's masculine

41 I must emphasise that the majority of these "ideal" men achieved their rank through their political and military achievements and they hailed, like the historian, primarily from the more modest levels of the landowning classes. See, e.g., Ammianus' descriptions of his patron, Ursicinus, master of cavalry in the East (15.13, 18.6–8), and Eastern Roman military commanders such as Sebastianus (30.10, 31.11–13) and Victor (25.5, 26.5, 27.5, 30.2).

42 Ammianus, *Res gestae* 21.16.3: "Valdeque raro contigerat, ut militarium alquis ad civilia regenda transiret."

43 Matthews, *Roman Empire of Ammianus*, 414–21.

identity. The former member of the elite officer corps of the *protectores domestici* provides his reader with a largely positive view of those Roman elites[44] and emperors, both Christian and non-Christian, who took on active roles in either the military or the political realms of Roman society. On the shoulders of such men, the Roman Empire could thrive once more.[45]

Eunapius also used his analysis of the Battle of Adrianople to relate what he saw as the failings of the Empire's leadership after the fall of his hero, the Emperor Julian.[46] Though only a small portion of Eunapius' history has survived, in what remains, it is clear that he saw the manliness or the unmanliness of the emperors and their soldiers as a key influence on the outcome of worldly events and the Empire's prosperity.[47]

The surviving fragments of Eunapius' history indicate that he primarily attributed the defeat at Adrianople to the Emperor Valens and those he considered as the less hawkish members of the Eastern Roman military high command. To the historian, the decision by these men to "allow" a large group of Goths to settle on Roman lands in 376 had triggered the disaster.[48] Eunapius

44 I use the more general term "elites" to denote those Romans who were wealthy enough to have received a secondary education.

45 See, e.g., Ammianus' (*Res gestae* 30.7.11) praise of the Christian emperor Valentinian I's warlike qualities, an emperor whom the historian generally characterises negatively elsewhere.

46 Breebaart, "Eunapius," 373, suggests that for Eunapius, "after Julian's death deterioration [in the Roman Empire] set in and ἀρετή was in decline."

47 The difficulty in creating "lost" histories from later citations is discussed in Brunt, "On Historical Fragments and Epitomes." For the pivotal role of τρῠφή (effeminacy, softness, luxury)—a common trait of unmanly men in Greek literature—in Eunapius' history, see Cameron, *Last Pagans of Rome*, 655–58.

48 Cf. the similar sentiments Ammianus expressed in *Res gestae* 31.4.6 (trans. Rolfe): "With such stormy eagerness on the part of insistent men was the ruin of the Roman world brought in." For modern historians' view of this migration and its impact upon the Empire, see Cameron, *Claudian*, 72–73;

explained that those in charge had not sanctioned this immigration with the well-being of the Empire in mind, but for their own selfish desires. To emphasise this point, Eunapius contrasted the virtuous and courageous Roman military men who wanted to uphold the "conventional" Roman foreign policy of forcefully blocking foreign peoples from settling freely onto Roman lands, and what he considered as the more passive policy undertaken by Valens and his successors of letting the Goths settle on their own terms.[49]

Eunapius claimed (truthfully) that Valens had granted the Goths "permission" to cross into Roman lands in order to supplement his own armies. In the historian's mind, at least the Eastern emperor had acted on a "jealous" desire to match his Western imperial rivals by bolstering the Eastern Roman army with Gothic recruits. Eunapius saved his harshest vitriol for those "pacifists" in the high command who had used the barbarian migration as an excuse to enrich themselves, while at the same time satisfying "their own lust" with their ill-gotten Gothic captives, both male and female. When describing the behaviour by some Roman commanders during the Goths' resettlement within the Empire, Eunapius decried:

> But one was smitten by a fair and pretty boy, another was taken by the beautiful wife of one of the captives, another was captivated by some maiden [...] Quite simply, each of them decided that he would fill his house with domestics and his farm with herdsman and sate his mad lust [ἐρωτικὴν λύσσαν] through the licence, which he enjoyed. Overpowered in this criminal and disgraceful manner, they received them (the Goths) with their weapons as if they were some long-standing benefactors or saviours.[50]

Goffart, *Barbarians and Romans*, 16–17.

49 Eunapius, *frag.* 42.
50 Eunapius, *frag.* 42. 31–40.

Most of his fifth-century readers would have readily understood the gendered implications found in the attack in this description. By discussing these officers' "mad lust," fondness for catamites, and uncontrolled avarice, Eunapius sought to highlight these soldiers' unmanliness. Such gendered criticism is not surprising in a culture that often saw fighting and leadership skills as intrinsically masculine characteristics.[51] Ancient Graeco-Roman moralists had long seen men's unrestrained sexual desire and/or activity towards both males and females as a sign of an effeminate lack of self-control.[52] Early Byzantine sources reveal a world where same-sex desire between men in any capacity was increasingly seen as shameful and unmanly.[53] Furthermore, as other studies on Graeco-Roman masculinity have shown, our classical sources frequently depicted the vice of avarice as a further tell-tale sign of an unmanly absence of self-mastery.[54]

Later Stoic and Christian thinkers often conformed to these older models of masculinity. We certainly find much of the late Roman and early Byzantine literature articulating the notion that a man's ability to restrain his sexual desires towards either gender, as well as a mastery of other "natural" impulses, such as avarice, represented a means of attaining a "true" masculine identity.[55] As specialists on later Roman sexuality have stressed, by the end of the fourth century, the tendency to equate a man's sexual restraint

---

51 Brubaker, "Age of Justinian," 428.

52 For a thorough discussion of the varied modern views on Roman men's sexual morality, see Martin, "Heterosexism and the Interpretation of Romans 1:18-32," 135–38; Williams, *Roman Homosexuality*. For Ammianus' attitude toward pederasty and same-sex desire in general, Masterson, *Man to Man*, 138–64; on the links between excessive womanising and effeminacy in the late Roman world, see Burrus, *Begotten Not Made*, 24–25.

53 Masterson, *Man to Man*, 1.

54 Conway, *Behold the Man*, 25–26.

55 Brubaker, "Age of Justinian," 431.

with notions of his manliness had grown even more pronounced.[56] In this period, Christian and non-Christian moralists increasingly attacked and condemned even formerly acceptable Graeco-Roman sexual practices.[57]

We discover further possible evidence of Eunapius' reliance on gendered invective in a passage from Zosimus that mirrors closely both the vocabulary and the content of an extant fragment from Eunapius.[58] In this section of his history, Zosimus condemned the manly virtues of Valens' army, claiming that under the emperor's watch, lax discipline and flawed training had led "the tribunes and soldiers" to be prepared only for retreat "and for effeminate and unworthy desires." Luckily, according to surviving accounts found in Eunapius and Zosimus, an ideal Roman soldier arrived and immediately took steps to salvage a military situation made critical by Valens' poor guidance.[59] Sebastianus, a Roman general who had formerly served under Julian, entered into Valens' service after "escaping" vicious eunuch advisors in what Eunapius and Zosimus both described as a corrupt Western regime.[60] In order to begin restoring the military discipline and "manliness" of Valens' army, Sebastianus chose a small group of two thousand soldiers to enter his specialised boot camp.[61] Through a combination of a strict training regime and Sebastianus' own manly example,

---

56 On the growing prominence of the ideal of sexual renunciation in late fourth- and early fifth-century Christian intellectual circles, see Brown, *Body and Society*; Kuefler, *Manly Eunuch*, 170; Brubaker, "Age of Justinian," 430.

57 See, e.g., Ammianus' (*Res gestae* 31.9.5) commentary on the pederasty of the Taifali. For the increasingly negative attitude towards pederasty in the later Roman Empire, see Kuefler, *Manly Eunuch*, 168–69.

58 Eunapius, *frag.* 44.1–4. For the close relationship between this section of Zosimus' history and Eunapius' history, see Blockley, 42, n. 103.

59 See, e.g., Eunapius (*frag.* 44.1) where the historian describes Sebastianus as an "exemplar of virtue" whose ἀρετή matched that of the ancient Roman heroes.

60 Eunapius, *frag.* 44.3.

61 Eunapius, *frag.* 44.4.

as Zosimus put it, Sebastianus' soldiers had attained "manliness out of effeminacy" (ἀρρενωπὸν ἐκ του θήλεος).[62] Given Zosimus' obvious debt to Eunapius, it is likely that this passage derived from one in Eunapius that expressed similar gendered sentiments.[63]

Wielding such gendered rhetoric would have helped to reassure Eunapius' readers. By placing much of the blame for the defeat at Adrianople on Valens' vice and select officers' lack of manly self-control, Eunapius avoided denigrating the Roman army as a whole by making the uncomfortable suggestion that the "barbarian" Goths may have overcome the Romans at Adrianople because of their better tactics and superior military might. For the conservative historian, the moral failings of a dead emperor and the "depraved" and unmanly behaviour by some members of the Eastern military hierarchy helped to explain the unthinkable.

In holding such a negative view towards the leadership of the imperial twin regimes in the East and the West, Eunapius may be seen as a spokesman for Eastern opinion opposed to the more conciliatory and—as the modern scholarly paradigm rightly contends—the Empire's more realistic foreign policies during the latter part of the fourth century.[64] During this era, it was becoming increasingly difficult for the Romans to dictate terms to the barbarian enemy on the battlefield. Many authors in this period, however, continued to base their understanding of foreign affairs on older military realities and literary models, paradigms that were habitually based on prejudicial gendered rhetoric.[65] As we observed in the previous chapter, the long-held material and

---

62 Zosimus, *New History* 4.23 (my trans.). According to Zosimus (*New History* 4.23–24), Valens, shortly after the "retraining" of some of his army at the behest of his advisors, failed to heed Sebastianus' "sound" military advice to avoid a direct confrontation with the Goths, a move that led to both of their deaths in the fateful battle.

63 Speck ("Wie dumm darf Zosimos sein?") questions the general consensus that Zosimus "slavishly" followed his sources.

64 Heather, *Goths and Romans*, 128–35.

65 Harlow, "Clothes Maketh the Man," 45–47.

strategic advantages that the Roman armies traditionally held over these foreign peoples, for many ancient authors, offered only a partial explanation for Roman supremacy. Indeed, several recent studies on Roman masculinity have convincingly demonstrated that the ancient literature regularly laid out the relationship between Romans and non-Romans along gendered lines.[66] For if in many ways woman represented the biological antithesis of man, then those considered as barbarians often personified the social inversion of Romans. Writers from the Republic to the early Byzantine Empire tended to equate the struggle between Romans and non-Romans—particularly Easterners—as a battle between the manly and the unmanly. Craig Williams associates this binarism with Roman attitudes towards masculinity. In his own words:

> A common theme in the sources of this period [from the second century BCE to the fourth century CE] is that true Roman men, who possess *virtus* by birthright, rightfully exercise their dominion or *imperium* not only over women but also over foreigners, themselves implicitly likened to women. An obvious implication is that non-Roman peoples were destined to submit to Rome's masculine *imperium*.[67]

Conservative intellectuals like Eunapius and Ammianus appeared sceptical about the effectiveness of diplomacy when dealing with foreign peoples. One finds in Eunapius' history the conventional conviction that these "barbarians" needed to be crushed in battle, and if not destroyed, at least cowed by the might of Roman arms before settling on Roman lands. Moreover, this belief in

---

66 See, e.g., Eckstein, *Moral Vision*, 119–25; Williams, *Roman Homosexuality*, 132–37; Kuefler, *Manly Eunuch*, 47–49, 285–86; McDonnell, *Roman Manliness*, 159–61; Conway, *Behold the Man*, 14.

67 Williams, *Roman Homosexuality*, 135.

the masculine supremacy of elite Roman men over their foreign rivals helps to explain why Eunapius and other writers from this age tended to depict many barbarian uprisings or invasions not as political or Roman military failures, but as acts of betrayal by Roman or non-Roman commanders, or the direct consequences of the moral failings and unmanliness of certain emperors and/ or their inner circle.[68] By utilising this familiar narrative, the conservative historian may have hoped to channel his audience's frustration with the way things were going into an antipathy towards the Theodosian emperors' regimes.

Ammianus and Eunapius, like many of the classicising historians that came after them, tended to take a critical view of the Roman emperors who ruled in the years before and after Adrianople.[69] Emperors from the pagan Carinus to the seminal Christian emperors Constantine I and Theodosius I attracted Eunapius' scorn.[70] Though Ammianus took a more balanced approach to his characterisations of the emperors, he too seemed to focus primarily on what he saw as the negative traits of rulers such as Diocletian, Constantius II, Valentinian I, and Valens.[71] For both historians, however, the apostate Emperor Julian offers a notable exception to this tendency. Julian's premature death on a military campaign in Persia in 363 for these historians marked

---

68 Cameron, *Claudian*, 74.

69 Treadgold, *Early Byzantine Historians*, 366–67.

70 As Sacks ("Meaning of Eunapius' History," 57) points out, Eunapius' criticisms of non-Christian emperors like Carinus (*frag.* 1.5.1), and positive description of the Christian Emperor Valentinian II, whom he described as "manly and just" (ἀρρενωπὸν καὶ δίκαιον, 3.58.1), give us room to question the general historical opinion in regards to Eunapius' anti-Christian stance. In fact, even in their highly negative portrait of Theodosius I, Eunapius/Zosimus recognised the emperor's ability to at times throw off his love of the hedonistic lifestyle and become an able military leader.

71 Note the inclusion of both Christian and non-Christian emperors on this list. On Ammianus' characterisations of the later Roman emperors, see Amirav, "Ammianus Stoicus."

the beginning of a difficult period of Roman history and served as another key event on the road to defeat at Adrianople and the Empire's subsequent misfortunes. For these historians and some other late Roman intellectuals, Julian is an exemplar of both late Roman leadership and heroic courage and manliness. We will explore some of these depictions of Julian in more detail below.

The Emperor Julian

As the last pagan Roman emperor, Julian has elicited both enormous interest and sharply divided attitudes amongst ancient and modern historians. The ancient gap between his non-Christian supporters and his Christian enemies has been matched by a similar polarisation among current scholars concerning his religious policies and military and political acumen.[72] Scholars have long recognised that non-Christian intellectuals like Ammianus and Eunapius frequently depicted Julian as both a model emperor and man.[73] We find, for instance, that in contrast to his own age, Eunapius remembered Julian's reign fondly "as one of sweetness and gold."[74] Ammianus, too, in his largely laudatory characterisation of Julian, seemed to cross the line from historian to panegyrist.[75] As one current historian comments, this glorification of the last pagan emperor is not difficult to

---

72 For Julian, see Bidez, *La vie de l'empereur Julien*; Browning, *Emperor Julian*; Bowersock, *Julian the Apostate*; Braun and Richer, *L'Empereur Julien*; Athanassiadi, *Julian an Intellectual Biography*; Smith, *Julian's Gods*; Tougher, *Julian the Apostate*.

73 Eunapius, *frag.* 1. For Ammianus and Eunapius' heroic presentation of Julian in their writings, see Breebaart, "Eunapius," 364; Tougher, *Julian the Apostate*, 8; Treadgold, *Early Byzantine Historians*, 70–71, 85. However, compare these accounts with Sack's ("Meaning," 55–56) arguments submitting that Eunapius, like Ammianus, could be critical of Julian.

74 Eunapius, *frag.* 2.15.

75 On the influence of panegyric in Ammianus' portrait of Julian, see Gartner, "Panegyrik."

understand coming as it does from these "pagan" conservative writers to whom Julian's reign represented "the last flowering of a pagan heritage in what had since become a Christian world."[76] Yet, we should object to this standard view. As even advocates of this position have recognised, the histories of Eunapius, Ammianus— and even more surprisingly—the early sixth-century Byzantine historian, Zosimus,[77] appear to have paid scant attention to Julian's religious policies, but concentrate instead on the apostate's use of his many virtues during his military campaigns.[78] Of course, the simplest answer we might give to queries about this omission is that the classicising historians made it a point to avoid religious issues, which they saw as inappropriate for a genre based on classical historiography. Ammianus and Eunapius may have found it dangerous to praise Julian's paganism when writing under staunch Christian emperors.[79] I must point out that this reluctance, however, did not keep Eunapius—and through him Zosimus—from attacking the religious policies of Christian emperors such as Constantine I and Theodosius I.[80]

76 Kuefler, *Manly Eunuch*, 20.

77 For this point in Zosimus and Ammianus, see Ridley, 169, n. 1, 173, n. 39. Zosimus compared his work to that of Polybius; however, where Polybius studied Rome's rise, Zosimus attempted to understand its fall. Zosimus argued that the Empire had deteriorated because it had abandoned paganism and allowed the barbarians to infiltrate its borders and take control of its armies, Zosimus *New History* 1.57.

78 Writing in the years during and shortly after Julian's reign, Libanius in his letters and orations revealed a greater interest in Julian's religious policies. Isabella Sandwell (*Religious Identity*, 218–24), however, proposes that Libanius was a sycophant who put his career before his religion.

79 Treadgold (*Early Byzantine Historians*, 74), while suggesting that some modern historians have overstated the dangers of writing negative portraits of living emperors, still argues that Ammianus' positive views on Theodosius I and his father may be proof that he was writing his history during Theodosius I's reign.

80 See, e.g., Zosimus, *New History* 2.29–38.

We must understand, as well, that Julian's eccentric brand of neoplatonic Hellenism held little appeal for most late Roman elites.[81] Even Julian's admirers criticised what they saw as the apostate's overzealous Hellenism. Ammianus labelled him "superstitious rather than truly religious" (superstitiosus magis quam sacrorum legitimus observator), remarking that he gave too much regard "to omens and portents." The historian only half joked when he quipped that Julian's addiction to animal sacrifice would have led to a "scarcity of cattle" if the emperor had survived his doomed Persian campaign. Ammianus also labelled as harsh Julian's ban on Christians teaching rhetoric and grammar.[82] Eutropius, a fourth-century non-Christian author of an abbreviated history of Rome from 753 BCE to 364 CE, who mostly praised Julian for his unique combination of military and intellectual virtues, also admonished the dead emperor for his persecution of "the Christian religion."[83]

When creating their idyllic portraits of Julian, these historians were not so much interested in reinforcing a divide between Christians and non-Christians, but in reiterating traditional ideals of martial manliness, leadership, and tolerance that would have appealed to the majority of their classically educated Roman audience, regardless of religious convictions.[84] In taking this stance, I follow current revisionist scholarship that proposes that the traditional belief of a great gulf between pagans and Christians in the age of Ammianus and Eunapius has been overstated. Peter Brown and Alan Cameron have convincingly shown that, by the opening of the fifth century, the common ground between pagans and Christians—based largely on their similar educational

---

81 Cameron, *Last Pagans of Rome*, 382.

82 Ammianus, *Res gestae* 25.4.16–20 (trans. Rolfe).

83 Eutropius, *Breviarium* 10.16.

84 Contra Treadgold (*Early Byzantine Historians*, 72), who, while admitting that Ammianus often disapproved of Julian's religious views, still insists that the historian's approval of the emperor was based on what Treadgold describes as their shared paganism.

background and shared cultural heritage—was more significant than the difficulties brought on by religious divide.[85] In addition, I also ally myself with those historians who reject the notion of Ammianus as a militant pagan.[86] With this in mind, I contend that these ancient historians' depictions of Julian as a prototypical manly Roman emperor—an ἀνδρεῖος βασιλεύς—would have been understood and largely approved of by early Byzantine Christians and non-Christians who had taken the time to read these intricate histories written in archaic prose.

For their characterisations of Julian, early Byzantine writers relied heavily upon the models of virtue and vice found in the classical literature that made up the foundations of these men's education.[87] Mirroring the emperor's own propaganda,[88] many of Julian's supporters made it clear in their writings that the apostate's ability to master the disparate virtues that had long defined the character of manly men and ideal leaders helped to ally him with the other heroes of the Greek and Roman past. This praise of the "philosopher king" Julian is similar to that of the seminal "good" emperor in late antiquity, the emperor Marcus Aurelius, whose reputation was built around his meditations and

85 See, e.g., the persuasive arguments found in Brown, *Power and Persuasion*; Cameron, *Last Pagans of Rome*.

86 Ammianus' attitude towards Christianity continues to provoke considerable scholarly debate. For the notion of Ammianus as a "militant pagan," see Barnes, *Ammianus Marcellinus*, 80; Kelly, *Ammianus*, 3. For Ammianus as a moderate and tolerant pagan, see Syme, *Ammianus*, 137–38; Matthews, Roman Empire of *Ammianus*, 436–45.

87 As a native speaker of Greek, Ammianus appears to have largely transposed the terminology used by Julian, Libanius, and Eunapius from Greek into Latin. A full discussion of the ways Ammianius' Greek lineage influenced his literary approach is discussed in Barnes, *Ammianus Marcellinus*, 174–77; Kelly, "Ammianus' Greek Accent."

88 On the use by Eunapius and Ammianus of Julian's personal account of his Western military campaigns in their histories, see Treadgold, *Early Byzantine Historians*, 46.

rather inflated assessments of his military and domestic policies.[89] The examples below should suffice to demonstrate how positive literary depictions of Julian closely adhered to categories of virtue and manliness extolled by the Stoic and neoplatonic schools of philosophy familiar to literate Christians and non-Christians in later Roman society.

Writing shortly after the emperor's death, Julian's friend, the esteemed Hellenic sophist Libanius (ca. 314–ca. 394), proclaimed that the emperor was more "restrained" (σωφρονέστερος) than Hippolyctus, as "just" (δίκαιος) as Rhadamanthys, more "intelligent" (συνετώτερος) than Themistocles, and "manlier" (ἀνδρειότερος) than Brasidas.[90] Most likely relying upon a lost section of Eunapius' history, Zosimus explained that, similar to other famous military leaders from the Roman past, Julian's soldiers had admired him for "the simplicity of his private life, his manliness in war [πολέμους ἀνδρεῖον], his self-control with regard to wealth" and his mastery of all "the other virtues."[91] Julian's ability to unite these intellectual and martial virtues induced even some of his Christian critics to acknowledge his ability to combine a sharp intellect with martial courage. The fifth-century ecclesiastical historian Socrates, for instance, called Julian "eminently distinguished for his learning," and praised him for his ability "to infuse courage [προθῦμία]" into the Roman soldiers.[92] St. Augustine of Hippo recognised that God had chosen Julian

89 Kuefler, *Manly Eunuch*, 27–29.

90 Libanius, *Or.* 18. 281 (my trans.).

91 Zosimus, *New History* 3.5.3. I have changed the translator Ridley's "courage in war" for πολέμους ἀνδρεῖον to "manliness in war." For the viability of extracting Eunapius' history and views from Zosimus, see Blockley, *Classicising Historians*, 97–106; Treadgold, *Early Byzantine Historians*, 82. Most historians accept Photius' view (*Bibliotheca* 98.2) that Zosimus merely condensed Eunapius' history and that Zosimus' "criticisms of the pious [Christian] Emperors," stuck closely to Eunapius' depictions.

92 Socrates, *HE* 3.1. For Socrates' surprisingly understanding attitude towards Julian, see Urbainczyk, "Vice and Advice," 313–15.

to be emperor, and even admitted that he admired the apostate's "gifted mind."[93]

Even Ammianus' more sober account of the ruler finds the historian claiming that Julian had mastered the cardinal "internal" and "external" virtues, traits that, according to these philosophical schools, defined both ideal masculinity and human excellence.[94] He lauded:

> Julian must be reckoned a man of heroic stature, conspicuous for his glorious deeds and his innate majesty. Philosophers tell us that there are four cardinal virtues: self-control, wisdom, justice, and courage; and in addition to these certain practical gifts: military skill, authority, good fortune, and liberality. All these Julian cultivated both singly and as a whole with the utmost care.[95]

93 Augustine, *De civitate Dei* 5.21, ed. and trans. Green, McCracken, and Wiesen.

94 Ammianus, *Res gestae* 16.1. In addition to criticising Julian's zealous Hellenism, Ammianus (*Res gestae* 25.4.17–18) considered Julian excessively verbose, and too eager for "the applause of the mob." He also censured Julian (*Res gestae* 273) for what he considered unjust executions of his enemies after becoming emperor.

95 Ammianus, *Res gestae* 25.4.1 (trans. Hamilton; I have changed Hamilton's "dignity" for *auctoritas* to "authority," his "prosperity" for *felicitas* to "good fortune," and his "generosity" for *liberalitas* to "liberality"): "Vir profecto heroicis connumerandus ingeniis, claritudine rerum et coalita maiestate conspicuus. Cum enim sint (ut sapientes definiunt), virtutes quattuor praecipuae, temperantia, prudentia, iustitia, fortitudo, eisque accedentes extrinsecus aliae, scientia rei militaris, auctoritas felicitas atque liberalitas, intento studio coluit omnes ut singulas."

Ammianus also praised Julian's restraint. Building upon Stoic codes that had long equated sexual modesty (*pudicitia*)[96] with manly self-mastery, the punctilious historian[97] emphasised that Julian's "inviolate chastity" (inviolata castitate)[98] after his wife's death reflected the "mature strength of his manhood" (adulto robore).[99] Libanius went further, claiming that the Christian hermits and Cynic philosophers' self-mastery paled in comparison to that of Julian.[100] The austerity depicted in the passages cited earlier would have appealed to late Roman readers, no matter their religious persuasion. In an age that regularly equated one's virtue and manliness with one's ability to contain sexual and emotional urges, this manly self-control highlighted for both Christians and non-Christians alike Julian's merit, masculinity, and right to dominion.[101]

Particularly in the histories of Ammianus and Eunapius, however, Julian the military man and leader takes centre stage. This emphasis is probably due to a combination of factors. First, as noted previously, for their imperial portraits both historians consulted Julian's own accounts of his military campaigns in Gaul; a report in which, even Eunapius admits, Julian seems to have gone a bit over the top in promoting his own military

96 As Rebecca Langlands (*Sexual Morality*, 3), points out, "*pudicitia* is a peculiarly Roman concept; there is no direct ancient Greek equivalent, in contrast to many Roman moral ideals, so it develops separately from the Greek philosophical tradition, although related to the Greek concepts of *sophrosyne* (self-control) and *aidos* (shame)."

97 For Ammianus' writings reflecting stricter views of "male *pudicitia*" than his early Roman predecessors, Kuefler, *Manly Eunuch*, 90–91.

98 Ammianus, *Res gestae* 25.4.2 (trans. Rolfe). Further praise of Julian's chastity is found in Socrates, *HE* 3.1; Libanius, *Or.* 18.179.

99 Ammianus, *Res gestae* 25.4.3 (trans. Rolfe).

100 Libanius, *Or.* 18.171.

101 Kuefler, *Manly Eunuch*, 78. Libanius (*Or.* 18. 301), for example, argued that Julian's superior virtues made it natural for him to rule over those "less well endowed."

exploits.[102] Furthermore, Eunapius relied upon Julian's physician Oribasius' "detailed memorandum of the deeds of the emperor."[103] This account, which the physician had composed expressly for Eunapius' use in his history, appears to have also concentrated mostly on Julian's heroic characteristics displayed in his military campaigns. Lastly, and most importantly, these conservative historians were simply following the conventional Roman literary attitude of praising "good" and "manly" emperors who excelled in performing their primary duties of either adding to "the realm of the Roman imperium" or protecting the Empire from barbarian incursions.[104] As I pointed out in the previous chapter, focusing on and applauding an emperor's martial prowess and deeds performed in battle had long served as a common and necessary motif in literary presentations of both model leadership and ideal manly conduct.

In many late Roman writings, Julian's ability to hone his manly virtues for the primary purpose of destroying the barbarian peoples who refused to submit to Rome's *imperium* represented one of Julian's foremost virtues. Ammianus, for example, commended Julian for using "his inborn vigour" (genuino vigore) to constantly dream "of the din of battle and the slaughter of barbarians." So too did Libanius give nodding approval to Julian's thirst for barbarian blood.[105] Julian commented, "An emperor delights in war" (Ἡδονὴ Βασιλεῖ πόλεμος).[106] Zosimus hyperbolically compared Julian's victory at the Battle of Strasbourg in 357 with the triumph of Alexander over the Persians.[107] In fact, some fifth- and sixth-century sources argued that Julian's death had led to

---

102 Eunapius, *frag.* 17.

103 Eunapius, *frag.* 15.

104 Themistius, *Letter of the Emperor Constantius* 18c (trans. Moncur).

105 Ammianus, *Res gestae* 16.1.1 (my trans.); Libanius *Or.* 13.29.

106 Julian, *frag.* 10 (trans. Wright).

107 Zosimus, *New History* 3.3.3.

the "barbarian onslaughts during the reigns of his successors."[108] Julian's refusal "to call upon the Goths for assistance" to fight the Empire's battles also attracted acclaim.[109]

Julian's adherence to these customary martial and manly ideals, according to his devotees, earned him the respect of both Romans and foreigners. As Libanius put it, Julian "was a hard man to his enemies and a hard man to those of his own troops who did not know how to conquer or die."[110] One observes evidence of Julian's "tough love" attitude with his soldiers in an anecdote found in Zosimus (again, most probably borrowed from Eunapius). In it, Julian punished the cowardice of some of his soldiers in battle by marching them through camp dressed in women's clothing. Zosimus contended that "for manly soldiers" (στρατιώταις ἀνδράσι) this was a punishment worse than *decimatio* (the traditional Roman response to cowardice).[111] Indeed, Zosimus and Eunapius, like other early Byzantine writers, emphasised in their works both the military and gendered aspect of ἀνδρεία. Following their ancient role models, ἀνδρεία served for these early Byzantine historians as a concept that could be opposed to femininity.

Of course, sentiments such as those found in the preceding examples represented literary devices for these authors, but this reality does not mean that Ammianus, Libanius, Eunapius, and Zosimus did not believe in the basic moral lessons behind such anecdotes. Living in an age where leaders such as Arcadius and Honorius mostly conducted their lives behind the secluded walls of imperial palaces while letting "barbarian soldiers" fight their

---

108 Libanius, *Or.* 18.290; Zosimus, *New History* 3.32.5. Though some of his detractors, Christian and non-Christian, argued the opposite: Themistius, *Or.* 5.66; Gregory of Nazianzus, *Against Julian* 5.15.

109 Libanius, *Or.* 18.169. Though, as Ammianus reveals (*Res gestae* 20.8.1), a Gothic contingent had served in Julian's forces.

110 Libanius, *Or.* 18.229 (trans. Norman): ἀλλ᾽ ἦν χαλεπὸς μὲν πολεμίοις, χαλεπὸς δὲ τῶν οἰκείων τοῖς οὐκ εἰδόσιν ἢ κρατεῖν ἢ πίπτειν.

111 Zosimus, *New History* 3.3.5.

wars, it is not difficult to understand why these historians may have found Julian's ability to instil manly courage into his soldiers and take a tough stance towards these "barbarians" admirable.

To many of these same late Roman intellectuals, a "passive" attitude at the top trickled down to the men they led in the Roman military. For example, in sharp contrast to their portrayal of the "war loving" Julian, Ammianus, Libanius, and Zosimus portrayed his rival Constantius II as unwarlike, and thus unmanly. In these men's mind, during Constantius II's watch the Empire became easy prey to barbarians. These writers repeatedly depicted Constantius II as cowardly, unmanly, and "soft" on barbarians.[112] Libanius made it clear that while Constantius II drained the Roman soldiers' ἀνδρεία, Julian restored it.[113] Libanius claimed that, in contrast to Julian, who loaded his camels with "weapons and books," Constantius II loaded his camels "with wine, unguents, and soft bedding."[114] Of Constantius II's soldiers, Julian famously said, "they knew only how to pray."[115] This sentiment on the part of Julian (and repeated on the pages of Zosimus' history)[116] did not mean to imply that good soldiers could not be Christians (a good number of Julian's soldiers were surely Christians), only that a zealous emphasis on religious ritual instead of military training led to decline in a soldier's efficiency, and even more dangerously, his masculine ἀνδρεία.[117]

112 Libanius, *Or.* 18.113; Ammianus, *Res gestae* 14.10; Zosimus, *New History* 2.55, 3.1.

113 Libanius, *Or.* 18.209–11.

114 Libanius, *Or.* 62.17.

115 Julian, *frag.* 5.

116 Zosimus, *New History* 3.3.2.

117 Note that Ammianus admonished the Eastern Roman cavalry commander Sebinian for being an inept commander because he wasted too much time on Christian rituals, while other more "reserved" Christian generals such as Jovinus (master of cavalry, 361–69), and Victor (commander in Julian's Persian campaign) are depicted positively. As we noted earlier, Ammianus saw Julian's excessive focus on his religious rituals as one of the emperor's

In the minds of many early Byzantine intellectuals, a combination of a leader's virtues and divine support led to the success of one's cause. On this concept Libanius wrote, "If you force a naturally virtuous [ἀρετῆς] man to live among drunken revelry, his goodness deserts him and he learns these vices instead of the honourable [τῶν καλῶν], and he lives with pleasure in them and loathes his previous life, and so habit becomes the ruin of his character."[118] Libanius went on to explain that it was a mélange of Julian's own manly influences, and the backing of the pagan gods, which had contributed to the Romans' unexpected victory at Strasbourg:

> Did Julian transform them into superior men from being naturally craven, like some deity infusing them with strength? Then what can surpass such superhuman ability? Or had their stoutness been made ineffective by their commanders' natural cowardice? Then what is more glorious to induce good men to demonstrate their full powers?[119]

Of course, there was nothing new in Libanius' conviction that the manly or unmanly conduct of the emperor or military leadership had a direct connection to the manliness or unmanliness of his subordinates. For the Romans, manliness was something that could easily be lost, but just as quickly restored. Anthropologists have shown how in many cultures manhood is not a status attained

---

serious flaws, suggesting that Ammianus disliked any type of ceremony, Christian or non-Christian, that he saw as a waste of time.

118 Libanius, *Or.* 18.209. I have changed the translator Norman's "good" for ἀρετῆς to "virtuous" and his "glories of virtue" for τῶν καλῶν to "the honourable."

119 Libanius, *Or.* 18.65 (my trans.): καίτοι πότερον φύσει κακοὺς ὄντας Ἰουλιανὸς ἐποίησε βελτίους ὥσπερ τις θεὸς μένος ἐμβαλών; καὶ τί μεῖζον τοῦ μεῖζον ἀνθρώπου δύνασθα; ἀλλὰ χρηστὰς φύσεις ἔβλαπτεν ἡγεμόνων κακία; καὶ τί κάλλιον τοῦ τοὺς ἀγαθοὺς εἰς ἐπιδειξιν ὧν ἴσχυον ἀγαγεῖν.

by entering "adulthood" but an elusive category that must be demonstrated or won.[120] The transitory nature of masculinity worked both ways: if "soft" living could quickly cause a Roman man to lose his masculine edge, then with a bit of effort on his part, as well as some prodding by "real" Roman men, courage, manliness, and, ultimately, Rome's masculine *imperium* could be restored.

An emperor's courage and ability to defeat an enemy on the field of battle, however, represented only an aspect of ideal leadership and true manliness. One sees evidence of this sentiment when Eunapius has Julian in a set-speech to his troops explain to both his men and the literary audience the qualities that separated the true manly Roman leader from a merely courageous military commander or barbarian king. Following rhetorical tradition, Julian claimed the most virtuous of men combined "gentleness [πραότητα] and moderation [σωφροσύνην] with courage [ἀνδρεία] and strength [ῥώμη]."[121] Echoing sentiments found in Julian's own writings, Eunapius praised the emperor for his perfect blend of force and restraint. In Eunapius' telling, Julian treated the barbarian enemy firmly yet fairly. Though Julian recognised that "manliness [ἀνδρεία], strength [ῥώμη] and physical force [κράτος]" played a vital role on the battlefield, he concluded that "justice [δικαιοσύνη] combined with authority was like a fountainhead of virtues [ἀρετῶν], which made even those far away manageable and obedient."[122]

Though the sentiments related above follow well-trodden classical ideals, and exaggerate Julian's military achievements somewhat, they are useful for our purposes because they show how Eunapius and many other contemporaries felt an ideal Roman emperor and soldier should behave towards "barbarians" in war and in peace. This is a line of argument repeated regularly

---

120 Gilmore, *Manhood in the Making*.

121 Julian, *Letter to Alypius* 404. I have change the translator Henderson's "courage" for ἀνδρεία to "manliness."

122 Eunapius, *frag.* 3.18.

in the classicising historians—the manly Roman uses his superior
ἀνδρεία to first dominate the barbarian on the battlefield, but
once victory has been achieved, however, the conquered enemy
could be shown mercy, and if they recognised Roman "justice,"
allowed to join the Roman army or to settle onto Roman territory.
Unless properly supervised, however, the barbarians could easily
fall back into "savagery." Therefore, one should not allow them to
maintain either their way of life (especially pastoralism) or their
pagan religion, but force them to adapt to Roman culture. In this
way, a Roman could use his manly resolve and self-controlled
adherence to justice to tame the "wild beasts."[123]

Despite the panegyrical views of the apostate by his supporters
found above, it is clear not everyone in the later Roman Empire
saw Julian as an ideal military leader or man. Ammianus was
likely countering such complaints. He recorded several instances
where Julian faced questions concerning his manliness and right
to rule. On one occasion, Ammianus related with some irony how
Julian's enemies (which included many of Constantius II's eunuch
advisors) within Constantius' court denigrated him as "Greek
dilettante" (litterionem Graecum) whose exaggerated military
exploits covered up his sedentary and timid nature.[124] In another
episode, when food fell scarce in 358, Julian's own soldiers in Gaul
ridiculed the future emperor as "a degenerate Greek from Asia and
a liar and a fool who pretended to be wise."[125] It is probably not
coincidental that many of these attacks remain aligned to typical

---

123 Cf. Procopius' account of Justinian's attempted Romanisation of the Tzani
(*Wars* 1.15.25).

124 Ammianus, *Res gestae* 17.11 (trans. Hamilton). As Ammianus explains in this
same section, the "most glorious actions" of great military men like Scipio
Aemilianus and Pompey tended to attract the envy of less accomplished
men.

125 Ammianus, *Res gestae* 17.9.3 (trans. Hamilton): "Asianum appellans
Graeculum et fallacem, et specie sapientiae stolidum." Cf. the criticisms of
Julian by the citizens of Antioch: Julian, *Misopogon* 37, 364C; Libanius, *Or.*
16.30.

Roman gendered prejudice. Indeed, these jibes appear to expose the prevailing concerns and the prejudices of soldiers who had long believed in the effeminacy of Easterners and the "softness" of the educated elite within the Empire.[126] Yet, Ammianus, who emphasised his own Greek identity[127] as well as his exploits as a soldier, made it clear to his readers that Julian quickly proved these detractors wrong.[128]

It is also important to point out that Julian's martial exploits and victories over the barbarians came as somewhat of a surprise to most Romans of the period, and even to Julian.[129] Contemporaries reported that the soldier-emperor Constantius II had sent Julian to Gaul with the expectation of his quick demise.[130] Some of these doubts concerning Julian's untested martial virtues appear related to existing teachings that contended that men who engaged in the higher echelons of intellectual endeavours needed to remove themselves from the concerns of the mundane world. Philosophers of the period were not expected to participate in warfare. In fact, in spite of the adulation of "philosopher kings" like Marcus Aurelius, in the ancient sources "true" philosophers were expected to avoid political lives. According to tradition, this independence allowed them to speak "truths" that others

126 See, e.g., *Panegyric of Constantine* 12 24.1, where the panegyrist contrasts Constantine I's victories over Western Roman rivals and Western barbarians with Licinius' victory in the Eastern half of the Empire over Maximinus "It is easy to conquer timid creatures unfit for war, such as the pleasant regions of the Greece and the charms of the Orient produce, who can barely tolerate a light cloak, and silken garments to keep off the sun, and who if they ever get into danger forget freedom and beg to be slaves."

127 Ammianus, *Res gestae* 20.3.4, 23.6.20, 25.2.5.

128 The method of a biographer highlighting an emperor's sexual restraint and martial virtues against opponents' gendered attacks had a long-established role in imperial biography. For this *topoi* in first-century biographers of Augustus see Conway, *Behold the Man*, 37–45.

129 Libanius, *Or.* 18.32.

130 Eunapius, *frag.* 14.1–2.

protecting their careers feared.[131] This reality may explain why Julian and his backers took such pains to portray him as reluctantly abandoning his intellectual pursuits to take on his military duties in Gaul and later the purple.[132]

Despite receiving some military training in his youth, Julian's martial acumen before his assignment to Gaul in 355 remained untested.[133] His devotees, however, made it clear to their audience that Julian was not only able to overcome such obstacles, but was inordinately adept at applying the alternative, yet positive, masculine attributes he had attained as a "philosopher" in his new political role. According to Eunapius, Julian's philosophical training at the Academy in Athens had come in handy during his subsequent political career, and had helped Julian to subdue unmanly[134] passions such as "the royal anger" (τὸν βασιλικὸν θυμὸν) that could undermine the reigns of less educated emperors.[135] Many ancient writers perceived a passion like "anger" (Latin *ira*) as an indication of a weak intellect, and consequently as a trait more common in the uneducated, barbarians, and women. Seneca, for instance, proclaimed that "anger [*ira*] is a most womanish [*muliebre*] and childish weakness."[136] Wielding

131 Sacks, "Meaning of Eunapius' History," 65.

132 Libanius, *Or.* 18.31, Eunapius, *Lives of the Philosophers* 476. Julian complained in a letter to former school friends in Athens about his having to abandon the pure delight "of pursuing philosophy at one's leisure without interruption." He only half joked in a letter, that after four years of living a "barbarian's life" in Gaul it was a wonder he could still understand Greek at all. Julian, *Letter to Eumenius and Pharianus* 441.

133 Ammianus, *Res gestae* 16.5.10.

134 As Colleen Conway explains (*Behold the Man*, 26–27), however, some Graeco-Roman moralists did perceive anger "as an active display of one's convictions—a manly act."

135 Eunapius, *frag.* 25.3. Cf. Eunapius' (*frag.* 44.5) description of Valens' "frenzied rage" (ἐκβαχεύω) when he ordered his soldiers to "unwisely" attack the Goths at the Battle of Adrianople.

136 Seneca, *De Ira* 1.13.5, 1.20.3, 2.19.4.

manly martial metaphors, the Emperor Marcus Aurelius declared that "anger is a mark of weakness as is grief; in both of them men receive a wound and submit to a defeat."[137] Ammianus echoed these sentiments above. He defined *ira* as "a long continued, sometimes permanent, ulcer of the mind, usually caused by weakness [*mollitia*] of the intellect; and they give for their opinion (the philosophers) the plausible ground that the sickly are more inclined to anger than the sound, women to men, the old to the young, and the wretched to the fortunate."[138]

Hence, Julian's superior intellect allowed him to control his passions better than less educated emperors or military commanders. When describing Julian's intellectual and martial virtues, Libanius underlined what he saw as the apostate's intrinsic advantage over less educated military commanders or emperors, commenting, "For he always had in his hands either books or arms, for he considered warfare to be greatly helped by philosophy, and that in an emperor ability to use his wits was more effective than belligerency."[139]

Such praise of Julian's easy commingling of these martial and intellectual talents probably represents more than just stock imperial rhetoric. It is important to point out that Roman intellectuals had long professed that one's education represented an essential step in one's "masculine formation." From at least the second century, wise instructors who functioned as conduits to masculinity played vital roles in the creation of manly Roman men.[140] Many of these same moralists advised that manliness and courage could be absorbed in the classroom. Even an intrinsically male characteristic like ἀνδρεία might be developed and honed by the instructor. As Karen Bassi notes, ἀνδρεία represented

137 Marcus Aurelius, *Ad se ipsum*, ed. Dalphen, trans. Staniforth.
138 Ammianus, *Res gestae* 27.7.4.
139 Libanius, *Or.* 18.72: ἀεὶ γὰρ εἶχεν ἐν χεροῖν ἢ βίβλους ἢ ὅπλα νομίζον μεγάλα πόλεμον ὑπὸ σοφίας ὠφελεῖσθαι καὶ μείζω γε φέρειν ῥοπέν βασιλέα βουλεύσθαι δυνάμενον ἢ μαχόμενον.
140 Conway, *Behold the Man*, 34.

"something that manly fathers seem particularly incapable of passing down to their biological sons."[141] These convictions provide reasons why some late Roman writers insisted that a literary education could serve as a critical component of a military leader's training.[142] Furthermore, we find Eunapius and Libanius explaining in their writings that an understanding of history provided a leader with the "blueprint" for success when fighting actual battles.[143] We do know that Julian employed his literary education to help him mimic the speeches of "generals of old" to motivate his own soldiers before battle.[144] So too it is likely that Julian read military manuals, since emperors and generals represented the expected audience for this popular early Byzantine genre.[145]

Although the accounts above may have exaggerated Julian's military prowess, they reflect widely held late Roman convictions concerning both idealised leadership and hyper-masculinity. By emphasising Julian's ἀνδρεία, as well as his intolerance for ἀνανδρία, his defenders were able to overcome accusations of unmanliness hurled at Julian by his naysayers, but also demonstrate to their literary audience the type of manly leader that was required to restore the Empire to its former glory. Traditional *topoi* centred on accepted categories of manly and unmanly behaviour, and therefore served to provide these writers with the means to depict Julian as both an ideal emperor and man.

These idealised portraits by Ammianus and Eunapius of Julian as a typical ἀνδρεῖος βασιλεύς are a reminder that late Roman

---

141 Bassi, "Semantics of Manliness," 200, 351.

142 For Ammianus' tendency to attribute some of Valens' vices to his lack of a proper education, see Amirav, "Ammianus Stoicus," 102.

143 Eunapius, *frag.* 44; Libanius, *Or.* 18.39.

144 Libanius, *Or.* 18.53.

145 Conor Whately suggests ("Genre and Purpose of Military Manuals") that military manuals like Vegetius' *Epitoma Rei Milataris* and the late sixth-century *Maurice's Strategicon* were meant to be read by the emperor and his generals.

intellectuals continued to esteem martial virtues as essential components of Roman masculinity and ideal leadership. Similar to the present-day American politicians who can appreciate, and at times appropriate, the über-masculine image of the American soldier for their own political needs, the majority of the demilitarised late Roman elites who read these accounts—if not necessarily wanting to emulate them on the field of battle—would certainly have appreciated Julian's mastery of many of the traditional martial and intellectual virtues that had long defined ultimate manliness in the Roman world. We should bear in mind as well that the Christian elites of the fifth century readily accepted such traditional secular themes. Moreover, as Alan Cameron has recently shown, by the time Eunapius and Ammianus published their histories, paganism was a spent force. By the close of the fourth century, the spread and the ascendancy of Christianity in both halves of the Empire was truly irreversible. As Cameron remarks, paganism had "died a natural death, and was already mortally ill before Theodosius (I) embarked on his final campaign."[146]

As a result, these secular writers represent Julian's "golden age" not so much in religious terms, but as a time when a "real" Roman man whisked out of the Academy in Athens unexpectedly stood up to the challenges presented by the Empire's internal and external foes. This message served as powerful propaganda for Julian in his own lifetime. Furthermore, as the histories of Eunapius and Ammianus reveal, this praise of Julian's militarism was an ideology that continued to resonate for late fourth- and early fifth-century Roman reading audiences wearied by a long line of Roman military failures and feeble, unwarlike, and unmanly emperors. So, even if strident Christians might attack Julian for his uncompromising religious beliefs, as well as the circumstances

---

146 Cameron, *Last Pagans of Rome*, 131. The most significant aspect of Cameron's argument for my argument in this chapter is his thorough rejection that Eugenius' war with Theodosius I represented a pagan revival undertaken on the behalf of an increasingly persecuted pagan senatorial elite in the West.

behind his premature death, the less ardent Christian, or more recent convert, probably would have admired Julian for his ability to combine virile displays of renunciation with traditional martial deeds that had long served as essential aspect of ideal leadership and manliness.

Evidence of this reality is reflected in Eunapius' claim that Julian's exploits had earned him "universal high repute" amongst the Romans who came to manhood in the generation after his death in 363, and the fact that church historians writing in the century after Julian's death still felt it necessary to undermine the apostate's lingering reputation for wisdom and manly courage.[147] Indeed, in early 550s Constantinople he was remembered and admired as an "outstanding man and indispensable to the state."[148] The early Byzantine readers of these histories could not help but be reminded how far the majority of Julian's successors had fallen short of his manly standard.

147 See, e.g., Socrates, *HE* 7.22.7–8; Theodoret, *HE* 3.21.

148 Jordanes, *Romana* 304 (trans. Regan): "Ipse siquidem vir egregius, et Rei Publicae necessarius."

Plate 7. Mosaic (ca. 500, Museo Arcivescovile, Ravenna, Italy) of Christ depicted in the military attire of a Roman emperor. He bears a cross and holds the Gospel showing the passage John 14:6 "I am the way, truth, and life."

V

THE WARS MOST PEACEFUL: MILITARISM, PIETY, AND CONSTRUCTIONS OF CHRISTIAN MANLINESS IN THE THEODOSIAN AGE

It is the struggles of the athletes of piety [εὐσεβείας
ἀθλητων] and their manliness [ἀνδρείας] that endured
so much, trophies won from demons, and over invisible
enemies, and the crowns at the end of all, that will endure.
Eusebius, *HE* 5.1.4

NO SINGLE MODEL OF IDEALISED MANLINESS CHARACTERISED early Byzantine constructions of men's heroic conduct. This point becomes readily apparent when one considers the diverse portraits of secular and religious heroes found in the early Byzantine scholarly tradition. At first glance, the courage and piety of the Christian martyrs described in the quotation above, or of a holy man, such as Daniel the Stylite (409–93), or of powerful bishops like Ambrose of Milan (ca. 339–97) and John Chrysostom (ca. 349–407) found in an early Byzantine church history may seem far removed from the acts of masculine bravery of the secular military heroes alluded to in the preceding chapters. Yet, as several recent studies on early Christian and Graeco-Roman masculinity have convincingly argued, the examples of idealised behaviour displayed by these men were all created by authors of a similar educational and cultural background, and consequently, though their representations of idealised men differed, they observed some of the same basic principles of heroic and manly conduct based, in part, on one's self-mastery and displays of "courage" in the face of adversity.[1]

From their religion's earliest days, Christian writers had necessarily engaged with the predominant gender ideologies of the Roman Empire, and especially, an ascendant Graeco-Roman masculinity that by the first and second centuries had increasingly accommodated multifaceted, and at times formerly more marginalised, pathways to a "true" masculine identity. This chapter explores some of the "revolutionary," aspects of what some modern academics describe as the rise and the growing dominance by the end of the fourth century of a new Christian masculine ideal.[2]

Though it remains outside this study's scope to retell in detail the Christianisation of the Empire, the rise of extreme asceticism, or the growing power and influence of holy men, monks, and bishops, the chapter opens by tracing the evolution of the Christian "hero" in the fourth century and his growing popularity in later Christian sources from the fourth and the fifth centuries. It seeks to demonstrate why some recent studies have attributed shifts in hegemonic Roman masculine ideology to these social and political developments. I will contend that while many of these influential modern studies have correctly uncovered how early Christian intellectuals both interacted and cleverly inverted dominant Graeco-Roman masculinities, they have, at times, overstated the impact as well as the innovative nature of Christian

---

1 Conway, *Behold the Man*, 175–84; Larson, "Paul's Masculinity," 85–97; Anderson and Moore, *New Testament Masculinities*.

2 Kuefler, *Manly Eunuch*, 286.

masculine ideology in this era. Moreover, despite the claims found in many of these same studies that martial virtues no longer played an essential part in shaping notions of heroic manliness in the fifth century, we will see once again that the waging of war and the acts of masculine bravery best demonstrated by Roman soldiers in "real" battles remained a crucial aspect of hegemonic masculinity in the Theodosian age.

God's Manliest Warriors

To appreciate the influence of the Christian heroic ideal on the fifth-century Eastern Roman Empire, it is necessary to outline briefly the evolution of the idealised Christian in the fourth century. Until this time, most Christian men and women had established their superiority by martyrdom. The martyrs (Greek for "witnesses") became the first Christian saints and heroes, both for their willingness to challenge the authority of the local pagan leaders and their eagerness to give up their lives for their religious convictions. Emulating the Graeco-Roman literary genre of biography that related the deeds of great philosophers, Roman political leaders, and military commanders, Christian writers in the second century began recording the deeds of these "saintly heroes."[3] These early works were the first examples of hagiography; their notions of ideal Christian conduct would have a tremendous impact in not only late antiquity, but also well into the Middle Ages.[4]

Current research has largely overturned the older scholarly view of early Christians as rigid pacifists, positing instead that from its earliest days Christian literature had readily paired irenic and

---

3 Krueger, *Writing and Holiness*, 5–6. For the steady popularity of Plutarch's (ca. 46–120 CE) biographies from the Roman and early Byzantine era, see Duff, *Plutarch's Lives*, 4–5.

4 Noble and Head, "Introduction," xxii–xxx.

militant ideologies.[5] Certainly, a deft intermingling of spiritual and physical warfare had always played a part in Christian ideology.[6] This process only accelerated in the post-Constantinian church.[7]

The authors of early saints' lives frequently compared the courage and manliness of martyrs with that of Roman soldiers. The original martyr stories focused regularly on the military aspects of their subject's execution.[8] As an example, one need only examine the second-century *Martyrdom of Saint Polycarp*, where God takes the place of the military commander by exhorting the Bishop Polycarp (69–155) when he entered the arena to face his execution: "Be strong Polycarp and play the man" (ἴσχυε, Πολύκαρπε, καὶ ἀνδρίζου).[9] The author presented Polycarp's death as heroic in the best Roman tradition. Roman and early Byzantine historians used similar gendered rhetoric and, indeed, vocabulary when depicting generals' pre-battle speeches to their troops.[10] The author therefore transforms a death that many Romans would have seen as passive and unmanly into a martial and manly demise. Whether or not one accepts that accounts of the persecution represented contemporary relations between Christians and imperial authority, for a religion that was both trying to fit in a Roman world and answering accusations of cowardice against its followers from the pagan establishment, these Christian examples

---

5   Brennecke, "An fidelis ad militiam converti possit"; Buc, "Christian Theology of Violence"; Shean, *Soldiering for God*; Conway, *Behold the Man*, 160–74.

6   Conway, *Behold the Man*, 176–81.

7   For the notion that a more militant and "more" violent Christianity was a particular feature of the post-Constantinian church, see Heim, *La théologie de la victoire d'Constantin à Théodose*; Gaddis, *There Is No Crime for Those Who Have Christ*; Sizgorich, *Violence and Belief in Late Antiquity*; Shaw, *Sacred Violence*.

8   Kuefler, *Manly Eunuch*, 110.

9   I use the version of the second-century *Life* found in Eusebius, *HE* 4.15.17, trans. Lake and Oulton. Cf. Eusebius, *HE* 6.8.7.

10   See, e.g., Procopius, *Wars* 6.23.32, 5.28.13, 6.12.20, 6.23.31.

of bravery served as a unifying force and a symbol of Christian courage and manliness.[11]

The fourth century also witnessed the birth of the genre of ecclesiastical history.[12] The seminal church historian, Eusebius (ca. 260–339) found it necessary to find alternatives to the pagan Roman Empire's reliance on secular literature and its cadre of non-Christian heroes.[13] It is critical always to keep in mind that early fourth-century Christian theologians like Eusebius were attempting to persuade a still largely non-Christian governing class that needed convincing. Michele Salzman summarises the situation: "A religion whose texts taught love for one's neighbours and humility, with strictures on wealth and notions of equality, did not, generally speaking, appeal to aristocrats." So, partially as a means of appeal to prospective or recent converts from the Roman upper classes fourth-century church leaders "fashioned the rhetoric of Christianity to make it pleasing to educated elite listeners."[14]

We discover evidence of this adaptation in Christian accounts of the martyrs. Since most late Roman elites expected their heroes to be "unyielding and warlike," it helps to explain why an idealised Christian had similar qualities—if, at times, only in a metaphorical sense.[15] Set against this background, we can understand why Eusebius, who essentially founded the genre of church history, infused his writings with heroic Christians who

11 Revisionists have challenged recently the validity of this portrayal of non-Romans' consistent persecution of Christians, suggesting that the majority of Christians felt little compunction to provoke imperial authorities, see, e.g., Moss, *The Myth of the Persecution*; Boin, *Coming out Christian*.

12 Good basic surveys of the Byzantine church historians are found in Chesnut, *The First Church Historians*; Treadgold, *Early Byzantine Historians*, 23–46, 121–75.

13 Eusebius, *HE* 5.1.1–4. On Eusebius in general, see Barnes, *Constantine and Eusebius*.

14 Salzman, *Christian Aristocracy*, 2, 201.

15 Julian, *Against the Galileans* 116 A.

showed his audience that through martyrdom Christians could act as gallantly and as bravely as any Roman legionary facing death on the battlefield. It is of course notoriously difficult to know the popularity or to pin down the exact makeup of the readership for this type of Christian literature, though it appears they reached a larger audience than their secular counterparts.[16] Though one might assume that Eusebius created his history primarily for fellow devout Christians, his introduction indicates that the bishop was addressing a more diverse group—one consisting of readers of more traditional secular history, potential converts, and even non-Christians critical of the genre of church history.[17] The readership for ecclesiastical history was not limited to devout Christians, but probably included a larger and more diverse audience of "the cultural elite and a wider group of less educated but still relatively literate civil and military officials and others" who liked to read all forms of history.[18]

Eusebius found it important to emphasise in his account the writings of earlier Christian theologians who had sought to refute claims by those labelled the "heathens" that the Christians facing public execution were "ignoble and unmanly" (ἀγεννεις καὶ ἄνανδροι).[19] In fact, Christian people's propensity for "piety" (εὐσεβείας) and the "courageous life" (καρτερία βίου), in the eyes of Eusebius and his sources, contributed to their excelling in "manly virtue" (καὶ ἀρετῆς ἀνδρεία).[20] He insisted that one

16 Urbainczyk (*Socrates*, 64–67), discusses the difficulty of pinpointing the size and the exact makeup of the readership of the early church historians. Cameron (*Procopius and the Sixth Century*, 116) and Kaldellis (*Procopius of Caesarea*, 235) contend that Procopius had read Eusebius' history, which would give us further evidence that not only devout Christians were interested in ecclesiastical history.

17 Eusebius, *HE* 1.1.6, 1.2.1.

18 Croke, "Uncovering Byzantium's Historiographical Audience," 33–34.

19 Eusebius, *HE* 5.1.34.

20 Eusebius, *HE* 1.4.7. I have modified the translator Lake's "courageous virtue" for ἀρετῆς ἀνδρεία to "manly virtue."

could compare the martyrs' courage to anyone immortalised for their ἀνδρεία "by Greeks or barbarians."[21] Roman intellectuals had long seen one's ability to handle pain with courage as a tell-tale sign of "true" manliness.[22] So when Eusebius or his source emphasised the martyrs' propensity to face dismemberment and worse with bravery typical of manly soldiers, they relied on an aspect of traditional hegemonic masculinity readily understood by their Christian and non-Christian audience.[23] As Philip Buc opines perceptively, "Christian martyrdom, far from being as a general rule pacifist or passive, was often enough bellicose and active." Certainly, a deft intermingling of spiritual and physical warfare had always played a role in Christian ideology. Buc argues that from its origins, "Christendom struggles simultaneously against physical enemies outside, against vices inside the human being and against vicious men inside Christendom—for instance, resident Jews, false brethren (falsi fratres, see Gal. 2.4), bad clergy, perverts, heretics—and against demons."[24]

In these spiritual battles, which Eusebius described as "the wars most peaceful" (εἰρηνικωτάτους πολέμους, 5.1.4) even a woman could become a "noble athlete" (γενναιος ἀθλητῆς, 5.1.19) or behave like God's "manliest warrior" (ὁ ἀνδρειότατος ὁπλομάχος, 6.41.16).[25] Despite following the common discriminatory attitude of the time that perceived women as the inferior sex, on certain occasions women's zealous faith in God could break down the boundaries between genders. By suffering the same contests as

21 Eusebius, *HE* 8.6.1: Πάντων δὲ ὅσοι τῶν πώποτε ἀνυμνοῦνται θαυμάσιοι καὶ ἐπ' ἀνδρεία βεβοημένοι εἴτε παρ'α "Ελλησιν εἴτε παρα βαρβάροις. We know too that Eusebius was familiar with these traditional models, see Eusebius, *Vita Constantini* 1.10, ed. Heikel.

22 E.g., Cicero, *Epist. Fam.* 5.17.3, discussed in Conway, *Behold the Man*, 29–30.

23 See, e.g., Ammianus (*Res gestae* 22.10.11) where the former soldier, who could be critical of Christians, expressed admiration for the Christian martyrs' courage.

24 Buc, *Holy War*, 23, 91.

25 I have changed the translator Oulton's "brave" for ἀνδρειότατος to "manliest."

men, Eusebius revealed that female martyrs "showed themselves no less manly than the men."[26]

Still, danger lurks for those looking for signs of "early Christian feminism" within texts composed by late Roman elites like Eusebius that remain highly misogynistic and regularly demand that women "must deny their sex" or "be like a man" to achieve sanctity.[27] As has been often times remarked, Roman intellectuals had long clashed over the idea that men and women possessed distinctive virtues. Particularly during the first and second centuries, many Stoic and Christian thinkers, influenced by ideas of symmetry, concluded that women were just as capable as men in cultivating essential and typically masculine virtues. In spite of these declarations of gendered egalitarianism, deeply ingrained misogynistic attitudes remained difficult for these intellectuals to overcome. Recent evaluations of these supposedly more philogynist writers have persuasively uncovered the dissonance between their idealistic philosophical claims, and the reality found in their texts. Much ink has been spilled on this topic. A divide persists within the field between those who see Byzantine women as relatively empowered—particularly in their roles as Christians and empresses—and those who suppose that Roman and early Byzantine societies remained "highly misogynistic" and androcentric.[28] For many late Roman theologians, the genderless ideal was quite simply the masculine ideal in disguise. The church fathers often cast exemplary Christians—male and female—as displaying masculine temperaments. One observes an example of this attitude expressed in a letter from Jerome (ca. 341–420)

---

26 Eusebius, *HE* 8.14.13 (trans. Oulton): αἱ δ᾽ αὖ γυναῖκες οὐχ ἧττον τῶν ἀνδρῶν ὑπὸ τῆς τοῦ θείου λόγου διδασκαλίας ἠρρενωμέναι αἵ μὲν τούς *autous* τοῖς *andrasin* ἀνδράσιν ἀγῶνας ὑποστᾶσαι ἴσα τῆς ἀρετῆς ἀπηνέγκαντο βραβεῖα.

27 Cameron, "Virginity as a Metaphor," 184–92; Salzman, *Christian Aristocracy*, 140–47.

28 Some noteworthy studies: Hallett, *Fathers and Daughters*; Lefkowitz, "Influential Women"; Cooper, *Virgin and the Bride*; Garland, *Byzantine Empresses*; James, *Empresses and Power*.

where he espoused the "manliness" of women whose dedication to perpetual virginity allowed women to transcend their gender's innately carnal and inferior nature. He wrote, "As long as woman is for birth and children, she is different from man as body is from soul. But when she wishes to serve Christ more than the world, she will cease to be a woman and will be called a man."[29] Ambrose of Milan went further, proposing: "She who does not believe is a woman and should be designated by the name of her sex, whereas she who believes progresses to perfect manhood."[30] To borrow the words of Karen Armstrong, "For Ambrose, salvation for a woman means shedding her femaleness and becoming fully human and fully adult, that is becoming male."[31] Statements like these illustrate for us once again the allure of the universalised masculine.

This is not to say that women did not play an important part in Roman and Byzantine society. Women from all levels of these cultures took on significant roles and, at times, wielded considerable power as political players, medical practitioners, scholars, and powerful religious patrons.[32] It is one thing, however, to say that the Romans and early Byzantines appreciated feminine virtues and produced powerful and influential women, but quite another to claim that this reality disproves that the Roman and Byzantine Empires remained at their cores androcentric cultures.

Women's influential roles in the late Roman and early Byzantine church did not lead to a less masculine centric culture. Instead of the genderless ideal preached by Paul, Christianity continued a

29 Jerome, *Commentarius in Epistolam ad Ephesios*, III, v (658), quoted in Schulenburg, *Forgetful of Their Sex*, 453. See too Augustine's (*Confessions* 9.4.8) declaration that though his "mother had the inherent weakness of a woman, she had the strong faith of a man" (matre adhaerente nobis muliebri habitu, virili fide).

30 Ambrose, *Expositio Evangelii secundum Lucam libri X*, n. 161, quoted in Schulenburg, *Forgetful of Their Sex*, 453.

31 Armstrong, "The Acts of Paul and Thecla," 87.

32 Cooper, "Gender and the Fall of Rome," 197–98.

more traditional misogynistic ideology better suited for recent converts among the non-Christian elite. On this development, Mathew Kuefler declares insightfully:

> An equal challenge was the willingness of some Christian men to acknowledge that the tradition of "no more male or female" meant that in order to pursue holiness as Christians they would have to abandon their masculine identity. The patristic model of Christianity proved successful, I have argued, because it was conservative in the truest sense of the word, preserving the classical tradition of a hierarchy of men over women and the clear-cut distinction between the two, a tradition otherwise brought into question by the many social changes of late antiquity.[33]

Accordingly, notwithstanding the significant roles that women from all social classes played in the early Byzantine world, the strict gender order of men over women proved persistent. Men's domination of the political hierarchy of the Eastern and Western churches is a reminder of the ceiling placed upon women in early Byzantium.[34]

Moreover, there was nothing new or specifically Christian in Eusebius' apparent rejection of "traditional standards of Roman masculine militarism." Early Christian intellectuals, like Paul, had long utilised the paradox where "weakness was strength and defeat

---

33 Kuefler, *Manly Eunuch*, 238–39.

34 James, *Empresses and Power*, 164–65. The actual authority wielded by these "Theodosian women" has attracted some recent debate. For example, Holum (*Theodosian Empresses*) and Chew ("Virgins and Eunuchs") see a great deal of influence, whilst Burgess and McEvoy point out, I believe rightly, that women from the Theodosian imperial family had far less authority and/or influence over internal and external politics than some suppose. See, Burgess, "Accession of Marcian," 47–48; McEvoy, *Child Emperor Rule*, 236.

was victory."[35] These New Testament authors in turn followed Stoic intellectuals in the early Empire who had embraced ἀνδρεία as a "quieter virtue" of "endurance and self-control rather than a perseverance of action." In fact, many of these same Stoic writers maintained that a seemingly passive death could be understood as manly if undertaken for a noble or honourable cause.[36]

New Champions of Christian Manliness

Despite the martyrs' continuing allure, by the fifth century this form of sacrifice had largely become outmoded.[37] There were several factors behind this change. When the Empire became Christian, two things occurred: first, the opportunities for a glorious death declined; secondly, because Christians joined the establishment, many of them found it unwise to treat the Roman government as an adversary. As Christianity's role in the Roman government grew, it also became essential for the church to control individuals who acted outside the established hierarchy, even charismatic heroes such as the martyrs.[38] In fact, before the martyr's decline, some Christians had adopted a new form of valour. In third- and fourth-century Egypt and Syria, an elite cadre became Christian heroes by pushing the limits of abstinence. Following New Testament examples of Jesus, who "escaped to the desert to pray in solitude,"[39] devout Christians like the Egyptian Anthony had set out alone from the cities of the Empire and into the deserts, determined to separate themselves from the physical

---

35 2 Corinthians 12:10.

36 Conway, *Behold the Man*, 77. For the influence of Stoic thought on Paul, see Engberg-Pedersen, *Paul and the Stoics*.

37 Martyr stories continued to be produced involving men and woman facing persecutions outside the Roman Empire, particularly in the Persian Empire, e.g., Sozomen, *HE* 2.9–14; Theodoret, *HE* 5.38.

38 Hall, "The Organization of the Church," 731.

39 Luke 5:16.

world's corruption.[40] Struggling against temptation, they battled to purify their bodies against the "demon of fornication" and fears of starvation. For these men isolated in the desert, conquering hunger became an even more difficult task than their struggle against lust. Many Christian intellectuals alleged that Adam and Eve's first sin had not been fornication, but their inability to resist eating the fruit from the Tree of Knowledge.[41] By persevering, these individuals became heroic models for the segment of devoted Christians who proclaimed that supreme men practised sexual abstinence, restricted their diet, and treated possessions, rank, and power with indifference.[42]

Some of Christian heroism's core appeal appears connected to its more inclusive nature. To some extent, the rise of the extreme ascetic was connected to concerns on the part of some Christians about Roman secular authorities' growing influence over fourth-century religious matters, as well as a rejection by these same intellectuals of the increased effect of "aristocratic status culture" on late Roman Christianity. Though the majority of these extreme ascetics hailed from the upper classes, some came from the peasantry, and some were female.[43] These humble backgrounds differed from classical Graeco-Roman and Germanic cultures that focused on men, emphasised a hero's lineage, and tended to look down on men of humble origins. Even though late Roman Christians from the upper classes rarely spoke of "universal salvation or egalitarian spirituality," Christian writers from the less privileged classes sometimes preached a less restricted theology.[44] These theologians rebelled against the traditional Roman attitude that a man's lineage and political accomplishments determined his *nobilitas* (distinction). *Nobilitas*, they claimed, served as a universal virtue and was open to all men, regardless of their social

40 Goehring, *Ascetics, Society, and the Desert*, 16.
41 See Brown, *Body and Society*, 220–21.
42 Rousseau, "Monasticism," 745.
43 Urbainczyk, *Theodoret*, 67–79.
44 Salzman, *Christian Aristocracy*, 218.

class. To accentuate their scorn for the Roman social order, these Christians gained acclaim by rejecting their family ancestry and joining Christ's family, thereby creating their own "aristocracy."[45] While most Christians could never hope to attain the strict perfection demanded by this new principle of heroism, by interacting with holy men or appealing to male and female saints they could gain a glimpse of God's flawlessness.[46]

Life of Anthony

The groundbreaking work describing these innovative Christian heroes was the *Life of Anthony*, probably composed by the Alexandrian bishop Athanasius around 357.[47] Written in simple Greek prose,[48] it sought to promote the devotion and the heroism of Anthony as an exemplar of the "extreme" ascetic life, and in this was largely successful. Anthony's biography, like much of the Christian literature of the day, was composed in a far simpler prose than its secular counterparts were. As a result, these Christian authors reached a far broader spectrum of late Roman literate society than their non-Christian counterparts. These Christian lives also concentrated on, and frequently praised, women and the poor—members of late Roman society who were typically neglected in the non-Christian literary tradition.[49] As Peter Brown puts it, "Anthony was the hero of the Panerémos, of the Deep Desert, the Outer Space of the ascetic world."[50] This work

---

45 This section owes much to Salzman, *Christian Aristocracy*, 200–19.

46 Brown, "Holy Men," 781–82.

47 Some scholars dispute that Athanasius composed the life, see Barnes, *Athanasius and Constantius*, 240, n. 64.

48 These issues are discussed in Cameron, *Christianity and the Rhetoric of Empire*, 147–49.

49 The modern literature on Anthony is vast. A helpful starting point is Brown, *Body and Society*, 213–40. An excellent survey on current historiographical controversies is found in Barnes, "Angel of Light."

50 Brown, *Body and Society*, 214–15.

both attracted potential converts to monasticism and served as a literary model for later hagiographers.[51] Yet, like ecclesiastical history, its readership included Christians and non-Christians.[52] Though a detailed analysis of this important text remains outside this study's scope, the metaphorical martial themes found in its opening chapters, as well as the influence this life has had on some modern scholars' conceptualisation of a "new Christian masculine ideal," deserve some comment.[53]

At its core, the story is one of transformation. The early chapters relate the time-honoured Roman account of a young adolescent male on the cusp of manhood, and the choices he must make to become an ideal citizen and a manly Roman man. Of course, what makes it special is the Christian twist on this conventional theme. Instead of becoming a productive member of civic society once his metamorphosis is complete, Anthony sought to reject it. In the end, his rejection is only partial. Anthony in fact communicates directly with many secular leaders of the day, including the emperor. In a similar vein to Eusebius' profile of the emperor Constantine I, Athanasius both followed and subverted the classical forms of biography.[54] Whereas the ancient generals, political leaders, and emperors in traditional biography had typically demonstrated their manliness and worth in war, Anthony must validate his merit in spiritual warfare.

Conflict, albeit of a spiritual and a metaphorical type, is rife in the early part of the *Life* where Anthony has to prove his worth. Athanasius portrayed a world where Anthony vied for supremacy with false Hellenic deities and the Devil. In the words of Claudia Rapp, "Anthony's progressive withdrawal into the desert amounted to nothing less than a territorial battle with the demons."[55] According to Athanasius, the demons whom Anthony

---

51 Rapp, *Holy Bishops*, 110.

52 For this diverse audience, see Cameron, "Form and Meaning," 78.

53 Kuefler, *Manly Eunuch*, 281.

54 Cameron, "Form and Meaning," 75.

55 Rapp, *Holy Bishops*, 110.

confronted in the tombs outside his home town and deep in the desert represented fallen angels who had tricked the Greek oracles into worshipping them as Hellenic deities.[56] It is likely then, that for Athanasius Anthony's numerous victories over these demons—spurred on by God's spirit within him—symbolised the Christians' triumph over the pagans and their "false" pantheon of gods. Anthony's role as a prototypical soldier of Christ dominates the early part of the biography.[57] Anthony, indeed, faced many of the same choices and challenges that a young Roman recruit would have confronted upon joining the Eastern Roman army—the abandonment of one's city and family to an often distant outpost at the fringes of the Empire, rigorous drilling to hone one's battle skills, and courage under the guidance of a commander who served as a conduit to courage and virtue.

The *Life of Anthony* demonstrates once again that Christian theologians repeatedly sought to associate their Christian heroes with traditional aspects of masculine martial *Romanitas*. Though this *Life* must at its core be understood as a work of Christian literature based on biblical allusions and mimesis,[58] it also adhered to some of the basic tenets of biography and traditional codes of masculinity based on one's self-mastery, courage in the face of danger, and the need to prove these skills in combat. In a culture that had long associated courage in warfare with manliness, and cowardice in battle with unmanliness, we can understand why proving one's bravery in even metaphorical struggles remained a fundamental aspect in the creation of any early Byzantine hero. In this we might suppose that the ability of these late Roman and

---

56 Athanasius, *Life of Anthony* 1.22, 1.33. For the influence of "Greek" culture on Athanasius' vision of these pagan deities and his view that the pagan gods were not imaginary but demons in disguise, see Endsjø, *Primordial Landscapes*.

57 It is, however, Anthony's responsibility as a "teacher" that plays the most prominent role in the biography. For this theme, see Rousseau, "Antony as Teacher."

58 Hägg and Rousseau, "Introduction."

early Byzantine writers to adopt, and at the same time adapt, these traditional codes was critical in gaining support from the classically educated elites in the fourth and the fifth centuries.

The extreme ascetic life exemplified by Egyptian monks such as Anthony, as well as the more city-linked asceticism popularised in the Syrian and Mesopotamian forms, proved attractive for a segment of devoted Christians in the latter half of the fourth and the fifth centuries—particularly in the Empire's Eastern half. Though the movement was probably never as popular or esteemed as some modern studies would have us believe, even Christians like Augustine who practised a more moderate form of asceticism felt attracted to its allure.[59] One finds that the early Byzantine historians—Christian and even some secular—thought that their audiences would be interested in the deeds of these holy heroes.[60] We find an example of this admiration in the fifth-century church historians. Sozomen populated his ecclesiastical history with a multitude of often-obscure holy men. In a remark that demonstrates that contemporaries could see these holy men as masculine as well as religious role models, Sozomen described Anthony as ἀνδρεῖος.[61] In fact, he praised all ascetics for their ability to "manfully" (ἀνδρείως) subjugate their passions and control what he described as their bodies' "natural weakness" (σώματος ἀσθενείαις).[62] The holy man's martial qualities in his spiritual battles also attracted notice. Another fifth-century church historian, Socrates of Constantinople—who assumed

---

59 Augustine, *Confessions*, 10.43.70 (trans. Pine-Coffin): "Terrified by my sins and the dead weight of my misery, I had turned my problems over in my mind and was half determined to seek refuge in the desert."

60 See, e.g., Procopius (*Wars* 1.7.7–8, 2.13.14–15). I agree with Geoffrey Greatrex's contention (*Rome and Persia at War*, 63, 87), that even if these accounts of Christian ascetics come from another source, Procopius' use of them indicates that both he and his audience were interested in the deeds of "holy heroes."

61 Sozomen, *HE* 1.13.6.

62 Sozomen, *HE* 1.12.3.

that most of his readers were familiar with Athanasius' account—largely ignored Anthony's ascetic traits, as well as his later deeds as the leader of his monastic community, but still found space in his truncated account to praise the saint for his combat with demons, and his ability to overcome their "wily modes of warfare."[63]

Anthony's spiritual battles offered a focal point for later hagiographers to emulate in their writings. The author of the life of a popular fifth-century pillar saint, Daniel the Stylite, revealed that early in his "career" the holy man fought demons in order to emulate "the model of asceticism" Anthony.[64] Whereas the Roman army's trumpet blast struck fear into the Empire's foes, in hagiography such as the *Life of Daniel*, the power of prayer enfeebled its spiritual enemies.[65]

The examples above, and others like it from hagiographical accounts of the period, attest to the attraction for some early Byzantine Christian intellectuals in representing the holy man as an exemplar of virtuous Christian behaviour, and at times courageous and manly men as well. Part of this appeal may have been the independent authority that sometimes allowed these individuals to act outside the restrictions of either the state or the religious establishment. These men often show up in secular and church histories as heroic men of great power and influence who stand up to secular and ecclesiastical authority, and even to the Empire's enemies.[66]

We do know, however, that some members of the clergy saw these independent holy men as a threat, or at least as individuals who the church needed to control. One way local bishops accomplished this aim was by seeking to prevent ascetics from wandering from place to place by recommending stability in a monastery.[67] In addition, it is important to emphasise that,

---

63 Socrates, *HE* 1.21.

64 *Life of Daniel the Stylite*, 14, ed. Delehaye, trans. Dawes and Baynes.

65 *Life of Daniel the Stylite*, 14–15.

66 See, e.g., Procopius, *Wars* 1.7.7–11.

67 Rousseau, "Monasticism," 775.

despite the fact that "independent" holy men continued to play an important role in the early Byzantine Empire, when compared to the clergy within the Empire's cities, their actual political authority and influence over theological debates were limited.[68] Indeed, by the close of the fourth century, we find Christian theologians more and more emphasising the heroic virtues of the clergy living within the cities.[69] The fifth-century bishop and ecclesiastical historian Theodoret of Cyrrhus stressed that living a virtuous life amongst the temptations of the Empire's cities represented a more difficult challenge than starving alone in the desert.[70] It is to the most powerful member of the early Byzantine clergy, the bishop, that we now turn.

Bishops

The bishop represented Christianity's involvement in, and responsibility to, the secular world. A bishop's power was heavily dependent on his moral superiority. As an exemplar of supreme Christian conduct, it was natural that a bishop's lifestyle would be compared to that of the holy men. Consequently, although many bishops were married when elected, the church's hierarchy frowned on subsequent sexual relationships, preferring virginal candidates.[71] In addition to his "ascetic authority," a bishop frequently wielded a great deal of "pragmatic authority."[72] As one finds with the example of the rather reluctant bishop, Synesius, bishops in the later Empire were often chosen because they hailed from the educated landowning elite, and therefore could be expected to use their social position and wealth to administer and look after their communities' well-being.[73]

68 Brown, *Authority and the Sacred*, 72–73.
69 See, e.g., Ambrose, *Epistula Extra Collectionem* 14.74.
70 Urbainczyk, *Theodoret*, 120–21.
71 Rousseau, "Bishops," 342.
72 Rapp, *Holy Bishops*, 23–55, 100–55.
73 Rapp, *Holy Bishops*, 17–18.

The episcopate offered Roman men other benefits. Their roles as spiritual and civic leaders at times provided bishops in the larger sees with direct access to the emperor and his inner circle—a place of power and decision making that was increasingly out of reach for even the most esteemed members of the Roman upper classes.[74] In the court-dominated world of the early Byzantine Empire, where political influence represented a highly valued commodity, this close contact with the imperial court allowed some bishops to become patronage brokers with considerable influence. Even though the majority of bishops in the smaller bishoprics scattered throughout the Empire could never hope to gain such intimate contact with imperial authorities, even these men from the Empire's backwaters could expect to send a missive on rather minor affairs direct to the eyes of the emperor or his consistory.[75] Therefore, while bishops remained largely subordinate to the emperor and his officials, as defenders of the local peace, advocates for their community's poor, sponsors of regional building projects, and protectors of the holy relics, many late Roman bishops became powerful men in their own right.[76]

We find evidence for the episcopate's growing power, as well as the need for some bishops to emphasise their moral authority over secular rivals in Bishop Ambrose's famous dispute with the Emperor Valentinian II (r. 383–92) and his mother the Empress Justina (ca. 340–ca. 390).[77] This confrontation, as well as his

---

74 Rapp, *Holy Bishops*, 260.

75 Millar, *Greek Roman Empire*, 60–62.

76 Brown, *Power and Persuasion*, 138–41.

77 The best introduction to Ambrose and his world remains McLynn. Valentinian II had become emperor in the aftermath of the Emperor Gratian's death fighting the usurper Magnus Maximus (383–88). Whilst recognising Valentinian II in his struggle against Magnus Maximus, Theodosius I at first left his Western counterpart to try and sort out his own affairs; indeed, the Eastern emperor had his own troubles trying to help his half of the Empire recover after disastrous defeat at the hands of the Goths in 378. Theodosius perceived Valentinian II to be more of a nuisance than a threat or rival.

disputes with Theodosius I, were well publicised in Western and Eastern sources of the period.[78] In his clash with the Western court, the Nicene Ambrose went to great lengths in his public writings to describe how his Christian faith had furnished him with the "tools" to deny an imperial order to abandon his basilica to the *Homoian* imperial court in the first half of 386.[79] Ambrose portrayed himself as a victim of imperial aggression. When the bishop and his supporters—who were guarding the basilica—found themselves surrounded by Valentinian II's soldiers, Ambrose declared, "If force is used, resistance I know nothing about [...] when I face arms, soldiers, Goths, even tears are my weapons; for such are the defences of a bishop." As in the case of the early Christian martyrs, his "weakness," however, was in actuality based on his superior courage. "Neither weapons nor do barbarians," Ambrose continued, "inspire fear in man who is not afraid of death, who is not held back by the inclinations of the flesh."[80] Though adorned with Christian values, behind some of Ambrose's prose is traditional Graeco-Roman masculine rhetoric extolling the unselfish manliness of men who treated their own deaths with scorn by standing up to "tyrants" for the good of others, or for their own "righteous" convictions.[81]

The ecclesiastical historian Rufinus portrayed the clash between Ambrose and the imperial family in gendered and martial terms. Emphasising Empress Justina's role, while deemphasising the child-emperor Valentinian II's part in the dispute, he wrote:

Ultimately marginalised to the point of despair, Valentinian killed himself rather than take the bullying of his barbarian henchman Arbogast.

78 Some Eastern Roman sources include, Sozomen, *HE* 7.13, 7.25, 8.4; Theodoret, *HE* 4.6, 5.17–18.

79 As Liebeschuetz notes (*Ambrose of Milan*, 130), it would have been difficult for the embattled Valentinian II to evict a Nicene bishop without provoking the Nicene Eastern emperor Theodosius I.

80 Ambrose, *Epist.* 75. 7, trans. Liebeschuetz.

81 Kaldellis, *Procopius of Caesarea*, 142.

In this war she assailed Ambrose, the wall of the church and its stoutest tower, harassing him with threats, terrors, and every kind of attack as she sought a first opening into the church she wanted to conquer. But while she fought armed with the spirit of Jezebel, Ambrose stood firm, filled with the power and grace of Elijah.[82]

The Milanese bishop, Rufinus went on, had sought to "ward off the empress's fury" not with "hand or weapon, but with fasts and unceasing vigils."[83]

It is also probably no coincidence that amidst this dispute, Ambrose "discovered" the relics of the martyrs Gervasius and Protasius.[84] Here he took a less passive stance, describing in a letter to his sister these dead saints' metaphorical "martial" qualities:

Thanks be to you, Lord Jesus, that in the holy martyrs you have raised for us such effective guardian spirits, at a time when your Church needs greater defenders. Let everybody take note what kind of champions I seek: champions who have the power to defend, but do not practise aggression. This kind of champion I have acquired for you, my holy people: champions to benefit everybody and harm no one. Such are the "defenders" to whom I pay court, such the soldiers whom I maintain, that is, not soldiers of the world, but soldiers of Christ.[85]

82 Rufinus, *HE* 11.15, trans. Amidon. Rufinus had spent many years in the Eastern half of the Empire and founded a monastery in Jerusalem. He translated many Greek works into Latin, including Eusebius' ecclesiastical history.

83 Rufinus, *HE* 11.16.

84 For the dates of these letters and a historical summary of the dispute, see Liebeschuetz, *Political Letters*, 124–35.

85 Ambrose, *Epist.* 77.10.

It is easy to see what Ambrose was trying to do; the military metaphor reinforced the bishop's claim for control of his church. Whereas the emperor and his soldiers ruled in the secular world, Ambrose implied here that he and the "soldiers of Christ" held sway in the spiritual one. Contemporaries of Ambrose once again presented the dispute in gendered terms. In reference to Ambrose's "triumph" over the Empress Justina, Augustine of Hippo declared that the discovery of the martyrs had allowed the Milanese bishop "to thwart a feminine fury, but also a royal one."[86]

A master of self-representation, Ambrose undeniably fashioned an image of the dispute that he wished to convey. Yet, passages like those discussed above—whether they are completely accurate or not—provide us with examples of how these classically trained orators created what one modern academic describes as a "Christian discourse," that could be wielded to promote the moral as well as the episcopate's political authority.[87] By adopting the Hellenic tradition of *parrhesia* (freedom of speech) that had formally granted the politically non-aligned philosopher the ability at times to speak "truthfully" to the emperor, bishops like Ambrose in the West and John Chrysostom in the East helped to establish the episcopate "as the arbitrator of imperial mercy."[88] Ambrose explained his vision of this role for bishops in a letter to Theodosius I: "It is not the part of an emperor to deny freedom of speech, so it is not that of a bishop to refrain from saying what he thinks."[89] With Ambrose, we have entered into a new stage for the Roman world's masculine power hierarchy. As Peter Brown comments, "We forget that this was the very first time a Latin bishop had raised his voice in such a tone when dealing directly with an emperor and that these certainties were first enunciated

---

86 Augustine, *Confessions* 9.7.16, quoted and trans. in Kuefler, *Manly Eunuch*, 135: "ad cohercendam rabiem femineam, sed regiam."

87 Cameron, *Christianity and the Rhetoric of Empire*, 139.

88 Brown, *Power and Persuasion*, 65–6, 111–13.

89 Ambrose, *Epist.* 74.2.

in situations where Ambrose was far from certain of success."[90] Though exaggerated for rhetorical effect, the sentiment expressed by Ambrose reflected the real power that bishops and holy men had throughout the Byzantine period to be listened to respectfully by the emperor and his representatives.[91] In a culture that frequently connected a man's masculine identity to his public authority, bishops could then feel and be seen by others as powerful and, at times, manly men.[92]

Of course, the instances of Ambrose standing up to the imperial regimes of Valentinian II and Theodosius I and emerging largely triumphant were exceptional, and possible primarily due to the Milanese bishop's mastery of northern Italian politics. So too was Ambrose fortunate to have in the case of Theodosius I an emperor who—though undoubtedly motivated to some extent by sincere religious convictions—also recognised the opportunities available in employing Christian rhetoric and ceremony as a political tool to help him manipulate public opinion.[93]

---

90 Brown, *Through the Eye of a Needle*, 121.

91 Liebeschuetz, *Ambrose and John Chrysostom*, 268.

92 For public authority and political virtues as an essential aspect of Roman masculine ideology, see Montserrat, "Reading Gender," 153–82; Kuefler, *Manly Eunuch*, 19–69; Harlow, "Clothes Maketh the Man," 44.

93 Neil McLynn (*Ambrose*, 323) argues plausibly that Theodosius' famous *ordo poenitentium* (public penance) in Milan at the behest of Ambrose in 391 for a massacre of citizens in Thessalonica the previous year does not represent an instance of an emperor bowing down to an increasingly puissant Christian church, as generally agreed, but is better understood as a mutually orchestrated political gesture that helped to transform "the catastrophe into a public relations triumph for the emperor." Liebeschuetz (*Political Letters*, 19, n. 3) labels McLynn's thesis as anachronistic, suggesting (*Ambrose and John*, 261) that Theodosius' penance was driven by genuine remorse and religious conviction, further positing that Theodosius' weak position in the West forced the emperor to allow himself to be "publically reprimanded." I favour McLynn's interpretation.

In 394, Theodosius defeated the Western usurper Eugenius (r. 392–94) and, however briefly, reunited the Empire under one emperor. Theodosius did not have long to celebrate, succumbing to dropsy while attending the games of the hippodrome in Milan on 17 January 395.[94] Ambrose was in the right place at the right time once again. Whatever the precise nature of the relationship between the emperor and the Milanese bishop,[95] Theodosius and his dynasty had secured Ambrose's loyalty. Forty days after Theodosius' death, Ambrose delivered in Milan the emperor's funeral address—a speech that would earn the bishop even greater fame. The audience consisted of a large number of military men who had only a few months earlier been fighting on opposing sides of a civil war.[96] The Western generalissimo Stilicho also lurked.[97] Merging classical and Christian forms, Ambrose beseeched the civilian and military audience to throw their support behind Theodosius' two young sons who were also in the audience—the eighteen-year-old Eastern emperor Arcadius and his eleven-year-old brother, and new Western emperor, Honorius:

> An emperor of such greatness, then, has withdrawn from us. But he has not wholly withdrawn; for he has left us his children, in whom we can both see and embrace him. Their age should not trouble us! The loyal support of his soldiers makes the emperor's age fully grown. For age is fully grown when strength is. This is reciprocal. For the faith

---

94 Socrates, *HE* 5.26.
95 Once again countering consensus, McLynn rejects (*Ambrose*, 330) the idea that Ambrose and Theodosius had a particularly close personal relationship.
96 McLynn, *Ambrose*, 357.
97 See, Cameron, *Claudian*, 38–45, for Theodosius' appointment of Stilicho as regent for Honorius, but the bogus nature of Stilicho's further claim of guardianship of the eighteen-year-old Arcadius, who had been ruling the East since Theodosius had left on campaign the previous year.

(*fides*) of the emperor produces strength in his soldiers.[98]

As Meghan McEvoy explains, "Ambrose's words should not be dismissed as mere rhetoric: he was making a real plea for military support which was not as yet assured."[99] The outlook expressed in the passage above underlines how nimbly Christian leaders like Ambrose could shift their language between the spiritual and material realms. A bishop, who we saw earlier guiding mystical armies, now sought to convince real soldiers to back the sons of an emperor whom many had only recently seen as an adversary. For Christian Romans, "warfare can be all at once literal, moral, and allegorical."[100]

Few later bishops would have the inclination, the courage, or most importantly, the opportunity, to emulate Ambrose's example.[101] Popular backing for a bishop meant little in the face of an imperial regime willing to use the military option. The Eastern emperors, in particular, "left little scope for independent initiatives by bishops." During Arcadius' reign, the patriarch of Constantinople John Chrysostom's attempts to emulate Ambrose's tactics against the imperial family backfired—ending with the bishop's death in exile. Though he had his ardent supporters, John's obstinacy during his time as patriarch seemed to have alienated "a powerful coalition of secular magnates, bishop, clerics, and monks."[102] Christian "extremists" who took on imperial authority could expect opposition from many quarters of early Byzantine society. We observe evidence of this reality when a later Byzantine historian related with relish the Emperor

98 Ambrose, *De obitu Theodosii* 6, trans. Liebeschuetz.

99 McEvoy, *Child Emperor Rule*, 146.

100 Buc, *Holy War*, 91.

101 For the similarities and dissimilarities between Ambrose and John's stands against the imperial family, see Liebeschuetz, *Ambrose and John Chrysostom*, 5.

102 Liebeschuetz, *Ambrose and John Chrysostom*, 229, 239, 266.

Arcadius' soldiers' slaughter of monks and other followers trying to protect John from banishment.[103]

We should therefore modify Mathew Kuefler's claim that Ambrose's "stands" against the emperors represented a "new manliness" in action. Kuefler overrates Ambrose's and other late Roman bishops' ability to make Roman emperors "submit to them."[104] I agree with Kuefler, however, that Ambrose's example—though extreme—casts needed light on the growing authority of bishops, and the need by some Christian authors to represent them as manly role models. Ambrose's embellished deeds certainly stimulated the imaginations of those fifth-century theologians seeking to curtail the emperor's dominant position within the church.[105] As Averil Cameron comments, "Religious authority in Byzantium remained contested."[106] Another modern scholar explains that later devout audiences embraced the notion that "a prince's impiety should be met by spiritual warfare."[107]

In their recollection of Ambrose, later Byzantine writers were much less interested in relating accurately the Milanese bishop's power relationship with the Roman emperors, than with providing a romanticised vision of the bishopric's independent religious authority. Much of this literature presented confrontational bishops like Ambrose as idealised Christians and as manly men. Sozomen, for instance, remembered Ambrose for the "manly [ἀνδρείως] and very holy way he represented his office."[108] For Sozomen, bishops need not make as dramatic a stand as Ambrose against the emperor to be seen as paradigms of Christian courage

---

103 Zosimus, *New History* 5.23. Although Sozomen (*HE* 6.18) decried the killing of John's supporters, he criticised John for his overzealous rebuke of the empress.

104 Kuefler, *Manly Eunuch*, 130.

105 Theodoret (*HE* 5.17) went to great lengths to make Ambrose's dispute against Theodosius I even more dramatic and confrontational.

106 Cameron, *Byzantine Matters*, 89.

107 Buc, *Holy War*, 24.

108 Sozomen, *HE* 6.24.6 (my trans.).

and manliness. Sozomen made it a point in his history to praise emperors who "never imposed any commands on priests," and praised bishops, who "manfully [ἀνδρείως] resisted the emperor" when he interfered in what the historian saw as the church's affairs.[109]

Consequently, for a ruling elite that greatly valued its social standing, by the fifth century holding an ecclesiastical office finally began to offer a pathway to not only religious fulfilment, but also to worldly and masculine prestige.[110] As Virginia Burrus sees it, by the end of the fourth century: "The Christian clergy are a new elite, and *officium*, in defining a higher moral duty in distinctly ascetic terms, also marks the privilege and responsibility of a ruling class."[111] The gradual triumph of Christian manliness, in her mind, came about because men who had formerly been "groomed for civic leadership" found manly roles within the church's hierarchy:

> Receding is the venerable figure of the civic leader and familial patriarch; approaching is a man marked as a spiritual father, by virtue of his place in the patrilineal chain of apostolic succession, and also as the leader of a new citizenry, fighting heroically in a contest of truth in which (as Gregory of Nyssa puts it) the weapon of choice is the "sword of the Word."[112]

109 Sozomen, *HE* 6.21 (my trans.). Sozomen here described an incident in 353 when the bishop of Rome Liberius, against Constantius II's wishes, refused to condemn the Bishop Athanasius. Ammianus (*Res gestae* 15.7) provides the secular alternative of the incident, seeing it as an example of Christian arrogance and of a bishop prying "into matters outside his province."

110 Salzman, *Christian Aristocracy*, 204–05. As Salzman notes (*Christian Aristocracy*, 132–33), members of the aristocracy had been somewhat reluctant in the fourth century to pursue careers within the church.

111 Burrus, *Begotten Not Made*, 178.

112 Burrus, *Begotten Not Made*, 4–5.

Reflecting on this development, Kuefler goes so far to claim: "It was as bishops, then, that men of the later Roman aristocracy rescued their political identities and their social superiority and found a new means to achieve manliness."[113] Even though we should remain cautious in making such extravagant claims as the two preceding ones, the rise of the holy men of the desert and the clerical authority in the cities played an important part in redefining men's roles in late antiquity.

A New Christian Masculine Ideal?

It is important to point out, however, that by designing a pathway to "true" masculine identities, these Christian men of the later Empire were simply retracing the steps that the demilitarised Roman elites had taken for centuries. As Colleen Conway remarks, there was little "new" about the Christian masculine ideal in late antiquity. She demonstrates, in fact, that New Testament authors responding to a "threatened masculinity" had drawn "on a variety of discourses on ancient masculinity that produced multifaceted Christological constructions."[114] As we observed in the writings of Eusebius and Ambrose earlier in this chapter, in the competitive and sometimes dangerous masculine- and military-centric world of the later Empire, Christian men at times felt the need to present themselves as courageous and manly while characterising their enemies as cowardly and unmanly. The Romans had long balanced their praise of the physical prowess and the acts of masculine bravery of its warriors with the cultivation of alternative forms of manliness based upon the more "civilised" masculinity of the literati.

Asceticism, best personified by exemplars of ideal Christian virtues like bishops, martyrs, monks, and holy men and holy women, certainly proved a popular theme in much of the Christian literature of the day. There is, no doubt, some truth in

---

113 Kuefler, *Manly Eunuch*, 125. Cf. Burrus, *Begotten Not Made*, 159–60, 178.
114 Conway, *Behold the Man*, 176, 183.

these views. As we have discussed, the fourth and the first half of the fifth centuries had witnessed major religious developments in the Eastern and Western halves of the Empire. As Fergus Millar so aptly puts it:

> The prominence, both in real life and in literature, of the ideal of abstinence, extreme physical self-denial, and devotion to piety, whether conducted individually, or in loose groups, or in tightly organized religous communities, could be thought to represent a revolution in the history of Christianity comparable to the conversion of Constantine itself.[115]

There was, however, no single Christian perspective on these issues. The enthusiastic views of extreme asceticism found in some of the writings of Athanasius, Ambrose, and John Chrysostom, that serve as the basis for many current studies on late Roman masculinity, must be balanced by other Christian and secular sources that provide more nuanced views or reject what they saw as radical views of the ideal Christian life, just as the praise of holy men in some sources must be offset by the writings of Christian theologians who sought to control these wandering ascetics. In fact, it must be pointed out that even those considered "rigorists" and advocates for a new Christian masculine ideal like the three theologians mentioned above frequently had more complex and/or malleable views on marriage, virginity, and the value of monks abandoning the world in search of ascetic perfection than some of the modern studies we have discussed recognise.[116]

Clearly, there is room for disagreement concerning the acceptance by the majority of Romans in the East and the West of a Christian masculine ideal based on extreme asceticism. Recent

---

115 Millar, *Greek Roman Empire*, 131–32.

116 For this evolution in John Chrysostom's theology, see Liebeschuetz, *Ambrose and John Chrysostom*, 174–84.

studies of late Roman manliness, in particular, state as established fact the idea that the sometimes rigorist views of masculinity espoused by the church fathers superseded more traditional forms of manhood. However, evidence from the period strongly suggests that a number of committed Christians in this period were hesitant to embrace a form of Christianity that appeared to ask them to reject many of the essential aspects of Roman culture.[117] As even Kuefler concedes, "many Christian men seemed content to remain in the world, despite the exhortation of their leaders to flee from it."[118]

In this instance, we should heed Anthony Kaldellis' warning that there is a danger of missing much of the diversity of early Byzantine society if one depends on a simplified image of "the universally pious Byzantine of (modern) scholarship."[119] As Warren Treadgold adds, it may well be that for many people in the early Byzantine Empire—perhaps even most—asceticism or holy men were something that many people knew very little about, or possibly were inclined to dismiss.[120] One needs to contrast this specialised influence of the holy heroes with the martial deeds of Rome's famous emperors and generals, which as we have observed represent a ubiquitous image throughout the early Byzantine age,

117 An example of such resistance to the ascetic ideal among even devout Christians is found in teachings of the fourth-century Western monk, Jovinianus, who rejected the need for ascetic living and the value of perpetual virginity, see Hunter, "Resistance to the Virginal Ideal." Even church fathers such as Augustine practised a more moderate form of asceticism than that promoted by rigorists like the desert fathers and Jerome. As Liebeschuetz shows (*Ambrose and John Chrysostom*, 177), Augustine in *De bono coniugali*, and *De sancta virginitate* sought "to distance himself from the extreme ascetic views of Jerome and the anti-ascetic views of Jovinian."

118 Kuefler, *Manly Eunuch*, 281.

119 Kaldellis, *Hellenism in Byzantium*, 169.

120 Treadgold asserts that he attaches "no great importance to holy men since most contemporaries seemed little interested in their deeds." Treadgold, *History of the Byzantine State*, 17, 263.

familiar to both the educated and the uneducated masses. Even if asceticism and a rejection of the secular world represented a new wave of Christian manliness, it is problematic to argue that it ever became the hegemonic code of masculinity, admired and followed by the majority of men in the early Byzantine period.

Moreover, it must be emphasised once again that it is a mistake to see Christians as pacifists with no concern for the Empire's security. Those considered rigorist Christians like John of Chrysostom, as J. H. W. G. Liebeschuetz makes plain, "accepted both the city and the Empire."[121] Christian theologians largely accepted Roman masculine ideals based heavily on martial virtues and courage in battle. Socrates, Sozomen, and Ambrose admired the "courage" of the emperor and his soldiers that, in the words of the Milanese bishop, led these men "to protect the country from barbarians in time of war."[122]

Even less convincing is Kuefler's idea that Roman men in the later Empire converted to Christianity as a means to "preserve the manliness of [Roman] men's identity." He continues:

> Roman men became Christians because they saw in Christian ideology a means of surmounting the gap between ancient ideals and contemporary realities. The men of late antiquity believed that their ancient counterparts had been martial conquerors, great statesmen, and commanding husbands and fathers. When compared to these ancient heroes, they could only be dismal failures. Christian ideology offered them an opportunity to recover their sense of greatness. As Christians, they could see themselves as indefatigable conquerors against evil, honored statesmen of the Church, and exacting spiritual fathers. The new masculine ideal presented itself to

---

121 Liebeschuetz, *Ambrose and John Chrysostom*, 207.
122 Ambrose, *De officiis* 1.129.

> them both as a repudiation of the classical heritage
> and as its ultimate fulfilment.[123]

To put it another way, military defeat forced Roman men to become Christians as a means of reclaiming their "lost" manliness. One finds, however, little evidence to back up Kuefler's claim that Roman men viewed themselves "as unmanly failures" or became Christians in an effort to recover their masculine legacy. Though more nuanced and subtle, such a view echoes Edward Gibbon's notorious contention that the acceptance of Christianity had weakened the Romans' martial spirit.[124] While I largely agree with Kuefler's contention that Christian ideology at times offered Roman men of the Late Empire another way of cultivating a "masculine" identity, this aim was surely not the reason most Romans chose to become Christians. Additionally, the prevalence of an ascetic manly ideal in the writings of many devout late Roman authors is simply no basis for proclaiming the triumph of a new Christian masculine ideal, even amongst dedicated Christians.

To the contrary, in a point that will be explored more fully in the chapters to come, one finds an increased militarism in the literary and visual sources of the fifth and sixth centuries, not a decline. As one specialist on the Eastern Roman army suggests, by the sixth century "the military was playing an increasingly important role in public and private life in the Eastern Roman Empire."[125] The emergence of what social historians describe as a Christian rhetoric of manliness did not mark the passing of classical forms of hegemonic masculinity based, in part, on martial virtues. Instead, it merely offered Christian men another avenue to promote their authority, as well as affirm their masculine identity to their peers, Christian and non-Christian.

---

123 Kuefler, *Manly Eunuch*, 287, 296. Although Kuefler's study deals predominantly with the Western half of the Empire, he suggests (*Manly Eunuch*, 9) that a similar process occurred in the East.

124 Cooper, "Gender and the Fall of Rome," 188.

125 Whately, "Descriptions of Battle," 354.

In order to see how fifth-century emperors were amalgamating these Christian qualities of manly *Romanitas* with more traditional martial forms, the next chapter shifts its attention to the tumultuous and "pious" reign of the Emperor Theodosius II (r. 408–50). Using Theodosius' reign as a pivot, it explores continuity and change in early Byzantine gender ideology. In particular, we look at how the fifth-century ecclesiastical and secular historians constructed images of Theodosius II that embodied a new Christian approach to strategies of leadership and manliness.

Plate 8. Remnants of the Golden Gate, Istanbul, Turkey.

VI

REPRESENTATIONS OF POWER
AND IMPERIAL MANLINESS IN
THE AGE OF THEODOSIUS II

Theodosius who succeeded his father Arcadius, was
unwarlike and lived a life of cowardice. He obtained peace
by money, and not by fighting for it.

Priscus, *frag.* 3

ON A SUMMER'S DAY IN 450, THE FORTY-EIGHT-YEAR-OLD
Eastern Roman emperor Theodosius II died of injuries sustained
in a horse-riding accident.[1] Such an end, hunting wild beasts,[2] was
a somewhat ironic demise for an emperor better known by most
modern historians for his ineffectual rule, monkish character, and
prominent role in Christological debates. Michael Kulikowski's

---

1   Theodosius died on 28 July of spinal cord injuries, see Marcellinus, *Chron.*
    s.a. 450; Malalas, *Chron.* 14.27 (366.19–367.5), ed. Thurn, trans. Jeffreys,
    Jeffreys, and Scott; Evagrius, *HE* 1.22; Theophanes, *Chron.* AM 5924.
2   Priscus (*frag.* 13) criticised Theodosius' fervour for wild-beast hunts. For the
    fifth-century Roman and Vandal elites' shared passion for the "manly pursuit
    of hunting" see Conant, *Staying Roman*, 53. On the quasi-military function
    of hunting, and the possibility that it was undertaken by Theodosius II as
    a means to counteract his non-martial image, see Lee, "Eastern Empire:
    Theodosius to Anastasius," 36.

recent assessment of the younger Theodosius is typical of the dominant scholarly view. In his own words: "Theodosius' interests ran no further than theology and ecclesiastical politics, and he was insulated from the task of governing by a thick layer of bureaucrats, who needed the imperial system to prosper but needed any particular emperor rather less."[3] Yet, despite his poor reputation in the historiographical tradition, Theodosius II had his admirers in early Byzantium. His great eloquence, it was said by one source, "made him loved by all Romans rich and poor."[4] Some recent revisionists have also somewhat rehabilitated Theodosius II's reputation. Jill Harries, for example, contends that a relative paucity of evidence has led to an unfair evaluation of Theodosius.[5] Whatever one's opinion about the younger Theodosius, his reign has deep implications for anyone interested in how Christian ideals were shaping notions of imperial leadership and masculinity.

The Pious Emperor

Born on 10 April 401,[6] Theodosius was the only son of Arcadius and Aelia Eudoxia, the daughter of the Frankish Western *magister militum* Bauto and a Roman mother.[7] In contrast to his feeble

---

3   Kulikowski, "Review." Cf., however, the generally more positive assessments found in Kelly, *Theodosius II.*

4   Malalas, *Chron.* 14.8 (358).

5   Harries, "*Pius princeps.*"

6   Marcellinus, *Chron.* s.a. 401.

7   Contra Treadgold (*History of the Byzantine State*, 87) we should reject as spurious contemporary rumours (Zosimus, *New History* 5.18.8) contending that Theodosius was not Arcadius' son, but the offspring of an affair between the empress and emperor's confidante, John. On the prevalence of such rumours in the "pious" reigns of the Theodosian emperors, see Holum, *Theodosian Empresses*, 64, n. 68.

father, his mother by all accounts was a remarkable woman.[8] A tough, determined woman, sometime after her father's death in 388 the future empress had arrived in Constantinople from the West where, in all probability at Theodosius' behest, the powerful family of the emperor's *magister militum* Promotus had adopted her. On 27 April 395, some four months after Theodosius I's demise, Arcadius married the relatively obscure Eudoxia. According to the historian Zosimus, a eunuch-advisor chose Eudoxia in order to thwart the growing ambitions of the Eastern *praetorian prefect* Flavius Rufinus (335–95),[9] who, not coincidentally, figures as the likely culprit behind Promotus' murder in 391.[10] Such a swift rise for the daughter of a non-Roman general acts as another apt reminder of the opportunities for family advancement available to those who chose a military career.

Arcadius for once had chosen wisely. The strong-willed Eudoxia wielded considerable influence in the political and religious arenas, a puissance that Arcadius recognised formally with her coronation as augusta on 9 January 400. A staunch Nicene Christian, it had been the empress who in 404 had brought about the exile and downfall of her erstwhile ally, John Chrysostom.[11] After giving birth to four children in rapid succession, Eudoxia, however, died attempting to deliver a fifth child on 6 October 404. With his assertive wife out of the way, the pliant Arcadius allowed his Eastern praetorian prefect Anthemius to become the virtual ruler of the Eastern Empire, a position that Anthemius held until his probable death around 415. On 1 May 408, Arcadius died, thus leaving the seven-year-old Theodosius as the vulnerable

---

8 Following the reconstruction of Eudoxia's life found in Holum, *Theodosian Empresses*, 53–78.

9 Zosimus, *New History* 5.3.

10 Zosimus, *New History* 4.51.

11 For the souring of what had originally been a good relationship between the empress and John, see Liebeschuetz, *Ambrose and John Chrysostom*, 231–38.

figurehead ruler of an Eastern Empire wracked by social, political, and religious discord.[12]

Few contemporaries seemed to have expected that the young Theodosius would enjoy a long reign.[13] Nevertheless, the young emperor survived and—notwithstanding many challenges—so did his empire. Whatever his faults as a political leader, Arcadius appears to have been a protective parent. Before his death, the emperor and his inner circle played a part in ensuring Theodosius' future survival. In order to assure his smooth accession, Theodosius had been named as the youngest ever augustus in 402. The child-emperor was also fortunate to be surrounded throughout his reign by an eclectic cadre of largely loyal and competent supporters, including eunuchs, military men, relatives, and perhaps even the Persian emperor Yazdgrid I (r. 399–420).[14] Although they would frequently squabble for pre-eminence amongst themselves, these advisors largely sought to safeguard Theodosius.[15]

Foremost of these early protectors was his eldest sister Pulcheria (ca. 398–453), who appears to have inherited her mother's leadership qualities and religious conviction. After taking a vow of chastity, she acted as her brother's guardian and confidante during the crucial second decade of the fifth century, a role she would continue to play off and on throughout her brother's long reign and even after when she agreed to lend

12 On the riots in 409 in Constantinople due to a shortage of bread, see Marcellinus, *Chron.* 409. For Honorius and Stilicho's intention to head to Constantinople to assert control over Theodosius, a move that would have likely led to another civil war, see Zosimus, *New History* 5.31.

13 For contemporaries' low expectations for Theodosius II's reign, see Sozomen, *HE* 9.6; Theodoret, *HE* 5.36.

14 On the possible kernel of truth behind Procopius' anecdote (*Wars* 1.2.1–10) suggesting that on his deathbed Arcadius had asked the Persian emperor to act as Theodosius' guardian (ἐπίτροπος), see Börm, "Procopius and the East."

15 On the ebbs and flows of these personal influences over Theodosius and his decision making, see Harries, "Men without Women."

legitimacy to Marcian's reign by marrying the former soldier on 25 November 450.[16] Largely insulated from the internal and external turmoil that threatened his rule, Theodosius spent his early years in the palace pursuing his studies with other youths from Constantinople's ruling elite.[17] Creating such intimate links with the leading families of Constantinople represents another important factor behind the emperor's long-term survival.

Similar to many upper-class Romans of the time, Theodosius and his family were sincere and dedicated Christians.[18] The literary and the visual sources from the reign offer ample evidence of this devotion.[19] This emphasis appears in the writings of the Eastern church historians whose literary genre flourished during the emperor's reign.[20] No less than five Greek authors continued Eusebius' church history. One specialist on the period remarks that contemporary descriptions of Theodosius II better resemble a late Roman holy man, bishop, or monk than an archetypal late Roman emperor.[21] For example, Socrates, whose generally fair and balanced account provides us with the reign's best narrative, informs his readers that the imperial family ran the palace like a monastery. He related that the emperor dedicated his days and

---

16 Pulcheria has attracted a great deal of scholarly interest, see Holum, *Theodosian Empresses*; Limberis, *Divine Heiress*; Angelidē, *Pulcheria*. For the late antique notion that sexual abstinence allowed women to "transcend their gender," see Schulenburg, *Forgetful of Their Sex*, 127–75.

17 Malalas, *Chron.* 14.3 (352).

18 One finds a lucid discussion of the imperial family's religious devotion in Millar, *Greek Roman Empire*, 35–36 and Rapp, *Holy Bishops*, 300. For a different perspective on Theodosius' religiosity, see Urbainczyk, *Socrates*, 33.

19 Holum, *Theodosian Empresses*, 101.

20 For some of the reasons for this abundance and popularity, see Cameron, "Empress and the Poet," 269–70; Treadgold, *Early Byzantine Historians*, 164–75.

21 Urbainczyk, *Socrates*, 145.

nights to prayer, fasting, and the study of sacred texts.[22] Another fifth-century writer tells us that Theodosius even wore a hair shirt—typical of extreme Eastern ascetics—underneath his royal garb.[23] Reneging on an earlier promise (*HE* 1.1.2–3) not to cross the line from historian to panegyrist, Socrates extolled what he saw as the emperor's "Christian" virtues:

> He evinced so much prudence, that he appeared to those who conversed with him to have acquired wisdom from experience. Such was his fortitude in undergoing hardships, that he would courageously endure both heat and cold; fasting very frequently, especially on Wednesdays and Fridays; and this he did from an earnest endeavour to observe with accuracy all the prescribed forms of the Christian religion.[24]

Here we encounter many of the characteristics of the standard bishop or holy man.[25] Throughout his history, Socrates presented an image of Theodosius II as a model leader of the church and the state. Theresa Urbainczyk has illustrated how drawing attention to the emperor's ascetic authority allowed Socrates to link the "unity of the Empire and the unity of the Church." Having the emperor conform to his vision of an ideal bishop's attributes promoted to Socrates' readers the controversial idea that the emperor represented the dominant, and indeed, the church's "rightful" leader. This stance by Socrates contrasted sharply with that of his fellow church historians, Sozomen, Theodoret, and Rufinus,

---

22 Socrates, *HE* 7.22.

23 John Rufus, *Life of Peter the Iberian*, ed. and trans. Horn and Phenix.

24 Socrates, *HE* 7.22.

25 As Conor Whately (pers. comms.) has pointed out to me, an ability to endure hardships like hot and cold courageously, however, had long been part of the rhetoric of the manly emperor or commander as *commilitones*.

who frequently supported the idea of the bishop as the primary authority in ecclesiastical affairs.[26]

Sozomen constructed a slightly more conventional portrait of Theodosius II as a quintessential Christian Roman emperor and man. In an introduction dedicated to the emperor, and most likely recited in front of the court in Constantinople, Sozomen's account quite naturally veered from historical to unabashed panegyric.[27] The resulting impression of Theodosius II differed little from encomia dedicated to the Emperor Augustus four and a half centuries earlier: he was courageous, militarily successful, devoted to God, sexually restrained, philanthropic, and benevolent.[28] In comparison to Socrates, who made only passing mention of the emperor's martial qualities, Sozomen claimed that Theodosius' days were filled with military training, physical exercise, and state affairs, while his nights were spent in study.[29]

While men had trained the young emperor in arms, horse riding, and letters, Sozomen attributed Theodosius' Christian piety and manly deportment to the upbringing and influence of his pious sister, Pulcheria. Amalgamating the traditional "womanly aristocratic" virtue of sisterly devotion with the newer

26 Urbainczyk, Socrates, 164–76. Urbainczyk likewise contends (Socrates, 158–59) that Socrates' ascetic image of Theodosius II served, in part, to counter Julian's lingering reputation as an ideal "philosopher-king."

27 Roman historians were expected to exaggerate the virtues and exploits of living emperors, see, e.g., Agathias, Histories preface, 18–20. Sidonius (Epist. 4.22), warned that the historian could "incur serious disfavour" for the requirement of the genre to recount the deeds of infamous men. However, I must add we do find in Procopius (Wars 1.24.39, 2.28.38–44, 7.1.30, 7.35.11) veiled and not so veiled criticisms of living emperors.

28 For the use of a similar combination of virtues in literary depictions of the Emperor Augustus, see Conway, Behold the Man, 65. On the "minor modifications" imposed by Christianity on these standard imperial virtues, see Brubaker, "Sex, Lies, and Textuality," 86; Kaldellis, Byzantine Republic, 165–89.

29 Sozomen, HE 9.1.

Christian emphasis on the "unparalleled dignity" of celibacy,[30] the historian applauded the emperor's elder sister for devoting "her virginity to God," and helping to guide "Theodosius into piety" by showing him the wisdom of constant prayer, respect for the clergy, and honouring the church with a steady stream of "gifts and treasure."[31]

Even though piety had always been one of the imperial virtues, Socrates and Sozomen, and other Christian sources from the period, emphasise this characteristic and other Christian qualities such as charity over the emperor's more "traditional" virtues such as courage, wisdom, and prudence.[32] In fifth-century Constantinople, religious and the secular rhetoric had coalesced. Following Old Testament precedents and contemporary hagiographical motifs, the church historians tended to attribute orthodox emperors' military victories to the power of piety and prayer.[33] We see evidence of this view in Sozomen's declaration that "Piety alone suffices for the salvation of princes; and without piety, armies, a powerful empire, and every other resource, are of no avail."[34] Socrates declared, that "any time war is raised, like David he (Theodosius II) had recourse to God knowing that he is arbiter of battles, and by prayer brought them to a prosperous issue."[35]

As Fergus Millar points out, theology and historiography were not the sole mediums that indicated that military success or failure depended on "proper" religious belief. One finds this view in "a large proportion of the laws issued by the Emperor."[36] How deeply Sozomen, Theodosius, and other Byzantines believed such

---

30 Salzman, *Christian Aristocracy*, 162–63; Sivan, *Galla Placidia*, 54.

31 Sozomen, *HE* 9.1.

32 For piety as an essential imperial virtue from the reign of Augustus, see Conway, *Behold the Man*, 45–46, 51, 59.

33 Cameron, *Last Pagans of Rome*, 96–99.

34 Sozomen, *HE* 9.1.

35 Socrates, *HE* 7.22.

36 Millar, *Greek Roman Empire*, 43.

rhetoric is more difficult to ascertain. Piety and prayer served as a legitimate complement to practical military strategies in a world where religion and politics intertwined.[37] Yet, throughout the Byzantine era, military preparation, strategy, tactics, good morale, and manly martial virtues continued to represent the surest means to achieve victory on the field of battle.

Few modern scholars, however, have been able to resist the temptation of seeing in such depictions a moving away from traditional martial virtues towards more Christian values such as asceticism, piety, and the power of providence. Since I will spend the remainder of this chapter rebutting aspects of these arguments, what follows are brief summaries, and a few initial comments and criticisms of some of their main claims. Theresa Urbainczyk's view is typical. She writes, "The Church became aware of the incongruity of celebrating military prowess in a Christian emperor and preferred to stress more conventional Christian qualities." This shift "in emphasis would also have had imperial approval."[38] Kenneth Holum proposes that this change in Christian imperial ideology had emerged in the reign of Theodosius II's grandfather, Theodosius I. He points to Christian literature surrounding Theodosius I's victory over his Western rival, Eugenius, at the Battle of Frigidus in 384 as evidence of this new ideology: "In that battle, contemporary authors stressed, the soldiers' weapons had accomplished nothing at all. Theodosius had mastered Eugenius through piety alone, his tears and prayers." According to Holum, in the reigns of his sons, Honorius and Arcadius, this Christian imperial dogma flourished. He concludes: "The new ideology owed much to the old, but the personal qualities on which victory depended had been transformed, from strategic ability and brute military strength to the emperor's Christian *eusebeia*."[39]

---

37 Kaldellis, *Byzantine Republic*, 196.

38 Urbainczyk, *Socrates*, 146. She, however, leaves open the possibility that this emphasis was taken out of necessity, since Theodosius II had no military virtues worth mentioning.

39 Holum, *Theodosian Empresses*, 50–51.

Peter Heather, too, points to a change in imperial ideology in the reign of Theodosius I. He argues more plausibly, however, that this emphasis on piety in the speeches of the court-propagandist, the Hellenic philosopher Themistius, represented a means to deal with changing political realities and military setbacks at the hands of the Goths in the years after Adrianople, as much as a real and permanent shift in imperial ideology.[40] I agree that this stress on the emperor's religious virtues, and the apparent rejection of the typical Roman adulation of brute force, seems to have been a response to Theodosius' rather embarrassing failure to crush the Goths, as well as the ensuing incorporation of many of these "barbarian enemies" into his armed forces. Before these defeats, Themistius had gone to great lengths to promote Theodosius' warlike qualities, and had expressed, in typical jingoistic and militaristic rhetoric, the emperor's need for revenge against the Goths for the setback at Adrianople.[41]

There are problems nevertheless with all of these approaches. First, the idea that piety and religious zeal had contributed to Rome's military successes was already a commonplace in the first century BCE when Cicero had proclaimed:

> It is in and by means of piety and religion, and this especial wisdom of perceiving that all things are governed and managed by the divine power of the immortal gods, that we have been and are superior to all other countries and nations.[42]

---

40 Heather and Moncur, *Philosophy and Empire*, 261–62.

41 Cameron, *Last Pagans of Rome*, 98–101.

42 Cicero, *Har. Resp.* 19, trans. Yonge: "sed pietate ac religione atque hac una sapientia, quod deorum numine omnia regi gubernarique perspeximus, omnis gentis nationesque superavimus." Cf. Horace, *Odes* 3.6.5, ed. and trans. Rudd. For a discussion of this link in the Republic and the early Empire, see Rich, "Roman Rituals of War," 542.

Second, as we saw earlier, examinations of the textual and visual sources that have survived from Constantius II's reign indicate that an imperial reliance on Christian virtues and imagery as a crucial aspect of imperial propaganda was not a Theodosian innovation. Despite the largely negative portrait found in Ammianus, we should recognise how deftly Constantius II balanced his military role with Christian engagement.[43] Finally, it is surely hazardous to rely largely on Christian writers' versions of battles like Frigidus and their visions of "pious" Roman emperors, as Holum does, as firm evidence of a cultural shift away from martial virtues as a key component of imperial ideology. Historians must take care when relying on ancient material with a spiritual rather than a historical agenda. As Alan Cameron rightly cautions, ecclesiastical history operated "on a theological rather than a historical plane"; secular wars and military victories were only of interest for the ecclesiastical authors "for the light they cast on the piety and orthodoxy of the victors."[44] This motive helps to explain why these Christian authors emphasised the bloodless and miraculous nature of Theodosius I's victory at Frigidus against the supposed pagan elements of Eugenius' forces.[45] It was only natural that these Christian sources, depending on Old Testament precedents (Joshua 6:20) as well as fourth-century trends in Christian hagiography and panegyric, would highlight the pivotal role that the "hand of God" played in the triumph of the "orthodox" and "pious" Theodosius, while marginalising both the numbers and the military qualities of his soldiers. Such a view probably had imperial approval. For Theodosius I and his heirs, a hard-fought contest between two rival Christian emperors heading evenly matched Roman armies of a similar religious makeup was perhaps better explained as a bloodless and providential triumph over a

---

43 See, e.g., Whitby, "Images of Constantius."

44 Cameron (*Last Pagans of Rome*, 103–09) disputes this "pagan" revival, contending that the wind miracle was the gradual "invention" of later Christian writers.

45 MacCormack, "Latin Prose Panegyrics," 169–72.

numerically superior Western army intent on re-establishing pagan worship.

Though I do not deny the worth—and the absolute necessity— of using theological sources in helping to reconstruct secular events in the murky late fourth and fifth centuries, some care must be taken. To proclaim the end of the relevance of the emperor and his soldiers' "brute military strength" as a key component of the Empire's well-being and as a key aspect of imperial ideology on such evidence is hazardous. Two late Roman authors less favourable to Theodosius I, Eunapius and the Christian historian Philostorgius (a church historian who opposed Theodosius I's Christological position), portrayed Frigidus "as just another triumph of the stronger over the weaker."[46] Hence, the marginalising of martial virtues and the trumpeting of Christian values promoted by late Roman Christian and imperial sources may simply represent the demands of one's literary genre and/or a response by imperial ideology to military setbacks and civil war.

The late fourth and fifth centuries had experienced an adjustment of the imperial image to emphasise emperors' ceremonial and religious roles.[47] Meaghan McEvoy lucidly discusses this development in her recent study on "child-emperors" from the accession of Gratian in 367 to the assassination of Valentinian III in 455, insisting correctly that this shift was undertaken for practical as much as religious reasons to better suit the non-martial Theodosian child-emperors: Arcadius, Honorius, Theodosius II, and Valentinian III. In this period, the emperors left military duties to those best able to command, their (mostly) loyal generalissimos. Although these military men largely remained faithful to the emperor, they certainly felt few qualms in eliminating their fellow Roman generals. The incessant factional rivalries that had defined the age had ultimately consumed potent fifth-century generalissimos like Stilicho, Bonifatius, Felix, Aëtius, and Aspar;

---

46 Cameron, *Last Pagans of Rome*, 111. Eunapius, *frag.* 60.1; Philostorgius, *HE* 11.2, ed. and trans. Amidon.

47 McEvoy, *Child Emperor Rule.*

so serving as a *magister militum* was more dangerous than being a non-martial emperor. Separating these vital and time-consuming civilian and military roles therefore made some sense. It created a certain amount of safety for these non-campaigning child-emperors; it seems more than coincidental that Honorius (r. 395–423), Theodosius II (r. 408–50), and Valentinian III (r. 425–55) represent some of the longest serving Roman emperors.

However, this move away from active martial virtues was not an entirely positive development for the fifth-century Theodosian emperors. As we will discuss more fully in the next chapter, this period famously witnessed an increase in both the menace and the magnetism of successful soldiers. The rise of fifth-century generalissimos—Roman and non-Roman—has long served as one of the most striking features of this age.[48] This change may also help to explain why, when looking back at the fifth century, Procopius described the Western generalissimos, Bonifatius and Flavius Aëtius, "as the last of the Romans." In contrast to the majority of fifth-century Western Roman emperors, whom he personified as effeminate weaklings, for Procopius these generalissimos represented exemplary masculine *Romanitas*.[49]

These generalissimos' authority often came at the expense of the emperors whom they served. Part of their growing prestige may be attributed to these generals monopolising military roles, and more vitally, manly martial *Romanitas*. While this modification allowed the Theodosians to survive a half-century of upheaval and military defeat, by eschewing their traditional military responsibilities, it shifted an element of power away from the emperor and into the hands of their generalissimos, who, as in the case of Bonifatius in the 420s, could "resist central

48 O' Flynn, *Generalissimos*; MacGeorge, *Late Roman Warlords*; McEvoy, *Child Emperor Rule*; Wijnendaele, *Last of the Romans*.

49 Procopius, *Wars* 3.3.15 (trans. Dewing). The Western soldier-emperor Majorian is one notable exception, Procopius praised him (*Wars* 3.7.4–6) hyperbolically as surpassing "in every virtue all who ever were emperors of the Romans."

authority successfully, without resorting to the traditional means of usurping the imperial office."[50] Increasingly able to lead armies loyal primarily to themselves, these quasi-independent warlords—Roman and non-Roman—avoided imperial control, and, as in the case of the *magister militum* Marcellinus in the 450s and 460s and Theoderic the Amal from the 470s to the 490s, could function simultaneously within and outside the imperial and Roman sphere.[51]

Nevertheless, it is once again important to emphasise that the Western and Eastern Roman emperors had never completely abandoned their symbolic and not so symbolic martial *Romanitas* as an aspect of their right to rule. Theodosius II sought to present himself as the face of Roman military victory. In a similar fashion to Justinian I in the next century, Theodosius II appeared to appreciate the importance of claiming "the credit for military successes." His religious devotion and his belief in providence certainly did not keep him from commissioning equestrian monuments of himself to commemorate "his" successes over the Persians 420/21 and the Huns 441/42.[52] Although the war with the Persians proved indecisive, Theodosius declared "victory" over the Persians in Constantinople on 6 September 421.[53] The emperor may have even initiated games to commemorate the "triumph."[54] It was in fact this image of Theodosius II as the Roman Empire's protector and the driving force behind the

---

50 Wijnendaele, *Last of the Romans*, 120.

51 On Marcellinus, see MacGeorge, *Late Roman Warlords*, 15–64; for Theoderic the Amal, see Arnold, *Roman Imperial Restoration*, 57–118. Indeed, Aëtius' ability to count on "outside" Hunnic support was one of the key elements behind his puissance.

52 On Theodosius' equestrian monument in Hebdomon just outside the capital, see Holum, *Theodosian Empresses*, 110. For the rather inconclusive outcome of these wars, yet the relative prosperity of the Eastern Empire at the close of Theodosius II's reign, see Millar, *Greek Roman Empire*, 62–83.

53 *Chron. Paschale* s.a. 421.4.

54 McCormick, *Eternal Victory*, 58, 119.

"triumphs" over the Huns and Persians that served as a prominent theme in Olympiodorus' secular history and is also found in the ecclesiastical histories of Theodoret, Sozomen, and Evagrius.[55]

In his early twenties, it looks as if Theodosius had begun to take an interest in political affairs. After Honorius' death in 423, the Western throne had sat empty for four months. This interregnum has caused some modern scholars to posit that Theodosius may have hoped to rule originally as a sole Augustus.[56] Political upheaval in North Africa and Rome, however, forced the emperor's hand. With the backing of powerful Western families and the generalissimo Flavius Castinus, the *primicerius notarium* (chief secretary of the Western court) John had seized the throne (20 November 423) in Rome.[57] Unwilling to relinquish his family's control in the West, Theodosius and his inner circle reacted swiftly.[58] In early 424, the emperor betrothed the then five-year-old Valentinian III, the son of Honorius' sister Galla Placidia and the former Western Emperor Constantius III (not recognised in the East), to his daughter Licinea Eudoxia.[59] The emperor subsequently named Valentinian III *Caesar* and raised him to the

---

55 Olympiodorus, *frag.* 43.1–2. Theodoret, *HE* 5.7.4–10; Sozomen, *HE* 9.6.1; Evagrius, *HE* 1.19. The pagan Olympiodorus' history, composed around 427, was dedicated to Theodosius II. For Olympiodorus' possible close relationship with Theodosius II and the Empress Eudocia, see Treadgold, "The Diplomatic Career and Historical Work of Olympiodorus of Thebes," 714, 723.

56 McEvoy, *Child Emperor Rule*, 228. Contra Millar, *Greek Roman Empire*, 55.

57 For a discussion on the complex politics surrounding this "usurpation," see Wijnendaele, *Last of the Romans*, 66–74; Pawlak, "L' usurpation De Jean."

58 I follow Jill Harries in rejecting the notion that eunuchs and the emperor's female relatives dominated this "inner circle." Harries, "Men without Women."

59 See, Matthews, *Western Aristocracies*, 377–81; McEvoy, *Child Emperor Rule*, 228. Galla Placidia had quarrelled with Honorius and fled to Constantinople in 421.

rank of *nobilissimus*.[60] Shortly afterwards, Theodosius launched a major military campaign that—despite initial setbacks—ultimately crushed the "usurper" and his faction, thus allowing Valentinian to be crowned Western emperor in an elaborate ceremony in Rome on 23 October 425, a coronation that Jill Harries has shown emphasised the Theodosian emperors' *Romanitas*.[61] A sure sign of this campaign's importance for Theodosius is the fact that the emperor had accompanied his army to Thessalonica, before an illness forced him to return to Constantinople.[62] Theodosius did, however, celebrate the triumph over John with a ceremony in Constantinople, and may, in fact, have been the first emperor to enter the city via the recently completed Golden Gate (plate 9), which in subsequent centuries would only be opened to honour an imperial victory.[63]

Military matters represented a major area of focus for Theodosius' regime throughout the 430s and 440s. In the years after Valentinian III's ascension, Theodosius and his army played a vital role in protecting the Western and Eastern regimes from their many enemies.[64] Priscus provides us with a famous description (circa 447)[65] of an Eastern Empire encircled by seething enemies:

> They were not only wary of starting a war with Attila, but they were afraid also of the Parthians [Persians] who were preparing for hostilities, the Vandals who were harassing the coastal regions, the Isaurians whose banditry was reviving, the Saracens who were ravaging the eastern parts of

60 Hydatius, *Chron.* s.a. 425; Olympiodorus, *frag.* 43.

61 Harries, *Law and Empire*, 64.

62 Socrates, *HE* 7.24, 25.

63 Madden, "Triumph Re-Imagined," 318.

64 Millar, *Greek Roman Empire*, 58.

65 Following the date for this fragment in Croke, "The Date of the 'Anastasian Long Wall' in Thrace."

their domain, and the Ethiopian tribes who were in the process of uniting.[66]

In the face of this myriad of threats—albeit exaggerated somewhat for literary effect—Theodosius' policy of paying off Attila and his Huns may at the time have been prudent foreign policy. Eventually his approach prevailed. Indeed, Theodosius may have had a better grasp of military affairs and greater political acumen than many modern scholars commonly assume. The emperor's reliance on barbarian and/or non-orthodox and pagan generals may have been a deliberate ploy undertaken to limit threats to his rule presented by charismatic "orthodox" Roman generals.[67]

Theodosius' reign was marked by near constant warfare. While the majority of his military campaigns were defensive, the Eastern Romans had planned to take back Vandalic North Africa. By attacking the Vandals, Theodosius and his inner circle likely sought to erase the shame and financial burden of losing most of North Africa in the 420s and 430s. Such a victory would have solidified his credentials as the protector of both the Eastern and the Western realms. A major Hunnic invasion of the Eastern Empire in 442, however, forced Theodosius to recall his fleet, which was preparing to transport his army to North Africa.[68]

Undeniably, military success represented an essential component of the ideology of both the state and the church in the Christian Eastern Roman Empire of Theodosius II.[69] By his reign, it had in fact become difficult to separate the two. Though exaggerated for rhetorical effect, the famous quotation from a sermon from 428 by the newly elected bishop of Constantinople, Nestorius, highlighted this intimate connection between

---

66 Priscus, *frag.* 10. Cf. Marcellinus, *Chron.* s.a. 441.

67 Lee, "Theodosius and His Generals."

68 A full discussion on Theodosius' attempts to present himself as the protector of the Western half of the Empire is found in McEvoy, *Child Emperor Rule*, 264–65.

69 For this point, see Millar, *Greek Roman Empire*, 39.

"orthodoxy" and military success: "Give me, King, the earth purged of heretics, and I will give you heaven in return. Aid me in destroying heretics, and I will assist you in vanquishing the Persians."[70] Socrates attributed the Eastern Romans' victory over the Persians to Christ's vengeful anger over the persecution of their Christian subjects.[71] Further evidence of this view is found in a letter from the bishop of Cyrrhus, Theodoret, to Theodosius' general, the Alan Aspar, promising "to implore our good Lord" to guard the Empire and make it a terror to its enemies.[72] It comes as no surprise, therefore, that the younger Theodosius, who as we have seen sought to justify and glorify his leadership of the church and the state, would have supported the creation of ideologies that portrayed him simultaneously as a model religious and secular leader.

The increasing fusion of church and government affairs that marked the politics of the Theodosian age is reflected in the writings of many contemporary Christian sources. In opposition to Holum's and Urbainczyk's conclusions about Christian writers' growing tendency to marginalise militarism, a wealth of evidence is found in the ancient testimony applauding the Roman emperors' and their soldiers' military prowess. One more example should suffice. In the following passage, the fifth-century Christian poet Prudentius celebrated Emperor Honorius' "Christian" Roman army's victory over the Goths:

> To lead our army and our empire we had a young warrior mighty in Christ, and his companion and father [-in-law] Stilicho, and Christ the one God of both. It was after worship at Christ's altar and

70 Socrates, *HE* 7.29.5. Socrates, in fact, used this speech to criticise Nestorius for his hard line against those the bishop considered heretics. Socrates portrayed many of the disputes that disrupted the church in the fourth and the fifth centuries as a waste of time.
71 Socrates, *HE* 7.20.
72 Theodoret, *Epist.* 139 (trans. Jackson).

> when the mark of the cross was imprinted on the
> brow, that the trumpets sounded. First before the
> dragon standards went a spear-shaft raising the
> crest of Christ. There the race that for thirty years
> had plagued Pannonia was at last wiped out and
> paid the penalty.[73]

As Michael Whitby aptly points out, "It is too easily forgotten that
the Christian God was chosen by Constantine as a God of Battles,
and that there are plenty of exempla of heroic warriors and much
smiting of enemies in the Old Testament – Gideon, Samson,
David, and Maccabees."[74] As we touched on in the previous
chapter, though imbued with pacifist themes the New Testament
also recognised the need for soldiers and, at times, supported
the Roman state's use of force.[75] These New Testament authors
appropriated imperial martial imagery for their own purposes.
Colleen Conway has demonstrated convincingly that the author
of Revelation, in particular, mirrored imperial martial aggression
by "presenting a violent side of his images of Christ."[76] Revelation
(19:11–21) famously culminates with a warrior rider (connecting
the Son of God with the Word of God) emerging from the heavens
on a white horse. This post-resurrection soldier-Christ armed
with a double-edged sword wears many crowns, "for he it is who
shall rule them with an iron rod, and tread the winepress of the
wrath and retribution of God the sovereign Lord." Commanding
heaven's soldiers against "the beast and the kings of the earth and
their armies," he throws the beast and the false prophet into a lake
of fire, and kills the rest with the "sword coming out of his mouth."

One observes further examples of this warrior-Christ in
late antique iconography. Merging biblical and Graeco-Roman
mythological motifs, the early sixth-century mosaic from the

---

73 Prudentius, c. Symmachus 2 II. 709–16.

74 Whitby (pers. comm.).

75 See, e.g., Luke 22:36; Romans 7:23, 13:4.

76 Conway, *Behold the Man*, 164–65.

Capella Arcivescovile in Ravenna (plate 8) offers a striking image of Christ as a Roman soldier-emperor. Trampling a viper and a lion, Jesus bears a cross in his right hand while his left holds the Gospel displaying the passage John 14:6 "I am the way, truth, and life" (Ego sum via, veritas et vita). For my reader, the figure offers another timely reminder of the dangers in seeing in this period a neat division between either the classical and the Christian or the martial and the irenic. Indeed, M. Shane Bjornlie has proposed recently that the artist combined the biblical triumph of David in Psalms (90:12–13) with "symbolic attributions of Hercules, who wrestled a serpent as a child and bore the hide of the Nemean lion."[77] If this assertion is true, then the mosaic deftly combined Christian, imperial, and mythological motifs of two revered heroic personages who fought for good against evil.[78]

The church fathers were fully aware of the paradoxical pairing of militarism and pacifism in scripture. Augustine of Hippo, who like other powerful bishops regularly kept in touch with local military commanders,[79] used the example of David to reassure the *comes Africae* Bonifatius that God valued the endeavours of Roman soldiers, supporting what the bishop famously described as just wars.[80] Devout fifth-century Christian intellectuals like

77 Bjornlie, *Politics and Tradition*, 250.

78 Michael Grant (*The Antonines*, 75) discusses the second- and third-century Roman emperors' individualistic adoption of Hercules' reputed martial and irenic traits.

79 The growth of letter writing as a symbol of increasing cultural ties between the Roman cultural elite and the Roman military high-command—Roman and non-Roman—from the second half of the fourth century is discussed in detail by McLaughlin, "Bridging the Cultural Divide," 253–79.

80 Augustine, *Epist. 189*. Augustine composed his *De civitate Dei* (*City of God*) chiefly as a rebuttal against non-Christian assertions that the Christianisation of the Empire had led to the barbarian invasions and the Goth Alaric's sack of Rome in 410. Although he largely dismissed in this work the importance as well as the long term impact of events in the secular world, as the example above shows, his political writings frequently took a far more pragmatic stand

Augustine had come to accept that "good" Christians could serve in the military and destroy Rome's enemies without committing a sin.[81]

Some of Augustine's Christian contemporaries went further. Sharing a view espoused by their model Eusebius, Sozomen and Socrates made it clear in their histories that the church's well-being remained linked inexorably to the Roman armies' military successes. Yet, Socrates and Sozomen included information on secular matters seemingly unlinked to church affairs in their accounts. Socrates, in particular, knew that this inclusion set his history apart from his model Eusebius (and in some ways his fellow ecclesiastical historians such as Theodoret).[82] This gradual move away from purely religious histories is not so strange considering that these ecclesiastical historians lived in a different age than their historiographical model. By the time these men composed their histories, the Christian Roman Empire was nearly a century and a half old; paganism was a spent force, and Christian symbolism and iconography were an important part of Roman military ideology. Whereas Eusebius' history had been largely a tale of the Christian church's fight against its external enemies, and in particular the "persecuting" pagan Roman emperors, the fifth-century ecclesiastical historians concentrated primarily on the battle against "heretics" within, and the integral relationship between

than his pastoral teachings. For Bonifatius and Augustine's relationship, and the generalissimo's sincere interest in religious doctrine, see Wijnendaele, *Last of the Romans*, 35. For an in-depth treatment on Augustine's view on warfare, persecution, and his concept of "merciful cruelty," see Mattox, *St. Augustine and the Theory of Just War*; Buc, *Holy War*, 13, 82, 89–90, 122–23.

81 Lee, *War in Late Antiquity*, 177–93.

82 Socrates' prefatory comments to book six suggests that some of his early readers had been critical of his heavy focus on secular matters. Fifth-century Christian intellectuals, like the Gallo-Roman Gaius Sidonius Apollinaris (*Epist.* 4.22), had warned that those serving within the church's hierarchy should avoid historical writing.

the Roman armies' successes and the church's prosperity.[83] To varying degrees, these ecclesiastical historians provided details on secular and military affairs and the actions of brave soldiers, and even offered accounts of "brave" Roman citizens taking up arms against foreign invaders.[84]

This inclusion was no accident. Socrates explained he included such formerly taboo topics for three primary reasons. First, and most important, as he put it, "whenever the affairs of the state were disturbed, those of the Church [...] were disturbed."[85] He continued by justifying his emphasis on the life and deeds of Roman emperors, I "continually included the emperors in these historical details; because from the time they began to profess the Christian religion, the affairs of the church have depended on them."[86] Next, and possibly most revealing, he thought (or perhaps hoped) that his reading audience would tire of an endless rehashing of doctrinal disputes.[87] Lastly, Socrates covered primarily what he saw as the religious aspects of warfare. For instance, he wrote several chapters on Theodosius II's war with the Persians. He argued that Theodosius had launched hostilities primarily in an effort to protect native and Roman Christians in Persia from what he described as an increased persecution.[88] Socrates attributed Theodosius' triumph to a combination of the Roman army's valour and Christ's vengeance upon the Persians.

---

83 Urbainczyk, *Socrates*, 150.

84 For just a few examples, Sozomen, *HE* 7.4, 9.5, 9.9. Socrates (*HE* 5.1) provided a vivid and enthusiastic account of the citizens of Constantinople taking up arms to defend the capital against the Goths.

85 Socrates, *HE* 5. pref.3.

86 Socrates, *HE* 5. pref. 9–10.

87 Socrates, *HE* 5. pref.5. This emphasis on secular events may imply a less devout Christian audience than one might expect for an ecclesiastical history.

88 However, Socrates also suggested (*HE* 18) that the Persians' forbidding of a group of Roman goldminers to return home and the plundering of Roman merchants represent the other *casus belli*.

Socrates' Theodosius was no soldier. Theodosius, according to Socrates, considered warfare a trifling matter best left to one's generals. More a man of peace than of war, this pious non-martial Theodosius is the one favoured in the ancient and modern traditions.[89] Yet, we should be careful not to mistake the well-known Byzantine contention that peace should be preferred to war as evidence of an unwarlike civilisation.[90] In spite of outwardly irenic tendencies, the smouldering embers of intolerance could be, and often were, stoked by Christian intellectuals into conflagrations of brutal intolerance. As Philippe Buc justly cautions, in early Christian rhetoric, "peace, *pax*, did not mean the absence of conflict but victorious conflict leading to right order and justice, *iustitia*."[91] In other words, though peace was preferable to war, internal enemies and strife within the Christian church and external threats by the Empire's foreign enemies consistently thwarted the achievement of a perfect Christian *imperium*. Therefore, while Theodosius II preached pacifism and religious tolerance, he spent most of his reign engaging in spiritual and material warfare.[92]

Due to the loss of much of the secular literature from the fifth century, our portrait of Theodosius II derives necessarily from the relatively abundant extant religious sources. This skewed ratio has probably tilted our view towards the pious Theodosius II somewhat.[93] Still, not all of the emperor's colleagues would have regarded piety as highly as these ecclesiastical historians

---

89 Socrates, *HE* 18, 20. Interestingly, Socrates, at the close of book 18, begins to tell the tale of the Roman general's martial deeds in combat, but cuts himself off with the reprimand that such tales were outside the scope of his genre.

90 E.g., Dennis, "Defenders of the Christian People."

91 Buc, "Christian Theology of Violence," 13.

92 For Theodosius' protracted struggle to ensure a "uniformity of Christian belief and practice," see Millar, *Greek Roman Empire*, 130–91.

93 Hence, Millar's masterful account of the reign relies heavily on the church historians and the *acta* of the oecumenical councils held during Theodosius II's reign.

did. Anthony Kaldellis has recently remarked cogently that "Some Byzantines thought piety was a more important virtue for their rulers to have, others less."[94] This appears to be the case with Theodosius II. For ecclesiastical writers, piety naturally represented his reign's defining feature. We have evidence that later critics of Theodosius' regime sought to turn this pious portrait on its head. For its negative representation of Theodosius II's court, the sixth-century chronicle of John Malalas utilised a late fifth-century source that concentrated heavily on the regime's "sexual politics."[95] In his chronicle, Malalas asserted scurrilously that Theodosius' passionate love for his handsome *cubicularius* Chrysaphius had led the emperor to allow the eunuch to run roughshod over imperial affairs.[96] Whether there was any fire beneath the smoke of this and other accusations against the Theodosians is difficult to say. Regardless of its accuracy, however, what better way to undermine an emperor whose reputation was based primarily upon his devout and pious life than to link him romantically to his key eunuch advisor? As we saw in the case of Eudoxia, exposing the Theodosians' alleged transgressions had long been a favourite tactic for the family's opponents.[97]

94 Kaldellis, *Byzantine Republic*, 193.

95 Wood, "Multiple Voices," 299.

96 Malalas, *Chron.* 14.18 (363). By successfully marginalising Pulcheria and the Empress Eudocia, the *spatharius* Chrysaphios (*PLRE* 2: 295–97) rose to dominance over Theodosius' political and ecclesiastical affairs in the 440s. Soon after Theodosius' death, Pulcheria had him executed (Marcellinus, *Chron.* s.a. 450).

97 On Galla Placidia's supposed sexual misconduct with her brother, the Emperor Honorius, see Olympiodorus, *frag.* 38. In another sensationalised passage, Malalas (*Chron.* 14.68 [356.17–58.4]) accused Theodosius II's wife of adultery with the emperor's childhood friend Paulinius. Eudocia, who retained her imperial title, had "retired" to Jerusalem in 441, where she would remain until her death in 460. For a full discussion of the factional rivalries and sexual innuendo that plagued Theodosius' court in the 440s, see Cameron, "Empress and the Poet."

Censuring the Theodosians for their dearth of martial virtues represented another avenue of attack for their detractors. While secular Byzantine historians unquestionably recognised the power of piety and providence in determining outcomes in battle, in their histories soldiers' virtues, armament, tactics, and strategy tend to represent the primary factors behind a victory or a defeat.[98] Priscus, one of the few fifth-century secular historians besides Olympiodorus to provide us with some details on Theodosius II's reign—albeit in a negative fashion—says very little in the fragments that survive about the emperor's piety, and nothing about the imperial regime's Christological views. Instead, he voiced his concerns that Theodosius' cowardice and dearth of martial virtues had caused him to prefer to pay off the Eastern Romans' enemies instead of facing them in battle.[99] As explained in chapter 3, Priscus designed a portrait of Theodosius II and his ministers as unmanly fops. In his history, probably composed during the second reign of the soldier-emperor Zeno, the younger Theodosius' unmanly vices had almost allowed the Empire to fall prey to the *andreios* Attila and his martial Huns.[100] Though we lack

98 See, e.g., Procopius (*Wars* 8.29.8–10, 8.30.1, 8.32.22–30) on the Battle of Taginae in 552. The church father's position on the role of providence in the world was never simple. Late Roman and early Byzantine Christians held divided positions on the providential meaning behind secular history. Augustine, while recognising that God controlled events in the secular world, famously rejected in *De civitate Dei* (e.g. 18.52.1, 20.11) the idea that a divine plan guided the worldly destiny of the *civitas terrena*. In a position that would gain the upper-hand in the Byzantine world, intellectuals like Eusebius (*HE* 4.26.7–8) and Orosius (*Against the Pagans*, 7.27) promoted the idea that a virtuous land could become a New Jerusalem and thus receive God's protection. For a full discussion of these issues, see Markus, *Saeculum*.

99 On Priscus' approval of anyone or group of peoples who took bold stands against barbarian peoples, see Thompson, *Attila and the Huns*, 189.

100 Priscus famously provided an account of his dealings with Attila, praising him as a stern yet just leader. He went on to submit (*frag.* 11) that "Although a lover of war, he was not prone to violence."

most of the text, it appears that the career diplomat had constructed the conventional binary contrast comparing the unmanly vices of Theodosius II and his generals and eunuch advisors with the more typically martial and masculine ideals displayed by the soldier-emperor Marcian, whose military background and strong diplomatic stance against the Huns had earned Priscus' praise.[101]

Such a gendered view of the Western Romans' fifth-century failures was common in sixth-century Western and Eastern sources. Looking back on the disastrous fifth century, East Roman and Italo-Roman writers placed the blame for the losses of the Empire's Western provinces squarely at the feet of the non-martial and effeminate fifth-century Theodosian emperors.[102] In his prologue to *Vandalic War*, for instance, Procopius theorised that Valentinian III had failed in his essential masculine task as the guardian of the state and of his family, and consequently both of his wards fell captive to the courageous Gaiseric[103] and his Vandals:

> Placidia, his mother, had raised this emperor and educated him in an effeminate manner, and because of this he was filled with evil from childhood. He associated mostly with sorcerers and astrologers, and he was an extraordinarily zealous pursuer of love affairs with other men's wives. He conducted himself in a most indecent manner, although he was married to a woman of exceptional beauty. Not only that, but he failed to recover for the empire anything that it had lost before, and he lost Libya in

---

101 Priscus, *frag.* 5.18–20. He also appreciated (*frag.* 53) Leo I's tough position against the Vandals, an attitude that Procopius shared in his narrative on Leo's regime.

102 For Justinian's attitudes towards his predecessors' failures in the West, *CJ*, 30.11.12, of April 535.

103 For Procopius' admiration of Gaiseric's wisdom and courage, see *Wars* 3.4.13–15.

addition and was himself killed. When he perished, his wife and children were taken captive.[104]

Writing in early 550s Constantinople, the self-proclaimed Goth Jordanes adopted a similar stance, claiming that the naming of Marcian as Eastern emperor in 450 had brought about the end of sixty years of "effeminate rule" (delicati decessores) for the Empire.[105] In sixth-century Ostrogothic Italy, the Italo-Roman writer Cassiodorus (ca. 490–ca. 583) wove a similar tale whereby the slack militarism of an unmanly regime brought about a decline in the Western Roman army's manly vigour. Cassiodorus proclaimed that Placidia, who had served as Valentinian III's regent from 423 to 437, had "feminised the soldiery through too much peace."[106] This passive and emasculated Western Roman rule stood in stark contrast with Cassiodorus' depiction of the "manly" martial rule of Amalasuintha (r. 525–ca. 534) and her Goths.[107] Such critiques demonstrate how many early Byzantines and

---

104 Procopius, *Wars* 3.3.10–13 (trans. Kaldellis): *Πλακιδία δὲ ἡ αὐτοῦ μήτηρ θηλυνομένην παιδείαν τε καὶ τροφὴν τὸν βασιλέα τοῦτον ἐξέθρεψέ τε καὶ ἐξεπαίδευσε, καὶ ἀπ᾽ αὐτοῦ κακίας ἔμπλεως ἐκ παιδὸς γέγονε. φαρμακεῦσί τε γὰρ τὰ πολλὰ καὶ τοῖς ἐς τὰ ἄστρα περιέργοις ὡμίλμει, ἔς τε ἀλλοτρίων γυναικῶν ἔρωτας δαιμονίως ἐσπουδακὼς πολλῇ ἐχρῆτο ἐς τὴν δίαιταν παρανομία, καίπερ γυναικὶ ξυνοικῶν εὐπρεπεῖ τὴν ὄψιν ἐς ἄγαν οὔσῃ. ταῦτά τοι οὐδέ τι ἀνεσώσατο τῇ βασιλείᾳ ὧν ἀφῄρητο προτερον, ἀλλὰ καὶ Λιβύην προσαπώλεσε καὶ αὐτὸς ἐφθάρη. καὶ ἐπειδὴ ἐτελεύτησε, τῇ τε γυναικὶ ταῖς τε παισὶ δορυαλώτοις γενέσθαι ξυνέπεσε.*

105 Jordanes, *Romana* 332 (my trans.), ed. Mommsen: "Regnum quod delicati; decessores prodecessoresque eius per annos fere sexaginta vicissim."

106 Cassiodorus (*Variae* 11.1.10, trans. Barnish): "qui provida dispositione libratus nec assiduis bellis adteritur nec iterum longa pace mollitur." I have changed the translator Barnish's "weakened" for *mollitur* to "feminised." For a full discussion of this passage and Cassiodorus' gendered views of the Goths and Eastern Romans, see Arnold, *Roman Imperial Restoration*, 48–51.

107 A vision of a "manly" and "sagacious" Amalasuintha that is very similar to that of Procopius (e.g., *Wars*, 5.2.3–4; *Secret History*, 16.1).

Italo-Romans rejected the idea that an emperor could "abandon" his martial role as the state's manly protector.

Moreover, the fact that the fifth century produced at least five other secular histories should serve as an important reminder that, in contrast to the West, historical writing continued to be a viable literary genre in the East. In addition, judging from their fragments and their sixth-century successors, these works appear to have focused on military affairs and the manliness of war. Candidus' lost history seems to have focused heavily on the future Emperor Basiliscus' military "successes and failures" in Africa.[108] Malchus, who probably wrote history during Anastasius' reign, also appears to have concentrated on the military reigns of Leo, Zeno, and Basiliscus.[109]

Fifth-century secular historiography portrayed military setbacks, not as acts of divine retribution, but primarily as tactical and/or moral failures. Priscus, for instance, blamed Leo I's failed campaign to recapture North Africa from the Vandals in 468 largely on its commander, the future "usurper" Basiliscus. According to Priscus, Basiliscus—through a combination of stupidity, treachery, and cowardice—failed to act decisively, and therefore allowed the noble and valiant Roman soldiers to suffer a disastrous defeat at the hands of the Vandals.[110]

None of this above is to argue that Christian values such as piety and providence did not play an important part in fifth-century imperial self-presentation and/or state war ideology. Idealised men and emperors needed to juxtapose their roles in the religious, political, and military spheres. As the next chapter will establish,

108 Candidus, *frag.* 1, ed. and trans. Blockley.

109 Malchus, *frags.* Contra Barry Baldwin's claim ("Malchus of Philadelphia") that Malchus' history sought to criticise the rampant militarism of Leo and Zeno's reigns, although critical of these reigns, far too little remains of his history to make such a sweeping conclusion. It seems peculiar, if Baldwin's thesis is correct, that Malchus would have made such an effort to portray Zeno as unwarlike and cowardly (e.g. *frag.* 5).

110 Priscus, *frags* 43, 53.1.

the soldier-emperors who came after Theodosius II frequently sought to emphasise their own orthodoxy and Christian virtues as an aspect of their civilised *Romanitas* and right to rule. These soldier-emperors prayed, fought, and ruled. By the fifth century, *Romanitas* and *christianitas* had unquestionably united to become an essential marker of Byzantine identity.[111] I only submit that the disappearance of much of the secular historiography from the fifth century must be remembered when one attempts to determine the extent of this era's focus on Christian virtues or a larger societal rejection of martial virtues and traditional masculine ideologies. The ecclesiastical material offers a valid, but partial vision of Theodosius II and fifth-century cultural politics. After all, imagine our view of the sixth century if the complete accounts we have from Procopius, Agathias, and Theophylact had disappeared or come down to us only in fragments like all of their fifth-century counterparts. The balance of the surviving sources is such as to give a false impression of a dramatic shift in the fifth century away from an imperial, as well as a larger societal, ideology of masculine *Romanitas* based on martial virtues. The infusion of the spiritual element into imperial war ideologies was a natural progression of the merging of the secular and the religious. As we have observed in this chapter, this fusion had gathered momentum in the fifth century. This development helps us understand why the majority of Romans believed simultaneously in the power of prayer and the power of military might as a means to defeat foreign enemies. Yet, practical military virtues would come to define the regimes of a long line of emperors after Theodosius II.

The Search for Martial Saviours

By the middle of the fifth century, we see a move back towards soldier-emperors. Indeed, the Western emperors Valentinian III and Majorian had been assassinated while trying to assert their right to martial hegemony. In his recreation of Valentinian III's

111 Rapp, "Hellenic Identity," 144.

infamous assassination of Aëtius in 454 at a financial meeting in Ravenna, Priscus luridly captured the disastrous consequences when a child-emperor grew wise enough to appreciate that he functioned merely as a puppet. Attempting to break free from these restraints, and egged on by his power-hungry advisor Petronius Maximus, the historian depicted the thirty-six-year-old emperor jumping from his throne and thundering at a dumbfounded Aëtius:

> That he would no longer endure to be abused by such treacheries. He alleged that, by blaming him for the troubles, Aëtius wished to deprive him of power in the West, as he had done in the East, insinuating that only because of Aëtius did he not go to remove Marcian from his throne.[112]

Catching the old general off guard, the emperor then struck the astonished Aëtius with his sword, while simultaneously his grand chamberlain Heraclius attacked with a cleaver he had hidden under his robes. Having slain the celebrated "conqueror" of Attila, neither Valentinian nor Heraclius had much time to bask in their victory; Aëtius' Hunnic supporters murdered the pair whilst the emperor was going to practise archery on the Campus Martius. Valentinian's assassination of a war hero and reliance on his eunuch advisor to help him perform the deed provoked an almost universally hostile response amongst contemporaries.[113] Hence, Valentinian's example reveals just how far power had shifted away from the emperor and into the hands of their generalissimos, at least in the West. Despite the disastrous outcome, Valentinian's attempt to take out his rival and effort to pursue a more martial

---

112 Priscus, *frag.* 30.

113 Sidonius, *Epist.* 7.359; Evagrius, *HE* 2.7. Interestingly, after describing Aëtius' "craven" murder, Priscus hypocritically praised Aëtius for cleverly arranging the assassination of his rival the Western *magister militum* Felix in 430.

role in order to gain the support of the military suggests that he understood too well that true power lay in the man who could drape himself in manly martial virtues.

The majority of Valentinian III's successors appeared to have learned this lesson. Reflecting the growing militarism of the Eastern and Western Roman ruling elites, military prowess represented the primary characteristic for the long line of non-dynastic emperors after 455. Alarmed by the inroads made by the "barbarians" in all corners of the twin regimes, by the middle of the fifth century, Romans from the East and the West appeared to have tired of the non-martial Theodosian emperors dominated by their martial "managers." The Gaul Sidonius Apollinaris (430–ca. 480–90), whose letters and speeches provide a vivid commentary on the state of the mid-fifth century Western Roman Empire, captured this mood in his panegyric delivered at the opening of 458 to the soldier-emperor Majorian:

> Ever since Theodosius [I] restored a joint authority to his patron's exiled brother [Emperor Gratian, r. 375–83], whose neck was broken by a hand destined to be turned against itself, my land of Gaul has even until now been ignored by the lords of the world, and has languished in slavery unheeded. Since that time much has been destroyed, for with the emperor, whomever he might be, closely confined, it has been the constant lot of the distant parts of a wretched world to be laid waste [...] Now our *princeps* [Majorian] is amending all this, and he advances to your wars by way of other wars, adding fresh forces from diverse peoples, for it is the going,

> not the fighting, that is hardest. But why do we
> waste time in words? He comes, he conquers.[114]

The point is unmistakable: in a violent age, the time had come to embrace an active martial emperor once more.[115]

Majorian fit the bill: a former *comes domesticorum* and *magister militum* under Aëtius, Majorian's aristocratic and martial background had made him an acceptable choice for Western elites, including those in Gaul, like Sidonius, who were still reeling after the overthrow of his father-in-law, the Gallo-Roman aristocrat Avitus, at the hands of Majorian and Ricimer in October of 456.[116] Writing during a time when central Roman control over Gaul was receding, Sidonius' propaganda rejected the Theodosians' non-martial rule, which had seen the Visigoths rise to dominance in his homeland. Speeches like the one above were meant to be flattering and over-the-top. Such public addresses, which Andrew Gillette has aptly described as "epic panegyrics," helped generalissimos such as Majorian to communicate directly with "the civilian elite,

---

114 Sidonius, *Panegyric to Majorian* 353–67: "ex quo Theudosius communia iura fagato reddidit auctoris fratri, cui guttura fregit post in se vertenda manus, mea Gallia rerum ignoratur adhuc dominis ignaraque servit. Ex illo multum periit, quia principe clauso, quisquis erat, miseri diversis partibus orbis vastari sollemne fuit. Quae vita placeret, cum rector moderandus erat? Contempta tot annos nobilitas iacult: pretium respublica forti rettulit invidiam. Princeps haec omnia noster corriget atque tuum vires gentibus addends ad bellum per bella venit; nam maximus isse est, non pugnasse labor. Terimus cur tempora verbis? Pervenit et vincit." For Sidonius' conviction that "proven military valour" represented a potential emperor's most important quality, see Arnold, *Roman Imperial Restoration*, 152, n. 42.

115 See, e.g., Sidonius, *Panegyric to Anthemius* 225–42.

116 For the mid-fifth century Western Roman elite's preference for imperial candidates who shared their "ennobling traits," see Arnold, *Roman Imperial Restoration*, 142–43. For the tendency of non-Romans like Attila taking pains to highlight their own royal pedigree in the face of Roman snobbery, see Priscus, *frag.* 15.2.

to massage opinion, and to generate and maintain support."[117] As a close relative of the former emperor who had gained the purple with the Visigoths' assistance, we may rightly suspect Sidonius' sincerity in praising a man who had played a key role in Avitus' downfall. As in most panegyrics, Sidonius' silences say as much as statements.[118]

Yet, despite the vacuous nature of its genre, Sidonius based his speech on Majorian's past, present, and future policies. Before Sidonius had delivered his panegyric, Majorian had been taking a keen interest in returning Gaul to the imperial fold. This policy had seen one potential Gallo-Roman usurper arrested and an imperial army besieging Lyon. Following his successes in Gaul, Majorian signed a truce with the Visigothic king, Theoderic II; he then turned his eyes to Spain and began planning his doomed campaign to retake Vandalic North Africa.[119]

Whatever Sidonius' true views concerning Majorian, his criticisms of the passive non-martial Theodosians were almost certainly heartfelt and indicative of the hopes of many Romans that an active soldier-emperor could rouse a moribund Western Roman Empire.[120] Such critiques of non-martial emperors demonstrate the limitations of non-martial and/or Christian virtues as the dominant aspect of imperial self-definition and *Romanitas* in the middle of the fifth century. Spiritual warfare and an emperor's piety could only take his realm so far.

With the prescience granted by hindsight, Sidonius' words may appear to us as nothing more than a dream. Majorian

117 Gillette, "Epic Panegyric," 288–89.

118 For possible cryptic criticisms of Majorian in the speech, see Rousseau, "Sidonius and Majorian."

119 Majorian had maintained a good reputation in sixth-century Byzantium. Procopius praised (*Wars* 3.7.4, trans. Kaldellis) his martial qualities, proclaiming hyperbolically that Majorian "surpassed in every virtue all who ever were emperor of the Romans."

120 Sidonius' nuanced attitude towards warfare is discussed by Sarti, *Perceiving War*, 91–93.

failed ultimately to deliver on his promise to rout the Vandals, and consequently he met his end at the orders of his *patricius et magister militum* Ricimer.[121] With Majorian's death, the last best chance to restore a durable centralised Western Empire evaporated. Of course, it is difficult to know whether a cohesive Western Empire would have survived even if Majorian had succeeded in recapturing North Africa. By the middle of the fifth century, the Western Empire had already become increasingly regionalised. We see the emergence of micro-Romes; Peter Heather has described this process as the gradual replacement of "central Romanness" with "local Romanness."[122]

From the vantage of 450s Italy, however, the situation in the West may not have seemed so futile. At the time Sidonius gave his panegyric to Majorian, the Eastern Romans were facing similar difficulties—ruled by a new emperor, the *tribunis militum*, Leo I. Indeed, Leo had risen to the purple under even more obscure circumstances than Majorian to suit the whims of the non-Roman generalissimo, Aspar, who like Ricimer preferred to rule behind the scenes. Yet, the Eastern Empire survived and eventually thrived. One prominent Byzantinist goes so far as to describe Leo I as "the first Byzantine emperor" and credits him and his successor Zeno with rescuing "Byzantium from becoming a plaything of the barbarians."[123] It is to these soldier-emperors' militarised regimes that we may now turn.

---

121 Priscus, *frag.* 6.36.2. Theophanes (*AM* 5954) names the patrician Remikios as the assassin. As Sidonius demonstrates (*Epist.* 1.10.11), Majorian's disgrace was not immediate; after his failure against the Vandals the emperor had returned to Gaul and once again took on his imperial role.

122 Heather, *Fall of Rome*, 432–43.

123 Treadgold, *History of the Byzantine State*, 847.

Plate 9. Missorium of Aspar (434) Florence, Italy,
Museo Archeologico Nazionale.

We need now an armed prince who in the manner of our sires will not order wars but wage them, one before whom land and sea will quake when he advances his standards.

Sidonius, *Panegyric to Anthemius* 2.382–86

VII

Emperors and Generals: Pathways to Power in the Age of Leo I

The sixth-century chronicle of John Malalas records a letter written purportedly by the Eastern Emperor Leo to his Western counterpart Anthemius.[1] Composed in the aftermath of Leo's infamous assassination of his Alan generalissimo and senior Eastern consul Aspar, in the summer of 471, Leo explained to his protégé that he had destroyed Aspar and his sons in order to be the one "who gives orders not takes them."[2] To avoid becoming a docile puppet, he advised Anthemius to immediately assassinate his supreme commander the Gotho-Sueve Ricimer and then eliminate Leo's rival the Roman noble and future Western

---

1 Bury ("Note on the Emperor Olybrius," 509) believed the letter to be genuine. Modern historians like Penny MacGeorge (*Late Roman Warlords*, 257) are more hesitant, regarding it as an embellishment, albeit a genuine reflection of the period's political realities.

2 For Aspar's status as Constantinople's oldest surviving consul, see also *Chron. Paschale* s.a. 467.

Emperor Olybrius (r. 472).[3]

Ricimer, however, anticipating this threat, had posted his soldiers at Rome's entrances.[4] One of these sentinels had intercepted Leo's *magistrianus* Modestus attempting to smuggle the incriminating letter to Anthemius. Alerted to the plot, Ricimer acted swiftly, summoning his nephew the *magister militum*—and future Burgundian king (r. 473–516)—Gundobad from Gaul. Priscus provides the further detail that after losing a pitched battle against Ricimer's forces, Anthemius' supporters had quickly abandoned the emperor and gone over to Ricimer.[5] Gundobad found Anthemius hiding amongst the beggars within the Church of the Apostle Peter; he then unceremoniously beheaded the cowering Western emperor.[6]

While we can rightly question aspects of this account's chronology and veracity, it sheds needed light on the factional rivalries that frequently defined turbulent mid-fifth century Roman politics. We should not see these disputes, however, as conflicts between noble Romans and rogue barbarian factions.[7] Scholars now generally accept that these men were not motivated by issues of ethnicity, but primarily by the tides of contemporary factional politics.[8]

Military elites dominated in this world.[9] Yet pure physicality represented only one element behind these men's ascendency. While dangerous and prone to acts of violence, the soldiers who

---

3 Leo had originally sent Olybrius to Rome with the hope to repair the rift between Anthemius and Ricimer.

4 On Ricimer, see Stein, *Histoire du Bas-Empire*, 371–95; O'Flynn, *Generalissimos*, 99, 104–28; MacGeorge, *Late Roman Warlords*, 165–269.

5 Priscus, *frag.* 64.

6 Malalas, *Chron.* 14.45 (373–75).

7 Elton, "Ilus and the Imperial Aristocracy."

8 Full discussion in Croke, "Dynasty and Ethnicity," 147–203. Contra Bury, *Later Roman Empire*, 339; Barnwell, *Emperor, Prefects, and Kings*, 43–45.

9 For the exaltation of the military classes over the class of civilian functionaries under Ricimer, see Sidonius, *Epist.* 1.9, and under Leo, see Malchus, *frag.* 3.

rose to the top in this competitive environment also depended on their wits and the intellectual side of their *Romanitas* to overcome their rivals. Indeed, defeating one's enemies in the world of public opinion was just as vital as besting them in armed conflict. We find valuable remnants of these clashes in the literature that survives from the age. This reality helps to explain why the Eastern Roman aristocrat Anthemius could be idealised both as an articulate manly martial aristocratic Roman or derided as a bumbling unmanly Greek, while the former soldiers Leo, Ricimer, and Aspar could be portrayed, on the one hand, as the Empire's martial manly protectors, and on the other hand disparaged as murderous, deceitful "barbarian" butchers.

We should see the letter above as a reflection of these propaganda wars. Reading the subtext of Malalas' account (echoed in Priscus), one finds that Anthemius' failure to check the control of "barbarians" like Ricimer had led to the Western emperors' increasing marginalisation and the rise ultimately of non-Roman rule in Italy. According to this paradigm, the Western half of the Empire fell because its emperors failed to stand up to these barbarian strongmen; in contrast, in the East, Leo I's assassination of Aspar and purge of his "Germanic" supporters had helped to assure East Rome's survival.[10] This view on the reasons behind the collapse of the West and the survival of the East found in writers such as Procopius is still followed by scholars that are more traditional.[11]

This chapter uses the militarised regimes of Leo I and Anthemius as a pivot to investigate the ways these men wielded "Christian,"

10 Philip Wood ("Multiple Voices," 301–03) reads this passage as an instance of Malalas being ironic, maintaining that the chronicler sought to paint a picture of Leo as a barbarian along the lines of Ricimer. I doubt that the rather clumsy historian Malalas was capable of such subtlety. So too did Malalas (and probably his source) rationalise Leo's elimination of the generalissimo, by maintaining that Aspar had been planning a rebellion.

11 Procopius, *Wars* 3.6, 4.6.1–21; Treadgold, *History of the Byzantine State*, 154–56; Heather, *Restoration of Rome*, 22.

martial, and civilised *Romanitas* as a means of highlighting their right to rule, while simultaneously marginalising their opponents as heretical and uncouth non-Romans. Particular attention will be paid to the rivalries and conflicts between Leo/Aspar and Anthemius/Ricimer.[12]

Unlike the absurd rhetoric describing the manly martial *Romanitas* of feeble puppet-emperors such as Honorius and Arcadius, the martial qualifications of these men is readily apparent. By scrutinising the careers of these men who had all risen to prominence from within the army, the chapter strives to uncover how these individuals truly—and not just rhetorically—garbed themselves in martial manliness. Far from accidental, the rise of these men as the primary players in the fifth-century Roman world represents a larger societal embracing of martial virtues. We shall see that the dominance of military men in these imperial regimes serves as inconvenient reminders for those who would argue that fifth-century Byzantine society was becoming less androcentric and/or turning away from traditional views of imperial leadership based on martial qualities.

Pathways to Power: Aspar and Leo I

The Emperor Marcian died on 27 January 457.[13] With his passing, so ended the Theodosian connection that had defined rule in

---

12 The precise chronology of many of the events discussed in this chapter remain disputed. In an effort to provide a free-flowing narrative, these debates are limited primarily to the footnotes.

13 Due primarily to his support of Chalcedon and tough stand against Attila's demands for tribute, later Orthodox Byzantine writers remembered Marcian as one of the "good" Roman emperors. See e.g., Marcellinus, *Chron.* s.a. 457; Procopius, *Wars* 3.4.11; Evagrius, *HE* 2.8. In contrast, Monophysite writers generally condemned Marcian. For a summary of these assessments, see Allen, *Evagrius Scholasticus*, 97–98.

the imperial East for the previous eight decades.[14] Many within Constantinople had probably expected that Marcian's son-in-law, the blue-blooded Anthemius, would be named successor.[15] Instead, ten days later at the Campus Martius in Constantinople, Leo was proclaimed emperor in front of a mixed audience of senators, imperial regiments (*scholai*), key members of the military, and, most symbolically, Anatolios, the archbishop of Constantinople. Despite the audience's chants insisting that each faction "demanded Leo as emperor," one suspects that many within the audience knew little about the grizzled soldier who was about to don the imperial diadem. When the crowd cried out in unison, "Leo *augoustos* may you always be victorious! He who has chosen you, may he guard you!"[16] some within the crowd might be forgiven for thinking that this protector was not the Christian saviour of the next line of the chant, but the Alan *magister militum* Flavius Ardabur Aspar, the driving force behind Leo's unexpected crowning.

Marcian (probably) and Leo (definitely) had been raised by Aspar (ca. 400–471).[17] Born around 401 in the Balkans, one fifth-century source described Leo as hailing from Dacia in Illyricum,

14 The Western emperor Olybrius (r. 472) had married to Valentinian III's daughter Placidia. Anthemius too retained the Theodosian link tenuously through his marriage to Marcian's daughter, Aelia Marcia Euphemia.

15 Though, writing nearly two decades later, Sidonius (*Epist.* 2 210–12) insisted that Anthemius did not want to become emperor at that time. Aspar most likely preferred the less connected, and consequently less dangerous, Leo.

16 Following the complete depiction of Leo's ceremony found in Constantine Porphyrogennetos, *De cerimoniis* 410–16.

17 For Aspar's role in Leo's rise, see Candidus, *frag.* 1; Jordanes, *Romana* 335; Procopius, *Wars* 3.5.7; Evagrius, *HE* 2.16. For Aspar's essential role in Marcian's ascension, I side with the arguments made by Burgess ("Accession of Marcian"). So too is the Isaurian generalissimo Flavius Zeno a possible player behind Marcian's rise, see Zuckerman, "L' Empire," 169–76. Cf., however, Chew ("Faction Politics"), who contends that the Empress Pulcheria was the primary player behind Marcian's accession. For

while sixth-century literature propose that he was of Bessian stock (the Bessi were an independent Thracian tribe).[18] Whatever his true heritage, Leo's career offers further evidence that for many fifth-century Romans from the Balkans, a career in the Roman army could offer a pathway to a better life.[19]

Unfortunately, we know virtually nothing about Leo's life before he became emperor. Though he was probably no obscure soldier, our sources do not record any major military victories or outstanding achievements.[20] All we can say with any certainty is that at the time of his accession, Leo was serving as a senior commander of the troops in Selymbria (modern Silivri in Istanbul district).[21]

Aspar's biography is easier to reconstruct. Of Gotho-Alanic descent, Aspar as a youth had undertaken a career in the Roman military.[22] Certainly, Aspar's rise to become the senior senator in Constantinople offers an instructive example on the ways a military career could facilitate a foreigner's climb up the Roman social ladder. His long if rather chequered military career spanned five decades. Scholars trace the Alans' service within the Eastern Roman army to the command of the Eastern *praetorian prefect*

a discussion on the variety of ways emperors could be proclaimed even when heirs of the former emperor survived, see Börm, "Born to be Emperor."

18 Candidus *frag.* 1; Malalas *Chron.* 14.35 (369); Jordanes, *Romana* 335. Writing shortly after Leo's reign, Candidus should be preferred. In fact, Malalas and Jordanes' contentions may represent later attempts to paint Leo as a barbarian cloaked in Roman clothing.

19 Whitby, "Emperors and Armies," 166. For a discussion of Balkan military culture, see Amory, *People and Identity*, 277–313.

20 Brian Croke ("Dynasty and Ethnicity," 151) rejects the commonly held notion that Leo was an "obscure soldier."

21 Candidus, *frag.* 1. Later sources describe him as a *comes et tribunis Mattiariorum*, Constantine Porphyrogennetos, *De cerimoniis* 91; *tribunis militum* see, e.g., Jordanes, *Romana* 335.

22 Candidus, *frag.* 1.

Rufinus at the close of the fourth century.[23] Although the Alans had been "Gothicised" in the late fourth and fifth centuries, their ancestry was Iranian not Germanic.[24] Aspar was no obscure barbarian auxiliary. While the exact details behind their rise are uncertain, Aspar's relatives held important commands under Theodosius II.[25]

As mentioned in the previous chapter, Aspar had served with his father, Ardabur (consul 427), in Theodosius II's short-lived and indecisive war (421–22) against the Persians. Having earned a reputation for martial prowess during the Persian campaign, in 424–25 the father and son were two of the three commanders that the Emperor Theodosius II sent to Italy to overthrow the Western usurper John.[26] After the capture of his father at sea by John's forces, Aspar rescued Ardabur by stealthily taking the formerly impregnable Ravenna.[27] In the summer of 425, the pair captured John in Aquileia, and then proceeded to torture the usurper before his execution.[28] We unearth hints of hostility towards this macabre display in the sentiment from a sixth-century source that "John was killed by the treachery, rather than the manliness, of Ardaburius and Aspar."[29]

---

23 Bachrach, *History of the Alans*, 41–42.

24 Goffart, *Barbarian Tides*, 90.

25 Lee, "Theodosius and His Generals," 90–108.

26 Olympiodorus, *frags* 43, 46; Malalas, *Chron.* 14.6 (356). Olympiodorus reveals (*frag.* 43) that the third commander, Candidianus, was primarily responsible for the triumph.

27 Socrates, *HE* 7.23; Olympiodorus, *frag.* 43.2. The ecclesiastical historian Socrates naturally focused on the miraculous aspects of Ravenna's capture, whilst the secular-minded Olympiodorus explained that the prisoner Ardabur had undermined John's position within the city before Aspar's arrival.

28 Procopius, *Wars* 3.3.9.

29 Marcellinus, *Chron.* s.a. 425: "Suprafatus Iohannes dolo potius Ardaburis et Asparis magis quam virtute occiditur."

However, Aspar's defeat of a large force of Huns led by the formidable fifth-century Western generalissimo Aëtius garnered later historians' respect.[30] In 431, Aspar joined Bonifatius in a game, but ultimately futile attempt to expel the Vandals from North Africa. The next year, somewhere between Carthage and Hippo, Gaiseric's forces inflicted a severe defeat on the Romans.[31] Shortly after the defeat, Valentinian III's mother Galla Placidia summoned Bonifatius to Italy, where she shortly afterwards named him supreme commander in the West (*magister militum*).[32]

Aëtius apparently had not taken kindly to Bonifatius' promotion, and at the close of 432 the two generalissimos' armies clashed outside Rimini. As one scholar notes, this battle was significant because "for the first time a civil war was fought not over who should be emperor, but over who should be the emperor's generalissimo."[33]

Despite achieving a narrow victory, shortly after the battle Bonifatius had succumbed to the wounds he may have received engaging Aëtius in single combat.[34] This left Aspar as the primary commander to regroup the Roman forces defending Carthage and

---

30 Cassiodorus, *Chron.* s.a. 425; Gregory of Tours, 2.8; Philostorgius, *HE* 12.4; Prosper, *Chron.* s.a. 425, ed. Mommsen; *Chron. gallica 452*, 100; Jordanes, *Romana*, 328.

31 Procopius, *Wars* 3.3.34–36. Perhaps in an effort to highlight the Alan's dishonour Procopius claimed mistakenly that Aspar had returned to Constantinople shortly after the devastating defeat.

32 For Bonifatius' recall to Italy, see Wijnendaele, *Last of the Romans*, 98–99; McEvoy, *Child Emperor Rule*, 246–48.

33 O'Flynn, *Generalissimos*, 80.

34 Marcellinus, *Chron.* s.a. 432. Wijnendaele sees Marcellinus' account as exaggerated but possible, since we have other examples of fifth-century Roman generals engaging in single combat with their enemies. I am more sceptical.

Roman North Africa from the unrelenting Vandals.[35] From 432–35 Aspar stayed in Carthage, where his army—for a time—held back the tide of the Vandalic advance. Aspar seems to have employed political skills to match his soldiership; he was probably present when the Vandals signed a treaty with the Western Romans in 435. The Romans ceded northern Numidia and parts of Africa Proconsularis; nevertheless, for the time being, Carthage and the majority of Africa Proconsularis remained under imperial control.[36]

Magister Militum et Consul

For his service in North Africa and probable role in negotiating the treaty with Gaiseric, in 434 Valentinian III had named Aspar Western consul.[37] This honour probably served a twofold purpose. First, awarding such a rank to an Eastern generalissimo would have functioned as a not too subtle warning to Western generalissimos like Aëtius not to aspire to acquire a diadem for themselves.[38] Second, as the third member of his kin-group the Adraburii to be named consul, it signalled to the Roman governing classes that Aspar and his relatives were now a respected political force.

We are fortunate to have a *largitio* plate commemorating Aspar's appointment. Such iconography reveals how quickly non-Roman

35 Prosper, *Chron.* s.a. 432; *Chron. gallica* 432. For the circumstances that led to this confrontation between the West's two supreme generalissimos, see Wijnendaele, *Last of the Romans*, ch. 5.

36 McEvoy, *Child Emperor Rule*, 255–56.

37 Bachrach, *History of the Alans*, 42, n. 47.

38 For this as a possible stratagem by Theodosius II and his inner circle, see McEvoy, *Child Emperor Rule*, 302. A fragment (13.2) in Priscus that describes Aëtius returning to Aspar a dwarf that the Huns had captured, suggests that the two former antagonists may have developed a friendship or at least kept in touch.

generals could display outward signs of their *Romanitas*.[39] The missorium (plate 7) depicts Aspar and his family in all their glory, declaring: FL [avius] ARDABUR ASPAR VIR INLUSTRIS COM [es] et MAG [ister] MILITUM et CONSUL ORDINARIUS. Aspar, bearded and wearing a tunic and a toga, holds up in his right hand the *mappa*, and in his left, a sceptre surmounted by two small busts of Theodosius II and Valentinian III. His son Ardabur standing, with the inscription ARDABUR IUNOR PRETOR, flanks him. Wearing a similar outfit to his father, Ardabur holds a *mappa* raised in his left hand, whilst saluting Aspar with his right hand. Two medallions looming above the pair contain the busts of Aspar's father Ardabur, consul in 427, and his relative Plintha, consul in 419.

As a recent study on the plate posits, its imagery offers evidence, not only on Theodosius II's and the Eastern Empire's dominance in Western affairs, but "The degree to which Aspar, an Alan and an Arian Christian, could be assimilated to Roman norms, at least iconographically." The missorium provides a "symbol of precisely this power and the dynastic aspirations of this eastern military family."[40] Such men were undoubtedly enjoying a more prominent role in fifth-century Roman society. Through loyal military service, in twenty short years, this Alan family had transitioned from barbarian auxiliaries to Roman elites. No other career could make Romans out of non-Romans so rapidly. No longer just fearsome barbarian auxiliaries, such iconography steeped in Roman aristocratic imagery broadcast to those in the highest circles of power in Constantinople and Italy that Aspar and his son shared in their civilised *Romanitas*.

The honours he received offer firm evidence that Aspar's initial "defeats" in North Africa had not been as catastrophic as later critics like Procopius maintained. Yet, in 439, Gaiseric had violated the accord from 435 and overrun Carthage and most of "Roman" North Africa. By 440, the Vandals were on Italy's

39 For the historical and archaeological backgrounds of the plate, see Bevan, Gabov, and Zaccagnino, "*Missorium*."
40 Bevan, Gabov, and Zaccagnino, "*Missorium*," 421.

doorstep, pillaging Sicily. In the face of this disaster, it is hardly shocking that Aspar's earlier achievements in Africa largely evaporated from public memory.

The Eastern Romans, however, never abandoned hopes of rebounding from this devastating defeat. As already discussed, Theodosius II's regime continued to display the will and the military capability to resist Vandalic expansion. While Aspar did not serve in the aborted naval campaign organised by Theodosius II and Valentinian III in 440 (or early 441) to drive the Vandals from North Africa, the five commanders that were chosen all had close ties to the generalissimo.[41] The details of Aspar's whereabouts in the 440s is more obscure. Priscus tells us that he was one of three commanders sent to counter Atilla and his Huns' thrusts into Eastern territory in 440.[42] These campaigns went poorly for the Eastern Romans, and 441 found Aspar negotiating a treaty with the Huns.[43] Two years later, however, Aspar and the Eastern Roman army suffered a further severe defeat at the hands of Attila's army. By the mid-440s, Aspar's star was on the wane.[44] Aspar was one of the commanders that Priscus derided for cowardice in the face of the Hunnic menace.[45] Relying on familiar literary tropes, the generalissimo's enemies maintained that these setbacks proved that despite his outward signs of *Romanitas*, Aspar remained an unreliable barbarian.[46] It seems, however, that by the time of Theodosius II's death, Aspar had once again regained the emperor's good graces, indeed, the sixth-century chronicler John

41 Bachrach, *Alans*, 46.

42 Pricus, *frag.* 9.4.

43 Marcellinus, *Chron.* s.a. 441.

44 Zuckerman ("L' Empire," 172–76) proposes that Aspar had been relieved of his command in 447. The Isaurian Flavius Zeno (not to be mistaken with the later emperor) then became the East's leading commander until his death around 451.

45 Priscus, *frag.* 9.3.

46 Priscus, *frag.* 14.85–90. For these Hunnic attacks in the East, see still Thompson, *Atilla and the Huns*, 76–86.

Malalas declared that Aspar was present when the dying emperor supposedly proclaimed that Marcian—a soldier who had served under Aspar—should be named his successor.[47]

The Contest

Although scholars continue to debate how significant a role Aspar played in Marcian's ascension, in the early years of Leo's reign he wielded a great deal of power, and may be seen as a shadow emperor.[48] This shared rule explains why when the bishop of Rome Leo I sought to confirm the new regime's stance on Chalcedon, he sent letters simultaneously to Leo and "the illustrious patrician Aspar."[49] Rather than rule himself, Aspar—like Ricimer—largely endeavoured to influence events behind the scenes. In establishing his influential role, he was successful during the reign of Marcian, if obviously less so during Leo's reign. Unfortunately for Aspar, Leo had an independent and—if early Byzantine sources are to be believed—a violent streak.

It did not take long for relations between Aspar and Leo to degenerate. Leo took his time, however, before making an aggressive move to eliminate his mentor. Aspar's long career and experience at cultivating his military patronage amongst Roman and non-Roman military men, at this point, probably would have made such a move suicidal. In particular, Aspar could rely on his Gothic *buccellarii* to suppress rapidly external or internal threats.[50] Moreover, we should not assume that Aspar and Leo feuded interminably throughout the 460s. Such a view may be anachronistic, since later Byzantine accounts naturally

---

47 Malalas, *Chron.* 14.27 (3.67). Cf. *Chron. Paschale* s.a. 450. We should dismiss Malalas' contention that Theodosius had named Marcian as his successor at this time.

48 Siebigs, *Leo I*, 201.

49 Leo, *Epist.* 153, trans. Hunt.

50 Wolfram, *The Roman Empire*, 197.

focused on the pair's disagreements that led ultimately to Aspar's assassination.

Whatever the precise nature of his relationship with Aspar, Leo soon began cultivating his independent authority. Revealing the mind of a deft tactician rather than the brute "butcher" his later critics would make him out to be, Leo at first concentrated on Christological issues. Polling the Eastern bishops and some Syriac ascetics on their views towards Chalcedon and suppressing an uprising by the council's detractors in Alexandria, Antioch, and Jerusalem were some of Leo's first official actions after he became emperor.[51]

In the view of his most recent biographer, Leo's focus in these early years on promoting his orthodoxy represented the opening salvos in Leo and the Arian Aspar's decoupling.[52] Leo supported Chalcedon while the Arian Aspar appeared to favour the Monophysites.[53] We should observe some caution, since we have a letter from 451 from the "orthodox" Theodoret of Cyrrhus to Aspar thanking him for recalling the bishop from exile.[54] These exchanges between generals and bishops were not limited to religious matters. As we saw in the case of Augustine and Bonifatius, by the mid-fifth century, high-ranking generals frequently engaged with leading bishops from both sides of the Christological divide on religious and secular matters.[55] Exchanging letters with Theodoret offers us another sign that Aspar had become a full-fledged member of what one scholar has

---

51 Marcellinus, *Chron.* s.a. 458; Theophanes, *Chron.* AM 5952; Evagrius, *HE* 2.10. For a discussion of the motivations behind Leo's initiative and the surviving responses found in the Codex Encyclius, see Kosiński, *Zeno*, 48–50.

52 Siebigs, *Kaiser Leo*, 478–90. Cf. Treadgold, *History of the Byzantine State*, 152.

53 Pseudo-Zachariah, *Chron.* 4.6.

54 Theodoret, *Epist.* 141. On Theodoret's reinstating at the Council of Chalcedon and subsequent orthodoxy, see Urbainczyk, *Theodoret*, 12–13.

55 Greatrex, "Government and Mechanisms of Control," 40.

recently described as a cultivated Roman "network of influence and power."[56] Moreover, Leo had attempted to reach a compromise with the obstinate Timothy before exiling the patriarch to Gangra in Paphlagonia, suggesting that Leo's primary strategy at this stage was one of tolerance and finding the common ground between Monophysites and Chalcedonians.[57]

This is not to say that Leo's stress on religious matters served no other political purpose. His emphasis on Christology probably aided in establishing Leo's credentials amongst Constantinople's ruling elite, while simultaneously highlighting Aspar's otherness. As a soldier from Thrace, many of Constantinople's elites would have regarded Leo as little better than a barbarian.[58] Certainly, soldier-emperors had long struggled to earn "their more aristocratic subjects' respect or loyalty."[59] The ruling classes may have needed some convincing that the former *tribunis militum* could brandish civilised Roman intellectual qualities to match his military credentials. Indeed, the threat of usurpation within the capital from a blue-blood aristocrat for many later fifth- and sixth-century Eastern Roman emperors was a greater risk than a potential rebellion from a general in the field.[60] "Proving" his orthodoxy, Leo could therefore declare himself to be authentically Roman. One prominent proponent of this theory, Philip Wood, explains:

> Leo and his allies held on to power in the teeth of such elite criticism. Their ability to do so may be

56 McLaughlin, "Bridging the Cultural Divide," 275.

57 Evagrius, *HE* 2.9–11; Pseudo-Zachariah, *HE* 4.5–9.

58 A view of Justinian found in Procopius, *Secret History* 6.1–3. For a similar condescending attitude towards the Emperor Anastasius amongst the upper-crust of Constantinople's' aristocracy, see Meier, *Anastasios*, 285.

59 On the necessity for these soldier-emperors to cultivate the intellectual sides of their *Romanitas* in order to be accepted by the ruling elite, see Arnold, *Roman Imperial Restoration*, 142–43.

60 Börm, "Justinians Triumph," 81.

found partially in their appropriation of the idea of being Roman and being Christian that was used by the Theodosian dynasty, and the creation of scapegoats, such as Aspar, against whom they could define themselves. [61]

To put it another way, by this period religion had become an increasingly central medium for men like Leo to promote their Christian *Romanitas*, while simultaneously painting their rivals as heretical barbarians.[62]

The emperor's creation in 460 or 461 of an elite palace guard, the *executibors*, has traditionally served as another sign of Leo's counterbalancing of Aspar's authority.[63] This gathering of soldiers linked to him personally continued when in 464 Leo named his brother-in-law Basiliscus *magister militum per Thracias*.[64]

Aspar appeared, however, to continue to hold the upper hand in the two men's power relationship. A devastating fire that struck Constantinople on 2 September 464 seems to have undermined some of the progress Leo had been making.[65] The leading role Aspar played and the kudos he received in later sources for his efforts to protect the city from the conflagration offers firm evidence concerning the Alan generalissimo's continuing puissance and popularity amongst Romans and non-Romans.[66] Constantinople's citizenry, on the other hand, apparently partially blamed Leo for the disaster. Emphasizing his role as a religious leader, Leo looked to placate Constantinople's terrified and superstitious citizens

---

61 Wood, "Multiple Voices," 310.

62 On Leo's persecution of pagans, see Theophanes, *Chron.* AM 5960.

63 Treadgold, *History of the Byzantine State,* 152.

64 Priscus, *frag.* 49; Theophanes, *Chron.* AM 5956.

65 On the fire, see Marcellinus, *Chron.* s.a. 465; Evagrius, *HE* 2.13. I follow Brian Croke "Dynasty and Ethnicity," 160, and Whitby and Whitby's (trans. *Chron. Paschale,* 87, n. 285) earlier dating. For the later date of 465, see Kosiński, *Zeno,* 64.

66 Candidus, *frag.* 1; *Chron. Paschale* s.a. 465; Theophanes, *Chron.* AM 5954.

who, as a later source tells us, during such natural catastrophes turned to religion (if only briefly) for answers.[67] A source close to his inner circle elucidates on the emperor's precarious situation in the fire's aftermath. Unable to match the active leadership of Aspar, the emperor and his wife led a procession to the pillar of the holy man Daniel the Stylite and beseeched the holy man: "This wrath was caused by our carelessness; I therefore beg you pray to God to be merciful to us in the future."[68] Leo's concern to appeal to the sentiment of Daniel offers testament to the influence holy men could exert on the government and public opinion.

Shortly after the fire, relations between Aspar and Leo had openly broken down.[69] In 466, Leo's support of the Sciri in their war with the Goths countermined Aspar's recommendation to remain neutral;[70] an example that might suggest that before this time Leo had usually followed Aspar's advice. In either 465 or 466, a whispering campaign initiated by the emperor and his inner circle played upon the traditional Roman distrust of non-Romans in positions of authority.[71] Leo accused Aspar's son Ardabur of giving away imperial secrets to the Persians and, as a result, dismissed him from the command he had held since 453. We are fortunate to have a source that provides some insight into the affair and Aspar's vulnerability to such propaganda. Composed

---

67 Agathias, *Histories* 5.5.1–5. Describing events after an earthquake, Agathias related how "charlatans and self-appointed prophets" had roamed the streets of Constantinople preaching "the end of the world." Agathias made it clear that most of this religiosity was short-lived and most returned to "play lip-service" to their devotion. One suspects that a similar hysteria enveloped the population after the earthquake in 464.

68 *Life of Daniel the Stylite* 55.

69 Candidus, *frag.* 1. Blockley (472, n. 3.) for the traditional idea that the dispute revolved around policy towards the Vandals or a political appointment. This also serves as evidence of the rehabilitation of Aspar's reputation under Anastasius.

70 Priscus, *frag.* 45.

71 For 465: Croke, "Dynasty and Ethnicity," 160. For 466: *PLRE* 2.136.

by an anonymous author sometime between 492 and 496, the *Life of Daniel the Stylite* provides an insider's view on the incident.[72] In view of its importance in shedding needed light on this affair and the rise of the Isaurian soldier Tarasicodissa—the future Emperor Zeno[73]—it is necessary to quote it in full:

> About that time a certain Zeno, an Isaurian by birth, came to the Emperor and brought with him letters written by Ardabur, who was then general of the East; in these he incited the Persians to attack the Roman State and agreed to cooperate with them. The Emperor received the man and recognizing the importance of the letters he ordered a Council to be held; when the Senate had met, the Emperor produced the letters and commanded that they should be read aloud in the hearing of all the senators by Patricius, who was Master of the Offices at that time. After they had been read the Emperor said, "What think you?" As they all held their peace the Emperor said to the father of Ardabur, "These are fine things that your son is practising against his Emperor and the Roman State." Aspar replied, "You are the master and have full authority; after hearing this letter I realize that I can no longer control my son; for I often sent to him counselling and warned him not to ruin his life; and now I see he is acting contrary to my advice. Therefore do whatsoever occurs to your piety; dismiss him from his command and order him to come here and he shall make his defence."

72 For this date for Daniel's *vita*, see Kosiński, "Leo II," 210.

73 Relying on the now lost sixth-century history of Eustathius, the late sixth-century historian Evagrius (*HE* 2.15) explains that this accusation by Zeno represented one of the primary factors behind his subsequent rise. For Zeno, see now the excellent study by Kosiński, *Zeno*.

> The Emperor took this advice; he appointed a successor to Ardabur and dismissed him from the army; then ordered him to present himself forthwith in Byzantium. In his place he gave the girdle of office to Jordanes and sent him to the East; he also appointed Zeno, Count of the Domestics.
>
> And the Emperor went in solemn procession and led him up to the holy man and related to him all about Ardabur's plot and Zeno's loyalty; others told him, too, how Jordanes had been appointed General of the East in place of Ardabur. The holy man rejoiced about Jordanes and gave him much advice in the presence of the Emperor and of all those who were with him then he dismissed them with his blessing.[74]

Obviously one must observe some caution since this quotation post-dates Aspar's death and passes down Leo's side of the dispute. Yet the episode offers enticing glimpses of how Leo's propaganda may have sought to move against his powerful rival. This account is certainly no frontal assault. Aspar, in fact, acts in the dignified manner befitting his status as Constantinople's senior consul, treating Leo respectfully and revealing his *Romanitas* by recalling his son to face his accusers in Constantinople rather than rebel against the state in "typical" barbarian fashion. Moreover, our author makes it clear that Leo had dismissed Ardabur on Aspar's recommendation.

Nevertheless, this incident was surely a serious blow to Aspar's prestige. Leo progressively and relentlessly chipped away at Aspar's hegemony. Jordanes' appointment as *magister militum*, to borrow the words of Brian Croke, not only "helped prise Jordanes loose from the patronage of Aspar," but showed how Leo was using the orthodox/Arian paradigm to achieve his

---

74 *Life of Daniel the Stylite* 55.

political goals. Indeed, the *Life*'s author emphasised the role that Daniel had played beforehand in converting the Arian Jordanes to orthodoxy.[75] Therefore, we can see that by using religion to drive a wedge between the Alan general and his co-religionists, the holy man and the emperor may have collaborated to undermine Aspar and his family.[76] Such alliances point to the complex web of factional alliances that marked 460s Constantinople's politics.[77]

Further evidence from Priscus suggests that some of Leo's propaganda attacked Ardabur's "manliness." It explained that although Aspar's son had done an admirable job defending Thrace from the "barbarians" in the early years of his command, eventually he had succumbed to a life of "self-indulgence and effeminate leisure."[78] Such sentiments concerning the dangers of the soft life for even the most martial of non-Roman and Roman commanders represents a commonplace in Roman and Byzantine literature.[79]

In 460s Constantinople, rhetoric and actual policy went hand in hand. Leo took further steps to marginalise a rival he cast as an untrustworthy barbarian. Leo and Zeno formalised their mutually advantageous relationship. In 466, the Isaurian married the emperor's daughter Ariadne.[80] It was in the aftermath of his marriage that Tarasicodissa the soldier became Zeno the

---

75 *Life of Daniel the Stylite*, 49.

76 Croke, "Dynasty and Ethnicity," 160.

77 Daniel and Leo did not always agree. The example of Daniel (*Life of Daniel the Stylite* 60, 61) coaxing the soldier Titus to take up the ascetic lifestyle, for instance, clearly irritated the emperor.

78 Priscus, *frag.* 19.

79 See, e.g., Procopius' contention (*Wars* 4.6.5–8) that their love of feasting, baths, and sexual pleasures had gradually eroded the Vandals' martial edge.

80 Croke, "Dynasty and Ethnicity," 172–73. The date of the marriage remains disputed. Kosiński (*Zeno*, 65) prefers 468, while Fox, "Life of Daniel," 191–92, suggests the year 469.

nobleman.[81] Zeno's rise continued. In the aftermath of Attila's son Dengizich's invasion of Thrace in 467, Leo appointed his new son-in-law *magister militum per Thracias* and sent him to thwart the incursion.

The Alan generalissimo, however, remained a potent threat to Leo's rule. Aspar served as a joint-commander of the campaign against Dengizich. [82] Although Aspar failed in his attempt to assassinate Zeno during this campaign, he succeeded in spooking Zeno, and the Isaurian fled to a semi-exile for the next four years.[83]

Aspar was not the only prospective challenger who the emperor had to deal with. In the spring of 467, Leo sent the blue-blooded Anthemius to Italy where he was named Western emperor outside Rome on April 12.[84] One can discern two other important reasons behind the appointment. First, it thwarted the Vandalic king Gaiseric's hopes to install his preferred candidate as Western emperor, Olybrius, whose wife Placidia was the sister of Gaiseric's daughter-in-law Eudocia.[85] Second, Leo probably hoped that Anthemius' extensive naval and infantry military background

---

81 Candidus, *frag.* 1; Evagrius, *HE* 2.15. Kosiński, *Zeno*, 59–64 discusses the modern disputes over Zeno's origins and original Isaurian name.

82 For Zeno's narrow escape from Aspar's assassination attempt, see, *Life of Daniel*, 65, who explains that Daniel had foreseen the attempt on Zeno's life. Cf. Theophanes, *Chron.* AM 5962. My interpretation of Zeno's exile relies on Croke, "The Date of the 'Anastasian Long Wall' in Thrace," 59–78. For the birth of Zeno's son Leo as a possible motivating factor behind Aspar's attempt on Zeno's life, see Kosiński, *Zeno*, 68.

83 The *Chron. Paschale* (s.a. 468) reveals that the *magister militum per Thracias* Anagastes slew Dengizich. Afterwards, the Hun's head was taken to Constantinople and then paraded along the main thoroughfare (the Mese), before being placed on a spike for public viewing.

84 Priscus, *frag.* 53.3.15–20; Marcellinus, *Chron.* 467.1; Theophanes, *Chron.* AM 5957.

85 *Chron. Paschale*, 90, n. 292.

would be useful with the planning and implementation of the Eastern emperor's imminent invasion of Vandalic Africa.[86]

A former *magister utriusque militiae*, consul, and patrician under Marcian, Anthemius' pedigree and proven military record made him an acceptable choice, at least at first, to Western elites.[87] Incapable of standing up to Leo's Eastern army,[88] the erstwhile shadow emperor Ricimer went along with the appointment and, at the close of 467, bound himself to the Western emperor by marrying Anthemius' daughter Alycia.[89]

Western Romans appeared hopeful—yet at the same time wary—that the uniting of Ricimer and Anthemius would help to remedy the factional disputes that had plagued the Western Empire since Valentinian's assassination in 455. Once again, Sidonius serves as our witness, recording with typical flair both the optimism and the financial consequences surrounding Ricimer and Alycia's nuptials:

> As yet, I have not presented myself at the bustling gates of Emperor or court official. For my arrival coincided with the marriage of the patrician Ricimer, to whom the hand of the emperor's daughter was being accorded in the hope of more secure times for the state. Not individuals alone, but whole classes and parties are given up to rejoicing [...] While I was writing these lines, scarce a theatre, provision-market, praetorium, forum, temple, or gymnasium but echoed to the cry of "Talassio"![90]

---

86 Candidus, *frag.* 2.

87 E.g., Sidonius, *Epist.* 2 193. Anthemius had achieved major victories over the Ostrogoths in Thrace sometime during 459–462 (Sidonius, *Epist.* 2 224–26, 232–35), and over the Huns in late 466 or early 467 (Sidonius, *Epist.* 2 236–42, 269–80).

88 MacGeorge, *Late Roman Warlords*, 234–35.

89 Priscus, *frag.* 64.

90 Sidonius, *Epist.* 1.5.10–11, 1.12–13.

So we can see that the marriage was undertaken for political reasons, indeed, a later source has Anthemius explain that he had agreed to the pairing, not out of any fear of Ricimer, but for the good of the Roman state.[91] By attaching his young daughter to the old general, Anthemius (and through him Leo) likely sought to contain the dangerous Ricimer, who in his lifetime would be behind the rise and fall of five Western Roman emperors.[92] Yet, despite the probability that he was compelled to accept Anthemius,[93] Ricimer doubtless also saw an opportunity. Not only could he connect his family to the Western imperial regime, while simultaneously thwarting Gaiseric's ongoing attempts to link his family to the Western imperial throne,[94] by supporting Leo's planned invasion Ricimer might finally see his Vandalic nemesis eliminated for good.

Ricimer may also have had the best interests of the Western imperial regime in mind. Having embraced the life of a Roman nobleman, Ricimer identified with the imperial cause; indeed, his arming of Majorian and of Anthemius suggests that he was willing

---

91 Ennodius, *Life of Epiphanius* 52.

92 Though we do know that his mother was the daughter of the Visigothic king Vallia (r. 415–ca. 418), the date of Ricimer's birth remains disputed. For a summary of these debates, see Gillette, "The Birth of Ricimer," 380–84. Gillette posits that Ricimer was born in 418, rather than the early 430s as advocated by some scholars.

93 For Leo forcing his choice on Ricimer, see Harries, *Sidonius*, 142. For Ricimer accepting Anthemius because he wanted to promote Italian interests by destroying the Vandals, see Flomen, "Ricimer," 13. O'Flynn, *Generalissimos*, 117.

94 The Vandals' sack of Rome and capture of the Empress Eudoxia and her daughters Eudocia and Placidia after Valentinian III's assassination in 455 was linked to the Vandalic king's attempts to protect the betrothal of his son Hunneric to Eudocia, see Marcellinus, *Chron.* s.a. 468; *Chron. Paschale* s.a. 455. Marcellinus (*Chron.* s.a. 455) and Theophanes allege that, objecting to marriage attempts, Eudoxia had asked Gaiseric for assistance.

to play second fiddle, if it helped Italy and the Romans' cause in the long run.[95]

If Alycia was the carrot in Anthemius and Leo's strategy to contain Ricimer, then the formerly independent warlord Marcellinus was the stick. Procopius explained that Leo and Anthemius had enticed Marcellinus to join Anthemius on his journey to Rome. Marcellinus and Ricimer, who had both served under Aëtius, appear to have been long-time rivals.[96] According to current thinking, Marcellinus had gone "rogue" after the assassination of Aëtius in 454 (though one new theory is that Ricimer's killing of Majorian caused the breach).[97] Whatever date one selects for the initial split, Ricimer could not have been happy that Leo and Anthemius had chosen Marcellinus to lead the Western army in the planned campaign to dislodge the Vandals from North Africa. Even more insulting, the Eastern emperor had granted Marcellinus the title of *patricus* (in 467 or 468), an honorific Majorian had given to Ricimer in 459 but Leo I had never recognised.

By the opening of 468, Leo's imperial power had reached its zenith.[98] Similar to Theodosius II's rhetoric from 425, Sidonius captured the vision of a Western regime protected by a dominant Eastern saviour:

> Emperor Leo, you surpass the deeds of your
> forerunners; for he who can command a man
> to reign towers above regal power. Now your

---

95 Ricimer's rise had begun in 456 with a victory in Sicily over the Vandals, see Priscus, *frag.* 31.1; Hydatius, *Chron.* 309.2. Historians continue to dispute the extent of Ricimer's Romanisation. For two opposing portraits, see Arnold, *Roman Imperial Restoration*, 16–20; MacGeorge, *Late Roman Warlords*, 299–300.

96 O'Flynn, *Generalissimos*, 117.

97 Full discussion in Kulikowski, "Marcellinus of Dalmatia."

98 Just how Leo had attained such a dominant position from the nadir of the fire in 464 is more difficult to ascertain.

> government will be more perfectly one, having thus become a government of two. All hail to thee, pillar of sceptred power, Queen of the East, the Rome of that region, no longer to be worshipped by the eastern citizen alone, now that you have sent me a sovereign prince.[99]

Although this statement above should not be seen as a ringing endorsement of Leo's meddling in Western imperial affairs,[100] placed alongside the passages discussed above from Procopius, this excerpt from Sidonius neatly highlights the growing aura of potency developing around Leo and his resurgent Eastern regime.

With Anthemius safely entrenched in Rome, Leo sent an embassy to the Vandal king Gaiseric demanding that the Vandals evacuate territories they had seized in Sicily and Southern Italy.[101] East Roman enmity against the Vandals had long been festering. Secure in the East, and with Ricimer's stranglehold on the Western government broken—at least temporarily—Leo prepared to strike Vandalic North Africa.[102] The next year (468), Leo launched his massive assault ostensibly to punish Gaiseric for his raids on Eastern and Western Roman lands in 467, which the

99 Sidonius, *Panegyric on Anthemius* 27–32 (trans. Anderson): "Auguste Leo; nam regna superstat qui regnare iubet: melius respublica vestra nunc erit una magis, quae sic est facta duorum. Salve, sceptrorum columen, regina Orientis, orbis Roma tui, rerum mihi principe misso iam non Eoo solum veneranda Quiriti."

100 For the speech's emphasis on continuing Western autonomy, see Harries, *Sidonius*, 149.

101 Marcellinus, *Chron.* s.a. 468. Procopius tells us (*Wars* 3.6.5) that Leo had made Anthemius emperor primarily to help him with his campaign against the Vandals.

102 The extent that Sidonius (e.g., *Panegyric of Anthemius* 485–520) aimed the flowery prose of his panegyric to Anthemius at Ricimer, however, offers firm evidence of the Gothic patrician's continued potency and fondness for praise of his *Romanitas*.

emperor claimed violated a treaty signed in 462.[103] In reality, Leo most likely sought a game-changing victory that would assure the long-term viability of his rule. Leo would certainly have the upper-hand over Aspar, who, as noted above, had been defeated several times by the Vandals.

The two imperial regimes had gathered a truly intimidating force. The enormous logistical efforts behind the ambitious attack offer firm evidence of the continuing military capabilities of the twin regimes when acting in unison. Although we should discount the figure of 100,000 ships given in one Byzantine source, clearly the attack represented an impressive display of logistical planning and enduring martial puissance.[104] Such a move reasserting Eastern control over Western affairs provides evidence of Leo's growing confidence.[105] Procopius explained that even the formidable Gaiseric feared Leo as an "invincible emperor" (ἄμαχον βασιλέα) and nearly capitulated before the Roman fleet had even set sail.[106]

Organised as a three-prong operation—with his eyes on Carthage—Marcellinus took Sicily.[107] Meanwhile, Basiliscus sailed the bulk of the Roman navy to meet the Vandal naval forces; lastly, a smaller fleet led by the Eastern *Comes rei militaris* Heracleius successfully occupied the Vandal stronghold of Tripolis. Heracleius and his army then set out towards Byzacena in order to link up with Basiliscus' troops when they arrived in Proconsular province. Basiliscus' forces, however, never reached North Africa. Whether through treachery or (more likely) incompetence, Basiliscus and

---

103 Priscus, *frag.* 52.

104 A point made by Merrills and Miles, *Vandals*, 122 on Theophanes, *Chron.* AM 5961. Procopius (*Wars* 3.6.1) provides a reasonable number of 100,000 for the combined number of men for the Western and Eastern forces.

105 Procopius, *Wars* 3.6.4.

106 Procopius, *Wars* 3.6.11. It is interesting that in his depiction of Belisarius' sixth-century Vandalic War, the situation was reversed: the pre-invasion Eastern Romans were the ones fearing the Vandals.

107 The circumstances behind this campaign are disputed, I follow largely Merrills and Miles' reconstruction (*Vandals*, 121–23).

the Byzantine armada suffered a humiliating defeat at the hands of the Vandals and their fire ships at Mercurium.[108] The defeat placed a severe strain on the Eastern Empire's finances.[109]

It is worth noting that Leo bears little of the responsibility for the naval rout in the accounts that survive. This absence may partially explain why fifth- and sixth-century emperors did not feel the need to direct campaigns in person. If the assault failed, a scapegoat could be found within the military, whilst if victory was achieved, the emperor could represent himself as the face of Roman victory. Surely, the example of the Western emperor, Majorian's aborted attempt to launch a military expedition against the Vandals in 460 and subsequent execution at the hands of Ricimer's henchmen, offered ample warning to Leo to proceed cautiously in the aftermath of the defeat.

Leo's storytelling machine probably kicked into gear straight away. It is likely no coincidence that two of Leo's prime potential rivals, Aspar and Basiliscus, bore the brunt of the blame for the fiasco. Procopius suggested that fearing the prestige that Leo would have gained from a reconquest of North Africa, Aspar had promised to make Basiliscus emperor if he sabotaged the campaign and took a bribe from Gaiseric.[110] This aside probably contains only elements of truth. As noted previously, the old trope of blaming a barbarian like Aspar for betraying the Empire to "fellow barbarians" was a literary commonplace. Therefore, while Aspar may have been wary of Leo gaining even further distinction,

---

108 Present-day historians (e.g., MacGeorge, *Late Roman Warlords*, 58) doubt the bribe account, placing blame for the defeat on Basiliscus' poor generalship. It is possible that Aspar may have been seeking to replace Leo with a more "malleable" Basiliscus.

109 John Lydus, *De Mag.* 3.43, discusses the long-term fiscal consequences of the failed campaign.

110 Procopius, *Wars* 3.6.14–15. Cf. Malalas, *Chron.* 14.44 (372); Theophanes, *Chron.* AM 5961; Jordanes, *Romana* 337.

it seems unlikely that he took, or truly had the capability to take, such drastic steps to hijack the campaign.[111]

The combat at Mercurium had its share of literature lauding Roman heroes for fighting on courageously in the face of betrayal and defeat. Different versions of these heroic narratives survive. A native of Antioch, John Malalas subscribes to the bribe account, declaring (inaccurately) that Basiliscus had fled at the start of the battle and was the only ship to escape the disaster.[112] His hero naturally is the Antiochene *magister militum* Damonicus, who—whilst Basiliscus fled—fought on bravely alone, until he was captured by the Vandals and flung fully armoured into the sea.[113] In contrast to what the historian described as Basiliscus' purposeful cowardice (ἐθελοκακήσας), in the admiring words of Procopius, the general John, "was one of the Romans who proved themselves brave men." Surrounded on his ship's burning deck, he slew the enemy without respite until—despite Vandalic guarantees of mercy—he "heroically" plunged into the sea.[114] As in the case of Adrianople a century before, such martial patriotism lauding the East Roman's spirited resistance probably helped to salve Roman pride wounded by the debacle. Such narratives imply that if their commander had not betrayed the Roman soldiers, they probably would have bested the Vandals in a "fair" contest of manly courage.[115]

---

111 The extant account of the bribe first appears in Priscus, *frag.* 53.1.

112 Relying on Priscus, Theophanes (*Chron.* AM 5961) contradicts Malalas, by explaining that Basiliscus' naval attack had started off well. Cf. Jordanes, *Romana* 337.

113 Malalas, *Chron.* 14.44 (373).

114 Procopius, *Wars* 3.6.

115 As Whately points out (*Battles and Generals*, 122–24), by blaming the Roman failure in 468 primarily on Basiliscus' cowardice and incompetence, Procopius was then able to show that under the guidance of an organised and brave general, Belisarius, the Roman victory in the 530s was fairly straightforward.

In spite of his largely successful campaign to divert blame, the defeat slowed Leo's political momentum. Aspar appears to have regained the upper-hand or at least equilibrium in the pair's relationship. The ninth-century Byzantine chronicler, Theophanes, maintained that in the aftermath of the reverse Leo had immediately recalled Basiliscus, Heracleius, and another commander, Marsus, to Constantinople in order to counteract a plot by Aspar.[116] Though Leo thwarted this conspiracy, Aspar escalated his pressure on Leo. Aspar probably instigated the *magister militum per Thracias* Anagastes' revolt in Thrace against Leo I in 469–70.[117] By 470, Aspar was powerful enough to have his son and former consul (459) Julius Patricus raised to *Caesar*. With Leo on his back foot, Aspar then arranged to have his son married to the emperor's daughter, Leontia.[118] Aspar's long-held hopes to have his Romanised son succeed Leo to the purple appeared possible once more.[119] Because of riots by those against an Arian taking the throne, Patricus had even agreed to convert to Chalcedonian Christianity before marrying Leo's daughter.[120]

Without his primary protector Zeno, Leo must have feared for his life.[121] It seems that the emperor had made the marriage pact with Patricus to buy some needed time.[122] Indeed, some sort of political stability appears to have returned to Constantinople by 471. Leo's eunuch-assassins seem to have taken Aspar and his

116 Theophanes, *Chron.* AM 5963. This evidence would seem to discount the idea that Basiliscus and Aspar were scheming together at this time or that the original rumour of their "alliance" stems from this date.

117 Priscus, *frag.* 56. A point discussed in Croke, "Dynasty and Ethnicity," 187.

118 Following the dates in Kosiński, *Zeno*, 68, although the dates for Patricus' honour and engagement may be 468/69, see Theophanes, *Chron.* AM 5961.

119 For these hopes, see Arnold, *Roman Imperial Restoration*, 159.

120 *Vita Marcela* 34.

121 On the pressure Aspar was able to exert on Leo due to the absence of Basiliscus and Zeno from Constantinople, see Kosiński, *Zeno,* 68.

122 Theophanes (*Chron.* AM 5963) suggests that Leo had raised Patricus to *Caesar* in order "to keep Aspar's good will."

sons by surprise when they ambushed them during a meeting of the grand council within the imperial palace (Patricus may have survived for a time). Leo's survival was still a near thing. In the aftermath of the murders, rioting broke out in the capitol. Aspar's supporters stormed the palace; the *execubitors* only fended them off with great difficulty.[123] The probability that Zeno only found it safe to return to the capital after Aspar's death offers further proof of just how dangerous a situation Leo was in before the assassinations.[124]

Views were mixed on the justice of this move. Distaste for the assassination is evident in some Byzantine sources.[125] The emperor's detractors used Leo's nickname "the butcher" as a slight.[126] Not everyone, however, condemned Aspar and his sons' elimination. As discussed earlier, we find praise of Leo and his firm stand against Aspar in Procopius. This stance probably reflects the type of anti-barbarian rhetoric that circulated during the years of Justinian's invasions of the "lost" Western provinces.[127] Others writing during Justinian's reign painted the assassination as an instance of an orthodox emperor righteously eradicating "an Arian, and his Arian family."[128]

123 Malalas, *Chron.* 14.38–40 (371.9–372.2).

124 For the notion that Zeno did not return to the capital until after the rebellion by Aspar's allies had been crushed, see Croke, "Dynasty and Ethnicity," 198, Kosiński, *Zeno*, 68, following the assertions found in *Life of Daniel Stylite*, 66; Theophanes, *Chron.* AM 5964. Contra Friell and Williams, *Rome That Did Not Fall*, 181, relying on Jordanes, *Romana*, 383.

125 E.g., Malalas, *Chron.* 371.9–372.2; Evagrius, *HE* 2.16.

126 Malchus, *frag.* 1; Candidus, *frag.* 2. Cf., however, Constantine Porphyrogennetos, *De cerimoniis* 2.18, where the epithet "Leo the Butcher" (Λεομαχέλλην) is used in a positive context.

127 Procopius, *Wars* 3.3–7.

128 Marcellinus, *Chron.* s.a. 471. A full discussion of this passage and similar sentiments in other Byzantine sources is found in Croke "Dynasty and Ethnicity," 199.

The Greek and the Goth: Anthemius and Ricimer, 468–72

Anthemius had a more difficult time regaining his footing after the defeat in 468. Predictable, since Anthemius had promised to restore the martial prestige of an enfeebled imperial West. Instead, only a year into his reign, the Western "Empire" teetered on the brink of oblivion, beset by financial and political threats. On the economic front, instead of filling the regime's coffers with spoils from Vandalic North Africa, the setback had left them bare.[129] Moreover, Anthemius faced a resurgent Vandalic threat to Sicily and Southern Italy, while in the north, Euric and his Visigoths tightened their grip on Gaul. As an outsider from the "Greek" Roman East, Anthemius depended on the support of Western Romans like Sidonius, who despite outward flattery, tended to distrust the notion of Eastern dominance over Western affairs. While they respected Eastern "Greeks" such as Anthemius for their cultivated *Romanitas* and, at times, military vigour, Western elites could quickly shift to use "Greekness" as a pejorative term.[130] Undoubtedly, these men were beginning to understand that Anthemius was not the promised saviour—so they began to look elsewhere. This shift is evident in a letter from Sidonius revealing that some Gallic elites were willing to conspire with Euric and

129 Candidus (*frag.* 2) provides the significant figure of sixty-four thousand pounds of gold and seven hundred thousand pounds of silver for the campaign. Candidus adds that Anthemius had contributed an unspecified additional sum through "confiscations."

130 For Western elites' positive and hostile attitudes towards East Romans in the age of Anthemius, see Arnold, *Roman Imperial Restoration*, 17–18, 143–47, 160. In his otherwise adroit assessment, Arnold underestimates the Eastern Romans' lingering reputation for martial *Romanitas*. This sentiment helps to explain why Ricimer never openly attacks Anthemius' martial qualities.

the Visigoths in the hope to eliminate a leader they dismissed as a "Greek emperor."[131]

Even with Anthemius' crumbling mandate, the emperor had his supporters amongst the Italo-Romans.[132] It is likely that some Western elites had granted Anthemius some leeway since he had not taken part in the debacle against the Vandals. Additionally, in 470 or 471, Leo had solidified his ties to the Western emperor by marrying his youngest daughter Leontia to Anthemius' son Marcian, an act that tied the "house of Leo" to Anthemius and the Theodosian line.[133]

What is more, Anthemius had not given up trying to stem the tide of the Visigothic advance in Gaul. Some scholars have seen in this policy a break with Ricimer, who perhaps realistically favoured an Italo-centric foreign policy.[134] Still seeking the victories he had promised at his coronation, and responding to Euric's attack on Clermont,[135] in 471 Anthemius had named his son Anthemiolius as joint-commander of a Roman army sent to confront the Visigoths in Gaul. This campaign, however, ended in

---

131 Sidonius, *Epist.* 1.7.5. The Roman senate had convicted former *praefectus praetorio Galliarum* (464–68), Arvandus, of treason in 468. He was not executed, but exiled. For the Arvandus affair and its influence on Sidonius' abandonment of his secular career to "reluctantly" take up the bishopric of Clermont in 470, see Harries, "Sidonius Apollinaris, Rome and the Barbarians."

132 Priscus, *frag.* 64.

133 Kosiński (*Zeno*, 69) prefers 470 for the marriage, while Friell and Williams (*Rome That Did Not Fall*, 181) suggest 471.

134 Flomen, "Ricimer," 15.

135 Ecdicius, the son of the former Emperor Avitus and Sidonius' brother-in-law, had led Clermont's original defence against Euric, see Sidonius, *Epist.* 3.3, 5.6.4.

disaster. All Anthemius received for his efforts was the death of his son and another crushing defeat.[136] Gaul was as good as gone.[137]

The combination of military debacles, Anthemius' distrust and subsequent purge of Ricimer's allies, and Alycia's failure to produce an heir, led to the final breakdown in Anthemius and Ricimer's already shaky "partnership." The exact details or dates are impossible to recover, but 470 saw the pair engaged in a rapidly escalating conflict for supremacy that split Italy into two quasi-independent regions.[138] Anthemius controlled Rome while Ricimer retreated with 6,000 of his men to his stronghold in Milan.[139]

Similar to the struggle between Leo and Aspar, Anthemius and Ricimer waged their war on two fronts. Before their soldiers unsheathed their swords, propagandists from each side appear to have launched smear campaigns against their rivals. Ennodius' *Life of Epiphanius* provides the best account of the murky months before hostilities between the two camps broke into open war. Writing a generation (ca. 502 or 503) after the initial confrontation, Ennodius undoubtedly simplified a complex story. I agree, nevertheless, with recent suggestions that Ennodius recounted some of the original rhetoric wielded by the two protagonists.[140]

Employing two set speeches, Ennodius records the Italo-Romans' emotive appeals for reconciliation between the two Western Roman power cliques priming for war. The scene opens in Ricimer's court in Milan. Meeting with a group of concerned Ligurian nobles, Ricimer acts in the dignified manner befitting a

136 *Gallic Chron. of 511* s.a. 471.

137 For Euric's military campaigns in early 470s Gaul, see Wood, *Merovingian Kingdoms*, 15–19.

138 MacGeorge (*Late Roman Warlords*, 215–19) provides a possible chronology of Anthemius and Ricimer's movements from 468–472.

139 For the significance of Anthemius residing and maintaining his power base in Rome, see Gillette, "Rome," 132–33, 151–52.

140 Kennell, *Ennodius*, 208; MacGeorge, *Late Roman Warlords*, 221; Arnold, *Roman Imperial Restoration*, 18.

Roman noble. He humbly acquiesced to the aristocrats' desires for peace, but doubted that the implacably hostile Anthemius would lay down his arms. Ricimer explained to the delegation the difficulty of trying to negotiate with an ill-tempered Anthemius, "Who can call back to senses an excitable Galatian and emperor? For when begged a favour, who does not control his temper with natural moderation, always loses control."[141] As we discussed earlier (chapter 3), anger and a lack of self-control had long served as defining traits of barbarians and unmanly men. Moreover, as Jonathan Arnold points out, "Galatian was more than just a reference to Anthemius' eastern origins, since (despite Hellenization) the Galatians were understood in antiquity to be Gallogrecians and hence only semicivilized."[142] Ennodius then has Ricimer and the Ligurian embassy cleverly paint a portrait of Anthemius as unmanly and un-Roman.[143] The nobles propose that the new bishop of Ticinum—and the hero of the hagiography— Epiphanius, might be an excellent choice to meet with the "unstable" Anthemius, since the bishop could tame "even wild beasts."[144] Furthermore, the saint "was worthy of veneration by every Catholic, Roman, and even 'the Greekling,' Anthemius."[145]

The scene then shifts to Rome. Anthemius listened respectfully to Epiphanius, but distrusted Ricimer's peaceful overtures. In

---

141 *Life of Epiphanius* 53, quoted and trans. in MacGeorge, 247–48: "Quis est qui Galatam concitatum revocare possit et princepem? Nam semper, cum rogatur, exuperat qui iram naturali moderatione non terminat."

142 Arnold, *Roman Imperial Restoration*, 18, n. 38.

143 I concur with Arnold (*Roman Imperial Restoration*, 15–19) that Ennodius' depiction of Ricimer is less hostile than his portrait of Anthemius, contra Stephanie Kennell's (*Ennodius*, 207–08) vision of a far more neutral Ennodius.

144 *Life of Epiphanius* 54, quoted and trans. in Arnold, *Roman Imperial Restoration*, 17: "cui et beluae rabidae colla submittunt."

145 *Life of Epiphanius* 54, quoted and trans. in Arnold, *Roman Imperial Restoration*, 17: "quem venerari possit quicumque si est catholicus et Romanus, amare certe, si videre mereatur, et Graeculus."

explaining the rift between the pair, the Western emperor, not surprisingly, focused on aspects of Ricimer's non-Roman identity. Relying on the traditional anti-barbarian rhetoric we have seen deployed by Roman elites throughout this study, Anthemius disparaged Ricimer as a pelt-wearing Goth (*pellito Getae*), feigning compromise, but driven by a barbarian's innate duplicity. Subtly criticising the bishop's naiveté, Anthemius asked Epiphanius rhetorically, "What raging fury among foreign peoples has he stirred up?" Indicating that he owed Ricimer nothing, the emperor listed the sacrifices he had already made to ensure the peace since he had taken the throne in 468. The greatest of which had been Anthemius granting Ricimer the honour of marrying his daughter. Anthemius emphasised that he had not arranged his marriage alliance with Ricimer out of fear,[146] but rather because of his "love for the *Republicae*." Somewhat anachronistically playing upon the ruling classes' traditional prejudices, the emperor highlighted the "shame" of marrying his daughter to Ricimer.[147] Nevertheless, the emperor relented to the bishop's plea, agreeing to a truce.[148] Yet if, as he suspected, the wily Goth had managed to deceive the bishop, Anthemius would march to war.

As we know from the opening of this chapter, civil war did ultimately erupt. However, other than to record Anthemius' death and remark that Ricimer had died of natural causes shortly after his victory, Ennodius provides no concrete details on the civil war. One must piece the story together through a number of

---

146 Malalas (*Chron.* 14.45 [373]) implied that it was natural for Anthemius to fear Ricimer, since he was a Goth.

147 As John Moorhead points out (*Theoderic in Italy*, 84, n. 77), a law of Valentinian I and Valens (CTh 3.14) had banned the marriage of Roman provincials and "barbarians." Yet, as we have seen, the fifth century had witnessed a number of marriages between non-Roman rulers and upper-class Roman women. For this trend, see Sorachi, *Ricerche sui conubia tra Romani e Germani*.

148 Gillette, "Rome," 133, suggesting March of 471 for Epiphanius' embassy to Rome and the subsequent truce.

unsatisfactory accounts. Sometime in late 471 or early 472 Ricimer and his army had moved south to besiege Rome, a siege that lasted five months. The failure of an imperial army returning from Gaul to lift the blockade and the deteriorating situation in Rome had forced Anthemius' backers to risk a fatal final confrontation with Ricimer's forces.[149]

With the benefit of hindsight, it is easy for us to suppose that Anthemius faced a hopelessly deteriorating position after 468. Yet, our sparse sources provide tantalising clues that this may not necessarily have been the case. The fact that he felt confident enough to send Anthemiolius with a significant armed force to Gaul amidst his split with Ricimer indicates that the emperor may have been better positioned at this stage than some scholars have suggested. Moreover, particularly after Aspar's elimination, Ricimer must have worried that Leo might intervene to shore up his alliance with Anthemius. Leo continued to pry into Western imperial affairs. With Aspar out of the way in 471, Leo had once again turned his gaze westward. Though too late to save Anthemius, in 474 Leo sent the *magister militum* of Dalmatia, Julius Nepos (r. 474–75), with troops to oust Glycerius, "a western-proclaimed Augustus whom Leo I regarded as a usurper."[150]

Yet, that Leo and Ricimer triumphed while Anthemius and Aspar perished is less important for our purposes than these men's remarkable ascendancy to the heights of Roman political life. We can discern in their rivalries these men's arduous and continuous quest to affirm their Roman authority. The rise of Ricimer, Aspar, and Leo demonstrates the allure of a military career for those Romans and non-Romans seeking to rise from relative obscurity. It was becoming increasingly difficult for non-militarised Romans to thrive in an increasingly militarised political world. Indeed, the need for a blue-blooded Roman like Anthemius to drape himself in martial virtues in order to be considered as a plausible candidate for the purple points to the vital role that martial virtues played in

149 Priscus, *frag.* 64.
150 McEvoy, "Between the Old Rome and the New," 252.

elite men's self-definition in the mid-fifth century imperial East and West.

Factional Politics

The fifth century was a world of rapidly changing political realities. This chapter has sought to penetrate beneath the context of normative cultural tropes found in the majority of our sources. Undeniably, men like Leo, Aspar, and Ricimer had much in common.[151] All had risen to prominence within the Roman military. Their "humble" backgrounds meant that these Roman soldier-emperors and their generalissimos needed to earn their more aristocratic subjects' respect and loyalty. In short, these soldiers strove to cultivate and promote simultaneously the intellectual and physical aspects of their *Romanitas*. This adaption of a multifaceted *Romanitas* worked both ways. In order to compete with these soldiers, the high-born Anthemius first had to prove his merit on the battlefield.

As we discussed in chapter 3, Roman civilisation had a long tradition of making Romans out of barbarians. Serving in the army helped to assimilate non-Romans and men from the lower strata into an imperial-state apparatus where civilian elites were used to admiring the ideals of manly soldiers. This process seems to have accelerated in the fifth century. In this militarised world, telling the difference between Romans and barbarians was becoming increasingly difficult. Certainly, evidence exists to suggest that Aspar may have been "Roman" enough for a diadem.[152] In 512, rioters in Constantinople considered Aspar's grandson Areobindus as a prospective alternative emperor.[153] The Emperor Zeno, who hailed from the semi-independent hinterland of Isauria, was probably far less attuned to cultivated aspects of

151 For the Emperor Zeno being far more of a barbarian than Aspar, see Goffart, *Barbarian Tides*, 38.

152 *MGH AA* 12.425.

153 Malalas, *Chron.* 16.9 (407).

Romanitas than the senior consul Aspar was.[154] Aspar and Ricimer were not the only cultivated non-Romans in late fifth-century Rome and Constantinople. Having spent his formative years as a hostage in Constantinople, the future ruler of Ostrogothic Italy, Theoderic the Amal, had probably received a more thorough education than either Leo or Zeno. In reference to the educated "Easterner" Theoderic's arrival in Italy, Jonathan Arnold has recently submitted, that "His situation thus closely resembled that of Anthemius or Julius Nepos, rather than that of the more obvious 'barbarian' strongmen Ricimer and Odovacer."[155]

So why did Aspar not just name himself emperor? The threat from the older families within the Eastern capitol may provide us an answer for why Aspar did not just make himself or one of his sons emperor or even a barbarian *rex* along the lines of the Ostrogoth Theoderic. Recent scholarship has provided several other reasons for this reluctance. Doug Lee (contra Arnold, Wood, and Mathisen) supposes that the likeliest explanation was that as an Alan and an Arian, Aspar, like Ricimer, could not rule themselves.[156] Procopius clearly expected his audience to believe that Aspar's Arianism and barbarian lineage disqualified him from the purple.[157] I think that some modern scholars have too readily dismissed Procopius' assessment. So too were links to the ruling regime important. Rather than destroy the reigning emperor, Stilicho, Aspar, and Ricimer sought to align their sons to the imperial family.

Perhaps his experience as an emperor-maker had led Aspar to bide his time, and therefore allow his son Patricus to take the throne with minimal dissent amongst the Eastern Roman ruling classes—dissent that indeed bubbled over only two months

154 Goffart, *Barbarian Tides*, 38.
155 Arnold, *Roman Imperial Restoration*, 148.
156 Lee, "Theodosius and His Generals," 108.
157 Procopius, *Wars* 3.6.3.

into the Isaurian Zeno's first reign.[158] As Brian Croke comments insightfully: "If, as an Arian, Aspar could not be emperor himself he could surely be the father of an emperor. This was Aspar's natural strategy for extending his influence and that of his family for the next generation."[159]

Aspar and Ricimer, moreover, may have preferred avoiding all the other obligations that went along with the imperial role. Olympiodorus asserted that Constantius III regretted giving up the relative freedom of his military command after he became Honorius' partner in 421.[160] Acting as general also allowed men like Aspar to keep themselves involved in both the Roman and non-Roman spheres of influence.

As Ralph Mathisen explains, especially in the West, the allure of the imperial office had declined markedly in the second half of the fifth century, therefore offering a partial explanation for why a powerful and seemingly ambitious man like Ricimer had little interest in becoming emperor himself:

> Ricimer saw emperors come and saw them go. As a patrician, he had all the benefits of being emperor—issuing laws and coins, being cited on equal terms with the emperors, and marrying an emperor's daughter—without any of the drawbacks—being burdened by court ceremony and being a ready target for assassination, not to mention being faced with the need to appoint a new patrician who would immediately become his own rival. Ricimer's authority was more greatly legitimated as Patrician and Master of Soldiers, an office for which barbarian origin and Arian affiliations, far from

---

158 John of Antioch, *frag.* 302. For Basiliscus' subsequent usurpation, and Zeno's struggles to thwart several rebellions in his second reign, see Kosiński, *Zeno*, ch. 4.

159 Croke, "Dynasty and Ethnicity," 157.

160 Olympiodorus, *frag.* 33.

being a possible hindrance, were virtually part of the job description.[161]

The theory cited above does not explain adequately, however, men such as Aspar's apparent reluctance, since in the East the imperial office appears to have been held in higher regard than in the West. It must be added that Ricimer, like Stilicho and Aëtius before him, faced the continual threat of assassination. Therefore, self-preservation does not seem a probable explanation.

The Roman/barbarian binary may be a construct of our sources. Such strict ethnic polarisation found in Priscus, Procopius, and others seems to be in dissonance with the realities of the day. Evidence suggests that Aspar could count on support amongst both Goths and Romans within the city of Constantinople.[162] So too, as we have seen, could a Romanised Ricimer depend on the backing of native Italians against Anthemius.[163]

Nonetheless, we should not dismiss all of these accounts describing the subtleties surrounding constructions of Roman and non-Roman identity. I am more inclined to believe that men like Theoderic and Aspar may have promoted their non-Romanness and, indeed, Gothic or Alan identity than some scholars. While Aspar gave his eldest son the Romanised name of Julius Patricus, the two sons he expected to follow in his footsteps were given the non-Roman names Ardabur and Hermineric.[164] It is doubtful that Aspar would have acclaimed Leo I as emperor in 457 if he was going to be seen as a barbarian. Zeno does not seem to have promoted his identity as an Isaurian, who, though technically

---

161 Mathisen, "Ricimer's Church in Rome," 324.

162 John Malalas' (*Chron.* 14.40) account of the riots that rocked Constantinople after Aspar's assassination would seem to suggest that Aspar had supporters from a segment of Constantinople's population, Roman and non-Roman.

163 A lucid discussion of this propaganda is found in Arnold, *Roman Imperial Restoration*, 16–20.

164 Arnold, *Roman Imperial Restoration*, 159.

Romans, were perceived by many Eastern Romans to be quasi-independent barbarians.[165]

So why did Leo succeed in eliminating his "barbarian" rival whereas his Western counterparts failed? Leo's success in eliminating his puppet-master Aspar has been explained by Doug Lee this way: Stilicho's decision at the opening of the fifth century to name a supreme commander of the Western Roman army stood in contrast to the East where five generals served to balance each other. Leo's astute manoeuvring to gain a powerful ally in the Isaurian Zeno also helped to protect him in the dangerous aftermath of the assassination.[166] Valentinian III had not taken similar precautions. Without anyone to defend him after he removed his generalissimo, as we saw in the previous chapter, Aëtius' Hunnic supporters quickly returned the favour.[167] So too had he eliminated a Roman general who had famously defeated Attila. The swift retaliation against such a murder is understandable. Leo had an easier time explaining his elimination of a man he painted as a traitorous barbarian. Leo emphasised, as well, Aspar's relatively poor record as a Roman commander. Valentinian III had a much more difficult time disparaging the Roman war hero Aëtius. Leo's close links to the military were also factor. As a former commander, Leo understood the dangerous whims of the military better than the blue-blooded "play-soldier" Valentinian. One suspects that Leo would have never have been naive enough to believe that in the wake of assassinating their revered leader Aëtius' soldiers would blindly follow him.

Finally, luck may have played a factor. Anthemius would have earned much political momentum if Basiliscus had attained a victory in a Vandalic North Africa that looked ripe for the picking. Although it may have been too late to save Gaul, the prestige and financial rewards of reclaiming the vital lands in North Africa may have bought Leo and Anthemius the time to unite the two

165 Lenski, "Assimilation and Revolt."
166 Lee, *From Rome to Byzantium*, 98–101.
167 Priscus, *frag.* 30.

halves of the Empire under one imperial family once again. We, of course, will never know. Yet the East, ultimately, did recover and thrive. To succeed the Empire called upon men with a more traditional military background than their fifth-century Theodosian predecessors. The soldier-emperors Leo and Zeno played a vital part in this rebirth.

Modern historians make more of Leo and Zeno's status as supposed barbarians than even their most ardent Byzantine opponents ever did. The fact that Aspar, Ricimer, and Theoderic remained "Arians" also seems noteworthy. If they wanted to be seen as Romans, why not just convert to the "Orthodoxy" of the day? If Aspar was ready to take this step in the case of his son, why not change as well if he truly wished to become emperor?[168] One answer can be provided. Such a step may have alienated these men from many of the non-Roman men who were their key supporters. Aspar, Theoderic, and Ricimer may have wanted to move swiftly between "Roman" and "non-Roman" worlds.[169] In fact, by the early sixth century, we find rulers like Theoderic not seeking to marry within the imperial family, but preferring to link themselves with other non-Roman dynasties.[170]

In closing, Leo's and Anthemius' legacies—good and bad— were defined largely by their relationships with their senior generalissimos. While Leo's detractors depicted the slaying of Aspar and his family as the work of a "butcher," and a sure sign of his unstable nature, later Byzantine historians, such as Procopius, admired Leo for taking a tough stand against Aspar—a

---

168 Theophanes (*Chron.* AM 5961) claimed (incorrectly) that Aspar at the coaxing of Patricus had also abandoned Arianism.

169 Penny MacGeorge (*Late Roman Army*, 301–02) makes this same point about Ricimer, Gundobad, and Odoacer.

170 For this growing preference, see Croke, "Dynasty and Aristocracy," 112. However, in the midst of his "reconquest" of Italy, Justinian arranged in 550 the marriage of his cousin Germanus to Theoderic's granddaughter Matasuntha, a move that was probably aimed at undermining Ostrogothic resistance in Italy.

barbarian cloaked in Roman clothing. Instead of witnessing a decline in traditional militarism, this chapter has shown that the fifth century witnessed an increased relevance of military men and the manly martial ideals they represented. As we shall see in the next chapter, Justinianic propaganda proclaimed the reconquests of Vandalic North Africa and Ostrogothic Italy as both the culmination and fulfilment of Leo's political aspirations. Indeed, sixth-century textual and visual media sought to depict these triumphs as a restoration of the natural order, whereby a reinvigorated Roman Empire and its manly soldiers restored the traditional Roman dominance over non-Roman peoples.

Plate 10. Late fifth- or early sixth-century Barberini ivory (Louvre, Paris, France) depicting a triumphant Roman emperor on horseback with a captive in tow. The emperor is probably Justinian, though Zeno and Anastasius I are possibilities as well. The horse rears over the female personification of earth, whilst Winged Victory crowns the emperor. Beneath the rider, barbarians cower. On the side panels, soldiers carry miniature victories.

Battle standards and captains, fierce nations and war's destruction I sing; treachery and the slaughter of men and hard toils. I sing of disasters in Libya and of an enemy broken in its might. [...] Once again the Muses want to sing of the sons of Aeneas. Peace is restored to Libya and takes its place here as wars draw to a close. Victory stands firm with its two wings shining. Now piety has turned its gaze upon the earth from heaven above. With Justice as her companion, Harmony, the joyful protectress, extends both arms in embrace and remakes the world. You, Justinian, sublime between them, rise from your lofty throne in your triumphs and, as joyful victor, lay down laws for these broken tyrants; for your renowned steps tread upon all these kings, and their purple now gladly serves Roman rule.

Corippus, *Iohannis* 1.1–19

VIII

CONTESTS OF MANLY VIRTUE
IN PROCOPIUS' *GOTHIC WARS*

> Show them, therefore, as quickly as possible that they are
> Greeks and unmanly by nature and are merely putting
> on a bold front when defeated, do not consent that this
> experiment of theirs proceed further.
> Procopius, *Wars* 8.23.25–26

FEW MILITARY CAMPAIGNS IN HISTORY HAVE ATTRACTED AS much attention as the Byzantine emperor Justinian's mid-sixth century "reconquests" of the Roman Empire's lost Western provinces against the Vandals in North Africa and the Goths in Italy. In the *History of the Wars*, the mid-sixth century historian Procopius provides a memorable description of the Empire's battles against the Persians in the East and the Western campaigns. In his account, Procopius attempted to place the sixth-century Romans' martial deeds alongside the accomplishments of the heroes of ancient Greek and Roman literature.[1] This chapter concentrates on one theatre of war, Italy, and examines how

---

1   For just two allusions in the *Wars* to the deeds of earlier Greek and Roman soldiers, see Procopius, *Wars* 1.1.6, 8.29.4–5. For a lucid exploration of this theme in Procopius' proem, as well as a discussion of how it differs from that of Thucydides, see Kouroumali, "Gothic War," 19–26.

Procopius used the field of battle as a means to comment on
the role that courage and manliness played in determining
the war's outcome. The conflict, in Procopius' telling, offered
the Byzantines the opportunity not only to regain Italy, but
also served as a means to test their military and manly virtues
against a worthy enemy, the Goths. I will suggest that issues of
manly ἀρετή and the age-old belief in the gendered dichotomy
between ἀνδρεία and ἀνανδρία play a significant role throughout
the account. We will see that Procopius' biographical details on
the Gothic monarchs and the Byzantine military hierarchy were
often gender-based and interlocked. Therefore, to comprehend
some of the significant themes found in the larger narrative, one
must understand both these character sketches' larger purpose
and the ways that Procopius drew on early Byzantine attitudes
towards gender and, in particular, idealised masculinity in their
construction. Indeed, *Wars* functioned, in part, as a means of
countering gendered propaganda emanating from Ostrogothic
Italy that sought to portray the Goths as manly protectors of Italy
whilst casting the Eastern Romans as unmanly Greeks.[2]

Justinian's "Reconquest"

In order to achieve a better understanding of the personalities
and the social and political changes that shaped Procopius' age
and his writing, it is necessary to describe briefly Justinian's
military campaigns.[3] Recent opinion favours the view that what
is commonly referred to as Justinian's "reconquest" resulted from

2 Jonathan Arnold (*Roman Imperial Restoration*, 141, n. 109) discusses this
gendered propaganda and suggests that Jordanes' *Getica*, like Procopius,
actively sought to invert this gendered invective.

3 One finds good accounts of Justinian's early career and reign in Moorhead,
Justinian; Evans, *Age of Justinian*; Meier, *Das andere Zeitalter Justinians*;
Leppin, *Justinian*; Bell, *Social Conflict*. For an insightful corrective to the
overly hostile view of Justinian permeating much of the recent historiography,
see Greatrex, "Perceptions of Procopius," 82–90.

opportunity, rather than a long-held plan to restore the Roman Empire's glory.[4]

Born Petrus Sabbatius, Justinian hailed from an impoverished Latin-speaking family from Tauresium in modern Macedonia. Like other ambitious Thracians seeking a better life, he and his uncle, the future Emperor Justin I, had first journeyed to Constantinople pursuing positions within the military.[5] Though their rise to the top of the Roman political hierarchy was not as smooth as the Byzantine evidence might suggest, the reigns of Justin I and Justinian I offer further evidence of the allure of these plum military positions for talented "new" men from the Empire's fringes.[6]

Whatever one's opinion concerning Justinian and his reign, his deft manipulation of early sixth-century East Roman politics proves that Byzantium rewarded men with keen intellects, regardless of their birth. Justinian appeared to recognise that his humble origins and largely titular military positions meant that

4   Heather, *Restoration of Rome,* 137–55; Brodka, "Prokopios von Kaisareia." For the notion that Procopius presented the Italian campaign as "a punishment of rebels" rather than a reconquest, see Boy, "History of Wars," 202–29.

5   Procopius (*Secret History* 6.1–4.) described a dirt-poor Justin walking to Constantinople during the reign of Zeno, seeking a position in the palace guard. Having risen to commander of the palace guards under Anastasius, Justin, probably in the early years of the sixth century, invited his nephew Petrus Sabbatius to join him in the capitol, where the childless Justin adopted the teenager as his son, who then changed his name to Justinian. An intriguing revision of Justin and Justinian's subsequent relationship is found in Pazdernik, "Quaestor Proclus."

6   One finds a sound discussion of the shadowy circumstances surrounding Justin's accession in 518 in Greatrex, "Early Years of Justin I's Reign."

his hold on power was tenuous.[7] Accordingly, when he became sole emperor after 1 August 527, Justinian took several steps to consolidate his authority. Under the guise of a classical renewal, he gradually increased imperial authority and simultaneously curtailed the aristocracy's power. He claimed for the first time that the emperor represented the *nomos empsychos* (the living law). In the *Digest,* he codified Roman law and refused to allow lawyers to change these laws. It became the emperor's duty to "resolve ambiguous juridical decisions."[8]

It is with Justinian that classical Rome fades away and a recognizable early medieval Christian state takes its place. Although Justinian played upon many Romans' hunger for the return of the glorious Roman past, he based his centralization, strict regimentation, and "classical Roman renewal" on Christian concepts. Justinian perceived himself as the head of the church and state, and he ruled as both a religious and a secular leader. No other emperor either before or after had such control over the church. It would be a mistake to see Justinian acting out these reforms purely from political necessity. Justinian was a devoted Christian, who truly abhorred "heresy."[9] Justinian thought of himself as a man who, along with his wife, the Empress Theodora, served as God's representative on earth. During the pagan era, the divinity of an emperor like Augustus isolated him from both his wife Livia and the general populace. Justinian's role as mediator between heaven and earth brought him closer to the people and to his wife.[10] Justinian assumed that for the good of the Empire, it was his duty to impose religious and legal conformity on his

---

7 For the titular nature of Justinian's military commands under Justin, see Lee, "Empire at War," 114. Yet, we should not underestimate the extent that Justinian experienced the day-to-day tasks of a soldier, particularly during Anastasius' reign.

8 Maas, *John Lydus and the Roman Past*, 15.

9 This zeal, however, did not stop him from adoring his Monophysite wife, Theodora.

10 Elsner, *Art and the Roman Viewer*, 180–84.

subjects. Before Justinian's reign, pagans had been allowed to serve in the bureaucracy as long as they kept their beliefs to themselves.[11] Justinian, however, felt compelled to stamp out the last vestiges of the old faith. In 528, he commanded that all pagans had three months to seek baptism. The next year he forbade the teaching of philosophy at the Academy in Athens. Pagan professors disillusioned with the Christianisation of the Empire fled to the more "enlightened" court of the Persian king Chosroes.[12]

Justinian's autocratic rule and his humble background guaranteed that there would be strong opposition to his rule among the populace, especially the nobility, many of whom remembered the reign of the Emperor Anastasius I as an era of relative religious freedom and prosperity.[13] In January of 532, the anti-Justinian faction felt strong enough to make its move. A crowd of people went to the home of Anastasius' nephew, Probus, in an attempt to name him emperor. Probus, perhaps purposely, was not there and the group burned down his house in frustration. In an attempt to appease the opposition, Justinian removed two unpopular officials from office. The emperor's rivals, however, took this gesture as a sign of weakness and awaited the proper opportunity to make their move. Their chance arrived when Justinian attended a race at the Hippodrome and tried to

11 However, as we noted in the previous chapter, the "outsider" Leo I had also stressed his orthodoxy and cracked down on those he considered pagans.

12 Brown, *Rise of Western Christendom*, 122. Agathias (*Histories* 2.31) points out that the philosophers quickly became disillusioned in Persia and returned to the Eastern Roman Empire in 531. Evans supports Agathias' account (*Age of Justinian*, 70). Averil Cameron is more sceptical (*Mediterranean World*, 134). Justinian launched three major persecutions against pagans during his reign, in 528–29, 545–46, and 562. The emperor sought to convert the remaining pagans both within and outside the empire, see John of Ephesus' account in *Pseudo-Dionysius of Tel-Mahre Chronicle*, trans. Witakowski, 76–78.

13 Bell, *Social Conflict*, 323–24. Yet, as we saw in the reigns of Leo and Zeno, such opposition by Constantinople's ruling elite to these low-born soldier-emperors was not unique to Justinian's regime.

placate the angry masses by giving a conciliatory speech. Both the Blues and the Greens, sporting factions that usually were bitter rivals, shouted down the emperor, and an uprising called the Nika revolt ensued.[14] According to Procopius, the emperor attempted to abandon the capital, but Theodora stiffened the emperor's resolve, and Justinian sent out his general Belisarius to punish the rebels. The *Chronicon Paschale*, an early seventh-century account, described Belisarius' ruthless counterattack, "The people remained mobbing outside the palace. And when this was known, the patrician Belisarius, the *magister militum*, came out with a multitude of Goths and cut down many [rioters] until evening."[15] Justinian never forgot the lesson of his near overthrow. Perhaps he knew that if he wanted to survive he could never again show any signs of weakness or compromise.

Justinian's actions cemented his power in Constantinople, and allowed him to conduct his campaigns to restore the lost provinces of the Western empire. The revolt, in truth, may have provided Justinian with the original impetus to launch his reconquest.[16] Moreover, a string of military victories had helped Justinian to secure his northern and eastern borders. Even before the Nika revolt, Byzantine armies had attained several important victories in these regions. In 530, for the first time in many years, the Byzantine army had defeated Persian forces in Armenia and Mesopotamia. The Empire attained further successes in the Balkans by defeating raiding Slavic and Bulgar forces. That same year, the Vandals deposed and imprisoned their king Hilderic and replaced him with his fiery nephew and heir, Gelimer. Although this overthrow disturbed Justinian, for the time being he could only warn Gelimer "not to exchange the title of king for the title of tyrant."[17] The next year, the Persians and the Romans fought to a standstill in the East. However, the Persian emperor Cabades

---

14 For a detailed account of the revolt, Greatrex, "Nika Riot."

15 *Chron. Paschale: 284-628 AD*, 117 (621).

16 Heather, *Restoration of Rome*, 137.

17 Procopius, *Wars* 3.9.11.

died in 531, and the new emperor, Chosroes, needing time to consolidate his power, readily agreed to a five-year truce with the Romans. With the dangerous Balkan and Persian frontiers secured, Justinian turned his attention to Africa.

Justinian employed both political and religious reasons to justify his attack on the Vandals.[18] In 533, claiming that he was protecting orthodox Christians from the dangers of an Arian usurper, the emperor sent Belisarius and his army of about 18,000 men to North Africa.[19] The landing caught the Vandals off guard. Although Gelimer attempted to block Belisarius' march on Carthage, the Roman army soundly defeated him. The Vandalic king fled, leaving his forces in disarray. Belisarius captured the city, and that same year he destroyed the remnants of the Vandal army at the Battle of Tricamerum. Although Gelimer escaped once more, in 534, he finally surrendered to Belisarius. Despite the seeming ease of the Byzantine victory over the Vandals, it would take another fifteen years to stamp out the local Berber tribes' stubborn resistance.

Defeating the Vandals gave Justinian the confidence to retake Italy from the Goths. The emperor secretly negotiated with Theoderic's daughter, Amalasuintha (regent to her son, King Athalaric, r. 526–34), to restore Italy to Roman rule. However, when Athalaric died in 534, political considerations forced Amalasuintha to reconcile with her cousin Theodahad (r. 534–36) and make him co-ruler. Theodahad, suspecting Amalasuintha's "treason" and perhaps hoping to ingratiate himself with the queen's enemies, had imprisoned her and then had her killed sometime in early 535.[20]

18 Procopius, *Wars* 3.9.10–13; Corippus, *Iohannis* 3.1–18, 3.260–313.

19 I agree, however with George Dennis ("Holy War," 34) that we should see Justinian's Western campaigns as "imperial" rather than "holy" wars.

20 Procopius, *Wars* 5.4.26–28; Jordanes, *Getica* 306. Cf., however, Procopius' (*Secret History* 16.5) claim that Theodahad had murdered Amalasuintha at Theodora's behest. The extent that Amalasuintha cooperated with Justinian is debatable, see Cooper, "Heroine and the Historian," 309.

Once again, Justinian used a "barbarian" king's unlawful usurpation of power as a pretext for Byzantine intervention. Soon after Amalasuintha's death, the emperor decided to take Italy and claimed the Gothic kingdom for himself.[21] Belisarius seized Sicily in 535. Justinian sent envoys to pressure the Goths to capitulate. Belisarius invaded Italy and, facing little resistance, easily captured Naples. Exasperated with Theodahad's inept leadership, in 536 the Goths killed him, replacing him with the general Vitigis (r. 536–40). Vitigis fared little better than Theodahad. His attempts to besiege Belisarius in Rome from 536 to 537 failed, and in 540 he surrendered Ravenna to Belisarius. Despite being sent to Constantinople in chains, Vitigis was allowed an honourable retirement in the capital.

Victory seemed to be within Justinian's grasp. Yet, in 540 things took a turn for the worse. Justinian's campaigns in North Africa and Italy had severely stretched the limits of the Eastern Romans' military power. In the same year, the Persian emperor Chosroes, fearing Justinian's growing puissance, violated the "endless peace." Persian troops quickly overwhelmed Syria's sparsely defended cities. Desperate to defeat the Persians, Justinian recalled Belisarius from Italy. While Belisarius had mixed success in his campaigns against the Persians, Justinian managed to sign another truce with Chosroes by agreeing to pay more tribute. The treaty with the Persians allowed Justinian to concentrate once more on conquering Italy. Ultimately, however, the payments reduced Byzantium's power in the East, allowing the Persians to become the dominant force in the region.

The year 540 also marked a turning point in Justinian's campaign in Italy. Even with Belisarius' victories, the Gothic army had refused to submit to Byzantine rule. In 541, the Gothic nobility appointed Totila (r. 541–52) as king. Totila, a relative of

21 Procopius, *Wars* 5.5.1. The idea that Justinian and Theodora manipulated Theodahad into murdering Amalasuintha in order to have a pretext to invade Italy remains controversial. A good up-to-date assessment of these shadowy events is found in Vitiello, *Theodahad*, 94–111.

the Visigothic king Theudis (r. 526–48), revitalised the Gothic army's fighting spirit. In a series of swift campaigns, he recaptured almost all of Italy. Finally, however, after a long and bitter struggle, Narses defeated Totila in 552, and by 554 the Eastern Roman army had overwhelmed the remnants of the Gothic forces. Victorious at last in Italy, in 555 Justinian sent an army to Spain, capturing the south-east corner of the Iberian Peninsula.[22]

For contemporaries, it may have looked as if Justinian had succeeded in restoring the Western half of the Roman Empire. In retrospect, however, the "reconquest" was the ancient Roman Empire's last gasp.[23] Victory in the West had come at a steep price. The vicious wars had devastated Italy, and many Italians began to perceive the Eastern Romans as foreign invaders.[24] Italy's depopulation also made it increasingly difficult for the Byzantine army to protect Italy from outside invaders, and in 568 the Lombards overran Northern and Central Italy.[25] Although the Eastern Romans managed to maintain a political presence in Italy until the eleventh century, they no longer treated it as if it were their ancient home, but simply as a frontier military province.[26]

In the end, Justinian failed to reinstate a united Roman Empire. The Empire's overextension had spread its defences thin. In the second half of the sixth century, Slavic invaders overwhelmed the Byzantine defenders and established permanent settlements in the Balkans. The Visigoths drove the Byzantines from Spain sometime between 623 and 625. Byzantine power in North Africa lasted until the Arabs took control at the end of the seventh

---

22 For the dates of these mostly undocumented campaigns in Spain, see Fossella, "Waiting Only for a Pretext."

23 See, e.g., Paul the Deacon, *Historia Romana* 16.23, where the eighth-century author described Justinian's reconquest as signifying the end of the Roman Empire.

24 Amory, *People and Identity*, 120.

25 Paul the Deacon, *Historia Langobardorum* 2.5–9.

26 Amory, *People and Identity*, 313.

century. Despite Justinian's attempts, the campaigns in the West ultimately only led to further decline.

Although one should be careful not to overstate the extent to which Justinian's reign should be defined by these military campaigns, the victories in North Africa and Italy were notable achievements. Correspondingly, they have played a crucial part in shaping ancient and modern perceptions of his reign.[27] The vestment that was placed over Justinian's coffin at his funeral in 565 depicted the emperor "in the midst of his court, trampling on the bold neck of the Vandal king" while the personifications of Libya and Old Rome looked on in approval.[28] To borrow the words of Averil Cameron, Old Rome "is treated in parallel with Africa as representing the two conquered provinces of the western empire."[29] That he chose to be buried amidst pictorial visions of "his" triumphs in the West provides solid evidence of the importance Justinian and those around him placed on his wars of reconquest.[30] Let us now turn to the seminal historian of those campaigns, Procopius.

---

27 Scott, "Chronicles versus Classicizing History." Scott maintains that historians relying too heavily on Procopius' *Wars* have overemphasised Justinian and the average Byzantine's interest in these campaigns and warfare more generally. I accede that a more balanced view of sixth-century Byzantine culture is important, but would submit one should not swing the pendulum too far the other way. Indeed, as we have seen, one finds an interest in military matters in a myriad of sixth-century sources and genres other than Procopius. For the importance of military matters in the sixth-century political philosophy, see Bell, *Three Political Voices from the Age of Justinian*, introduction, 50–54.

28 Corippus, *In laudem Iustini Augusti minoris* 1.288–90.

29 Cameron, "Old Rome and New Rome," 19.

30 Whately (*Battles and Generals*, 158–59) provides a summary of the recent debates surrounding the peripheral importance of the Italian campaign in comparison to Justinian's wars in Persia, the Balkans, and North Africa.

Procopius

Ordinarily, one might consider it problematic to rely on one historian's work as an accurate reflection of his society. There are, however, several important reasons for choosing Procopius as the main source for his era and as a good example of how early Byzantine gender ideologies were constructed. Procopius has, arguably, long been the most important and widely read early Byzantine historian.[31] The *Wars*, *Buildings*, and *Secret History* are the primary, and at times the only, sources for events in the crucial reign of Justinian. In their accounts of the era, eminent historians like J. B. Bury have paid Procopius the ultimate compliment by summarising large sections of the *Wars*. Procopius' writings were popular during his own lifetime as well; the historian claims that the history found an audience in every part of the Empire.[32] His focus on military affairs and the Byzantine soldiers' martial deeds seems to have appealed to prevailing literary tastes.[33] Though the audience for such a detailed prose account of Justinian's campaigns could never have been large, its Byzantine readership probably included influential Greek-speaking members of the bureaucracy

31 Procopius has received much needed attention in the past twenty-five years. Cameron (*Procopius and the Sixth Century*) and Kaldellis (*Procopius of Caesarea*) provide thorough reviews of the earlier literature and interesting, if at times opposing, ideas on Procopius' religion, methods, intentions, and merits as a historian. Treadgold's (*Early Byzantine Historians*, 176–226) short study provides a good basic summary of the content of *Wars* as well as some interesting insights into Procopius' possible creative process. For a thorough and thoughtful rundown and critique of Procopian scholarship in the last fifteen years, see Greatrex, "Recent Work on Procopius"; "Perceptions of Procopius."

32 Procopius, *Wars* 8.1.1.

33 For the popularity of military matters and the praise of military men in a variety of literary genres in the sixth century, see Rapp, "Literary Culture under Justinian"; Whately, "Militarization."

and the military high command.[34] Procopius may too have recited his work in front of larger and less-educated audiences, who, as Brian Croke reminds us, "were no less used to formal rhetoric and found these works enjoyable."[35] The *Wars* also influenced other early Byzantine historians. Agathias, Procopius' continuator, who accused some of his fellow sixth-century writers of composing histories that demonstrated a "flagrant disregard for the truth and no concern for historical accuracy," in contrast, complimented Procopius for his precision and reliability.[36] This praise was not limited to secular historians. The sixth-century ecclesiastical historian Evagrius, who paraphrased large sections of the *Wars* for his own history, revealed the esteem in which Procopius was held: "Procopius has set forth most assiduously and elegantly what was done by Belisarius, when he commanded the Eastern forces and by the Romans and Persians when they fought each other."[37] The regard in which contemporary historians held him and his popularity amongst an influential segment of early Byzantine society indicates that his history was considered accurate and suggests that his paradigms of heroism, masculinity, and *Romanitas* were ones that his readership could appreciate.

Procopius witnessed many of the events he described and knew many of the people that helped to shape events in his history. In 527, the historian had been appointed as *assessor* (legal secretary) to Belisarius, the newly appointed commander

---

34 For this probable audience, see Treadgold, *Early Byzantine Historians*, 189; Croke, "Uncovering Byzantium's Historiographical Audience," 33. For capabilities for early Byzantine generals to read Greek and Latin military texts, see Whately, "The Genre and Purpose of Military Manuals."

35 Croke, "Uncovering Byzantium's Historiographical Audience," 32.

36 Agathias, *Histories* preface 16–22.

37 Evagrius Scholasticus, *HE* 4.12. Admittedly, as Whitby points out in his introduction (*The Ecclesiastical History of Evagrius Scholasticus*, xxxi–xxxii), Evagrius shifts the focus of Procopius' secular military narrative in order to highlight the providential aspects of the episodes he borrows.

of the Eastern forces.[38] For the next thirteen years, Procopius accompanied Belisarius on his military campaigns in the East against the Persians, to the West in Africa against the Vandals, and in Italy against the Goths. Writing Belisarius' speeches, letters, and military reports seems to have represented some of Procopius' primary duties, suggesting that some of his material on earlier battles and set speeches given by Belisarius may be more accurate than some scholars would have us believe.[39] After 540, the two parted ways, and we lose track of the historian's exact location. We do not know if he joined Belisarius' campaign against the Persians in 541, though he was present the next year when the plague struck in Constantinople. It is probable that after 542 he no longer witnessed the events he described, but relied on Byzantine diplomatic records and on his contacts in the Byzantine army and within the Italian senate.[40]

Scholars have long noted the *Wars'* literary character and, for some, Procopius' excessive moralising and heavy emphasis on a rather limited number of virtues and vices to describe his leading characters hinder any attempts to discover these people's actual personalities or to uncover the "real" history of the age.[41] It is true that Procopius could shift chronology and distort the truth in an

---

38 Procopius, *Wars* 1.12.24. Most historians believe that Procopius was a lawyer, Tinnefeld, "Prokopios [3]"; Codoner, *Procopio de Casarea*, 11–12; Greatrex, "Lawyers and Historians," 151. However, James Howard-Johnston argues that Procopius was an engineer/architect, Howard-Johnston, "The Education and Expertise of Procopius."

39 As suggested by Cameron, *Procopius and the Sixth Century*, 186–206.

40 On these contacts in Italy, see Evans, *Procopius*, 31–36. For Procopius and Agathias' use of oral sources, see Whitby, "Greek Historical Writing," 46. On Procopius' use of official and oral sources, see Cameron, *Procopius and the Sixth Century*, 136, 156; Greatrex, *Rome and Persia at War*, 62–64. Procopius also used written material. Unfortunately, like many ancient historians, he failed to specify which writers he consulted.

41 Ljubarskij, "Quellenforschung"; Cameron, *Procopius and the Sixth Century*, 12.

effort to create a more dramatic narrative.[42] Yet, though rhetoric undeniably influenced his writings, as Conor Whately has recently suggested, "facts underline his descriptions."[43] Procopius, indeed, largely followed the literary guidelines found in his preface, which maintained "that while cleverness was appropriate for rhetoric, story-making was appropriate for poetry, and truth for history."[44]

Others sources from the period largely corroborate Procopius' depictions of individuals and peoples such as the Persians and the Goths.[45] Moreover, we should not criticise Procopius too heavily for his penchant to stretch the truth or "recreate" the thoughts of his main players in an effort to create a more didactic account. Ancient historians cared less than their modern counterparts do about seeing men like the emperors and generals as "real" men or learning about their private lives.

This is not to say that we learn nothing about the private lives of Byzantines in Procopius' writings. Particularly in *Secret History*, Procopius investigated the private lives of his power couples: Belisarius/Antonina and Justinian/Theodora. He did so, however, primarily as a means of explaining setbacks in Belisarius' and Justinian's public lives. Additionally, just as many of his fellow early Byzantines did, Procopius made the point in his writings that a combination of fate, circumstances, God, demons, and men's vices and virtues helped to determine events in the secular

---

42 A discussion of some of these "untruths" and the role that such deceptions play in Procopius' writings is found in Kaldellis, *Procopius of Caesarea*, 32–34.

43 Whately, *Battles and Generals*, 20.

44 Procopius, *Wars* 1.1.4. Cf. Thucydides, *Peloponnesian War* 1.21; Agathias, *Histories* preface 4–12.

45 For Procopius as a relatively accurate source on the Persians, see Börm, *Prokop und die Perser*. On the Goths, see Vitiello, *Theodahad*.

world.[46] Therefore, for Procopius, providing a detailed or accurate account of the foreign policies or the intricate strategic and tactical motivations of the Gothic and Byzantine leadership was not as important as his observations on how the moral characteristics of his key players influenced the outcome of battles. This emphasis helps to explain why the historian filled his writings with numerous character sketches of the soldiers who played an integral part in Justinian's various military campaigns.[47] The remainder of this chapter will focus on Procopius' characterisations of the Gothic monarchs and the Byzantine soldiers in the *Gothic Wars*.

Theoderic: The Manly Protector

Procopius opened the *Gothic Wars* by relating his version of events that had led to Theoderic and the Goths' rise to power in Italy. Procopius explained that his history would be a story of three protagonists: the Goths, the Italians, and the Romans.[48] Military

---

46 Undeniably, fate (τύχη) plays an important, if complex, role throughout the *Wars*. Kaldellis (*Procopius of Caesarea*, 199) goes so far as to claim that for Procopius there was "no reward for nobility in the world, only the twists and turns of *tyche*." I agree with Treadgold's assertion (*Early Byzantine Historians*, 223), however, that men's virtues played an essential role in determining events, and that for Procopius "fate, whether personified or not, could represent the will either of God or of the demons, it amounted to little more than a rhetorical device. Only God, the demons, or men determined what happened." Cf. Brodka, *Die Geschichtsphilosophie in der spätantiken Historiographie*, 40–45.

47 As we will see, however, contemporary sources frequently corroborate Procopius' depictions of the personalities and the deeds of the key players in his history.

48 Procopius, *Wars* 5.1.1–2: "I shall now proceed to the Gothic War, first telling all that befell the Goths [Γότθοις] and Italians ['Ιταλιώταις] before this war." In the next sentence, he described the Eastern Roman Zeno, as "the reign of Zeno in Byzantion [βυζαντίω]." Although Procopius used the term "Byzantion" (for residents of Constantinople) or at times "Greek" to describe the Eastern Romans, the historian's preferred term was "Roman."

matters and men's martial virtues play a key role in Procopius' prologue. Indeed, the decline of the "native" Western army and the demilitarisation of the Italian populace, according to the historian, represented one of the primary reasons for the loss of Italy. Similar to Synesius' argument from nearly a century and a half before, in Procopius' eyes as the Western army's barbarian make-up grew stronger the native element grew weaker. In Procopius' opinion, these "barbarians" had no grasp of Roman law and little respect for the "native" population. Barbarian control of the army led to the Western Romans' inability to protect themselves from the "foreigners" who "tyrannically" demanded a share of the lands of Italy.[49] Under the last Western Roman emperors' inept rule, the "barbarian" generals became the true power behind the throne. In 476, a group of these rebellious barbarians proclaimed one of these strongmen, Odoacer, king. Odoacer then deposed the Western Roman emperor Romulus, whom Procopius does not name.

In contrast to the Western Romans, who accepted barbarian rule and domination of the army, Procopius suggested that the Eastern Romans' continued adherence to a martial lifestyle and control over their armed forces had allowed them to continue to utilise the barbarians as their pawns. One finds an example of this paradigm in Procopius' description of the Eastern Roman emperor Zeno's adept use of allied barbarians to punish his enemies. In Procopius' version of events, Zeno convinced Theoderic the Amal to gather his forces in Thrace and the Balkans, and then march into Italy and eliminate Odoacer. Procopius depicted this confrontation as

He also distinguished (e.g., *Wars* 5.1.26) between Goths and Italians in the post-Roman kingdom. Amory (*People and Identity*, 120) asserts that in the later part of the fifth century Western Romans began calling themselves *Itali* in order to distinguish themselves from the Eastern Romans. He further proposes that this development broke down some of the social barriers between the Western Romans and the Goths.

49 Procopius (*Wars* 3.5.12–13) described a similar land-grab by the Vandals in North Africa.

something more than a clash between two "barbarian" peoples. He, in fact, made an effort of "de-barbarising" Theoderic somewhat. He highlighted the Goth's patrician rank and the fact that Theoderic had attained "consular office in Byzantium."[50] After a fierce struggle, Theoderic slew Odoacer and took control of Italy. Despite emphasising his subordinate position to the Roman emperor and his role as a barbarian "king" (ῥήξ, *Wars* 5.1.26), Procopius made the rather extraordinary claim in a work that would have been read in imperial circles that Theoderic held the qualities appropriate "to one who is by birth an emperor."[51] The historian even blamed Theoderic's "unjust" execution of the Roman senators and consuls, Boethius and Symmachus, partly on the treachery of his advisors.

Throughout the *Gothic Wars*, Procopius portrayed Theoderic's reign as a "golden age."[52] In a theme that marks many of his subsequent portraits of the Gothic leadership, Theoderic frequently acted the opposite way one might expect of a barbarian *rex*.[53] The Gothic king undoubtedly treated the Italians with justice and compassion, especially in comparison with what Procopius portrayed as the Vandals' tyrannical rule in North Africa and of Odoacer's short reign in Italy. Procopius certainly respected the Gothic king's martial qualities. Theoderic ruled as a military leader and, in Procopius' view, part of his success stemmed from his ability to provide stability and a renewed sense of military

---

50 Procopius, *Wars* 5.1.9.

51 Procopius, *Wars* 5.1.29. Jonathan Arnold (*Roman Imperial Restoration*, 90) goes so far to say that "Theoderic's reign [...] constituted much more than simply that of a king along the same lines as Odovacer or other 'barbarian' kings of the West. He was a *princeps Romanus*, or Roman emperor, acknowledged as such by his own subjects and presented as such, though in a deferential and conciliatory manner, to the East." Cf., however, the more restrained views found in Moorhead, *Theoderic in Italy*, 77–78.

52 See, e.g., Procopius, *Wars* 7.9.10, 7.21.12, 23.

53 For Procopius' use of such inversions in his accounts of the Gothic rulers, see Halsall, "Funny Foreigners," 106–11.

pride to the Western Romans. Procopius' portrait also revealed the Gothic king's mastery of the "intellectual" virtues that allowed a good leader to treat his subjects justly. *Wars* emphasised that Theoderic's mingling of "wisdom and manliness" (ξυνέσεώς τε καὶ ἀνδρίας) allowed him to both "observe justice" (δικαιοσύνης), and to protect Italy from barbarian invaders. These traits earned Theoderic "the love of the Goths and the Italians."[54]

When describing Theoderic's Italy, one thing that the Gothic and the Byzantine sources seemed to agree on was the notion that the Italo-Romans lacked the manly courage and martial virtues to protect their native land.[55] Italo-Roman authors frequently repeat the notion that the Goths should do the fighting while the native Italians basked in tranquillity. Cassiodorus commented that "While the Gothic army wages war, let the Roman be at peace."[56] When describing Theoderic's move into Italy in 489 with his army, Ennodius of Pavia (ca. 473–521) declared, "The empress of the world, Rome, was demanding you [Theoderic] restore her."[57] The Goths personify active manliness. Cassiodorus explained that for the Goths "strife is needed, since a warlike race like ours delights to prove their courage."[58] It is only against this background that one can appreciate some of the gendered themes found in *Gothic Wars*.

The question of whether the Italians owed greater loyalty to their current "protectors," the Goths, or to the Byzantines, represented a recurrent theme in the *Gothic Wars*. From Procopius'

---

54 Procopius, *Wars* 5.1.27–29: ἔρως τε αὐτοῦ ἔν τε Γόθοις καὶ Ἰταλιώταις.

55 Procopius, *Wars* 3.3.10–13, 7.11.12–14. Arnold (*Roman Imperial Restoration*, 125–42) offers an insightful discussion on this paradigm from the Gothic and Italo-Roman perspective.

56 Cassiodorus, *Variae* 12.5.4 (trans. Barnish): "dum belligerat Gothorum exercitus, sit in pace Romanus."

57 Ennodius, *Panegyric to Theoderic* 7.30 (trans. Haase).

58 Cassiodorus, *Variae* 1.24.1 (trans. Hodgkin): "Innotescenda sunt magis Gothis quam suadenda certamina, quia bellicosae stirpi est gaudium comprobari: laborem quippe non refugit, qui virtutis gloriam concupiscit."

perspective, this issue of fidelity had little to do with the Eastern and Western Romans' shared past, and more with which side, Goth or Byzantine, could both better protect the "non-martial" Italians from foreign threats and treat them "justly."[59]

These are remarkable views for an Eastern Roman writer to express. Most of Procopius' readers would have probably understood the irony that a man deemed a barbarian *rex* seemed the only man capable of protecting Italy from barbarian invaders.[60] Procopius repeatedly provided nuanced views of foreign peoples he generally labelled as barbarians. While, at times, he displayed the traditional Graeco-Roman distrust of "barbarians," overall his attitude towards foreign peoples like the Goths and the Vandals appears quite enlightened. Geoffrey Greatrex argues that Procopius' sympathetic portrayal of the Goths mirrored other sixth-century writers' flexible attitude towards "barbarians," and reflected the blurring of boundaries between Eastern Romans and foreign peoples in the sixth century. So besides the fact that these sentiments may have represented Procopius' true feelings towards the Gothic monarch, I can think of three other possible reasons for such effusive praise.[61] First, this flattering description of Theoderic may represent a barb aimed at Justinian, whose humble origins, lack of battle experience, and inability to fend off

---

59 See, e.g., Procopius, *Wars* 7.4.16, 7.9.10–15, 7.30.24.

60 Western propaganda frequently described the native Italians as needing Gothic protection from the barbarians, e.g., Ennodius, *Panegyricus dictus Theoderico* 12.69.

61 Greatrex, "Roman Identity in the Sixth Century." See too Anthony Kaldellis' comment (*Procopius of Caesarea*, 221) that Procopius "treated Romans and barbarians impartially, condemning the former as often as he praised the latter." Cf., however, Averil Cameron (*Procopius and the Sixth Century*, 239) who argues that Procopius attempted to preserve the "established order" by creating "a strong demarcation between civilised peoples and barbarians," and Goffart (*Barbarian Tides*, 94–96) who uses Procopius' account of the Heruls to make the larger claim that Procopius wanted to expel all the barbarians from the Roman Empire.

barbarian incursions into Byzantine territory earned Procopius' scorn in *Secret History*.[62] Second, it may be a veiled insult aimed at the native Italians, who in Procopius' mind were incapable of protecting their own lands. Finally, it allowed Procopius to represent Theoderic as a manly archetype whose character could be compared to those of his Gothic successors and the leading Byzantine generals, and in particular, Belisarius.

Procopius based much of his esteem for Theoderic on the monarch's ability to combine the virtues of an idealised political and military leader. It was, however, Theoderic's martial virtues that the historian appeared to have admired most. At the close of his biographical sketch, in fact, Procopius explained that it was Theoderic's ability to make "himself an object of terror to all of his enemies" that contributed to his lasting legacy.[63]

Athalaric: Boys to Men

For Procopius, Theoderic's strong leadership helped to unify the Goths. So too had the king largely succeeded in maintaining the bond between Italians and Goths. The historian's descriptions of the king's flawed successors revealed the difficulty of maintaining this unity. Though Procopius does not mention him, the unexpected death in 522 of Theoderic's son-in-law and chosen heir, the Visigothic-warrior Eutharic, had thrown the aging king's succession plan into disarray.[64] On his deathbed, necessity had compelled Theoderic to name his ten-year-old grandson

---

62 As Kaldellis points out (*Procopius of Caesarea*, 60), one may also make comparisons with Procopius' negative portrait of Justinian in *Secret History*, where the historian described the Eastern Emperor as a land-hungry tyrant.

63 Procopius, *Wars* 5.1.31. Procopius praised Belisarius for being an object of fear amongst his soldiers. See, e.g., Procopius, *Wars* 3.12.8–22, 6.8.1–18.

64 Vitiello, *Theodahad*, 50–51. On Eutharic, see Moorhead, *Theoderic in Italy*, 86, 93, 98–99, 108; Arnold, *Roman Imperial Restoration*, 215–18.

Athalaric[65] as his heir. He then appointed his daughter and the boy's mother Amalasuintha (ca. 495–535), as regent.[66] Amalasuintha was the daughter of Theoderic's second wife Audofleda, the Merovingian king Clovis' sister. Yet, despite the oaths they had sworn to Theoderic, some within the Gothic aristocracy had a difficult time accepting a dynastic succession dependent solely on the Amal line.[67] It took time, however, for this resentment to boil over. In Procopius' telling, the early years of Amalasuintha's regency were a relatively peaceful and stable time for Italy.[68] By distancing herself from some of the less tolerant policies of Theoderic's final years (proof too that Procopius' praise of Theoderic may not have been completely heartfelt), Amalasuintha sought to restore harmonious relations between the Goths and the Romans. Procopius declared that she protected the Romans from the Goths' "mad desire to wrong them" (ξυνεχώρησεν ἐς τὴν ἐκείνους ἀδικίαν ὀργῶσιν). Additionally, attempting to reconcile herself to the senate, she had returned Symmachus' and Boethius' confiscated lands to their families.[69] Amalasuintha and her supporters reigned supreme, yet trouble lurked in the hearts of Gothic men spurned by the new regime.[70]

Procopius compressed the ten-year period of Athalaric's rule into a didactic tale that appears to unfold over a much shorter

65 Following Procopius, *Wars* 5.2.1; Jordanes, *Romana* 367. Contra Jordanes' claim in *Getica* (304) that Athalaric was eight years old when Theoderic had died.

66 Jordanes *Getica* 304; Cassiodorus, *Variae* 8.2–7.

67 Heather, *Goths*, 250–55.

68 Procopius explained (*Wars* 7.21.12) that by 550 many Goths recalled the years of Theoderic and Athalaric's rule fondly.

69 Procopius, *Wars* 5.2.5–6.

70 Herwig Wolfram claims (*History of the Goths*, 336) that these men were Gothic hardliners who took a tough stance against Constantinople. He suggests that members of this faction, who probably included Theodahad among its members, realised by late 532/early 533 that they needed to gain control over Athalaric before he reached his majority.

period.[71] According to Procopius, the struggle began as a dispute over the proper way to educate Athalaric. Amalasuintha felt compelled to raise the boy as a Roman aristocrat.[72] She sent him to a Roman school of letters and hired three "prudent and refined" (ξυνετούς τε καὶ ἐπιεικεῖς) Gothic tutors to further educate the future king.[73] Procopius illustrated how this decision created a backlash among some members of the Gothic nobility who wanted to raise the boy in "the barbarian fashion." He wrote:

> All the notable men among them gathered together, and coming before Amalasuintha made the charge that their king was not being educated correctly from their point of view nor to his own advantage. For letters, they said, are far removed from manliness [ἀνδρίας], and the teaching of old men results for the most part in a cowardly [δειλὸν] and submissive spirit. Therefore the man who is to show daring [τολμητήν] in any work and be great in renown ought to be freed from the timidity [φόβου] which teachers inspire and to take his training in arms [...] "Therefore, O Queen," they said, "have done with these tutors now, and give to Athalaric some boys of his own age to be his companions, who will pass through the period of youth with him and thus give him an impulse toward that excellence [τὴν ἀρετὴν], which is in keeping with the custom [νόμον] of barbarians."

The "martial" faction emphasised the "dangers" of a literary education by claiming that Theoderic refused to allow the Goths to send their children to school. They suggested that he took this

71 Discussed in Amory, *People and Identity*, 156.

72 For further evidence of Amalasuintha's adulation of classical learning, see Cassiodorus, *Variae* 10.3.

73 Procopius, *Wars* 5.2.7.

stance because he believed that a literary education would cause them "to despise sword or spear."[74] One assumes that Procopius and his contemporary audience were aware of the flawed logic of this argument, since Procopius told his audience about Theoderic's daughter Amalasuintha's and his nephew Theodahad's excellent classical educations.[75] So too did this "martial faction" support ultimately the unmanly Plato-loving non-soldier Theodahad. While this discrepancy and other incongruences in his history may be the result of Procopius' reliance on rhetorical themes and disregard for the "truth," it is also possible that he purposefully has the "martial" Goths tell a known non-truth. As we will see throughout the remainder of this chapter, Procopius often utilised such inaccuracies in his set speeches as a means of later undermining the speakers' overall argument.

In this stylised episode, Procopius transformed an internal Gothic power struggle into a didactic debate about the proper way to educate young men. While simplifying a complex political dispute, Procopius provided his audience with the differences— real and imagined—between Roman and Gothic methods and beliefs about the best way to transform boys into manly men.[76] Each of the Gothic factions implied that boys travelled a long and hazardous path to manhood. The two sides only differed on the best methods to overcome these obstacles. The "conservatives" preached that in order to instil courage in a young man, he needed

74 Procopius, *Wars* 5.2.11–17.

75 John Malalas (*Chron.* 15.9 [383]) explained that Theoderic had received an education during his years in Constantinople, a point that Procopius—with his focus on the Gothic king's early embracing of Byzantine culture—may have known. So too did Theoderic's panegyrist Ennodius (*Panegyricus dictus Theoderico* 3.11) declare that Theoderic had received an education in Constantinople. Cf. Theophanes (*Chron.* AM 5977). Contra *Anonymus Valesianus* 12.61. Theoderic's role in providing the women in his family with a proper Roman education is discussed in Vitiello, *Theodahad*, 45–46.

76 Of course, many young men from the Byzantine literate classes would have also received military training as an essential part of their upbringing.

to be surrounded by companions of a similar age and "take his training in arms," while Amalasuintha and the Goths presumably following Roman traditions focused on the development of a boy's mind.[77] Notwithstanding its obvious rhetorical aspects, this episode has some historical basis. Evidence from the Gothic side supports Procopius' characterisation of Amalasuintha as being devoted to Roman literature. For example, in a letter to the Roman senate, Amalasuintha espoused the benefits of a Roman education by suggesting that literary learning allowed the warrior to discover "what will strengthen him with courage; the prince learns how to administer his people with equity."[78] In the Graeco-Roman tradition, a literary education could both enhance one's martial skills and hone one's innate ἀνδρεία.[79] As we discussed in chapter three, one's education had served both as an indicator of one's civilised *Romanitas*, but also one's manliness. Although we know very little about what constituted a "Gothic" education, we know that officers' children received substantial military training, and that Gothic society's upper echelon embraced the soldier's life.[80] As mentioned above, we know that Theoderic had hoped originally to have a fellow warrior-king succeed him. Therefore, Procopius may have been aware of Theoderic's dilemma in appointing a martial successor.

Evidence, however, from the remainder of Athalaric's biography compels us to consider his words more carefully. Procopius clearly rejected the Goths' contention that a young

---

77 Procopius, *Wars* 5.2.11–17.
78 Cassiodorus, *Variae* 10.3.4 (trans. Barnish). The entire passage reads: "Accessit his bonis desiderabilis eruditio litterarum, quae naturam laudabilem eximie reddit ornatam. ibi prudens invenit, unde sapientior fiat: ibi bellator reperit, unde animi virtute roboretur: inde princeps accipit, quemadmodum populos sub aequalitate componat: nec aliqua in mundo potest esse fortuna, quam litterarum non augeat gloriosa notitia."
79 Connolly, "Like the Labors of Heracles," 287, 328.
80 Amory, *People and Identity*, 96. For the Goths' military ethos, see Heather, *Goths*, 322–26; Whitby, "Armies and Society," 472.

man's curriculum should involve military training alone. The historian, in fact, responded to the barbarians' claims about the unmanliness of a Roman education, by demonstrating how Athalaric's exposure to the "customs of the barbarians" produced a "failed man." Fearing her political rivals, Amalasuintha dismissed the tutors and replaced them with a group of Gothic boys who, like Athalaric, "had not yet come of age."[81] Predictably, in Procopius' view, this decision proved disastrous. Instead of providing Athalaric with an inclination towards manly ἀρετή, his comrades only enticed the future king "to drunkenness and to intercourse with women" (μέθην καὶ γυναικῶν μίξεις). Qualities that we have already seen in the classical tradition represented typical vices of not only barbarians, but of unmanly men as well.[82] For Procopius, Athalaric's inability to control both his drinking and sexual appetites marked him as flawed and, ultimately, unmanly.

Procopius closed his didactic tale by showing how Athalaric, having abandoned Amalasuintha and a "civilised" way of life, fell victim to this "debauched" Gothic lifestyle and died of a wasting disease brought on by the overindulgence in wine and the relentless pursuit of women.[83] Procopius appears to have wanted to highlight the folly of permitting mere boys to educate a future

---

81 Procopius, *Wars* 5.2.18–20.

82 Procopius, *Wars* 5.2.19. Cassiodorus hints about Athalaric's alcoholism in the *Variae*, see Barnish, introduction to *Variae*, 16. Procopius revealed that an addiction "to the disease of drunkenness" (μέθης νόσῳ) was particularly prevalent among barbarian peoples (*Wars* 4.4.29, 6.1.28, 7.27.5–6). This point is illustrated when Procopius praised the Herul Pharas for his energetic and serious nature, but noted sarcastically: "For a Herulian not to give himself over to treachery and drunkenness, but to strive after uprightness, is no easy matter and deserves abundant praise" (*Wars* 4.4.29). The susceptibility of barbarian armies to drunkenness served as a topos in classical literature. This drunkenness made "barbarians" unreliable soldiers. For instance, Polybius (*Histories* 11.3) partly blamed the Carthaginians' defeat in Spain on the Gauls' drunken state during the Battle of Metauras (207 BCE).

83 Procopius, *Wars* 5.4.4.

king about manly ἀρετή. Torn between two worlds, Athalaric
fell short of becoming either a Gothic warrior or a cultivated
Roman aristocrat. This account, however, is less a tale about the
"impossibility" of amalgamating "Roman" and "Gothic" ideals,
as has been suggested by one recent study,[84] but more a way of
comparing and contrasting the Romans' and the Goths' martial
and manly qualities. We shall see that each time a Goth made a
claim of masculine and martial superiority, shortly afterwards
Procopius "proved" the assertion patently false. One may observe
this paradigm in the case of Athalaric. It could hardly be clearer,
in Procopius' mind it was his "barbarian" and not his "Roman"
education that turned Athalaric into a leader with an unmanly
lack of self-control.

Amalasuintha: Manly Woman

Procopius repeated his gendered theme with a slight twist
in his depiction of Amalasuintha. In the *Wars* and the *Secret
History,* Procopius described Amalasuintha as "an aristocrat
and a queen."[85] He continued by illustrating her beauty and wit
(Procopius' praise may be a jibe at the Empress Theodora).
Procopius attributed many of Amalasuintha's virtues, however,
to her "extraordinary masculine bearing" (μεγαλοπρεπὲς καὶ
διαφερόντως ἀρρενωπόν).[86] By overcoming her enemies' attempts
to usurp her control over Athalaric, she earned Procopius' praise
for not acting "woman-like" and feebly giving way to her enemies.[87]
The historian claimed that the queen overcame the "limitations"
of her sex and took on the qualities of an ideal and manly leader.

---

84 Kaldellis, *Procopius of Caesarea*, 108.
85 For a similar gendered presentation of Amalasuintha in Cassiodorus'
    Variae, as well as a full discussion on the historical context of the gendered
    relationship between Amalasuintha and Theodahad, see La Rocca, *"Consors
    regni."*
86 Procopius, *Secret History* 16.1.
87 Procopius, *Wars* 5.2.21.

Similar to his praise of Theoderic's intelligence and manliness, Procopius proclaimed that she was wise, just, and "displayed very much a masculine nature" (τῆς δὲ φύσεως ἐς ἄγαν τὸ ἀρρενωπὸν ἐνδεικνυμένη).[88]

Because it seems to go against his assertions elsewhere that "masculine" women transgressed nature, Procopius' depiction of Amalasuintha as a "manly woman" needs some further explanation. The first five chapters of *Secret History*, in fact, traced the calamitous consequences of allowing women to take on men's dominant masculine roles in the political and the private arenas. A closer examination of Procopius' description of Amalasuintha's character reveals, however, that she fits into his and classical Graeco-Roman literary visions of femininity.[89] Despite her manly virtues, Amalasuintha's leadership depended on men's support, and Procopius portrayed her as a defenceless woman in need of Justinian's protection. When her political position became too tenuous she attempted to hand "over the power of the Goths and Italians to the Emperor Justinian, in order that she herself might be saved."[90] Although Amalasuintha ruled briefly within her own kingdom, she remained subordinate to Justinian and dependent upon men within the Gothic aristocracy for her survival.[91] Only under exceptional circumstances should women take on masculine roles; Procopius suggested that Amalasuintha faced such a situation at the outset of Athalaric's reign when she needed to take on an active role in order to protect her family from its enemies within Gothic Italy.[92]

---

88 Procopius, *Wars* 5.2.3 (my trans.).

89 A point made by Kaldellis, *Procopius of Caesarea*, 144–45.

90 Procopius, *Wars* 5.3.13.

91 Frankforter, "Amalasuntha, Procopius and a Woman's Place," 42.

92 Procopius, *Wars* 5.2.10–18. A similar instance (*Wars* 1.24.32–39) of this paradigm occurs when Theodora stiffened Justinian's resolve during an uprising known as the Nika revolt, convincing him not to flee Constantinople but to remain in the capital and fight. Garland (*Byzantine Empresses*, 32–33) regards this episode as an instance of Theodora taking on a masculine and

Procopius' portrait of Amalasuintha seems to have followed closely her actual characteristics and political manoeuvring. We know, for instance, that Amalasuintha had received an excellent classical education. Cassiodorus proclaimed, "In what tongue is her learning not proven? She is fluent in the splendour of Greek oratory; she shines in the glory of Roman eloquence."[93] Though she was politically more autonomous than Procopius allowed, Italian sources confirm the historian's assertion that Amalasuintha had largely supported Justinian's invasion of Vandalic North Africa.[94]

An examination of Procopius' depiction of the Amazons from book eight of the *Gothic Wars* adds further insight into his attitudes towards Amalasuintha's or any woman's ability to take on what he considered "masculine" responsibilities. He made it clear that the Amazons were not "a race of women endowed with the qualities of men," but the remnants of a people whose men had been destroyed in war. Fear of their people's annihilation, not a reversal of human nature, had forced these women to embrace "manly valour" (ἀρρενωπὸν), by arming themselves and performing "a deed of the utmost courage" (ἄριστα ἔργα ἀνδρεῖα).[95] According to Procopius, although women like the Amazons and Amalasuintha could put on temporarily a "masculine nature" and perform heroic deeds, it went against the natural order. Sheer necessity had compelled both the Amazons and Amalasuintha to take on masculine roles. In the case of the Amazons, the death of

martial role. I side with Averil Cameron (*Procopius and the Sixth Century*, 65), however, that the speech is better understood as an example of the traditional "protective wife" supporting and defending male family members. Cf. *Wars* 3.13.24 where Procopius praised Belisarius' wife Antonina—a woman he attacked ruthlessly in *Secret History*—for saving her husband's life and helping avert a disaster by safeguarding a warship's water supply.

93 Cassiodorus, *Variae* 10.1.6 (trans. Barnish): "qua enim lingua non probatur esse doctissima? Atticae facundiae claritate diserta est: Romani eloquii pompa resplendent."

94 Arnold, *Theoderic*, 300.

95 Procopius, *Wars* 8.3.7 (my trans.).

all of their male soldiers drove them to take up arms to face their enemies. Similarly, after Theoderic's death, a lack of suitable male heirs and the rather exceptional attempt to maintain the Amal line forced Amalasuintha to fill the void and take on a leading role in protecting her son and the Italian people from the barbarous elements in the Gothic leadership. For Procopius, this reversal of gender roles had its limits. While Amalasuintha and the Amazons could for a time display manly valour and emulate the excellence of men, without the support of real men they all were fated to die young.

This reliance on traditional Greek literary conceptions of "manly women" helps to explain why Procopius depicted Amalasuintha's taking on a masculine role positively, whilst he attacked Theodora and Antonina in *Secret History* for doing the same thing by stepping outside their gender constraints.[96] It seems likely that, in Procopius' mind, as a "barbarian" Amalasuintha could more easily break established gender roles. Indeed, in the classical tradition "manly women" were largely a foreign phenomenon. In addition, manly women ruled typically in places where men were unmanly.[97] One may presume then that Procopius' depiction of Amalasuintha was based on these traditional precedents, and as such, Procopius used her manliness as a means to, on the one hand, praise the Gothic queen and, on the other, to comment on the character defects of her male rivals to the Gothic throne and, in particular, her royal colleague after Athalaric's death, the Gothic king Theodahad (r. 534–36).

---

96 Cameron (*Procopius and the Sixth Century*, 199–200) censures Procopius for this seeming inconsistency.

97 Harrell, "Marvellous *Andreia*," 83.

Theodahad: Unmanly Man

After Athalaric's death, political necessity had pushed Amalasuintha to name her cousin Theodahad co-ruler.[98] Playing the gender card, Jordanes posited that fearing that "she might be despised by the Goths on account of the weakness of her sex," Amalasuintha had reluctantly named Theodahad as her co-ruler.[99] In Procopius' truncated version of the co-regency,[100] Amalasuintha's demise was not related to her gender, but was due primarily to the fact that she had underestimated her cousin's resentment concerning an earlier reprimand by the queen that had forced Theodahad to return lands that he had confiscated from the Italian nobility. Simplifying what was probably a drawn out affair, Procopius explained that Theodahad had imprisoned the queen and then, following the advice of the "martial" Gothic faction seeking revenge for earlier "wrongs," had her strangled at his private fortress on Lake Bolsena in Tuscany on or around 30 April 535.[101] This move, which provided Justinian with a

---

98 As Vitiello points out (*Theodahad*, 61), as a legitimate Amal heir Theodahad represented the best available choice "to save the kingdom and maintain power." Amalasuintha may have hoped to flee to the East once Theodahad was secure on the throne.

99 Jordanes, *Getica* 306: "Tum mater, ne pro sexus sui fragilitate a Gothis sperneretur, secum deliberans, Theudahathum consobrinum suum germanitatis gratia arcessitum a Tuscia, ubi privatam vitam degens in laribus propriis erat, in regno locavit."

100 Vitiello (*Theodahad*, 95–98) relates the fuzzy period of the co-regency.

101 Following Justinianic propaganda in support of the reconquest, Jordanes (*Getica* 306) claimed that Theodahad's murder of Amalasuintha had broken this bond between Roman and Goth.

convenient excuse to invade Italy, upset many Italo-Romans and Goths.[102]

Though the modern political scientist might see Theodahad's manoeuvring as the actions of a prudent and astute politician, Procopius depicted these deeds as evidence of Theodahad's unstable and unmanly nature. Procopius used his rather banal characterisation of Theodahad as another example of men destroying their ἀρετή, by failing to balance study and military training:

> There was among the Goths one Theodahad by name, son of Amalafrida, the sister of Theoderic, a man already of mature years, versed in the Latin literature and the teachings of Plato, but without any experience whatever in war and taking no part in active life [δραστηρίου], and yet extraordinarily devoted to the pursuit of money [φιλοχρηματίαν]. This Theodahad had gained possession of most of the lands in Tuscany, and he was eager by violent methods to wrest the remainder from their owners.[103]

Procopius did not necessarily criticise Theodahad for his love of learning, but primarily for his failure either to emulate the virtues he had learned in writers such as Plato, or to balance his

---

102 Procopius, *Wars* 5.4.28. In *Secret History* 16.1–5, Procopius provided a different version, suggesting plausibly that Theodora was behind Amalasuintha's death. Theodahad therefore was attempting to ingratiate himself to the Eastern regime. Cassiodorus (*Variae* 10.20–21) adds credence to Procopius' claim.

103 Procopius, *Wars* 5.3.1.

zeal for literature with a zest for the military life.[104] Theodahad, in fact, represented the antithesis of the ideal ruler praised by Plato, who typically rejected φιλοχρηματία and safeguarded his subjects' property.[105] Theodahad, then, represents an anti-Theoderic.[106] It is important to point out, however, that Procopius did not necessarily see the Gothic king's hunger for land grabs as a barbarian trait. In *Secret History*, Procopius condemned Belisarius for similar "crimes" in Italy. Procopius saw both instances as examples of unmanly behaviour.[107]

Procopius did not necessarily fault Theodahad for his attempt to become a Romanised Goth; Procopius, who claimed Theodahad was by "nature unmanly" (φύσει ἄνανδρος), criticised the Gothic king for allowing his love of learning to thwart his fighting spirit.[108] When the Gothic king faced the prospect of confronting Justinian's invading forces, Procopius described how Theodahad's lack of a "firm mind," combined with his fear of war, caused Theodahad to enter into a state that Procopius described as "the antithesis of boldness."[109]

Behind much of this rhetoric is the ancient idea linking indecision and a fickle mind to unmanliness and vice. Procopius

104 Kaldellis (*Procopius of Caesarea*, 110) contends that Procopius presented Theodahad as a failed "philosopher king," proposing that this analogy reveals the influence of Plato's *Republic* on Procopius' perceptions of ideal and non-ideal kingship.

105 Plato, *Republic* 391C.

106 Despite its rhetorical aspects, Procopius' presentation of Theodahad as a greedy, Plato-loving, non-martial Gothic *rex* is corroborated by Cassiodorus. For his lack of military experience, see Cassiodorus, *Variae* 10.31; his education, Cassiodorus, *Variae* 10.3, 11.13.4; his greed for other people's lands, Cassiodorus, *Variae* 8.28, 10.3.

107 Procopius, *Secret History* 5.4–7.

108 Procopius, *Wars* 5.9.1.

109 Procopius, *Wars* 5.7.11. I have changed the translator Dewing's "opposite extreme of unspeakable boldness" for ἀντικαθίστη θράσος to "the antithesis of boldness."

demonstrated that Theodahad's inability to be "steadfast," display a "fighting spirit," to live an "active" life (δραστήριος), or to observe "justice" exposed him as "unmanly." Using Theodahad as an example of an "unmanly" leader allowed Procopius to lay bare the difficulties and the perils of blending the "manliness" of a warrior-king with the finer refinements of Roman civilisation.[110] Such a view of the Gothic *rex*—though exaggerated—appears reflective of Theodahad's actual personality. Cassiodorus corroborates Procopius' vision of Theodahad as an educated Goth who had avoided what both modern and ancient historians consider a mandatory Gothic military education.[111]

According to Procopius, kind yet "soft or effeminate" rulers were often too weak to face the rigours of war. This softness, however, was not always due to one's civilised *Romanitas*. He described the Vandalic king Hilderich (r. 523–30), as "easily approachable" and "altogether gentle" towards Christians and all of his subjects. However, when faced with battle, his "softness in war" (πόλεμον μαλθακός) forced Hilderich to rely on his nephew Homer, the "Achilles of the Vandals," to fight his battles. It is also important to mention that Procopius frequently praised the manliness and fighting abilities of Roman generals like Justinian's cousin the *magister militum* Germanus, an *ex consule* and *patricus*, who would have surely received both training in military skills and a formal education in letters.[112] So too, as we will see below, does Procopius frequently praise other generals, Roman and barbarian, for displaying martial qualities based upon their civilised *Romanitas*. Thus, I reject current thinking, which postulates that Procopius saw Theodahad's indecision, failure to grasp

---

110 Procopius, *Wars* 3.9.1.

111 Vitiello (*Theodahad*, 27–29) suggests that perhaps some physical impairment had prevented Theodahad from the "prerequisite" Gothic military education. This goes too far, it seems more plausible that, as their hold on Italy seemed assured, some Gothic elites would willingly abstain from the "prerequisite" military training.

112 Procopius, *Wars* 7.40.9. Cf. Corippus, *Iohannis* 3.195–217.

philosophy, and obsessive materialism as necessarily "barbarian" traits, but more as tell-tale markers of his unmanly nature and a trait that could afflict equally Romans and non-Romans.[113]

With Theodahad's "unmanly" reign, the "martial" Gothic faction's accusation that a Roman education made a leader unmanly seemed to come true.[114] Yet, like many themes in the *Wars*, the answer may not be so straightforward. Theodahad's inability to adhere to the virtues found in the literature he read was not necessarily a natural result of his "barbarian" nature.[115] As we observed in the cases of Amalasuintha and the Gothic tutors, Procopius knew of "barbarians" who could learn the finer nuances of a Roman literary education. Procopius, moreover, had read widely, drawing material from a number of earlier authors. Certainly, the classical Greek and Roman literature that Procopius was familiar with provided examples of barbarians who had mastered a Hellenistic education.[116] It is also essential to point out once again that the martial faction had supported Theodahad's overthrow of Amalasuintha. Procopius, who exhibited a sense of humour in *Wars*, probably would have expected his educated readers to appreciate this quirk of fate. I suggest, then, that Procopius' portrait of Theodahad represented only the opening salvo in his exploration on the similarities and the differences

---

113 E.g., Halsall, "Funny Foreigners," 106; La Rocca, "*Consors regni,*" 140.

114 Vitiello, *Theodahad*, 51.

115 As Vitiello, points out, Theodahad would have read Plato in a Latin translation. He also theorises that Theodahad potentially had an "intellectual" relationship with Boethius, see Vitiello, *Theodahad*, 55–56.

116 See, e.g., Julian's description (*Mispogon* 351A–351C) of his "barbarian" tutor Mardonius, who the emperor credited both for his early love of classical literature and his manly deportment. The second-century writer, Lucian (*The Skythian*, 1.3, trans. Kilburn), too made it clear that he knew "Celts and Scythians," who despite their barbarian births "could become indistinguishable from Athenians" through their *paideia*. Procopius' familiarity with, and grasp of, classical literature is discussed in Greatrex, "Classical Past."

between Gothic and Roman notions of virtue and manly courage. The remainder of his account of the Italian campaigns tells the tale of Gothic kings who, on paper at least, represented the martial and manly archetype of the barbarian warrior-king espoused in these early rhetorical set pieces. It is to these "martial" Gothic leaders that we now turn.

Vitigis and Belisarius: The Fine Line between Manliness and Unmanliness

Exasperated with Theodahad's disastrous and unmanly leadership, the Goths replaced him with the celebrated warrior Vitigis (r. 536–40).[117] Procopius explained that the new king faced a difficult political situation. An ongoing conflict with the Franks in the north, coupled with Belisarius' invasion in the south, meant that Vitigis needed to cope with the dangerous prospect of a two-front war (a peril that Procopius knew that the Byzantines would soon face themselves). Having replaced the inactive and unmanly Theodahad, Vitigis emphasised in a speech to his troops that his hesitancy to confront straightaway the Byzantine forces stemmed from tactical necessity rather than any effeminate fear of war:

> The success of the greatest enterprises, fellow soldiers, generally depends, not upon hasty action at critical moments, but upon careful planning [...] For the title of the coward [δειλίας], fittingly applied, has saved many, while the reputation for bravery [ἀνδρείας] which some men have gained at the wrong time, has afterward led them to defeat [...] For a man's worth [ἀνδρός ἀρετὴν] is revealed

117 Procopius, *Wars* 5.11.5. Vitigis had earned his military reputation with an important victory over a combined Gepid and Herul army in 530. The Goths murdered Theodahad in December 536 shortly after Vitigis' coup. For an account of these events, see Wolfram, *History of the Goths*, 340–43.

by his deeds, not at their commencement, but at their end.[118]

Other scholars have noted the importance of this particular speech for understanding Procopius' account of Vitigis' reign and the *Gothic Wars'* main themes. Similar to many of *Wars'* set-speeches, this outwardly innocuous address allowed Procopius to foreshadow future events.[119] The speech contains two important Procopian themes in the *Gothic Wars* concerning masculine ideology and good leadership. First, an ideal leader needed to see the larger picture, and base his military decisions, not to achieve personal glory, but on what would, in the long-term, benefit his soldiers and his cause. A man needed to remain steadfast— even if others labelled his strategy cowardly or effeminate. On numerous occasions in the *Wars* when leaders responded to attacks on their manliness with reckless displays of courage, disaster soon followed.[120] Second, like many ancient intellectuals,

118 Procopius, *Wars* 5.11.12–22. This speech mirrors Vitigis' own propaganda, e.g., Cassiodorus *Varia* 10.31 (trans. Barnish): "I was chosen not in the privy chambers, but in the wild open field. I was not sought among the subtle debates of sycophants, but as the trumpets blared" (Non enim in cubilis angustiis, sed in campis late patentibus electum me esse noveritis, nec inter blandientium delicate colloquia, sed tubis concrepantibus sum quaesitus). La Rocca (*"Consors regni,"* 141) discusses the gendered aspects of this letter.

119 Kaldellis, *Procopius of Caesarea*, 32.

120 The following examples demonstrate this point. Procopius illustrated (*Wars* 1.18.19–26) how an accusation of "softness" drove Belisarius to abandon his prudence before the Battle of Callinicium in April of 531. Impassioned by their Lenten fast, the Christian soldiers felt that the eve of the holiday represented the opportune time to engage the Persian army. Belisarius attempted to forestall their ardour by pointing out that "a large number of you have come on foot and all of us are fasting." Instead of heeding Belisarius' advice, the soldiers and officers insulted Belisarius to his face by accusing him of "softness" ($\mu\alpha\lambda\theta\alpha\kappa\delta\nu$) that had destroyed their "fighting zeal" ($\pi\rho o\theta\upsilon\mu\dot{\iota}\alpha\varsigma$). Against his better judgment, Belisarius gave into their insults

Procopius commented frequently on the fine distinction between rashness and courage.[121] In classical Greek θράσος describes either recklessness or valour. Aristotle had considered ἀνδρεία as "the attributes of a man whose actions demonstrate a moderate negotiation between 'boldness' [θάρσος] and 'fear' [φόβος]." As Karen Bassi puts it, "the *andreios* man neither fears too much or too little."[122] A man's capacity to maintain this precarious balance depended largely upon his ability to suppress his natural urges to either launch a rash attack or turn tail in a cowardly retreat. These distinctions regularly separated the manly from the unmanly in the classical literary tradition. Procopius used the term in both senses.[123] On the one hand, desperate circumstances often drove men to take reckless yet ultimately courageous and manly actions; on the other hand, unthinking acts of rashness revealed weakness and unmanliness, and led regularly to men's downfall.[124] These concepts unquestionably represented a primary theme throughout the *Gothic Wars*, in which Procopius went to great

---

by reassuring his troops, "that now he was of good courage [θαρσεῖν] and would go against the enemy with a better hope." The Eastern Roman army went on to suffer a devastating defeat at the hands of the Persians. In another example from *Wars*, the Heruls launched an unjust and ultimately disastrous war against the Lombards, when their leader, Rodolphus, succumbed to his peoples' taunts that he was "effeminate and womanlike" (μαλθακόν τε καὶ γυναικώδη, *Wars* 6.14.11).

121 Some examples include, Procopius, *Wars* 5.20.8, 6.23.29–30. Cf. Thucydides, *Peloponnesian War* 2.40.3.

122 Aristotle, *Eudemian Ethics* 1228a26–30a37, 1230a26–33, quoted in Bassi, "Semantics of Manliness," 52–53.

123 For the influence of Aristotle on Procopius' writings, see Kaldellis, *Procopius of Caesarea*, 149, 212, 220. For the impact of Aristotle on late antique culture in general, see Wildberg, "Philosophy in the Age of Justinian," 324–28.

124 For a description of how desperation could evoke unprecedented deeds of manly courage, see Procopius, *Wars* 6.21.30–33, 8.35.21.

lengths to compare and contrast the leadership styles of Belisarius and Vitigis.[125]

An early example of these tests of our protagonists' manliness and courage came when Vitigis advanced on Rome with his revitalised army. Hoping to buy some time before reinforcements from the East arrived, Belisarius and his soldiers sought to stall the Gothic advance by making "a display of their own daring [θάρσους]."[126] Procopius use of θάρσος here signals to the reader that this first contest between the revitalised Goths and the Romans would represent a test of a less rational type of courage. Without a doubt, Belisarius acted somewhat out of character, and made the unusual decision for an early Byzantine general to fight as a common soldier.[127] Belisarius and his men made the perilous decision to meet a group of Goths in a face-to-face trial of their martial prowess. In fact, Belisarius' intellectual prowess, which represented one of his primary advantages over his "barbarian" opponents, played a minimal role in this fighting.[128] It was probably no coincidence that in a contest based on θάρσος, the fighting was on foot, brutal, and hand-to-hand. Procopius seemed to be of two minds about this choice of combat; he admired Belisarius' courage, but, in the historian's own words, "The cause of the

---

125 More than just literary tropes, Byzantine military manuals such as the late sixth-century *Strategikon* of Maurice repeat many of the same generalship mantras found in Procopius, suggesting that the historian's views reflected actual Byzantine military practices.

126 Procopius, *Wars* 5.17.18.

127 The late sixth-century military guidebook, Maurice's *Strategikon* 2.16, 7.1–15, trans. Dennis, advised against commanders fighting amongst the front ranks: "We would not allow the general to take part personally in raids or other reckless attacks. These should be entrusted to other competent officers. For if one of the subordinate officers blunders or fails, the situation may be quickly straightened out. But if the leader of the whole army fails, his fall can open the way to complete disaster."

128 On the importance of a general's intellect in determining the outcome of battles, see Maurice, *Strategikon* 2.1.

Romans was thrown into great danger, for the whole decision of the war rested with him."[129] Here the narrative takes a Homeric turn.[130] In Procopius' telling, any Goth with a claim to ἀρετή made a beeline towards Belisarius. As the focal point of the fighting and the narrative, Belisarius displayed all the martial skills typical of a Homeric hero; he slew enemies left and right. However, even the mightiest warrior at times needed assistance. Luckily for the general and for the Romans' cause, Belisarius' personal guards made a display of ἀρετὴν that, as Procopius somewhat hyperbolically described it, "had never been shown by any man in the world to this day." The "undermanned" Byzantines, according to Procopius, met the enemy on their own terms in basic hand-to-hand combat and showed that they were more than a match for the Goths' martial valour. In Homeric fashion, the historian praised the fighting prowess and heroic conduct of the Goths as well as the Romans.[131] Procopius discussed the loss of many notable fighters on each side. Yet, in the end, Belisarius and his men's superior ἀρετή won out, and the vanguard of "barbarians" fled back to their main army.[132] Belisarius and his men, however, were not yet quite out of danger because the Gothic cavalry remained unchecked. Here, in Procopius' mind, Belisarius made the more responsible decision; he fled back to the safety of Rome. Pursued closely by the enemy, Belisarius arrived at the gates of Rome only to find that the "Italians manning the gates of the city" thought that the general had died in battle. Accordingly, fearing a ruse, they refused the general and his men entry into the city. Only quick thinking on the part of Belisarius saved the day and,

129 Procopius, *Wars* 5.18.5.

130 Whately "Descriptions of Battle," 304.

131 Procopius made special mention (*Wars* 5.18.29–33) of the fighting prowess of Belisarius and a Gothic warrior, Visandus Vandalarius.

132 Procopius, *Wars* 5.18.16.

after one last dangerous skirmish, Belisarius and his men gained entrance into Rome.[133]

"Trapped" in the city of Rome, Belisarius and the Byzantines appeared to be at the mercy of the marauding Goths preparing to lay siege. Here, Procopius split the narrative's perspective three ways: Goth, Italian, and Byzantine. The Goths and the Italians saw the situation similarly—the Goths expected an easy victory, and the Italians dreaded what they saw as the inescapable storming of Rome and their inevitable punishment for their unfaithfulness to their "masters" the Goths.[134] On the other hand, Belisarius remained smugly confident. To build tension, Procopius took his time to explain Belisarius' optimism. In fact, everything seemed to point to an easy Gothic victory. Once again, however, not everything was quite as it appeared. Certainly, Procopius made it clear that the Romans could not trust their Italian "allies." Brimming with confidence, the Goths attempted to undermine the alliance and the confidence of the Italians guarding the Salarian Gate by belittling the manliness of their "allies" in Belisarius' army:

> He [Vacis] began to reproach the [inhabitants of Rome] Romans for their faithlessness to the Goths and upbraided them for the treason which he said they had committed against both their fatherland and themselves, for they had exchanged the power of the Goths for Greeks [Γότθων δυνάμεως Γραικοὺς] who were not able to defend them, although they had never before seen any men of the Greek race come to Italy except actors of tragedy and mimes and thieving sailors.[135]

---

133 Procopius later (*Wars* 5.27.25) described this skirmish as an Eastern Roman defeat.

134 Procopius, *Wars* 5.19.1.

135 Procopius, *Wars* 5.18.40–41. On this passage and the pejorative use of the term *Graikoi*, see Kaegi, "Procopius the Military Historian," 79–81.

Vacis' portrait of Belisarius and his men as "Greeks" reflected contemporary Gothic propaganda. This set-speech illustrates that perhaps one way that the Gothic leaders may have attempted to gain the Italian Romans' support in their war against the Byzantine Empire was by trying to sever the Western and Eastern Romans' sense of a shared identity and history. By calling Belisarius' heterogeneous army "Greeks," Vacis not only split the two sides, but also played upon the traditional Roman belief that Greek soldiers were soft, lazy, and reluctant to fight in "a real man's war."[136] Vacis' suggestion that Greek culture produced only actors and mimes aroused another Roman prejudice. For the Romans, the performing arts represented the dangers of civilised luxury. They considered actors, singers, and dancers as particularly effeminate and representative of a weak and unmanly culture.[137] Procopius' version of Vacis' speech implied, because of their warrior traditions, that it was natural for the Goths to presuppose that they were not only more valorous than the Byzantine soldiers, but also manlier. Such rhetoric had defined Theoderic's regime from its beginning.[138]

---

136 Williams, *Roman Homosexuality*, 62–70, Kuefler, *Manly Eunuch*, 47, discuss the Greeks' reputation in the Roman literary tradition for an unmanly love of luxury and the "soft" life. Near the close of the *Gothic Wars* (*Wars* 8.28.2), another Gothic commander provides us with a more accurate picture of Justinian's forces, describing Narses' army as a "heterogeneous horde of barbarians."

137 Williams, *Roman Homosexuality*, 135–39.

138 As Jonathan Arnold has observed (*Restoration of the Roman Empire*, 117), the Goths and Italians went to great lengths to paint themselves as "true" Romans, whilst depicting the Eastern Romans as unmanly Greeks. Arnold writes: "Goths and Gothicness represented martialism, the old Roman virtue of *virtus* (the very source of the term virtue), which meant 'manliness' or 'courage'. *Virtus* was an ideal that the Romans had seemingly lost, becoming overly effeminate (perhaps even overly Greek), yet which until recently had been most Roman indeed."

Though it is probable that Procopius made up the details in Vacis' speech, its inclusion at this stage of the narrative appears purposeful. As one recent paper has proposed, Procopius seemed to have meant for Vacis' address to be "ironic and incongruous, in that a barbarian is accusing the citizens of Rome of that stereotype of barbarism, unfaithfulness."[139] While this argument may be true, I suspect that Procopius' larger objective was to highlight the Goth's dismissive conviction that they were facing an unmanly threat from Belisarius and his men. The Goth's vision of the Italians as untrustworthy was largely accurate. In fact, in Procopius' telling, they were prone to switch sides and betray both the Goths and the Byzantines.[140] The statement that would soon be proven false was Vacis' contention that Belisarius and the Eastern Roman army would not be able to protect the Italians. Procopius likely sought to rebuff this misconception.

Without doubt, Procopius rejected the notion that the Byzantines lacked the courage or the manliness to defend Rome. In Procopius' mind, it was the Italians who were the "true" non-martial people unable to protect their native land. In fact, throughout the narrative the Goths and the Romans at least agreed on one point: the idea that the Italians were a soft and an unmanly people in need of protection.[141] As the situation in Rome deteriorated, Procopius noted that the Italians were completely unprepared for the rigours of a siege. Because the civilians and the Italian soldiers guarding the city were convinced that Vitigis' army would soon defeat Belisarius, fear took hold throughout the city. They railed against Belisarius and his men, questioning the general's decision to confront the Goths before reinforcements had arrived. The Italians also ridiculed Belisarius for his advice "to take courage [θαρσεῖν], and to look with contempt upon

---

139 Halsall, "Funny Foreigners," 110.
140 See, e.g., Procopius, *Wars* 7.4.16.
141 See, e.g., Procopius, *Wars* 3.3.10–13, 7.11.12–14.

the barbarians." So too did they scoff at the general's supreme confidence that he would easily conquer the Goths.[142]

In another set-speech, the Gothic ambassadors who met with Belisarius and the Roman senators shortly after this debate expressed Procopius' attitudes about the overconfident Goths and the meek Italians. Addressing Belisarius with a group of Roman senators looking on, the Gothic envoy, Albis, highlighted the two aspects of θάρσος. "Rashness [θάρσος] is different from courage [ἀνδρεία]," he proclaimed, "for rashness, when it takes possession of a man, brings him into danger with discredit, but bravery bestows upon him an adequate prize in a reputation for valour [ἀρετῆς]." The Gothic diplomat suggested mockingly that if Belisarius and his men had attacked the Goths outside the gates of Rome because of a belief in their ἀνδρεία, then by all means they should take the opportunity to "play the manly man" (ἀνδραγαθίζεσθαι) in battle against the Goths. However, if, as the Gothic envoy believed, the Romans had been temporarily possessed by "rashness" (θράσει) when they decided to make that attack, then the Goths would give them the opportunity to "repent [...] the reckless undertaking." The emissary concluded his speech with a final attempt to get the Byzantines to capitulate by requesting that Belisarius "not cause the sufferings of these Romans [Italians] to be prolonged any further, men whom Theoderic fostered in a life not only of soft luxury [βίῳ τρυφερῷ] but also of freedom, and cease your resistance to him [Vitigis] who is master both of the Goths and the Italians."[143]

Belisarius scorned the notion that the city of Rome belonged to anyone but its rightful owners, the Romans. Procopius showed Belisarius asserting that he was made of sterner stuff than the feeble Italians were, retorting in heroic language, "As long as Belisarius lives, it is impossible to relinquish the city."[144]

142 Procopius, *Wars* 5.18.4.
143 Procopius, *Wars* 5.20.9–12. I have changed Dewing's "play the man" for ἀνδραγαθίζεσθαι to "play the manly man."
144 Procopius, *Wars* 5.20.18.

According to Procopius, when the envoys returned to camp, Vitigis asked his representatives what sort of man they faced in Belisarius. The envoys replied that the Goths would never be able to make Belisarius relinquish the city by frightening him. With the description above, we can see how Procopius used seemingly trite rhetorical set battle pieces, repetitive vocabulary, and bombastic set speeches to set up his reader for the combat and the "lessons" to come. The Goths who had met with Belisarius and his men had only just realised what Procopius and his readers already knew, the fact that Belisarius and his men were not the unmanly or "rash" men the martial Goths had been expecting to rout easily in battle. Once again, we find that the Gothic version of the situation given in a dramatic set-speech represented the polar opposite of the reality. In fact, we are soon to learn that the Goths represent the rash side, and that Belisarius was motivated not by θάρσος, but by a justified belief in his side's superior ἀνδρεία.

As the battle for Rome opened in earnest, the more intellectual and strategic Belisarius came to the fore. When the general noticed the approaching Goths' siege engines, he chuckled to himself and restrained his men from attacking until he gave the order. The Italians, still expecting the worst, accused Belisarius of feigned bravery and of purposefully avoiding battle. Belisarius knew, however, that his defensive position had given his archers a significant advantage over the Goths lumbering along with their siege engines. When Belisarius finally gave the go ahead to fire, his bowman decimated the Goths.[145] As Procopius explained, the calculating Belisarius had exploited the "simplicity of the barbarians."[146] Having lost previously in brutal hand-to-hand warfare, the Goths proved even less of a match for the Romans' material, tactical, and strategic superiority. After Procopius related often-gruesome scenes of battle, Belisarius and his men

---

145 Whately, *Battles and Generals*, 181–87, discusses Procopius' emphasis on the prowess of Belisarius' archers and the advantage that it gave to the Byzantines during the Italian campaign.

146 Procopius, *Wars* 5.27.27.

emerged triumphant. Procopius painted a vivid picture of the shift in morale. Ebullient in victory, the Byzantines sang the praises of Belisarius and collected their spoils, while the humiliated Goths "cared for their wounded and bewailed their dead."

Procopius described how this setback transformed Vitigis into an impetuous and, ultimately, an unmanly man. Made increasingly desperate by his numerous setbacks at the hands of Belisarius' forces during his siege of Rome, Vitigis launched a hopeless attack against the Byzantine army.[147] The Gothic king sent five hundred equestrians against the Byzantine commander Bessas' one thousand cavalry. It was a dreadful decision. Procopius explained that Vitigis had failed to "account for the difference between the two armies in point of equipment of arms and of practice of warlike deeds."[148] The battle ended in a rout, with only a few soldiers returning to the Gothic camp. Vitigis chastised the survivors, "insisting that cowardice [τῷ ἀνάνδρῳ] had caused their defeat." Three days later, continuing to fume irrationally, Vitigis selected another five hundred men and "bade them to make a display of valorous [ἀρετῆς] deeds against the enemy." The astute reader harks back to Vitigis' speech at the opening of his reign preaching the necessity of preparation before battle and the benefits of seemingly unmanly retreats. Inevitably, for Procopius, the Romans' numerical and tactical superiority allowed them to rout the imprudent enemy "without any trouble." While the Goths lamented that these defeats proved that "fortune stood against them," Belisarius provided a more mundane explanation for the Byzantines' victories. He advised that the Romans' and their allies, the Huns', use of mounted bowman had provided their crucial edge over the Goths, who lacked experience in this

---

147 Probably in an effort to create a more vivid didactic narrative, Procopius ignored several Gothic victories during the year-long siege that began in February 537. Wolfram (*History of the Goths*, 344–45) discusses these omissions.

148 Procopius, *Wars* 5.27.15.

type of warfare.[149] The reader knows that Procopius throughout his narrative has provided a third reason. He had shown that the Goths had underestimated both the martial capabilities and the manly virtues of their foes, the Byzantines.

After relating Vitigis' increasingly irrational behaviour, Procopius immediately exposed how the Byzantines' growing confidence made them susceptible to hubris. On the cusp of breaking the Goths' fighting spirit, Belisarius once again succumbed to his soldiers' pressuring.[150] Elated with their numerous triumphs over the Goths, the Roman army coaxed a reluctant Belisarius "to risk a decisive battle with his whole army." Belisarius replied that his hesitance to fight a decisive battle resulted, not because he detected any "softness" (μαλακίαν) in his men, nor because he "was terrified at the strength of the enemy" (τῶν πολεμίων κατορρωδήσας τὴν δύναμιν), but because his current strategy of skirmishing was going so well.[151] Belisarius opined, "When one's present affairs are going to one's satisfaction, it is inexpedient to change to another course of action." However, after witnessing his men's enthusiasm, Belisarius relented:

> Since I see that you are eager for this danger, I am filled with confidence and will never oppose your ardour [ὁρμῇ] [...] I see that the present moment is also in our favour, for it will, in all probability, make it easier for us to gain mastery over the enemy, because their spirit has been enslaved by what has gone before. For when men have often met with misfortune, their hearts are no longer

149 Procopius, *Wars* 5.27.15–29.

150 As Geoffrey Greatrex explains (*Rome and Persia at War*, 179–80, n. 30), common tradition allowed Roman generals to solicit and accept advice from their commanders.

151 Belisarius avoided major engagements with the Gothic army. Of course, Narses ultimately defeated the Goths by seeking just such a confrontation.

wont to thrill even slightly with manly valour
[ἀνδραγαθίζεσθαι].[152]

The Romans went on to suffer a defeat on the Plain of Nero. Belisarius' lapse of judgment helped end any hopes for a quick victory over the Goths, indicating that even at this early stage of his history Procopius detected some flaws in Belisarius' ability to lead men.[153] An ideal general did not care what his men thought of him, but rather based his tactics purely on what advantages might be gained for his forces and the Byzantine Empire.[154]

Like his earlier lapse against the Persians, Belisarius' failure, however, proved to be temporary. Vitigis failed to follow up his victory. Unable to penetrate Rome's defences, and facing the threat of a Byzantine attack on the Gothic royal city of Ravenna, the Gothic king abandoned the siege in March 538. He retreated with his army first to Ariminum, and then to Ravenna—where he would spend the next two years facing an increasingly deteriorating situation. Vitigis failed in his attempt to secure allies against the Byzantines. His efforts to relieve his forces besieged in Auximum and in Faesulae came to naught as well.[155] Finally, in late

152 Procopius, *Wars* 5.28.6–14.

153 Most scholars agree with Cameron's contention (*Procopius and the Sixth Century*, 8, 15, 52–54) that as the Italian campaign dragged on, Procopius developed an increasingly negative attitude towards Belisarius. Kaldellis posits, however, that an underlying negativity towards Belisarius is found throughout the *Wars*, see Kaldellis, "Procopius' *Persian War*," 255–56. As Conor Whately has suggested to me (pers. comm.) it seems Procopius' opinion of the general shifts in terms of his military successes or failures.

154 Procopius' portrait of Belisarius as a man easily influenced by others is similar to his negative portrait of the general in *Secret History*. In this work, Procopius censured Belisarius for allowing his wife Antonina to take on the masculine role in their relationship, believing that by draining his *andreia*, she had inhibited Belisarius' effectiveness as a general. Full discussion in Stewart, "*Andreios* Eunuch-Commander Narses," 15–17.

155 Procopius, *Wars* 6.24.1–16, 6.26.2–13.

539, Belisarius and his army arrived at the gates of Ravenna. The besieger became the besieged.

Procopius revealed how these events gradually transformed Vitigis from an esteemed soldier at the outset of his reign into a leader reviled by his former supporters for his "unmanly" (ἀνάνδρως) leadership and "ill fortune" (ἀτυχῶς) by its end.[156] Vitigis' response to setbacks was markedly different from Belisarius' usual quick recoveries from his mistakes or military setbacks. Fearing that their opponents might think the Goths had succumbed to "indolence" (ῥαθυμία),[157] Vitigis called on the Goths starving in Auximum and Faesulae "to endure manfully" (φέρειν ἀνδρείως).[158] Yet, when the Gothic leader faced his own peril, he acted in a decidedly unmanly manner. Instead of resisting Belisarius' siege, Vitigis desperately sought a way out of his predicament by seeking a truce with the Byzantines.[159] Finally, after a series of failed negotiations between the two warring parties, Belisarius managed to capture Vitigis and most of his entourage by feigning to accept the Gothic nobles' offer to declare him Western emperor.[160]

Procopius concluded book six with a rather melancholy description of the vanquished Gothic forces marching downtrodden through the streets of Ravenna in May of 540.[161]

156 Procopius, *Wars* 6.30.5.

157 Procopius, *Wars* 6.26.8 (trans. Kaldellis).

158 Procopius, *Wars* 6.26.13.

159 Procopius, *Wars* 6.28.27, 6.29.2. Procopius believed that a man could not act courageously or manly when he was starving. See, e.g., *Wars* 8.23.15–16. Cf. Maurice, *Strategikon* 8.2.28: "The general achieves the most who tries to destroy the enemy's army more by hunger than by force of arms."

160 Procopius, *Wars* 6.29.18.

161 The pessimistic tone of this passage stands in stark contrast from the triumphant rhetoric of the earlier material on the first siege of Rome. Procopius here openly questioned the role that ἀρετή played in determining battles, which he attributed to the whims of "some divine power" (δαιμόνιον). Kaldellis (*Procopius of Caesarea*, 196) argues that this sentiment reflected

Procopius indicated the Gothic soldiers' humiliation was made complete when their wives—seeing the small numbers and the ordinary stature[162] of the Byzantine soldiers who had captured the city—belittled their husbands for their "unmanliness" (τὴν ἀνανδρίαν), and spat in their faces.[163] The fact that Vitigis allowed himself and his army to be captured by the Romans seemed a particularly cowardly and unmanly way for a Gothic leader to meet his end. Before his victory over the Byzantines on the Plain of Nero, Vitigis had exclaimed that "noble men [ἄνδρες γενναῖοι] consider that there is only one misfortune (in battle)— to survive defeat at the hands of the enemy."[164] Vitigis even said that Theodahad had received a "blessed" (ὄλβιον) end to his life because "he was privileged to lose both his sovereignty and his life at the hands of his own men."[165] Procopius probably used these earlier comments by Vitigis as a means of highlighting the

Procopius' "true" feelings concerning the supremacy of *tyche* over men's ἀρετή. Procopius appears to have inserted this passage to create a bridge between the shifting tones of books six and seven. In fact, it appears closely related to the ideas espoused by Totila (*Wars* 7.21.5–7) that Procopius ultimately proves mistaken. Treadgold (*Early Byzantine Historians*, 204–05) postulates that in 545, with the war dragging on, Procopius altered the end of book six by adding more pessimistic material, and in turn took material from book six to open book seven. Belisarius' triumphal entry into Constantinople in 540 and Procopius' subsequent encomium appears misplaced at the opening of book seven, and was probably meant to be the original finishing point for book six, and in fact the entire account.

162 It is worth emphasising that the Byzantine army had many Goths and other "barbarian" peoples fighting in it, so this emphasis on the size discrepancy of the men in the two armies seems to be more of a rhetorical flourish by Procopius to promote his views that the Goths viewed the Byzantines as unmanly.

163 Procopius, *Wars* 6.29.32–34. I changed the translator Dewing's "cowardice" for ἀνανδρίαν to "unmanliness."

164 Procopius, *Wars* 5.29.9.

165 Procopius, *Wars* 5.29.6.

ignominy of his end.[166] Vitigis suffered the dual disgrace of losing both his sovereignty and freedom at the hands of his enemies; even worse, he fled into captivity without even making a final stand. Vitigis' assertion at the outset of his reign that a man's worth was revealed by his deeds, not at their beginning, but at their end, had come back to haunt the Gothic king. The Goths' apparent martial and "manly" supremacy had proven inferior to the tactical, the material, and the martial manliness of the Byzantine soldiers.

Totila: Theoderic Reborn or Barbarian Belisarius?

Belisarius' victory over Vitigis appears to have represented the original terminus for the *Gothic Wars*.[167] The narrative drives to what looks like a logical climax, with Vitigis' defeat and Belisarius' triumphal return to Constantinople. The theme of a "manly" and "heroic" Roman army defeating a worthy Gothic foe would have made a suitable ending to *Wars*. Events on the ground seemed to have interfered with Procopius' well laid out didactic tale. As discussed earlier, the year 540 marked a turning point in Justinian's reconquest of Italy. The naming of Totila as king revitalised the Gothic army's fighting spirit and led to the near defeat of the Byzantines. Procopius now had to deal with a resurgent Goth nation and the recall of his idol, Belisarius. How did the historian explain such a reversal of fortune? Without a doubt, the mercurial nature of *tyche* and the power of God to determine events play a greater role in books seven and eight than they did in books five and six.[168] Procopius, however, once again blamed Roman failure primarily in the familiar moralising terms. Procopius did not attribute the Roman defeats after 540 on the whims of fate or a deficiency of courage, nor did he suggest that they resulted

166 This section also foreshadows both Totila's shameful death and Teïas' heroic death at the close of the *Gothic Wars*.

167 Treadgold, *Early Byzantine Historians*, 204.

168 Discussed in Kaldellis, *Procopius of Caesarea*, 198–204.

from strategic failures. Instead, he treated these losses as arising from moral failures on the part of the Byzantine military high command and the imperial administration.[169] We should take Procopius at his word when he explained that the "insatiable" greed of certain members of the Byzantine high command in Italy and within the Byzantine treasury[170]—not the caprice of fortune—represented the primary reason "the entire fabric of Roman power was utterly destroyed in a short space of time."[171] Once more, in Procopius' mind, the "rightful" rulers of Italy would be the side that juxtaposed martial capabilities with a policy of restraint and justice towards the Italians. The tide of battle shifts in the Goths' favour as the Byzantine generals and administration succumbed to jealousy, greed, bickering, and injustice.[172]

Totila is the undisputed hero of book seven.[173] As Belisarius and the Byzantines' fortunes decline, Totila and the Goths' fortunes improve. Totila, in this part of the *Gothic Wars*,

169 Procopius (e.g., *Wars* 7.12.1–11) also blames the seeming disinterest of Justinian in the Italian campaign and a failure to pay Belisarius' troops as a reason for the Goths' resurgence. Modern scholarly consensus contends that for Justinian, the war in Italy was as minor theatre of war in comparison to Thrace, North Africa, and the troublesome eastern boundary with Persia. For a discussion of this point, see Whately "Descriptions of Battle," 259.

170 Procopius declared (*Wars* 7.1.33) that the Byzantine treasury's refusal to pay the soldiers in Italy was a primary reason for a decline in the Byzantine army's fighting prowess, not a lack of courage or the superior martial virtues or tactics of Totila and his men.

171 Procopius, *Wars* 7.1.24. I thus reject Kaldellis' claim (*Procopius of Caesarea*, 198–200) that, in this section, the historian sought to reject the idea that *Wars* were won, not by justice or soldiers courage, but primarily by the whims of *tyche*.

172 See, e.g., Procopius, *Wars* 7.3.15–22.

173 Procopius' admiration for Totila is commonly seen as genuine. See, e.g., Cameron, *Procopius and the Sixth Century*, 190, 197; Moorhead, "Totila"; Kaldellis, *Procopius of Caesarea*, 198. Cf., however, Pazdernik, "Belisarius' Second Occupation of Rome."

encapsulates nearly all of the leadership qualities and virtues found in Procopius' encomium on Belisarius at the opening of book seven.[174] Procopius had much to say in this section about Totila's mastery of copious political and martial virtues. Like many of his royal predecessors, Totila was formidable in battle.[175] Similar to Theoderic, Totila was also energetic and wise. Totila, however, exhibited some "civilised" qualities not typical in a barbarian king—even Theoderic. Procopius at various times in the narrative described Totila as "restrained" (σωφροσύνη), "humane" (φιλανθρωπίαν), "gentle" (πρᾷόν), and "just" (δίκαιος).

Totila also gave the Byzantines respect. In Procopius' version of his first address to his downtrodden men, though not overawed, Totila recognised that the Goths faced a "contest" (τὸν ἀγῶνα) for their very existence against a formidable and worthy Byzantine opponent. This speech contains little of the bravado and none of the condescending gendered rhetoric found in earlier Gothic warriors' set speeches denigrating the manliness and courage of his foes. Totila explained to his men, that in order to defeat the Byzantines, the Goths would have to match their "usual spirit of manly courage" (ἀνδραγαθίζεσθα) in battle with deeds of justice and acts of humane self-restraint in their relations with the Italians. He attributed earlier Gothic defeats against the Byzantines to his predecessors' lack of concern for justice, which caused God to turn against them.[176] He too made an effort to treat his captured

---

174 As argued by Kaldellis, *Procopius of Caesarea*, 194. Amongst many other virtues, the historian described (*Wars* 7.1.1–21) Belisarius as "gentle" (πρᾷόν), "generous" (φιλοδωρότατος), protective of civilians' land, sexually "restrained" (σωφροσύνης), "courageous" (εὔψυχος), "daring" (εὐτολμοτατος), and "steadfast" (ἀσφαλεῖ) in war, without being rash.

175 For the fear Totila's fighting prowess induced in the Eastern Roman soldiers, see Procopius, *Wars* 7.6.19. For the Romans' lack of spirit and courage after a long line of defeats at the hands of Totila and his men, see Belisarius' letter (*Wars* 7.12.3–10) to Justinian begging the emperor for reinforcements, money, and supplies.

176 Procopius, *Wars* 7.4.10–18.

foes well, a shrewd policy that Procopius showed led many Byzantine soldiers to desert to the Gothic side.[177]

This strategy proved successful. The bulk of the first half of book seven focuses on the Goths' gradual retaking of Italy. Instead of providing a detailed account of the various battles and sieges that decimated Italy over the next five years, Procopius concentrated instead on Totila's philanthropy and deep regard for justice. Two examples should serve to demonstrate this emphasis. Shortly after Totila's first capture of Rome in 546, Procopius reported how Totila felt obligated to protect Rome's aristocratic women from acts of revenge and from sexual violence:

> Now the Goths, on their part, were eager to put Rusticiana to death, bringing against her the charge that after bribing the commanders of the Roman army, she had destroyed the statues of Theoderic, her motive in so doing having been to avenge the murder not only of her father Symmachus, but also of her husband Boethius. But Totila would not permit her to suffer any harm, but he guarded both her and all the Roman women safe from insult, although the Goths were extremely eager to have intercourse [κοίτην] with them. Consequently, not one of them had the ill fortune to suffer personal insult, whether married, unwed, or widow, and Totila won great renown for moderation [σωφροσύνη] from this course.[178]

As a modern scholar notes, Totila's reputation for σωφροσύνη "is scarcely a virtue one would associate with a barbarian."[179] Totila's civilised σωφροσύνη definitely distinguishes him from typical barbarian leaders, and even the manly and wise Theoderic. It

177 E.g., Procopius, *Wars* 7.12.9, 7.16.19.
178 Procopius, *Wars* 7.20.29–31.
179 Moorhead, "Totila," 382.

seems more than coincidental that the women that Procopius chose to describe Totila protecting were none other than Boethius' wife and Symmachus' daughters—the two men that the historian had revealed earlier had been "unjustly" executed by Theoderic. Procopius would surely have expected his readers to remember these earlier "crimes." Totila, as described by Procopius, thus represents a better version of Theoderic. Procopius once more deftly combined historical events with his own moralising themes to produce an edifying tale that interlocks each of his biographies of the Gothic royalty.[180]

We uncover further evidence that Procopius sought to differentiate Totila from a typical rough-hewn "Gothic" king or military man in another anecdote from the same period. An unnamed Italian accused one of Totila's bodyguards of violating his virgin daughter; the Gothic king imprisoned the soldier. This prompt punishment, in the words of Procopius, alarmed "the most notable men among the barbarians" (τῶν Βαρβάρων οἱ δοκιμώτατοι). They requested that Totila release the soldier and dismiss the charges, since the assailant was an "active" (δραστήριος) man and "a capable warrior" (ἀγαθος τὰ πολέμια). Totila, however, "gently and with no excitement" (πράως τε καὶ ταραχῇ οὐδεμιᾷ) refused, declaring that what they "called kindness [φιλανθρωπίαν] in reality was lawlessness [παρανομίαν]." The Gothic king proclaimed that "the act of committing a sin and that of preventing the punishment of those who have committed sin, are in my judgment on the same plane." The nobles relented and, not long afterwards, Totila executed the Goth.[181] Procopius had no qualms in presenting Totila as a man willing to follow justice and "lawful order" over the concerns of powerful members of the

---

180 The sixth-century *Liber Pontificalis* (61.7) related Totila's reputation for restraint in protecting the Italo-Romans from his army's retribution when he captured Rome for the third time in 549. Cf., however, the less positive views of Totila found in Marcellinus, *Chron.* s.a. 545; Jordanes, *Romana* 382; Gregory the Great, *Dialogues* 2.14–15, 3.12. 13.

181 Procopius, *Wars* 7.8.12–25.

Gothic hierarchy. This desire to protect the Italians from harm was a trait that Totila shared with the other Gothic ruler who appreciated Roman law, Amalasuintha. It certainly distanced him from the Gothic "hardliners."[182]

Soon after the capture of Rome, one senses a gradual modification in Procopius' idealised characterisation of Totila.[183] Though still capable of great deeds of moderation, the king also lashes out more frequently against the Italians and those he perceived as his enemies.[184] In Procopius' telling, Totila's long line of victories over the Byzantines also eroded some of his previous respect for his foes. In my view, the shift prepares the reader for the re-emergence of Belisarius and the gradual revival of Byzantine fortunes to come in the second half of book seven.

Once again, Procopius employed a set-speech to mark this change. Shortly after his storming of Rome, Totila gathered all of his men together for an address. The king explained to his men that at the outset of the "contest, the Goths had gathered a well-supplied host of two hundred thousand most warlike soldiers [...] Yet, with all this in our favour, we were vanquished by five thousand Greeks, and for no good reasons were stripped of our power and everything else that was ours." [185] "But now," he continued, "though reduced to a small number" and meagrely armed, they had defeated an enemy "twenty-thousand strong." Totila pondered how this inexplicable event had occurred. Whereas, in

---

182 It also seems to undermine Narses' claim (*Wars* 8.30.5) shortly before the Battle of Busto Gallorum that Totila had no regard for justice or Roman law.

183 One finds earlier signs of a less controlled and more "barbaric" Totila even before the siege of Rome. Procopius explained (*Wars* 7.15.13–16) that Totila had become so agitated with the bishop Valentinus during an interrogation that he chopped off both of the bishop's hands.

184 One finds a further example of Totila's dangerous fury in his desire to destroy Rome, which was only thwarted by a letter from Belisarius, see *Wars* 7.30.20–24. Cf. *Wars* 7.20.23–25.

185 Whately ("Descriptions of Battle," 350–54), discusses Procopius' use of often widely discrepant troop numbers as a narrative device.

his previous set-speech, he had attributed success in battle to a combination of martial prowess and just behaviour, Totila now claimed that the Goths' superior ἀρετή, numbers, and armament and supplies had played little part in their resurgence. Instead, he decreed that God had supported the Goths because under his rule they had paid a "greater honour to justice" than in previous times. He concluded the speech with a warning that the Goths needed to continue to act justly, "for if you change your course, God too will instantly change his favour and become hostile to you. For it is not his wont to fight with a race of men or a particular nation, but with such as show the greater honour to justice."[186] Immediately after giving this stark warning, however, Totila called on members of the Roman senate and, in Procopius' words, admonished them "as an angry master might be expected to say in upbraiding men who have become his slaves." He reprimanded them for allowing "the Greeks to attack their fatherland and for forgetting the prosperity they had attained under Gothic rule."[187]

Totila's less conciliatory attitude, the power of God, and the whims of *tyche* represent only some of the elements of causation at play in this section. The reader soon learns that in the spring of 547, Belisarius with "courage" (τόλμα) and deeds of ἀρετή retook Rome from the Goths.[188] The Byzantines then successfully defended the city from Totila's furious counter-attack.[189] Procopius plainly rejected Totila's assertion that ἀρετή and courage played no part in deciding events. Yet again, he had rebuffed Totila's dismissive suggestion that the Goths were better fighters than the "Greeks" were. Though the reader will have to wait until the end of book eight, Totila's further claim, that the Goths' small numbers and

186 Procopius, *Wars* 7.21.4–12. I have changed the translator Dewing's "Greeklings" for Γραικῶν to "Greeks."

187 Procopius, *Wars* 7.11.12–16.

188 For the Thucydidean parallels in Procopius' account of Belisarius' retaking of Rome from Totila, see Pazdernik, "Belisarius' Second Occupation of Rome," 208.

189 Procopius, *Wars* 7.24.1–26.

shortage of armament were actually beneficial to their cause, would also be undermined. As the reader will eventually learn, the Byzantines' better weaponry, greater numbers, and superior ἀρετή ultimately turn out to be Totila's undoing.[190] Indeed, by the close of book seven, and throughout much of book eight, it was the Byzantine soldiers fighting "manfully" (ἀνδρείως) and the Goths acting disgracefully and forgetting their "courage."[191]

A key turning point in the Italian war originated from Totila's need to engage the Romans at sea, a form of combat that, Procopius believed, put the Goths at a disadvantage.[192] Not coincidentally, this section follows Procopius' famous digression concerning the Italo-Romans' preservation of "the ship of Aeneas, the founder of the city."[193] Justinianic propaganda indeed explicitly described the emperor and his soldiers as "the sons of Aeneas."[194] So, it is likely that this anecdote is not superfluous to the historian's larger didactic tale. Procopius reported how the Goths under Totila had built their own fleet of 300 vessels to attack Greece. According to Procopius, despite some initial successful raiding and the capture of Narses' supply ships, this fleet failed to do any serious damage

---

190 Procopius, *Wars* 8.32.7–11.

191 See, e.g., the acts of Byzantine ἀρετή and ἀνδρεία at *Wars* 8.23.34 (Roman soldiers' fighting "manfully" [ἀνδρείως]), 8.29.22–23 (Roman soldiers make a "display of valour" [δήλωσιν ἀρετῆς] that surpasses all others), 8.32.11 (Romans and "barbarian allies" at the Battle of Busto Gallorum show a common προθυμία and ἀρετή). Whilst examples of Gothic cowardice are found at *Wars* 8.23.36 (Goths make a "disgraceful" [αἰσχρὰν] retreat), 8.24.3 (Goths in fear after suffering disgraceful defeat), 8.30.7 (Gothic soldiers terrified before the Battle of Busto Gallorum), 8.32.19 (Gothic soldiers make a panicked retreat at Busto Gallorum).

192 So too, according to Procopius (*Wars* 8.26.7), did Justinian's decision to refocus on the Italian campaign after years of "neglect" contribute heavily to the Byzantines' resurgence and ultimate victory.

193 Procopius, *Wars* 8.22.9–16.

194 Corippus, *Iohannis* 1.1–10. George W. Shea proposes (*Iohannis*, intro., 2) that the North African author Corippus cast himself as Justinian's Vergil.

to the Eastern Romans' cause.[195] The point is unmistakable; the
Goths were only playing at being martial sailors. Procopius'
conscious appeal to a distinguished Roman naval past thus served
a larger narrative purpose.

Who then in the historian's mind were the "true" heirs of
Aeneas? Surely not the feeble Italo-Romans, who, as Procopius
had shown throughout his *Gothic Wars*, had preserved merely a
token of their native martial and nautical past, while abandoning
the manly virtues found in the soldier's life.[196] Only after describing
Totila's naval campaigns in the Mediterranean Sea, and another
seemingly innocuous depiction by Procopius on the geography
found in Homer's writings (*Wars* 8.22.16–29), and the description
of another mythical ancient vessel (this one the ship that had
taken Odysseus home to Ithaca in the *Odyssey*), does the reader
finally find out who the true heirs of Aeneas are: the Eastern
Roman force led by John and Valerian.[197] Procopius' account of
the subsequent naval battle provides the key to understanding the
earlier digression on Aeneas' ship.

Procopius deployed two set speeches to set up the combat
and the lessons to come. The speeches by John and Valerian are
straightforward and Thucydidean.[198] The Romans must wage the
battle to protect their supply lines. The commanders proclaim
that "ἀρετή cannot dwell together with hunger, since nature will
not permit a man to be starving and to play the manly man at the

---

195 Procopius, *Wars* 8.22.17–32. Procopius later contradicts himself by depicting
continued Gothic naval puissance (*Wars* 8.24.31).

196 For the use of naval power in the sixth century and the growth of the
Byzantine navy, see Cosentino, "Constans II and the Byzantine Navy."

197 Homer, *Odyssey* 13.157–87. This Homeric reference is probably no accident
since Procopius declared in his introduction to *Wars* (1.1.6) that he had
composed his history in order to place the martial deeds of the sixth-century
Romans alongside the accomplishments of the heroes of Homer. For a
discussion of this theme in Procopius' proem, as well as a discussion of how
it differs from that of Thucydides, see Kouroumali, "Gothic War," 9–26.

198 For these links with Thucydides, see Whately, *Battles and Generals*, 202.

same time." Indeed, even if the Roman troops decided to behave cowardly, the Roman commanders bleakly reminded them that there would be little chance of escape, since the Goths controlled the land and the sea.[199]

This straightforward advice by the Roman commanders stands in stark contrast to the Goths' subsequent harangue. Lest we forget the gendered aspect of the dispute found throughout *Gothic Wars*, Procopius had the Gothic naval commanders exhort their men "To show therefore as quickly as possible that they [the Eastern Romans] are Greeks and unmanly [ἄνανδροι] by nature and are merely putting on a bold front when defeated, do not let this bold experiment of theirs proceed further." "For unmanliness [ἀνανδρία]," the Goth continued, "when merely despised, proceeds to flaunt itself still more, because rashness just by continuing comes to be devoid of fear."[200] Here the Gothic leader harkens back to old Theoderican and, indeed, Western Roman propaganda that sought to disparage the Eastern Romans as unmanly Greeks.[201] The experiment discussed is nothing less than Justinian's entire reconquest.

The Gothic commanders' condescending attitude toward the Eastern Romans proves to be misplaced.[202] The battle concludes with an overwhelming Eastern Roman victory. John and Valerian's men turn out to be manly Romans, not unmanly Greeks. Conversely, Procopius exposed the Gothic soldiers as the real cowards. After providing a rather muddled account of the naval battle, Procopius explained to his readers, "the barbarians,

199 Procopius, *Wars* 8.23.14–22. I have changed the translator Dewing's "to be brave" for ἀνδραγαθίζεσθαι to "play the manly man."

200 Procopius, *Wars* 8.23.23–28. I have changed the translator Dewing's "Greeklings" for Γραικοί to "Greeks" and "cowardice" for ἀνανδρία to "unmanliness."

201 Arnold, *Roman Imperial Restoration*, 141, 153.

202 Procopius often utilised such inaccuracies in his set speeches as a means of later undermining the speaker's overall argument. See, e.g., Procopius, *Wars* 5.18.40–41, 5.20.9–12, 7.21.4–12.

through their lack of sea fighting, began to carry on the combat in great disorder." The Roman navy had come a long way since the opening of the campaign against the Vandals in 533, where in book three of *Wars*, Procopius had described the Eastern Romans' "mortal dread of seafighting" (κατωρρωδηκύτες τε τὴν ναυμαχίαν).[203] In the remainder of *Gothic Wars* the Eastern Romans fought "manfully," while the Goths acted in a frequently unmanly manner.[204]

What Procopius deemed as a major turning point in the entire Italian campaign, in reality was not that decisive a victory. The historian's ensuing account, in fact, undermines his hyperbolic suggestion that the Battle of Senogallia "broke the spirit and weakened the power of Totila and the Goths."[205] As Maria Kouroumali posits, this distortion probably indicates Procopius' fuzzy knowledge of naval warfare and his ignorance of the actual military manoeuvring and tactics used by both sides during the final stages of the campaign.[206] One may provide a further explanation. It seems probable that such a naval victory better fit Procopius' larger didactic tale. Although such a solution may trouble those hoping to understand the actual events at the close of the war, it sheds valuable light on Procopius' attitude towards Justinian's reconquest. Indeed, it points to a more optimistic vision of the campaign's final years than some scholars have allowed.

Despite his faults and his deteriorating military position, Totila retained his military skills. When describing Totila's display of martial dexterity before the fateful Battle of Busto Gallorum, Procopius did little to hide his admiration for the bellicose king's prowess and intimidating persona. He wrote:

203 Procopius, *Wars* 3.14.2. Cf. *Wars* 3.10.5.

204 See, e.g., the acts of Byzantine ἀρετή and ἀνδρεία at *Wars* 8.23.34, 8.29.22–23, 8.30.1, 8.32.11. While examples of Gothic shame and cowardice are found at *Wars* 8.23.36, 8.24.3, 8.30.7, 8.32.19.

205 Procopius, *Wars* 8.23.42: αὕτη διαφερόντως ἡ μάχη τό τε φρόνημα καὶ τὴν δύναμιν Τουτίλα καὶ Γότθων κατέλυσεν.

206 Kouroumali, "Gothic War," 337–40.

> First of all, he was not reluctant to make an exhibition to the enemy of what kind of man he was. The armor in which he was clad was abundantly plated with gold, and the ample adornments that hung from his cheek-plates as well as from his helmet and spear were not only of purple [the colour of the Roman emperors] but in other respects befitting a king, marvellous in abundance.

Attempting to delay the Romans until his reinforcements arrived, Totila performed a "dance under arms" upon his horse and "hurled his javelin into the air and caught it again as it quivered above him, then passed it rapidly from hand to hand, shifting it with consummate skill." Totila brandished many of the martial skills one would expect from a man raised for battle. Procopius remarked that Totila was "like one who has been instructed with precision in the art of dancing from childhood."[207]

This display of fighting prowess before the battle, however, did Totila and the Goths little good against the well-supplied and supremely confident Byzantines. The intelligent Byzantine eunuch-general Narses alertly refused to accept Totila's ruse that he would fight in eight days hence; Narses correctly prepared his men to fight the next day. Narses made it clear to his men before battle that his side held all the tactical and strategic advantages. They had greater numbers, better equipment, and superior ἀρετή.[208] Although generals in Procopius' set speeches often overstated their side's advantages before battle, these comments by the eunuch Narses prove prescient. In the battle, the Byzantine

---

207 Procopius, *Wars* 8.31.18–21 (trans. Kaldellis). This anecdote appears to be another reference to the Goths' focus on providing a martial education to their children. As Philip Rance ("Battle of Taginae," 451) aptly warns, however, we should not see this display as an example of Totila's "barbarian" martial manliness. Byzantine military officers in this era were well versed in such displays.

208 Procopius, *Wars* 8. 8.29.8–10, 8.30.1.

army overwhelmed the Gothic forces, slaying the king and most of his men.[209] In Procopius' description, *tyche* and/or God play little role in deciding the outcome of the actual events on the ground.[210] The immediate cause of the Goths' defeat was, in fact, straightforward; Procopius attributed the trouncing to Totila's "folly" in risking his men in battle when the Byzantines held all the material and tactical advantages.[211] Furthermore, Totila's decision to forego using bows and any other weapon except spears proved critical. In contrast, Narses' army made use of a variety of weapons, and were thus able to adapt to the shifting circumstances of combat.

The manner of Totila's death, however, clearly shocked Procopius. For a historian obsessed with causation, he provided a somewhat incoherent explanation for the Gothic king's seemingly ignoble death.[212] In Procopius' most reliable version of the Gothic king's demise, Totila died while escaping the frontlines. Procopius saw Totila's conduct as a cowardly act.[213] His somewhat muddled attempts to find a palatable explanation for Totila's cowardly behaviour encapsulates the anxieties of a man unable to understand such behaviour in a man who, though not perfect, had always faced danger with courage. Procopius made it clear that such seismic shifts in human nature or secular events troubled him. They were only comprehensible if one saw them as acts of God, demons, or *tyche*. One can agree with Procopius that Totila's

209 Cf. Procopius, *Wars* 7.35.2.

210 Procopius, *Wars* 8.32.22–30. Though at the end of the battle Procopius agreed with Narses' attribution (*Wars* 8.33.1) of victory to God.

211 Rance, "Battle of Taginae," 472.

212 For Procopius' befuddlement at the "cowardice" (δειλίαν) of Totila, see *Wars* 8.32.28–30.

213 Procopius provided two versions of Totila's death. In the first account (*Wars* 8.32.22–28), Totila fled during the rout, and subsequently received a mortal wound while retreating. In the second and, according to Procopius, less credible version (*Wars* 8.32.33–36), Totila was struck by a missile while fighting as a common soldier.

end "was not worthy of his past deeds." Though undeserving, a "martial" Gothic king had yet again failed to obtain a glorious death in battle.

Teïas' Manly Death

For some modern readers, the *Wars* concludes tragically.[214] Procopius' depiction of the final battle in the *Wars*, at Mons Lactarius, certainly portrayed each side sympathetically. Surprisingly, the defeated Gothic leader Teïas earns Procopius' greatest praise. After Totila's death, the Goths' desperate situation had forced them to seek a "virtuous death" (θανατιάω ἀρετή). Their "despair of the situation," explained Procopius, represented the primary reason for the Goths' "extraordinary courage" (εὐτολμίαν).[215] Although he praised both sides' conduct during the struggle, Procopius reserved his highest acclamation for the Gothic king, exclaiming that Teïas' actions compared to those of "heroes of legend" (λεγομένων ἡρώων). Meeting his end heroically, Teïas, "easily recognised by all, stood with only a few followers at the head of the phalanx." The Gothic leader slew so many Romans that he needed to keep replacing his shields as they filled with enemy spears. Finally, after several hours of constant fighting, Teïas perished as he attempted to exchange another shield with his bodyguard.[216]

With his heroic death in battle, Teïas at last obtained the type of noble and manly demise that had eluded all of the previous Gothic kings in the *Gothic Wars*. This idealised literary version of his death may suggest that Procopius and his Byzantine readership may not have viewed Teïas' demise or the Goths' defeat as heart breaking. Procopius followed traditional literary models that made it clear that defeat in battle was not shameful or tragic as

214 E.g., Kaldellis, "Procopius' *Persian War*," 257.
215 Procopius, *Wars* 8.35.20–21 (my trans.).
216 Procopius, *Wars* 8.35.21–30 (I have changed Dewing's "courageous" for εὐτολμίαν to "extraordinary boldness").

long as one faced it with honour.[217] Procopius' account clearly has a literary ring to it. It also suspiciously ties up some of the loose threads in his narrative. First, Teïas' death in battle permitted Procopius to show a member of the Gothic royalty dying as Vitigis said they wished, in battle. Second, a gallant final clash featuring two worthy opponents fighting, in the words of Procopius, "with the fury of wild beasts," made a fitting terminus for an account that strove to describe and compare the Goths and the Romans' martial and manly virtues. While appreciating the fighting qualities and, indeed, the manliness of the Goths, the historian had confirmed the Byzantines as the superior and the manlier side. In the end, the Goths' martial prowess had proven inferior to the organization, leadership, weaponry, and manly ἀρετή and ἀνδρεία of the Byzantine soldiers. Finally, and most importantly, though unspoken, Procopius had fulfilled his stated purpose at the *Wars'* outset, which was to relate the worthiness of the martial deeds and the prowess of the contemporary Roman soldiers to his Byzantine audience. By defeating a martial and heroic foe like the Goths, Procopius had succeeded in establishing that Justinian's soldiers were at least the equals of their ancient counterparts. One should consider Procopius' depiction of the Battle of Mons Lactarius and, indeed, the entire *Gothic Wars* in this context.[218]

217 For this concept in Aristotle, see Bassi, "Semantics of Manliness," 54, and in Polybius, see Eckstein, *Moral Vision*, 42–43.

218 Of course, it is important to point out that the individual who had achieved these two dynamic victories over the Goths, Narses, was a eunuch. For some of my readers, the presence of a eunuch in such an essential military role may seem to undermine the connection made throughout this book between martial virtues and hegemonic masculinity. In Procopius' telling, however, Narses' identity as a castrate did little to hinder his military acumen. Although Procopius depicted Narses, at times, as vain, jealous, insubordinate, and petty, the historian generally respected Narses for being a successful and resourceful commander. So even though Procopius perceived Narses as an anomalous example of a eunuch (e.g., *Wars* 6.13.16–17), he certainly sees him as a man. Indeed, Procopius reported with little sense

Procopius' overall estimate of Justinian's reconquest is therefore far less gloomy than some assert.[219] As we have seen, context and sequence matter. One should be careful not to focus primarily on the criticisms, while ignoring the praise. Although there are certainly negative representations of Justinian's campaigns, Byzantine soldiers, and warfare more generally in *Wars* and *Secret History*, Procopius largely followed the sixth-century Constantinopolitan interpretation that "Roman legitimacy was in the East."[220] Indeed, in *Wars*, positive descriptions of Justinian's military campaigns and Byzantium's soldiers far outnumber the negative ones. As a historian seeking the "truth" behind failures and triumphs, Procopius naturally combined high praise with sharp criticisms of military men like Totila, Belisarius, and Narses.

Most importantly, Procopius' contemporaries and later Byzantines made no mention of the historian's supposed hostile attitude towards the return of Roman power in the West. For example, writing in the reign of Justin II (r. 565–74), Procopius' continuator Agathias perceived *Wars* to be pro-reconquest, asserting that they described how "Sicily, Rome, and Italy cast off the yoke of foreign domination, and were restored to their ancient

---

of irony that Narses' supporters in the officer corps hoped that the eunuch would achieve his own fame through "deeds of wisdom and manliness" (ἔργα ξυνέσεώς τε καὶ ἀνδρείας, *Wars* 6.18.7). Procopius' presentation of Narses does not indicate that just any eunuch could become an able military commander, only that in certain instances, just as one can find manly women and restrained barbarians, one can indeed find a vigorous and, indeed, an *andreios*-eunuch. A full discussion of Procopius and other early Byzantine attitudes towards Narses is found in Stewart, "*Andreios* Eunuch-Commander Narses," 1–25.

219 E.g., Kaldellis, "Procopius' Persian War," 274; Cameron, *Procopius and the Sixth Century*, 190; Bjornlie, *Politics and Tradition*, 102–09.

220 Goffart, *Barbarian Tides*, 54.

way of life."[221] This represents a common view of the reconquest in the East. We come across similar rhetoric at the famous close of Jordanes' *Getica*:

> And now we have recited the origin of the Goths, the noble line of the Amali and the deeds of brave men. The glorious race yielded to a more glorious prince and surrendered to a more valiant leader [...] Justinian and his consul Belisarius shall be named and known as Vandalicus, Africanus, and Geticus.[222]

Here, like generations of barbarians before them, the martial Goths have submitted honourably to the superior martial *Romanitas* of Justinian and Belisarius.

Causation and Manly Virtues

Wars has no perfect men. This reality has less to do with Procopius' disdain for the role that men's virtues played in determining worldly events, and more to do with his Christian belief that all men were flawed.[223] Yet, despite his likely belief in the Christian principle of original sin, Procopius also populated his work with heroic and manly characters drawn from the pages of classical literature. In a work that focused on warfare and the deeds of soldiers, not surprisingly then, in Procopius' mind a "manly man"

---

221 Agathias, *Histories* preface 30: οὐδέ γε ὅπως Σικελία τε καί Ῥώμη καί Ἰταλία τοὺς ἐπήλυδας ἀποβαλοῦσα βαρβάρους πάλιν ἤθεσι πατρίοις μετεκοσμεῖτο. Cf. Photius, *Bibliotheca* 63.

222 Jordanes, *Getica* 315 (trans. Mierow): "Haec hucusque Getarum origo ac Amalorum nobilitas et virorum fortium facta. Haec laudanda progenies laudabiliori principi cessit et fortiori duci manus dedit, cuius fama nullis saeculis nullisque silebitur aetatibus, sed victor ac triumphator Iustinianus imperator et consul Belesarius Vandalici Africani Geticique dicentur." Cf. John Lydus, *On Powers* 3.55; Corippus, *Iohannis* 3.281–313.

223 Treadgold, *Early Byzantine Historians*, 214–15.

(ἀνὴρ ἀνδρεῖος) was a military man.[224] Moreover, in a history that provided a balanced view of the virtues and vices of both foreigners and Romans, one's ethnicity did not predetermine one's manliness. The men who best personified the political and martial virtues esteemed by Procopius were, on the Roman side, Belisarius and Germanus, and on the barbarian side, Theoderic, Totila, and, if only briefly, Teïas.

Although it is difficult to know with certitude if Procopius' opinions on causation and the importance of individuals' martial virtues and manliness in determining secular affairs were representative of larger societal views, as we saw above, a number of his contemporaries lauded the exploits of Justinian's military campaigns and soldiers. *Wars* provides evidence of the continuing admiration of the soldier's life as an exemplar of the manly life in the sixth-century Byzantine Empire. Indeed, for Procopius the manly deeds of courage and self-restraint performed in the theatre of war by military men like Theoderic, Totila, Belisarius, and Germanus set a standard of masculine excellence that was difficult for their civilian counterparts to equal.

---

224 E.g., Procopius, *Wars* 7.40.9.

Plate 11. The David Plates, ca. 613–30. Nine silver pieces depicting Old Testament scenes from the life of the Hebrew King David. Metropolitan Museum of Art, New York City, New York.

IX

CONCLUSION:
LINGERING MANLY *ROMANITAS*
IN BYZANTIUM

Why did you assume you were addressing an assembly
of women, insulting our nature as well as our race? With
words you misrepresent deeds, bringing shame on the
council. Did you not realize that you were pouring forth
disgraceful words in the presence of men [ἀρρένων]? Or do
you not see an assembly of Roman people, proud of their
zeal, vigorous in arms, knowledgeable in their experience
of danger and providence for future advantage?
Theophylact, *History* 2.14.3

THE EXCERPT ABOVE COMES FROM WHAT WOULD PROVE TO BE
the last Greek history composed in the grand classical style for
more than three centuries.[1] The Egyptian Theophylact published
his work in the euphoric period surrounding the soldier-emperor
Heraclius' emphatic victory over the Persians in 628—a brief

1   For some possible reasons for this decline in almost all genres of Greek
    secular literature, see Whitby "Greek Historical Writing," 66–74;
    Treadgold, *Early Byzantine Historians*, 348–49, 393–99; Croke, "Uncovering
    Byzantium's Historiographical Audience," 34–35. On the disappearance of
    stone inscriptions, see Whittow, "Early Medieval Byzantium and the End of
    the Ancient World."

interlude of triumphant calm before the sudden emergence of the Arab menace in the 630s that saw the near snuffing out of the Byzantine Empire.[2] The sudden disappearance after 640 of many genres of secular literature and inscriptions, as well as the Muslims' emergence as a new religious and political rival in this period,[3] demarcates the dawning of a new age.[4] I have chosen the era of Theophylact's history to conclude this investigation for these reasons, as well as the obvious martial aspect and gendered implications of the passage. The set-speech from which this quotation is drawn certainly touches on two of this book's primary themes: the primacy of military matters and the manliness of war. In the anecdote, which describes the Roman response to an Avar invasion of Thrace in 587, the historian constructed a debate between two Roman soldiers, one a tribune and the other a grizzled veteran. The deliberation provides the reader with both the standard commentary on the fine lines between courage and rashness and the familiar linking of traditional martial virtues to masculinity. The tribune suggested that it was best to avoid directly confronting the Avars, whilst the veteran advocated a more aggressive approach. The older soldier wins the debate with his refrain that Rome's rise to world dominance had been due to its men's embrace of the rigours and courageous virtues of the soldier's life.[5] His assertion from the rhetorical opening of the speech that bold action on the battlefield helped to prove that Roman soldiers' souls were "masculine" (ἄρρενας) like their

2   Theophylact's career and the date of composition and publication of his history are discussed in Whitby, *Emperor Maurice and His Historian*, 39–45.

3   For the seventh-century conquests of Byzantine territory as primarily a Muslim, not an Arab phenomenon, see Howard-Johnston, *Witness to a World Crisis*, 527. On the idea that Islam's formation and subsequent "militant ideology" represented a "late antique" phenomenon, see Hoyland, "Early Islam as a Late Antique Religion."

4   On the transformative nature of this age for Byzantium, see Haldon, *Byzantium in the Seventh Century*.

5   Theophylact, *History* 2.14.6.

bodies serves as an important final reminder for my readers of how conceptualisations of the Roman soldier's life remained linked intimately to masculine ideology.[6] According to Theophylact, "courage" in battle represented a sure sign of "manliness," whereas "cowardice" in the face of war indicated that one had fallen into the realm of "effeminacy."[7]

We have seen such motifs before. Indeed, the emotive rhetoric associating traditional Roman codes of masculinity with idealised visions of the soldier's life is so common in the Roman and the early Byzantine sources that the modern reader is tempted to skip over such grandiloquence to get to the "relevant" parts. Ancient and modern scholars have quite rightly criticised Theophylact for his heavy reliance on "extravagant metaphors, sententious artistry, and ornate rhetoric."[8] Yet, as I have argued throughout this study, an exploration of these standard themes helps one to understand these early Byzantine texts and the society that produced them. Although such anecdotes' heavy reliance on standard rhetoric and stock heroes and villains may tell one very little about the combatants' "real" personalities, or the actual debates among the Roman soldiers before battle, they provide important insights

6 Theophylact, *History* 2.14.1: "Men of Rome, unless you would belie the name by your actions; men, that is if your souls [ψυχάς] are masculine [ἄρρενας] like your body. Even though the tribune is expert at high-flown talk and at confusing the issue, nevertheless deeds are more vigorous than words and do not tolerate empty sounds." I have changed the translators' "hearts" for ψυχάς to "souls."

7 Theophylact, *History* 3.13.4: "Comrades—you are my comrades both in toils and tumults because of the war—the engagement is established as a test of virtue [ἀρετῆς] and vice [κακίας], and is the arbiter of souls: for this day will either convict us of effeminate [θηλυπρεπὲς] cowardice [δειλίας], or with garlands and glorious triumphs will proclaim our manly [ἀρρενωπὸν] bravery [εὐτολμίας]." I have changed the translators' "courage" for ἀρετῆς to "virtue" and "cowardice" for κακίας to "vice."

8 Whitby, introduction to Theophylact, *History*, 28. For a later Byzantine view, see Photius, *Bibliotheca* cod. 65.

into wider societal attitudes towards gender and masculinity. The episode above, for instance, relied on the traditional appeal of the manly Roman soldier and the conventional disdain for the cowardly and effeminate man.

Martial virtues and images of the soldier's life continued to represent an essential aspect of masculinity and *Romanitas* in the early Byzantine period. This is not to say that the masculinity of soldiers represented the only type of heroic manliness in this period. As was discussed in chapters 4 and 5, alternative pathways to achieving "true" manliness had long been a feature of masculine ideology in the late Roman and the early Byzantine period. Extreme ascetics, courageous martyrs, fearless philosophers, and powerful political and church leaders were all, at times, compared favourably to military men. Christian historiographical concepts like providence and miracles played a role in the classicising histories of Procopius, Menander Protector, and Theophylact.[9] To borrow the words of Jonathan Conant, "at the end of antiquity Roman identity had come to be defined along multiple axes, the most prominent of which included politics, high culture, and religion."[10] Militaristic ideologies featured in all three realms.

Traditional hegemonic masculinity, secured in acts of masculine bravery in warfare, unquestionably proved resilient in the early Byzantine period. One need not serve in the military to perceive the soldier's life as an exemplar of the manly life. Civilian elites admired the manliness of war and the masculine deeds of the Empire's soldiers. As Theophylact had the Bishop Domitianus of Melitene explain to a group of soldiers headed off to fight the Persians:

> Let no one receive a scar on his back: the back
> is incapable of seeing victory. In the contest be
> united in spirit more than body, comrades in toils

9 For this role in Theophylact and his sixth-century predecessor, Menander Protector, see Whitby, "Greek Historical Writing," 44.

10 Conant, *Staying Roman*, 377.

but not in cowardice. Let him who has not taken up the inheritance of danger be disowned. In death reach out for victory. Trophies are bought with wounds and blows. Sloth provides no glory. There is nothing sweeter than death in war, for if there is no advantage in growing old and being struck down by wasting disease, assuredly it is more appropriate for you heroes to die in the battle-line while you are young, reaping glory in your tombs. For nature is unable to make fugitives immortal.[11]

Scholars have long recognised how Heraclius' wars against the Persians and Muslims neatly synthesised traditional secular and religious rhetoric.[12] This pairing is understandable since the martial and devout Heraclius was a by-product of a Byzantine world that inextricably interwove the political with the spiritual. Faced with a fight for its very survival, Heraclius' Byzantium naturally ramped up the religious bombast. As Walter Kaegi suggests, Heraclius "was emphasizing participation and even deaths in this war as a means to heaven." Nonetheless, we would be wise to heed Kaegi's further warning, that Heraclius' military campaigns were "no simple religious crusades." They were "multidimensional" conflicts "of which religious zeal was only one aspect."[13]

As we have observed in the previous chapters, these important developments of the seventh century had firm roots in earlier times. Unquestionably, however, the deft intermingling of spiritual and secular codes of warfare and masculinity had evolved somewhat over the years. The fifth-century Theodosian emperors'

11 Theophylact, *History* 5.4.8–9.
12 On the increasing focus in Heraclian propaganda in the Persian war based on religious themes, see Alexander, "Heraclius, Byzantine Imperial Ideology, and the David Plates"; Whitby, 'Defender of the Cross"; Stoyanov, *Defenders and Enemies*. For Byzantine attitudes towards "crusade" and "holy war," see Koder and Stouraitis, *Byzantine War Ideology*.
13 Kaegi, *Heraclius*, 126. Cf. Dennis, "Holy War," 31–39.

lack of military experience and prowess had little place in a world where the Empire's very survival was on the line. In 611, Heraclius had broken with precedent by leading the Roman army into battle against the Persians. The emperor had probably taken this step out of necessity since the Persian forces at this time were marauding freely within large swathes of Byzantine territory. In this highly charged climate, Heraclius' propaganda naturally fell back on Old Testament and classical examples of warrior-leaders protected by God, manfully defending their religion and their lands.

The set of nine seventh-century silver plates known as the David Plates (e.g., plate 11, left: "fight between David and Goliath"), which illustrate various Old Testament scenes from King David's life, offer us visual evidence of elements of this propaganda. Modern research suggests that the scenes depicted on the plates intentionally provide direct analogies with events from Heraclius' Persian war. Ruth Leader, for example, posits that the use of "imperial costumes and settings" represents the designer's attempts to invoke "a visual analogy between the kingdom of Israel and the Roman Empire."[14] Such iconography parroted similar motifs found in Heraclian literature. As Mary Whitby explains, contemporary writers such as George of Pisidia took a keen interest in depicting Heraclius as a military leader who, through a combination of God's guidance and his own courage, wisdom, clemency, and mildness achieves "not only personal, but also cosmic salvation."[15] This model of strong spiritual convictions and traditional active militaristic leadership would continue to play an essential role in imperial self-definition throughout the Byzantine period. Indeed, the majority of Byzantine emperors who followed Heraclius served as actual rather than merely symbolic warriors; two-thirds of these emperors had "led troops before or after their accession."[16]

---

14 Leader, "David Plates Revisited," 413–14.

15 Whitby, "Defender of the Cross," 263.

16 Treadgold, *Byzantium and Its Army*, 1, 214.

Byzantium's foes also wielded gendered religious rhetoric to endorse their own rights to dominion. Facing the trauma of first the Persian invasions and then the Islamic conquests, the Roman population's loyalty in these war-stricken territories was severely tested. Propaganda emanating from both the Persians and the Muslims appealed, in part, to the Roman subjects' admiration of virile manliness best represented by the soldier's life. The seventh-century Armenian historian Sebeos, for example, has a Muslim commander accepting the surrender of parts of the Eastern Roman Empire scoff at the protective power of Christ and the cross. Recording what seems to be a genuine ultimatum from the caliph,[17] the historian wrote:

> If you wish, he said, to preserve your life in safety, abandon that vain cult which you learned from childhood. Deny that Jesus and turn to the great God whom I worship, the God of our father Abraham. Dismiss from your presence the multitude of your troops to their respective lands. And I shall make you a great prince in your regions and send prefects. I shall make an inventory of the treasures and order them to be divided into four parts: three for me, and one for you. I shall provide you with as many soldiers as you wish, and take tribute from you, as much as you are able to give. But if you do not, that Jesus whom you call Christ, since he was unable to save himself from the Jews, how can he save you from my hands?[18]

The tactic used by the Muslim commander above, of criticising the unmanliness of Christ's crucifixion should cause little surprise, since, as Colleen Conway states, "it was Jesus' death that

---

17 Howard-Johnston, *Witness to a World Crisis*, 91.
18 Sebeos, *The Armenian History of Sebeos* 50 (170), trans. Thomson.

most called his masculine honor into question."[19] In fact, despite multifaceted attempts by the New Testament to portray Christ's crucifixion as a manly act similar to examples in the Graeco-Roman noble death traditions, many Christian Romans appeared reluctant to embrace these more pacifist strains of Christ's masculinity.

This sentiment helps to explain why in the first thousand years of the church's history the figure of the dead Christ was almost never shown. Christian tradition seemed reluctant to portray Christ as a suffering man, preferring to emphasise his divine power (e.g., plate 8).[20] As Felicity J. Harley-McGowan explains, there was "a fundamental hesitancy on the part of Christians to approach this particular narrative, but also an inherent lack of creativity in formulating iconography for the representation of critical episodes from that narrative, such as the Crucifixion or the Resurrection."[21] This hesitancy was not limited to visual iconography. One finds early Byzantine writers like Eusebius largely ignoring details of the crucifixion, concentrating instead on Jesus' rebirth, and focusing on the "treachery" committed by the Jews in Christ's condemnation.[22] The same is largely true as well for the fourth- and fifth-century church fathers from both halves of the Roman Empire.[23]

Sebeos, however, subtly addressed the Muslim commander's denigration of Christ's martial vigour. Likely writing between 656–61, a period when an internal divide within the Muslim world

---

19 Conway, *Behold the Man*, 177.

20 The transformation from "triumphant" to "suffering" Christ in both literary and visual forms has attracted much interest, see e.g., Morris, *Discovery of the Individual*; Chazelle, *The Crucified God*; Viladesau, *The Beauty of the Cross*. Boin (*Coming Out Christian*, 50–53), considers some of the reasons behind early Roman Christians' reluctance to embrace images of the "crucified" Christ.

21 Harley-McGowan, "The Narration of Christ's Passion," 223.

22 Eusebius, *HE* 1.2.

23 See, e.g., Bain, "Four Interpretations of Biblical Crucifixion Narratives."

stalled its expansion, Sebeos went on to relate the Byzantines' "glorious" victory over an Arab naval attack on Constantinople in 654—a victory that the historian attributed to God and the "pious prayers" of the Emperor Constans II (r. 641–68). We know, of course, that this respite was only temporary, and that Byzantium survived by the thinnest of margins.

Historians have long admired the Byzantines for their resilience in the face of near extinction at the hands of a seemingly relentless Muslim foe. These perilous circumstances have tended to shape opinions of the age as one of doom and gloom. James Howard-Johnston echoes the voice of modern consensus when he insists that a long series of military defeats at the hands of the Muslim armies had convinced many Byzantines that the hand of God was against them:

> Each successive defeat likewise impressed on Christians the plain truth that the Muslims were indeed agents of the Lord and that the End of Time was approaching. No wonder then that the morale of an army might suddenly plummet or that a whole province might submit once there was no prospect of help from field forces. There was also no point in continuing resistance from the cities, doomed as it was to failure and likely to cost their ruling elites all their suburban villas, gardens, and orchards.[24]

There is definitely some truth in this view. To devout seventh-century Byzantines like Maximus Confessor, the long line of Muslim victories served as a sure sign that the coming of the Antichrist was at hand.[25] Yet more can be said. Clearly, we should not place all of the ebbs and flows of Byzantine fortunes at the feet of eschatological and apocalyptical Christian belief. If apocalyptic

---

24 Howard-Johnston, *Witness to a World Crisis,* 473. Cf. Donner, *Muhammad and the Believers,* 14–17; Reinink, "Pseudo-Methodius."

25 Maximus Confessor, *Ep.* 14, ed. Migne, 540B.

paralysis represents the primary factor behind the Muslims' triumphs and the Byzantines' failures in the second half of the seventh century, it does little to explain Byzantine resilience in the same period and at the siege of Constantinople in 717–18. Surely if the majority of Byzantines believed wholeheartedly that the long line of Arab victories and territorial conquests served as a "true" sign that God had turned against them, Constantinople's citizens and its armies would have bowed down to the inevitable. On the contrary, they innovated, resisted, and survived.

As is well known, the seventh-century Byzantines' ability to adopt political reforms and adapt "new" military technologies helped them to survive the initial shock of the rapid Muslim advance. The use of the incendiary compound we call "Greek-fire" represented a crucial factor in the Byzantine's capacity to resist the Muslim naval attacks on Constantinople.[26] So too did the resettlement of Slavs during Constans II's reign into areas of Anatolia depopulated by the Arab invasions play a part in Byzantium's defence. Furthermore, Constan's refinement of the basic elements of what would become by the eighth and the ninth centuries the *themata* (a division of Roman territory into separate military provinces, whereby a general [*stratēgos*] held civilian and military power) assisted in ensuring the East Romans' long-term survival.[27] Such practical tactical and organisational innovations demonstrate that political and military leaders did not place Byzantium's survival purely in the hands of God, but continued to seek practical solutions to the military dilemmas they faced.

A lingering sense of manly martial *Romanitas* offers a further explanation for Byzantine endurance in the face of extinction. Romans—Christian and pagan—had a long record of overcoming

---

26 On the current debates surrounding the development and effectiveness of this weapon, see Haldon, "Greek Fire."

27 The literature on the origins and extent of the implementation of the thematic administration in the seventh century is vast. For good introductions, see Lilie, "Die zweihundertjährige Reform"; Haldon, *Byzantium in the Seventh Century*, 208–53.

foreign foes in similarly dire situations. One cannot help but suspect that a combination of a continued belief in the resilience of Roman military virtues and the practical need to survive represent the primary factors behind Byzantium's continued resistance and century-long battle back to relevance.

The eventual emergence of the post-imperial kingdoms of the West may be partially attributed to the gradual severing of the local ruling elite's Roman identity from the Roman state.[28] As Patrick Amory explains, by the opening of the seventh century, this decoupling led to the eventual disappearance in the Empire's Western periphery of a united "Roman" culture dictated by Constantinople:

> The eventual failure of Justinian and his successors to retain the allegiance of Africa and Italy and finally, after Phocas, the Balkans, was partly a result of the inadequacy of imperial ideology to draw together the varied elites of new frontiers into a single homogeneous cultural, religious and political culture determined by Constantinople.[29]

In contrast, Byzantine emperors found more success dominating the political and religious culture in the Empire's Eastern heartland. In contrast to their Western counterparts, even during the darkest days the majority of Eastern elites continued to link their Romanness to the Roman state in Constantinople. Shared ideals such as a lingering belief in manly martial *Romanitas*, then, provide a partial explanation for Byzantine resilience and longevity.[30]

Certainly one finds evidence of the influence of cultural memory in later Byzantine historians. Anguishing over his

---

28 Conant, *Staying Roman*, 377.

29 Amory, *People and Identity*, 313.

30 Leyser ("Introduction") discusses the ways such shared convictions hold societies together during periods of political rupture.

contemporaries' failure to live up to the martial masculine
prowess and ideals of his Republican Roman forbearers, the
eleventh-century Byzantine aristocrat and historian Michael
Attaleiates encapsulates the appeal of a continuing belief in the
vital connection between martial virtues, manly *Romanitas*,
and the prosperity of the Roman state that we have explored
throughout this monograph. When explaining the reasons behind
his Roman forebear's greatness, he opined:

> For the noble Romans of that time did not strive for
> money and the acquisition of wealth but simply for
> renown, the demonstration of their manliness, and
> their country's safety and splendour.[31]

This conscious appeal to the virtues of the Republic reveal the
extent that a later Byzantine like Michael could identify with
his non-Christian Roman past. Michael sees himself as one of
the "modern Romans" (Τοῖς δὲ νῦν Ῥωμαίοις) admiring the
manly martial virtues of his pagan "Roman ancestors" (οἱ πάλαι
Ῥωμαῖοι).[32] A mutual veneration of the manly values found
in the soldier's life united these ancient and modern Romans.
His Republican forebears may not have shared all of Michael's
Christian values, but they embraced both the manly and martial
virtues that represented a fundamental facet of their shared
Romanitas. An ability to tap into this Roman cultural memory
represents a key factor in Byzantium's longevity. In this process,
the state was not essential. Indeed, the social bonds among

---

31 Michael Attaleiates, *History* 27.11, Greek text according to the edition of
 Tsolakis, *Michaelis Attaliatae Historia*, 169–70. Cf. *Miguel Ataliates, Historia*,
 ed. Perez Martin, trans. Kaldellis and Krallis: Οὐ γὰρ πρὸς ἀργύριον καὶ
 πλούτου ἐπίκτησιν οἱ εὐγενέστατοι Ῥωμαῖοι τὸ κατ᾽ ἐκεῖνο καιροῦ ἠγωνίζοντο,
 ἀλλὰ δι᾽ εὔκλειαν μόνην καὶ ἀνδρίας ἐπίδειξιν καὶ τῆς ἰδίας πατρίδος σωτηρίαν
 τε καὶ λαμπρότητα.

32 For this theme in Michael's history, see Kaldellis, "A Byzantine Argument";
 Neville, *Heroes and Romans*.

aristocrats were particularly important during periods when the state's authority waned. In these times of crisis, the ruling elites could become the voice of the social order. By conjuring a view of aristocratic power and Roman identity that stretched back to the Roman Republic, Michael thus vividly roused his fellow members of the social hierarchy. This helps us to understand why in the East a societal value like manly martial *Romanitas* remained largely impervious to the tides of political and communal change.

Therefore, I suspect that for many Byzantines defeat at the hands of their enemies did little to shake the entrenched notion that "Roman" greatness had been earned by the blood of its battle-hardened soldiers. The theatre of war continued to provide one of the easiest places for men in Byzantine civilisation to prove not only their courage, but also to express their enduring manly *Romanitas*.

BIBLIOGRAPHY

Primary Sources

Agathias. *Agathiae Myrinaei Historiarum Libre Quinque.* Edited by Rudolf Keydell. Berlin: De Gruyter, 1967.

—. *The Histories.* Translated by Joseph D. Frendo. New York: De Gruyter, 1975.

Ambrose. *Ambrose of Milan: Political Letters and Speeches.* Translated by John H. W. G. Liebeschuetz. Liverpool: Liverpool University Press, 2006.

—. *De officiis.* Edited and Translated by Ivor J. Davidson. Oxford: Oxford University Press, 2002.

Ammianus Marcellinus. *The Later Roman Empire, A.D. 354-378.* Translated by Walter Hamilton. London: Penguin, 1986.

—. *Res Gestae.* Edited and Translated by John C. Rolfe. 3 vols. Cambridge, MA: Harvard University Press, 1935–39.

Anonymus Valesianus. In volume 3 of Ammianus Marcellinus' *Res Gestae*, edited and translated by John C. Rolfe, 506–69. Cambridge, MA: Harvard University Press, 1952.

Aristotle. *History of Animals.* Translated by Arthur L. Peck. 3 vols. Cambridge, MA: Harvard University Press, 1965.

Arrian. *Anabasis of Alexander.* Translated by Peter A. Brunt. 2 vols. Cambridge, MA: Harvard University Press, 1929.

Athanasius of Alexandria, *The Life of Anthony and the Letter to Marcellus.* Translated by Robert Gregg. Mahwah, NJ: Paulist, 1980.

Attaleiates, Michael. *The History*. Translated by Anthony Kaldellis and Dimitris Krallis. Cambridge, MA: Harvard University Press, 2012.

Augustine. *City of God*. Edited and Translated by William M. Green, George E. McCracken, and David S. Wiesen. 3 vols. Cambridge, MA: Harvard University Press, 1957–68.

—. *Confessions*. Translated by R. S. Pine-Coffin. London: Penguin, 1961.

The Book of the Pontiffs (Liber Pontificalis). The Ancient Biographies of the First Ninety Roman Bishops to AD 715. Translated by Raymond Davis. 2nd ed. TTH 6. Liverpool: Liverpool University Press, 2000.

Candidus. *frags*. In *The Fragmentary Classicising Historians of the Later Roman Empire: Eunapius, Olympiodorus, Priscus, Malchus, and Candidus*, edited and translated by Roger C. Blockley. 2 vols. Volume 2, 464–73. Liverpool: Francis Cairns, 1983.

Cassiodorus. *Cassiodori Senatoris variae*. In MGH AA 12, edited by Theodor Mommsen, 10–392. Berlin: Weidmann, 1894; partial translation by Thomas Hodgkin. *The Letters of Cassiodorus Being a Condensed Translation of the Varia of Magnus Aurelius Cassiodorus Senator*. London: Henry Frowde, 1886; partial translation by S. J. B. Barnish. *The Varia of Magnus Aurelius Cassiodorus Senator*. TTH 12. Liverpool: Liverpool University Press, 1992.

Chron. gallica. Edited by Theodor Mommsen. MGH AA 9, CM 1, 615–66. Berlin: Weidmann, 1892–28.

Chron. Paschale. Edited by Ludwig Dindorf. Bonn: Weber, 1832.

Chron. Paschale: 284–628 AD. Translated by Michael Whitby and Mary Whitby. TTH 7. Liverpool: Liverpool University Press, 1989.

Cicero. *De officiis*. Translated by Walter Millar. LCL 30. Cambridge, MA: Harvard University Press, 1913.

—. *The Orations of Marcus Tullius Cicero*. Translated by Charles D. Yonge. London: Bell & Sons, 1891.

Claudian. *Claudian*. Translated by Maurice Platnauer. LCL 135. 2 vols. Cambridge, MA: Harvard University Press, 1922.

Claudius Mamertinus. *The Emperor Julian: Panegyric and Polemic*. Translated by Samuel Lieu. TTH 2. Liverpool: Liverpool University Press, 1986.

—. *Gratiarum action suo Juliano imperatori*. Edited by D. Lassandro. Turin: Pavaria, 1992.

Codex Theodosianus. Edited by Theodor Mommsen and Paul M. Meyer. Berlin: Weidmann, 1905.

The Theodosian Code. Translated by Clyde Pharr. Princeton: Princeton University Press, 1952.

Constantine Porphyrogennetos. *The Book of Ceremonies. With the Greek Edition of the Corpus scriptorum historiae Byzantinae (Bonn, 1829)*. Translated by Ann Moffatt and Maxeme Tall. 2 vols. Brisbane: Australian Association for Byzantine Studies, 2012.

Corippus. *In laudem Iustini Augusti minoris*. Edited and Translated by Averil Cameron. London: Athlone, 1976.

—. *The Iohannis or De Bellis Libycis of Flavius Cresconius Corippus*. Translated by George W. Shea. Lewistone: Edwin Mellen Press, 1988.

Dialogue on Political Science. In *Three Political Voices from the Age of Justinian: Agapetus, Advice to the Emperor, Dialogue on Political Science, Paul the Silentiary, Description of Hagia Sophia*, translated by Peter N. Bell, 123–88. Liverpool: Liverpool University Press, 2009.

Dio Cassius. *Roman History*. Translated by E. Cary et al, LCL. 9 vols. Cambridge, MA: Harvard University Press, 1979.

Dio Chrysostom. *Dio Chrysostom. 1: Discourses 1–11*. Translated by James W. Cohoon. LCL 257. Cambridge, MA: Harvard University Press, 1932.

Ennodius. *Ennode de Pavie: Lettres*. Edited and translated by Stéphane Gioanni. 2 vols. Paris: Les Belles Lettres, 2006–10.

—. "Ennodius' Panegyric to Theoderic the Great. A Translation and Commentary." Translated by Barbara S. Haase. MA thesis, University of Ottawa, 1991.

—. *Magni Felicis Enodii Opera*. Edited by Friedrich Vogel. MGH AA 7. Berlin: Weidmann, 1885.

Eunapius. *Lives of the Philosophers*. Translated by Wilmer C. Wright. LCL 134. Cambridge, MA: Harvard University Press, 1921.

—. *Universal History*. In *The Fragmentary Classicising Historians of the Later Roman Empire: Eunapius, Olympiodorus, Priscus, and Malchus*, edited and translated by Roger C. Blockley, 2–150. 2 vols. Volume 2. Liverpool: Francis Cairns, 1983.

Eusebius. *Ecclesiastical History*. Translated by Kirsopp Lake and John E. L. Oulton. LCL 153. 2 vols. Cambridge, MA: Harvard University Press, 1926–1932.

—. *Life of Constantine*. Translated by Averil Cameron and Stuart G. Hall. Oxford: Clarendon, 1999.

—. *Vita Constantini*. In *Eusebius Werke*, edited by Ivar A. Heikel. Volume 1. GCS. Leipzig, 1902.

Eutropius. *Breviarium*. Translated by Harold W. Bird. TTH 14. Liverpool: Liverpool University Press, 1993.

Evagrius Scholasticus. *The Ecclesiastical History of Evagrius Scholasticus*. Edited by Joseph Bidez and Léon Parmentier. London: Methuen, 1898.

—. *The Ecclesiastical History of Evagrius Scholasticus*. Translated by Michael Whitby. TTH 33. Liverpool: Liverpool University Press, 2000.

Fragmentary Classicising Historians of the Later Roman Empire Text, Translation and Historiographical Notes. Translated by R.C. Blockley. Liverpool: F. Cairns, 1981.

Galen. *On the Natural Faculties*. Translated by Arthur J. Brock. LCL 71. Cambridge, MA: Harvard University Press, 1916.

Gregory the Great. *The Dialogues of St. Gregory the Great*. Edited and translated by Edmund G. Gardner. London: Warner, 1911.

Gregory Nazianzen. *Two Invectives against Julian*. Translated by Charles W. King. London: Bell and Sons, 1888.

Herodian. *BH*. Translated by Charles R. Whittaker. LCL 454 and 455. 2 vols. Cambridge, MA: Harvard University Press, 1969–70.

Herodotus. *Herodoti Historiae*. Edited by Karl Hude. Oxford: Clarendon, 1927.

—. *The Histories*. Translated by Alfred D. Godley. LCL 117. 4 vols. Cambridge, MA: Harvard University Press, 1920–25.

Hippocrates. *Airs, Waters, Places*. Translated by William H. S. Jones. LCL 147–150. 8 vols. Cambridge, MA: Harvard University Press, 1972.

Historia Augusta. Edited and translated by David Magie. LCL 3 vols. Cambridge, MA: Harvard University Press, 1921–31.

Homer. *Homeri Opera*. Edited by David B. Monro and Thomas W. Allen. Oxford: Clarendon, 1920.

Horace. *Odes and Epodes*. Edited and translated by Niall Rudd. LCL 33. Cambridge, MA: Harvard University Press, 2004.

Hydatius. *Chron*. In *The Chronicle of Hydatius and the Consularia Constantinopolitana: Two Contemporary Accounts of the Final Years of the Roman Empire*, edited and translated by Richard W. Burgess, 70–123. Oxford: Clarendon, 1993.

In Praise of Later Roman Emperors: The Panegyrici Latini: Introduction, Translation, and Historical Commentary, with the Latin Text of R.A.B. Mynors. Edited by Roger A. B. Mynors, translated by C. E. V. Nixon and Barbara S. Rogers. Berkeley, CA: University of California Press, 1994.

John Lydus. *On Powers or the Magistracies of the Roman State*. Edited and translated by Anastasius C. Bandy. Philadelphia, PA: American Philosophical Society, 1983.

John Malalas. *The Chronicle of John Malalas*. Translated by Elizabeth Jeffreys, Michael Jeffreys, and Roger Scott. Melbourne: Australian Association for Byzantine Studies, 1986.

—. *Ioannis Malalae Chronographia*. In *Chronographia*, edited by Hans Thurn. Berlin: de Gruyter, 2000.

John Rufus, *The Lives of Peter the Iberian, Theodosius of Jerusalem, and the Monk Romanus*. Edited and translated by Cornelia

B. Horn and Robert R. Phenix. Atlanta, GA: Society of Biblical Literature, 2008.

Jordanes. *The Gothic History of Jordanes*. Translated by Charles C. Mierow. Oxford: University Press, 1915.

—. *Iordanis Romana et Getica*. Edited by Theodor Mommsen. MGH AA 5.1. Berlin: Weidmann, 1882.

Joshua the Stylite. *The Chronicle of Joshua the Stylite*. Translated by John W. Watt and Frank R. Trombley. TTH 32. Liverpool: Liverpool University Press, 2000.

Julian. *Works*. Edited and translated by Wilmer C. Wright. LCL. 3 vols. Cambridge, MA: Harvard University Press, 1913–23.

Justinian, *Digest of Justinian*. Edited and translated by Alan Watson. 2 vols. Philadelphia, PA: University of Pennsylvania Press, 1997.

Lactantius. *Divine Institutes*. Edited and translated by Anthony Bowen and Peter Garnsey. TTH 40. Liverpool: Liverpool University Press, 2003.

Libanius. *Antioch as a Centre of Hellenic Culture as Observed by Libanius*. Translated by Albert F. Norman. TTH 34. Liverpool: Liverpool University Press, 2000.

—. *Selected Orations*. Edited and translated by Albert F. Norman. LCL 451 and 452. 2 vols. Cambridge, MA: Harvard University Press, 1969.

Life of Daniel the Stylite. In *Three Byzantine Saints*, translated by Elizabeth Dawes and Norman H. Baynes, 7–71. Oxford: Blackwell, 1948.

Lucian. *The Scythian or the Consul*. Translated by K. Kilburn. LCL 430. Cambridge, MA: Harvard University Press, 1959.

Malchus, *frags*. In *The Fragmentary Classicising Historians of the Later Roman Empire: Eunapius, Olympiodorus, Priscus, and Malchus*, edited and translated by Roger C. Blockley, 402–62. 2 vols. Volume 2. Liverpool: Francis Cairns, 1983.

Marcellinus. *The Chronicle of Marcellinus: A Translation and Commentary (with a Reproduction of Mommsen's Edition of the Text)*. Translated by Brian Croke. Sydney: Australian Association for Byzantine Studies, 1995.

Marcus Aurelius. *Ad se ipsum*. Edited by Joachim Dalphen. Leipzig: Teubner, 1979.

—. *Meditations*. Translated by Maxwell Staniforth. London: Penguin, 1964.

Maurice. *Das Strategikon des Maurikios*. Edited by George T. Dennis and Ernst Gamillscheg. Vienna: Verlag der Österreichischen Akademie der Wissenschaften, 1981.

—. *Maurice's Strategikon: Handbook of Byzantine Military Strategy*. Translated by George T. Dennis. Philadelphia, PA: University of Pennsylvania Press, 1984.

Maximus Confessor. *Epistolae*. In *PG* 91, edited by Jacques Paul Migne, cols 363–649. Paris: Migne, 1860.

Menander Protector. *The History of Menander the Guardsman*. Translated by Roger C. Blockley. Liverpool: Francis Cairns, 1985.

Menander Rhetor. *Menander Rhetor*. Edited and translated by Donald A. Russell and Nigel G. Wilson. Oxford: Clarendon, 1981.

Michael Attaleiates. *The History*. Translated by Anthony Kaldellis and Dimitris Krallis. Cambridge, MA: Harvard University Press, 2012.

—. *Michaelis Attaliatae Historia*. Edited by Eudoxos Tsolakis. Athens: Academia Atheniensis, 2011.

—. *Miguel Ataliates: Historia*. Edited by Inmaculada Pérez Martín. Madrid: Consejo Superior de Investigaciones Científicas, 2002.

Olympiodorus of Thebes. *History*. In *The Fragmentary Classicising Historians of the Later Roman Empire: Eunapius, Olympiodorus, Priscus, and Malchus*, edited and translated by Roger C. Blockley, 152–220. 2 vols. Volume 2. Liverpool: Francis Cairns, 1983.

Orosius. *Pauli Orosii Historiarum adversum paganos*. Edited by Karl F. W. Zangemeister. Vienna: Gerold, 1882.

—. *Seven Books against the Pagans*. Translated by Andrew T. Fear. TTH 54. Liverpool: Liverpool University Press, 2010.

Paul the Deacon. *Historia Langobardorum*. In MGH SRL, edited by Georg Waitz, 12–187. Hannover: Hahn, 1878.

—. *Romana*. In MGH AA 2, edited by Hans Droysen, 183–224. Berlin: Weidmann, 1879.

Panegyrici Latini. Edited by Roger A. B. Mynors, *XII Panegyrici Latini*. Oxford: Clarendon, 1964.

Philostorgius, *Church History*. Edited and translated by Philip R. Amidon. Leiden: Brill, 2007.

Philostratus. *Lives of the Sophists*. Translated by Wilmer C. Wright. LCL 134. Cambridge, MA: Harvard University Press, 1921.

Photius. *Photius Bibliothèque*. Edited and translated by René Henry. 8 vols. Paris: Les Belles Lettres, 1959–77.

Plato. *Meno*. Translated by Walter R. M. Lamb. LCL 165. Cambridge, MA: Harvard University Press, 1967.

—. *The Republic*. Translated by Desmond Lee. London: Penguin, 1955.

Polybius. *The Histories*. Edited and translated by William R. Paton. LCL 128, 137, 138, 159, 160, 161. 6 vols. Cambridge, MA: Harvard University Press, 1923.

Priscus of Panium. *History*. In *The Fragmentary Classicising Historians of the Later Roman Empire: Eunapius, Olympiodorus, Priscus, and Malchus*, edited and translated by Roger C. Blockley, 222–400. 2 vols. Volume 2. Liverpool: Francis Cairns, 1983.

Procopius of Caesarea. *Buildings*. In *Procopii Caesariensis opera omnia*, vol. 4: *De Aedificiis*, edited by Jakob Haury, revised by Gerhard Wirth. Leipzig: Teubner, 1963; translated by Henry B. Dewing. LCL 343. Cambridge, MA: Harvard University Press, 1940.

—. *Secret History*. In *Procopii Caesariensis opera omnia*, vol. 3: *Historia arcana*, edited by Jakob Haury, revised by Gerhard Wirth. Leipzig: Teubner, 1963; translated by Henry B. Dewing. LCL. Cambridge, MA: Harvard University Press, 1940.

—. *Wars*. In *Procopii Caesariensis opera omnia*, vols 1–2: *De Bellis*, edited by Jakob Haury, revised by Gerhard Wirth. Leipzig:

Teubner, 1962–63; translated by Henry B. Dewing. LCL 48, 81, 107, 173, 217. 5 vols. Cambridge, MA: Harvard University Press, 1940.

Prosper, *Chron*. Edited by T. Mommsen, *Prosper Tironis epitome Chron*. In CM, 3 volumes. Berlin, 1892–98, I, 341–99.

Prudentius, *Against Symmachus 2. Crowns of Martyrdom. Scenes from History. Epilogue*. Edited and translated by H. J. Thomson. LCL 398. Cambridge, MA: Harvard University Press, 1961.

Pseudo-Dionysius of Tel-Mahre Chronicle (Known Also as the Chronicle of Zuqnin) Part III. Translated by Witold Witakowski. TTH 22. Liverpool: Liverpool University Press, 1996.

Pseudo-Zachariah Rhetor. *The Chronicle of Pseudo-Zachariah Rhetor*. In *Church and War in Late Antiquity*, edited by Geoffrey Greatrex and translated by Robert R. Phenix and Cornelia B. Horn. TTH 55. Liverpool: Liverpool University Press, 2011.

Rufinus. *Church History*. In *Eusebius Werke. Zweiter Band, zweiter Teil, Die Kirchengeschichte*, edited by Eduard Swartz and Theodor Mommsen, revised by Friedhelm Winkleman. Berlin: Akademie Verlag, 1999.

—. *The Church History of Rufinus of Aquileia, Books 10 and 11*. Translated by Philip R. Amidon. Oxford: Oxford University Press, 1997.

Les saints stylites. Edited by Hippolyte Delehaye. Paris: Picard, 1923.

Seneca. *Moral Essays: De Providentia. De Constantia. De Ira. De Clementia*. Translated by John W. Basore. LCL 214, 254, 310. 3 vols. Cambridge, MA: Harvard University Press, 1928–35.

Sebeos. *The Armenian History of Sebeos*. Translated by Robert W. Thomson. TTH 31. 2 vols. Liverpool: Liverpool University Press, 1999.

Sidonius Apollinaris. *Poems and Letters.* Translated by William B. Anderson. LCL 296 and 420. 2 vols. Cambridge, MA: Harvard University Press, 1936.

Socrates. *The Ecclesiastical History of Socrates.* Translated by Edward Walford. London: Bohn, 1853.

—. *Sokrates Kirchengeschichte.* Edited by Günther C. Hansen and Manja Širinjan. Berlin: Akademie Verlag, 1995.

Sozomen. *The Ecclesiastical History of Sozomen.* Translated by Edward Walford. London: Bohn, 1855.

—. *Historia ecclesiastica = Kirchengeschichte.* Edited by Joseph Bidez and Günther C. Hansen. Berlin: Akademie Verlag, 1995.

Synesius. *The Letters of Synesius of Cyrene.* English translation by Augustine Fitzgerald. Oxford: Oxford University Press, 1926.

—. *On Kingship.* In *The Essays and Hymns of Synesius of Cyrene,* translated by Augustine Fitzgerald, 133–39. London: Oxford University Press, 1930.

—. *Synesii Cyrenensis opuscula.* Edited by Nicola Terzaghi. Rome: Typis Regiae Officinae Polygraphicae, 1944.

—. *Synésius de Cyrène.* French Translation by Antonio Garzya and Denis Roques. 3 vols. Paris: Belles lettres, 2000.

Tacitus. *Annals.* Translated by Clifford H. Moore and John Jackson. LCL 111, 249, 312. 3 vols. Cambridge, MA: Harvard University Press, 1925–37.

Themistius. *Politics, Philosophy, and Empire in the Fourth Century: Selected Orations of Themistius.* Translated by Peter J. Heather and David Moncur. TTH 36. Liverpool: Liverpool University Press, 2001.

Theodoret of Cyrrhus. *Kirchengeschichte.* Edited by Léon Parmentier and Günther C. Hansen. 3rd ed. Berlin: Akademie-Verlag, 1998.

Theophanes. *The Chronicle of Theophanes Confessor: Byzantine and Near Eastern History AD 284-813.* Translated by Cyril A. Mango and Roger Scott. Oxford: Oxford University Press, 1997.

—. *Theophanis chronographia*. Edited by Carl de Boor. Hildesheim: G. Olms, 1963.

Theophylact Simocatta. *T. Simocattae Historiae*. Edited by Carl de Boor and revised by Peter Wirth. Stuttgart: Teubner, 1972.

Thucydides. *History of the Peloponnesian War*. Translated by Charles F. Smith. LCL. 4 vols. Cambridge, MA: Harvard University Press, 1919.

Vergil. *Aeneid*. Translated by Stephen J. Harrison. Oxford: Clarendon, 1991.

Vegetius. *Epitome of Military Science*. Translated by Nicholas P. Milner. TTH 16. Liverpool: Liverpool University Press, 1993.

Vita Marceli. Edited by Gilbert Dagron, "La Vie ancienne de saint Marcel l'Acémète." *Analecta Bollandiana* 85 (1968): 271–321.

Zosimus. *Zosime, Histoire Nouvelle*. Translation by François Paschoud. 3 vols. Paris: Les Belles Lettres, 1971–89.

—. *New History*. Translation by Ronald T. Ridley. Brisbane: Australian Association for Byzantine Studies, 1986.

Secondary Sources

Adshead, Katherine. "Thucydides and Agathias." In *History and Historians in Late Antiquity*, edited by Brian Croke and Alanna M. Emmett, 82–87. Sydney: Pergamon Press, 1983.

Alchermes, Joseph D. "Art and Architecture in the Age of Justinian." In *CCAJ*, edited by Michael Maas, 343–75. Cambridge: Cambridge University Press, 2005.

Allen, Pauline. "Contemporary Portrayals of the Byzantine Empress Theodora (A.D. 527-548)." In *Stereotypes of Women in Power: Historical Perspectives and Revisionist Views*, edited by Barbara Garlick, Suzanne Dixon, and Pauline Allen, 93–103. New York: Greenwood Press, 1992.

—. *Evagrius Scholasticus, the Church Historian.* Leuven: Spicilegium sacrum Lovaniense, 1981.

Alexander, Suzanne S. "Heraclius, Byzantine Imperial Ideology, and the David Plates." *Speculum* 52 (1977): 217–37.

Amirav, Hagit. "Ammianus *Stoicus*? Reflections on Rulership, Tyranny, and Power in *Res Gestae*." In *From Rome to Constantinople: Studies in Honour of Averil Cameron*, edited by Hagit Amirav and Bas Ter Haar Romeny, 85–104. Leuven: Peeters, 2007.

Amory, Patrick. *People and Identity in Ostrogothic Italy: 489-554.* Cambridge: Cambridge University Press, 1997.

Anderson, Janice. C., and Stephen D. Moore, eds. *New Testament Masculinities.* Atlanta, GA: Society of Biblical Literature, 2003.

Angelidē, Christina. *Pulcheria: La Castita Al Potere.* Milan: Jaca Book, 1998.

Armstrong, Karen. "The Acts of Paul and Thecla." In *Feminist Theology: A Reader*, edited by Ann Loades. Louisville, KY: Jaca Book, 1990.

Arnold, Jonathan J. *Theoderic and the Roman Imperial Restoration.* Cambridge: Cambridge University Press, 2014.

—. "Theoderic's Invincible Mustache." *JLA* 6 (2013): 152–83.

Athanassiadi, Polymnia. *Julian an Intellectual Biography.* London: Routledge, 1992.

Bachrach, Bernard S. *A History of the Alans in the West: From Their First Appearances in the Sources of Classical Antiquity through the Early Middle Ages.* Minneapolis, MN: University of Minnesota Press, 1973.

Bain, Andrew M. "Four Interpretations of Biblical Crucifixion Narratives in the Latin West, c. 350-430." PhD thesis, Queensland University, 2007.

Baldwin, Barry. "Malchus of Philadelphia." *Dumbarton Oaks Papers* 31 (1977): 91–107.

Barnes, Timothy D. *Ammianus Marcellinus and the Representation of Historical Reality.* Ithaca, NY: Cornell University Press, 1998.

—. "Angel of Light or Mystic Initiate? The Problem of the Life of Antony." *JTS* 37 (1986): 353–68.

—. *Athanasius and Constantius, Theology and Politics in the Constantinian Empire.* Cambridge, MA: Harvard University Press, 1981.

—. *Constantine and Eusebius.* Cambridge, MA: Harvard University Press, 1981.

—. *The Sources of the Historiae Augusta.* Brussels: Latomus, 1978.

Barnish, Samuel J. B. "Transformation and Survival in the Western Senatorial Aristocracy, c. A.D. 400-700." *Papers of the British School at Rome* 56 (1988): 120–55.

Barnish, Samuel, A. Doug Lee, and Michael Whitby. "Government and Administration." In *CAH.* Vol. 14, *Late Antiquity: Empire and Successors A.D. 425-600,* edited by Averil Cameron, Bryan Ward-Perkins, and Michael Whitby, 164–206. Cambridge: Cambridge University Press, 2000.

Barnwell, Paul S. *Emperor, Prefects, and Kings: The Roman West, 395-565.* Chapel Hill, NC: University of North Carolina Press, 1992.

Barton, Carlin A. *Roman Honor: The Fire in the Bones.* Berkeley, CA: University of California Press, 2001.

—. *The Sorrows of the Ancient Romans: The Gladiator and the Monster.* Princeton, NJ: Princeton University Press, 1993.

Bassi, Karen. "The Semantics of Manliness in Ancient Greece." In *Andreia: Studies in Manliness and Courage in Classical Antiquity,* edited by Ralph M. Rosen and Ineke Sluiter, 25–58. Brill: Leiden, 2003.

Beckmann, Martin. *The Column of Marcus Aurelius: The Genesis & Meaning of a Roman Imperial Monument.* Chapel Hill, NC: University of North Carolina Press, 2001.

Breebaart, Abraham B. "Eunapius of Sardes and the Writing of History." *Mnemosyne* 32 (1979): 360–75.

Behr, John. *Asceticism and Anthropology in Irenaeus and Clement.* Oxford: Oxford University Press, 2000.

Bell, Peter N. *Social Conflict in the Reign of Justinian: Its Nature, Management, and Mediation.* Oxford: Oxford University Press, 2013.

Bidez, Joseph. *La vie de l'empereur Julien.* Paris: Société d'édition Les belles lettres, 1930.

Binns, John. *Ascetics and Ambassadors of Christ: The Monasteries of Palestine 314-631.* Oxford: Oxford University Press, 1994.

Bjornlie, Michael S. *Politics and Tradition between Rome, Ravenna and Constantinople: A Study of Cassiodorus and the Variae, 527-554.* Cambridge: Cambridge University Press, 2013.

Bleckmann, Bruno, and Timo Stickler, eds. *Griechische Profanhistoriker des fünften nachchristlichen Jahrhunderts.* Historia Einzelschriften. Stuttgart: Franz Steiner Verlag, 2014.

Boin, Douglas. *Coming out Christian in the Roman World: How the Followers of Jesus made a Place in Caesar's Empire.* London, Bloomsbury, 2015.

Boswell, John. *Christianity, Social Tolerance, and Homosexuality: Gay People in Western Europe from the Beginning of the Christian Era to the Fourteenth Century.* Chicago: University of Chicago Press, 1980.

Bowersock, Glen W. *Julian the Apostate.* London: Duckworth, 1978.

Bowersock, Glen W., Peter Brown, and Oleg Grabar, eds. *Late Antiquity: A Guide to the Postclassical World.* Cambridge, MA: Belknap Press of Harvard University Press, 1999.

Boy, Renato Viana, "*History of Wars*: Narratives of Crises in Power Relations between Constantinople and Italy in the Sixth Century." In *Byzantium, Its Neighbours and Its Cultures*, edited by Danijel Dzino and Kenneth Parry, 209–22. Brisbane: Australian Association for Byzantine Studies, 2014.

Börm, Henning. "Born to be Emperor: The Principle of Succession and the Roman Monarch." In *Contested Monarchy*, edited by Johannes Wienand, 239–64. Oxford: Oxford University Press, 2015.

—. "Justinians Triumph und Belisars Erniedrigung. Überlegungen zum Verhältnis zwischen Kaiser und Militär im späten Römischen Reich." *Chiron* 43 (2013): 63–91.

—. "Procopius and the East." In *Brill's Companion to Procopius*, edited by Mischa Meier. Leiden: Brill, forthcoming. Braun, René, and Jean Richer, eds. *L'Empereur Julien: De l' histoire à la legend.* Paris: Société d'édition Les belles lettres, 1978.

—. "Procopius, His Predecessors, and the Genesis of the *Anecdota*." In *Antimonarchic Discourse in Antiquity*, edited by Henning Börm, 305–45. Stuttgart: Franz Steiner Verlag, 2015.

—. *Prokop und die Perser: Untersuchungen zu den römisch-sasanidischen Kontakten in der ausgehenden Spätantike.* Stuttgart: Franz Steiner, 2007.

Brennecke, Hanns C. "'An fidelis ad militiam converti possit?' [Tertullian, de idolo latri 19.1]. Frühchristliches Bekenntnis und Militärdienst im Widerspruch." In *Die Weltlichkeit des Glaubens in der Alten Kirche: Festschrift für Ulrich Wickrt zum siebzigsten Geburtstag,* edited by Barbara Aland and Christoph Schäublin, 179–232. Berlin: De Gruyter, 1997.

Brodka, Dariusz. *Die Geschichtsphilosophie in der spätantiken Historiographie. Studien zu Prokopios von Kaisareia, Agathias von Myrina und Theophylaktos Simokattes.* Frankfurt: P. Lang, 2004.

—. "Prokopios von Kaisareia und Justinians Idee der Reconquista." *Eos* 86 (1999): 243–55.

Brooten, Bernadette J. *Love between Women: Early Christian Responses to Female Homoeroticism.* Chicago: University of Chicago Press, 1996.

Brown, Peter. *Augustine of Hippo.* Berkeley, CA: University of California Press, 2000.

—. *Authority and the Sacred: Aspects of the Christianisation of the Roman World.* Cambridge: Cambridge University Press, 1995.

—. *The Body and Society: Men Women and Sexual Renunciation in Early Christianity.* New York: Columbia University Press, 1988.

—. "Holy Men." In *CAH*. Vol. 14, *Late Antiquity: Empire and Successors A.D. 425-600*, edited by Averil Cameron, Bryan Ward-Perkins, and Michael Whitby, 781–810. Cambridge: Cambridge University Press, 2000.

—. *Power and Persuasion in Late Antiquity: Towards a Christian Empire*. Madison, WI: University of Wisconsin Press, 1992.

—. *The Rise of Western Christendom: Triumph and Diversity AD 200-1000*. Oxford: Oxford University Press, 1996.

—. "The Saint as Exemplar in Late Antiquity." *Representations* 1.2 (1983): 1–25.

—. *Through the Eye of a Needle: Wealth, the Fall of Rome, and the Making of Christianity in the West, 350-550 AD*. Princeton, NJ: Princeton University Press, 2012.

—. *The World of Late Antiquity AD 150-750*. London: Thames and Hudson, 1971.

Brown, Truesdell S. *Gentlemen and Officers: Imperial Administration and Aristocratic Power in Byzantine Italy, AD 554-800*. London: British School at Rome, 1984.

Browning, Robert. *The Emperor Julian*. London: Weidenfeld and Nicolson, 1975.

Brubaker, Leslie. "The Age of Justinian: Gender and Society." In *CCAJ*, edited by Michael Maas, 427–47. Cambridge: Cambridge University Press, 2005.

—. "Sex, Lies, and Textuality: The Secret History of Prokopios and the Rhetoric of Gender in Sixth-Century Byzantium." In *Gender in the Early Medieval World: East and West, 300-900*, edited by Leslie Brubaker and Julia M. H. Smith, 83–101. Cambridge: Cambridge University Press, 2004.

Brunt, Peter A. "On Historical Fragments and Epitomes." *Classical Quarterly* 30 (1980): 477–94.

Buc, Philippe. *Holy War, Martyrdom, and Terror: Christianity, Violence, and the West*. Philadelphia, PA: University of Pennsylvania Press, 2015.

Burgess, Richard W. "The Accession of Marcian in the Light of the Chalcedonian Apologetic and Monophysite Polemic." *Byzantion* 86/87 (1993/94): 47–68.

Burgess, Richard W., and Michael Kulikowski. "The Historiographical Position of John Malalas: Genre in Late Antiquity and the Byzantine Middle Ages." In *Die Weltchronik des Johannes Malalas*, edited by Mischa Meier, Christine Radtki, and Fabian Schulz, 93–117. Stuttgart: Franz Steiner Verlag, 2016.

Burgess, William D. "Isaurian Factions in the Reign of Zeno the Isaurian." *Latomus* 51 (1992): 874–80.

Burrus, Virginia. *Begotten Not Made: Conceiving Manhood in Late Antiquity*. Stanford, CA: Stanford University Press, 2000.

Bury, John B. "A Note on the Emperor Olybrius." *English Historical Review* 1 (1886): 507–09.

—. *History of the Later Roman Empire: From Arcadius to Irene, 395 to 800*. 2 vols. London: Macmillan and Co., 1889.

Butler, Judith. *Bodies That Matter: On the Discursive Limits of "Sex."* New York: Routledge, 1993.

Bynum, Caroline W. *The Resurrection of the Body in Western Christianity in Western Christianity, 200-1336*. New York: Columbia University Press, 1995.

Cameron, Alan. *Circus Factions: Blues and Greens at Rome and Byzantium*. Oxford: Clarendon, 1976.

—. *Claudian: Poetry and Propaganda at the Court of Honorius*. Oxford: Clarendon, 1970.

—. "The Empress and the Poet: Paganism and Politics at the Court of Theodosius II." *Yale Classical Studies* 27 (1982): 217–89.

—. *The Last Pagans of Rome*. Oxford: Oxford University Press, 2011.

—. "The Probus Diptych and Christian Apologetic." In *From Rome to Constantinople: Studies in Honour of Averil Cameron*, edited by Hagit Amirav and Bas Ter Haar Romeny, 191–202. Leuven: Peeters, 2007.

Cameron, Alan, Jacqueline Long, and Lee Sherry. *Barbarians and Politics at the Court of Arcadius*. Berkeley, CA: University of California Press, 1993.

Cameron, Averil. *Agathias*. Oxford: Clarendon, 1970.

—. *Byzantine Matters.* Princeton, NJ: Princeton University Press, 2014.

—. *Christianity and the Rhetoric of Empire: The Development of Christian Discourse.* Berkeley, CA: University of California Press, 1991.

—. "Form and Meaning: The *Vita Constantini* and the *Vita Antonii.*" In *Greek Biography and Panegyric in Late Antiquity*, edited by Tomas Hägg and Philip Rousseau, 72–88. Berkeley: University of California Press, 2000.

—. *The Mediterranean World in Late Antiquity, AD 395-600.* London: Routledge, 1993.

—. "Old Rome and New Rome: Roman Studies in Sixth Century Constantinople." *Transformations of Late Antiquity: Essays for Peter Brown*, edited by Philip Rousseau and Emmanuel Papoutsakis, 15–36. Burlington, VT: Ashgate, 2009.

—. *Procopius and the Sixth Century.* London: University of California Press, 1985.

—. "Virginity as a Metaphor: Women and the Rhetoric of Christianity." In *History as Text: The Writing of Ancient History*, edited by Averil Cameron, 175–205. London: Duckworth, 1988.

Canepa, Matthew P. *Two Eyes of the Earth: Art and Ritual of Kingship between Rome and Sasanian Iran.* Berkeley, CA: University of California Press, 2009.

Chazelle, Celia M. *The Crucified God in the Carolingian Era.* Cambridge: Cambridge University Press, 2001.

Chesnut, Glenn F. *The First Church Historians: Eusebius, Socrates, Sozomen, Theodoret, and Evagrius.* 2nd ed. Macon, GA: Mercer University Press, 1986.

Chew, Kathryn. "Virgins and Eunuchs: Pulcheria, Politics and the Death of Emperor Theodosius II." *Historia: Zeitschrift für Alte Geschichte* 55.2 (2006): 207–27.

Cohen, Edward. "The High Cost of *andreia* at Athens." In *Andreia: Studies in Manliness and Courage in Classical Antiquity*, edited by Ralph M. Rosen and Ineke Sluiter, 145–66. Leiden: Brill, 2003.

Conant, Jonathan. *Staying Roman: Conquest and Identity in Africa and the Mediterranean, 439-700*. Cambridge: Cambridge University Press, 2012.

Connell, Raewyn W. *Masculinities*. Berkeley, CA: University of California Press, 1995.

Connolly, Joy. "Like the Labors of Heracles: *Andreia* and *Paideia* in Greek Culture under Rome." In *Andreia: Studies in Manliness and Courage in Classical Antiquity*, edited by Ralph M. Rosen and Ineke Sluiter, 287–317. Leiden: Brill, 2003.

Constable, Giles. *The Reformation of the Twelfth Century*. Cambridge: Cambridge University Press, 1996.

Conway, Colleen M. *Behold the Man: Jesus and Greco-Roman Masculinities*. Oxford: Oxford University Press, 2008.

Cosentino, Salvatore. "Constans II and the Byzantine Navy." *BZ* 100.2 (2007): 577–603.

Cooper, Kate. "Gender and the Fall of Rome." In *A Companion to Late Antiquity*, edited by Philip Rousseau, 187–99. Oxford: Blackwell, 2009.

—. "The Heroine and the Historian: Procopius of Caesarea on the Troubled Reign of Queen Amalasuentha." In *A Companion to Ostrogothic Italy*, edited by Jonathan Arnold, M. Shane Bjornlie, and Kristina Sessa, 296-315. Leiden: Brill, 2016.

—. *The Virgin and the Bride: Idealized Womanhood in Late Antiquity*. Cambridge, MA: Harvard University Press, 1996.

Croke, Brian. "The Date of the 'Anastasian Long Wall' in Thrace." *GRBS* 20 (1982), 59–78.

—. "Dynasty and Aristocracy in the Fifth Century." In *CCAA*, edited by Michael Maas, 98–124. Cambridge: Cambridge University Press, 2014.

—. "Dynasty and Ethnicity: Emperor Leo and Ethnicity and the Eclipse of Aspar." *Chiron* 35 (2005): 147–203.

—. "Justinian's Constantinople." In *CCAJ*, edited by Michael Maas, 60–86. Cambridge: Cambridge University Press, 2005.

—. "Uncovering Byzantium's Historiographical Audience." In *History as Literature in Byzantium*, edited by Ruth Macrides, 25–53. Burlington, VT: Ashgate 2010.

Dagron, Gilbert. *Empereur et prêtre. Étude sur le 'Césaropapisme' Byzantine.* Paris: Gallimard, 1996.

Davies, Glenys. "Greek and Roman Sculpture." In *The Oxford Companion to Classical Civilization*, edited by Simon Hornblower and Antony Spawforth, 651–53. Oxford: Oxford University Press, 1998.

Demandt, A. "The Osmosis of Late Roman and Germanic Aristocracies." In *Das Reich und die Barbaren*, edited by Evangelos K. Chrysos and Andreas Schwarcz, 75–86. Vienna: Böhlau, 1989.

Dennis, George T. "Defenders of the Christian People: Holy War in Byzantium." In *The Crusades from the Perspective of the Byzantine and Muslim World*, edited by Angeliki E. Laiou and Roy P. Mottahedeh, 31–40. Washington, DC: Dumbarton Oaks Research Library and Collection, 2001.

Deslauriers, Marguerite. "Aristotle on *Andreia*, Divine, and Sub-Human Virtues." In *Andreia: Studies in Manliness and Courage in Classical Antiquity*, edited by Ralph M. Rosen and Ineke Sluiter, 187–211. Leiden: Brill, 2003.

—. "Sex and Essence in Aristotle's Metaphysics and Biology." In *Feminist Interpretations of Aristotle*, edited by Cynthia A. Freeland, 138–67. University Park, PA: Pennsylvania State University Press, 1998.

Devijver, Hubert. "Les milices équestres et la hiérarchie militaire." In *La hiérarchie (Rangordnung) de l'armée romaine sous le haut-empire*, edited by Yann Le Bohec, 175–91. Paris: De Boccard, 1995.

Donner, Fred McGraw. *Muhammad and the Believers: At the Origins of Islam.* Cambridge, MA: The Belknap Press of Harvard University Press, 2010.

Duff, Tim. *Plutarch's Lives: Exploring Virtue and Vice.* Oxford: Clarendon, 2000.

Eckstein, Arthur M. *Moral Vision in the Histories of Polybius.* Berkeley, CA: University of California Press, 1995.

Edwards, Catharine. *The Politics of Immorality in Ancient Rome.* Cambridge: Cambridge University Press, 1993.

—. "The Suffering Body: Philosophy and Pain in Seneca's Letters." In *Constructions of the Classical Body,* edited by James Porter, 252–68. Ann Arbor, MI: University of Michigan Press, 1999.

Eich, Peter. "Militarisierungs- und Demilitarisierungstendenzen im dritten Jahrhundert n. Chr." In *The Impact of the Roman Army,* edited by Lukas de Blois, 511–15. Amsterdam: J. C. Gieben, 2001.

Eikenberry, Karl W., and David M. Kennedy. "Americans and Their Military, Drifting Apart." *The New York Times* 26 May 2013 http://www.nytimes.com/2013/05/27/opinion/americans-and-their-military-drifting-apart.html

Elm, Susanna. *Virgins of God: The Making of Asceticism in Late Antiquity.* Oxford: Oxford University Press, 1994.

Elsner, Jaś. *Art and the Roman Viewer: The Transformation of Art from the Pagan World to Christianity.* Cambridge: Cambridge University Press, 1995.

—. *Imperial Rome and Christian Triumph.* Oxford: Oxford University Press, 1998.

Elton, Hugh. "Defence in Fifth-Century Gaul." In *Fifth-Century Gaul: A Crisis of Identity,* edited by John F. Drinkwater and Hugh Elton, 167–75. Cambridge: Cambridge University Press, 1992.

—. "Ilus and the Imperial Aristocracy under Zeno." *Byzantion* 20 (2000): 394–407.

—. "Off the Battlefield: The Civilian's View of Late Roman Soldiers," *Expedition* 10 (1997): 42–50.

Endsjø, Dag Øistein. *Primordial Landscapes, Incorruptible Bodies: Desert Asceticism and the Christian Appropriation of Greek Ideas on Geography Bodies, and Immortality.* New York: Peter Lang, 2008.

Engberg-Pedersen, Troels. *Paul and the Stoics*. Edinburgh: Clark, 2000.

Evans, James A. S. *The Age of Justinian: The Circumstances of Imperial Power*. London: Routledge, 1996.

—. "The Dates of Procopius' Works." *GRBS* 37 (1996): 301–20.

—. *The Empress Theodora: Partner of Justinian*. Austin, TX: University of Texas Press, 2002.

—. "The 'Nika' Rebellion and the Empress Theodora." *Byzantion* 54 (1984): 380–82.

—. *Procopius*. New York: Twayne, 1972.

Flomen, Max. "The Original Godfather: Ricimer and the Fall of Rome." *Hirundo, the McGill Journal of Classical Studies* 8 (2009–10): 9–17.

Foss, Clive. "The Empress Theodora." *Byzantion* 72 (2002), 141–76.

Fossella, Jason. "Waiting Only for a Pretext: A New Chronology for the Sixth-Century Byzantine Invasion of Spain." *Estudios Bizantinos* 1 (2013): 30–38.

Foucault, Michel. T*he History of Sexuality*. Vol. 1, *An Introduction*. Translated by Robert Hurley. New York: Vintage, 1979.

—. *The History of Sexuality*. Vol. 2, *The Use of Pleasure*. Translated by Robert Hurley. New York: Vintage, 1985.

—. *The History of Sexuality*. Vol. 3, *The Care of Self*. Translated by Robert Hurley. New York: Vintage, 1988.

Fox, Robin Lane. "The Life of Daniel." In *Portraits: Biographical Representation in the Greek and Latin Literature of the Roman Empire*, edited by M.J. Edwards and Simon Swaine, 175–225. Oxford: Clarendon, 1997.

Foxhall, Lin, and John Salmon. *When Men Were Men: Masculinity, Power and Identity in the Classical Tradition*. London: Routledge, 1998.

Frank, Richard I. "*Scholae Palatinae*: The Palace Guards of the Later Roman Empire." *Papers and Monographs of the American Academy in Rome* 23 (1969), 201–19.

Frankforter, A. Daniel. "Amalasuntha, Procopius and a Woman's Place." *Journal of Women's History* 8 (1996): 41–57.

Gaddis, Michael. *There Is No Crime for Those Who Have Christ: Religious Violence in the Christian Roman Empire*. Berkeley, CA: University of California Press, 2005.

Garland, Lynda. *Byzantine Empresses: Women and Power in Byzantium, AD 527-1204*. London: Routledge, 1999.

Gartner, Hans. "Panegyrik und zu Ammians Charakteristik des Kaisers Julian." *AbhMainz, Geistes- und Sozialwiss. Kl.* 10 (1968): 499–529.

Geary, Patrick J. "Barbarians and Ethnicity." In *Late Antiquity: A Guide to the Postclassical World*, edited by Glenn W. Bowersock, Peter Brown, and Oleg Grabar, 107–129. Cambridge, MA: Belknap Press of Harvard University Press, 1999.

Geiger, Joseph. *The First Hall of Fame: A Study of the Statues in the Forum Augustum*. Leiden: Brill, 2008.

Gillette, Andrew. "The Birth of Ricimer." *Historia* 44 (1995): 380–84.

—. "Epic Panegyric and Political Communication in the Roman West." In *Two Romes: Rome and Constantinople in Late Antiquity*. Edited by Lucy Grig and Gavin Kelly, 265–90. Oxford: Oxford University Press, 2012.

—. "Rome, Ravenna, and the Last Western Emperors." *Papers at the British School at Rome* 69 (2001): 131–67.

Gilmore, David D. *Manhood in the Making*. New Haven, CT: Yale University Press, 1990.

Gleason, Maud W. *Making Men: Sophists and Self-Presentation in Ancient Rome*. Princeton, NJ: Princeton University Press, 1995.

Goehring, James E. *Ascetics, Society, and the Desert: Studies in Early Egyptian Monasticism*. Harrisburg, PA: Trinity Press International, 1999.

Goffart, Walter. *Barbarians and Romans*. Princeton, NJ: Princeton University Press, 1980.

—. *Barbarian Tides: The Migration Age and the Later Roman Empire*. Philadelphia, PA: University of Pennsylvania Press, 2006.

—. *The Narrators of Barbarian History: Jordanes, Gregory of Tours, Bede, and Paul the Deacon A.D. 550-800*. Princeton, NJ: Princeton University Press, 1988.

—. "Zosimus, The First Historian of Rome's Fall." *The American Historical Review*. 76.2 (1971): 412–41.

Grant, Michael. *The Antonines: The Roman Empire in Transition*. London: Routledge, 1994.

Greatrex, Geoffrey. "The Classical Past in the Classicising Historians." In *The Reception of Classical Texts and Images*. Vol. 1 *Reception within Antiquity*, edited by Lorna Hardwick and Stanley Ireland, 40–56. Milton Keynes: The Open University, 1996.

—. "The Dates of Procopius' Works." *BMGS* 18 (1994): 101–14.

—. "The Early Years of Justin I's Reign in the Sources." *Electrum* 12 (2007): 99–112.

—. "Government and Mechanisms of Control, East and West." In *CCAA*, edited by Michael Maas, 26–43. Cambridge: Cambridge University Press, 2014.

—. "Lawyers and Historians in Late Antiquity." In *Law, Society and Authority in Late Antiquity*, edited by Ralph Mathisen. Oxford: Oxford University Press, 2001.

—. "The Nika Riot: A Reappraisal." *JHS* 117 (1997): 60–86.

—. "Perceptions of Procopius in Recent Scholarship." *Histos* 8 (2014): 76–121 (*Addenda*) 121a–121e.

—. "Recent Work on Procopius and the Composition of Wars VIII." *BMGS* 27 (2003): 45–67.

—. "Roman Identity in the Sixth Century." In *Ethnicity and Culture in Late Antiquity*, edited by Stephen Mitchell and Geoffrey Greatrex, 267–92. London: Duckworth, 2000.

—. *Rome and Persia at War: 502-532*. Leeds: Francis Cairns, 1998.

—. "Stephanus, the Father of Procopius of Caesarea?" *Medieval Prosopography* 17 (1996): 122–45.

Gregory, Timothy E. *Vox Populi: Popular Opinion and Violence in the Religious Controversies of the Fifth Century A.D.* Columbus, OH: Ohio State University Press, 1979.

Hägg, Tomas, and Philip Rousseau, eds. *Greek Biography and Panegyric in Late Antiquity*. Berkeley: University of California Press, 2000.

—, "Introduction: Biography and Panegyric." In *Greek Biography and Panegyric in Late Antiquity*, edited by Tomas Hägg and Philip Rousseau, 1–28. Berkeley: University of California Press, 2000.

Hagl, Wolfgang. *Arcadius Apis Imperator: Synesios van Kyrene und sein Beitrag zum Herrscherideal der Spätantike*. Stuttgart: F. Steiner, 1997.

Haldon, John F. *Byzantium and the Seventh Century: The Transformation of a Society*. Cambridge: Cambridge University Press, 1990.

—. "'Greek Fire' Revisited: Recent and Current Research." In *Byzantine Style, Religion and Civilization: In Honour of Sir Steven Runciman*, edited by Elizabeth Jeffreys, 290–325. Cambridge: Cambridge University Press, 2006.

—. *Warfare, Society and State*. London: UCL Press, 1999.

Hall, Edith. *Inventing the Barbarian: Greek Self-Definition through Tragedy*. Oxford: Clarendon, 1989.

Hall, Stuart G. "The Organization of the Church." In *CAH*. Vol. 14, *Late Antiquity: Empire and Successors A.D. 425-600*, edited by Averil Cameron, Bryan Ward-Perkins, and Michael Whitby, 731–44. Cambridge: Cambridge University Press, 2000.

Hallett, Judith P. *Fathers and Daughters in Roman Society: Women and the Elite Family*. Princeton, NJ: Princeton University Press, 1984.

Halperin, David M. "One Hundred Years of Homosexuality." In *One Hundred Years of Homosexuality and Other Essays on Greek Love*, 15–40. New York: Routledge, 1990.

Halsall, Guy. "The Barbarian Invasions." In *The New Cambridge Medieval History*, Volume 1: c. 500–700, edited by Paul Fouracre, 35–55. Cambridge: Cambridge University Press, 2005.

—. "Funny Foreigners: Laughing with the Barbarians in Late Antiquity." In *Humour, History, and Politics in Late Antiquity and the Early Middle Ages*, edited by Guy Halsall, 89–113. Cambridge: Cambridge University Press, 2004.

Harley-McGowan, Felicity J. "The Narration of Christ's Passion in Early Christian Art." In *Byzantine Narrative, Papers in Honour of Roger Scott*, edited by John Burke, Penelope Buckley, Kathleen Hay, Roger Scott, and Andrew Stephenson, 221–32, 536–38. Melbourne: Australian Association for Byzantine Studies, 2006.

Harlow, Mary. "Clothes Maketh the Man: Power Dressing and Elite Masculinity in the Later Roman World." In *Gender in the Early Medieval World: East and West, 300-900*, edited by Leslie Brubaker and Julia M. H. Smith, 44–69 Cambridge: Cambridge University Press, 2004.

Harrell, Sarah. "Marvellous *Andreia*: Politics, Geography, and Ethnicity in Herodotus' *Histories*." In *Andreia: Studies in Manliness and Courage in Classical Antiquity*, edited by Ralph M. Rosen and Ineke Sluiter, 77–94. Leiden: Brill, 2003.

Harries, Jill. *Law and Empire in Late Antiquity*. Cambridge: Cambridge University Press, 1999.

—. "Men without Women: Theodosius' Consistory and the Business of Government." In *Theodosius II: Rethinking the Roman Empire in Late Antiquity*, edited by Christopher Kelly, 67–89. Cambridge: Cambridge University Press, 2013.

—. "*Pius princeps*: Theodosius II and Fifth-Century Constantinople." In *New Constantines: The Rhythm of Imperial Renewal in Byzantium, 4th-13th Centuries: Papers from the Twenty-Sixth Spring Symposium of Byzantine Studies, St Andrews, March 1992*, edited by Paul Magdalino, 35–44. Brookfield, VT: Variorum, 1994.

—. *Sidonius Apollinaris and the Fall of Rome, AD 407-485*. Oxford: Clarendon, 1994.

—. "Sidonius Apollinaris, Rome and the Barbarians: A Climate of Treason?" In *Fifth-Century Gaul: A Crisis of Identity*, edited by John F. Drinkwater and Hugh Elton, 298–308. Cambridge: Cambridge University Press, 1992.

Harris, Leonard. "Honor: Emasculation and Empowerment." In *Rethinking Masculinity: Philosophical Explorations in Light of Feminism*, edited by Larry May and Robert A. Strikwerda, 275–88. Lanham, MD: Rowman & Littlefield, 1992.

Harrison, Thomas, ed. *Greeks and Barbarians*. New York: Routledge, 2002.

Hartog, François. *The Mirror of Herodotus: The Representation of the Other in the Writing of History*. Translated by Janet Lloyd. Berkeley, CA: University of California Press, 1988.

Heather, Peter. *The Fall of the Roman Empire: A New History*. Oxford: Oxford University Press, 2005.

—. *Goths and Romans, 332-489*. Oxford: Oxford University Press, 1991.

—. *The Goths*. Oxford: Blackwell, 1996.

—. "Migrations." *Networks and Neighbours* 3.1 (2015): 1–19.

—. *The Restoration of Rome: Barbarian Popes and Imperial Pretenders*. London: Oxford University Press, 2013.

Heather, Peter, and David Moncur. *Philosophy and Empire*. Liverpool: Liverpool University Press 2001.

Heim, François. *La théologie de la victoire de Constantin à Théodose*. Paris: Beauchesne, 1992.

Helgeland, John, Robert J. Daly, and J. Patout Burns. *Christians and the Military: The Early Experience*. Philadelphia, PA: Fortress Press, 1985.

Herrin, Judith. "In Search of Byzantine Women: Three Avenues of Approach." In *Images of Women in Antiquity*, edited by Averil Cameron and Amélie Kuhrt, 167–89. Detroit: Wayne State University Press, 1983.

Hexter, Ralph. "John Boswell's Gay Science: Prolegomenon to a Re-Reading." In *The Boswell Thesis: Essays on Christianity, Social Tolerance, and Homosexuality*, edited by Mathew Kuefler, 35–56. Chicago: University of Chicago Press, 2005.

Hobbs, Angela. *Plato and the Hero: Manliness and the Impersonal Good*. Cambridge: Cambridge University Press, 2000.

Holum, Kenneth G. "The Classical City in the Sixth Century: Survival and Transformation." In *CCAJ*, edited by Michael Maas, 87–112. Cambridge: Cambridge University Press, 2005.

—. *Theodosian Empresses: Women and Dominion in Late Antiquity*. Berkeley, CA: University of California Press, 1982.

Hopkins, Keith. *Conquerors and Slaves*. Cambridge: Cambridge University Press, 1978.

Hornblower, Simon, and Antony Spawforth, eds. *The Oxford Companion to Classical Civilisation*. Oxford: Oxford University Press, 1998.

Howard-Johnston, James. "The Education and Expertise of Procopius." *Antiquité tardive* 8 (2000): 19–30.

—. *Witness to a World Crisis: Historians and the Histories of the Middle East in the Seventh Century*. Oxford: Oxford University Press, 2010.

Hoyland, Robert. "Early Islam as a Late Antique Religion." In *The Oxford Handbook of Late Antiquity*, edited by Scott Fitzgerald Johnson, 1053–77. Oxford: Oxford University Press, 2007.

Hunter, David G. "Resistance to the Virginal Ideal in Late Fourth-Century Rome." *JTS* 48 (1987): 45–64.

James, Liz. *Empresses and Power in Early Byzantium*. London: Leicester University Press, 2001.

Jones, Arnold H. M. "The Caste System of the Later Roman Empire." *Eirene* (1970): 79–96.

—. *The Later Roman Empire, 284-602: A Social, Economic and Administrative Survey*. 3 vols. Oxford: Blackwell, 1964.

Kaegi, Walter E. *Byzantium and the Decline of the West*. Princeton, NJ: Princeton University Press, 1968.

—. *Heraclius, Emperor of Byzantium*. Cambridge: Cambridge University Press, 2003.

—. "Procopius the Military Historian." *Byzantinische Forschungen* 15 (1990): 53–85.

Kaldellis, Anthony. "A Byzantine Argument for the Equivalence of All Religions: Michael Attaleiates on Ancient and Modern Romans." *International Journal of the Classical Tradition* 14 1/2 (2007): 1–22.

—. *The Byzantine Republic: People and Power in New Rome*, Cambridge, MA: Harvard University Press, 2015.

—. *Hellenism in Byzantium: The Transformation of Greek Identity and the Reception of the Classical Tradition*. Cambridge: Cambridge University Press, 2007.

—. *Procopius of Caesarea: Tyranny, History, and Philosophy at the End of Antiquity*. Philadelphia, PA: University of Pennsylvania Press, 2004.

—. "Procopius' *Persian War*: A Thematic and Literary Analysis." *History as Literature in Byzantium*, edited by Ruth Macrides, 253–74. Burlington, VT: Ashgate, 2010.

—. "The Religion of Ioannas Lydos." *Phoenix* 57 (2003): 300–16.

—. "Things Are Not What They Are: Agathias Mythistoricus and the Last Laugh of Classical Culture." *Classical Quarterly* 53 (2003): 295–300.

Kelly, Christopher, ed. *Theodosius II: Rethinking the Roman Empire in Late Antiquity*. Cambridge: Cambridge University Press, 2013.

Kelly, Gavin. "Ammianus' Greek Accent." *Talanta* 45 (2013): 67–79.

—. *Ammianus Marcellinus the Allusive Historian*. Cambridge: Cambridge University Press, 2008.

Kennell, Stefanie A. H. *Magnus Felix Ennodius: A Gentleman of the Church*. Ann Arbor, MI: University of Michigan Press, 2000.

Koder, Johannes, and Ioannis Stouraitis, eds. *Byzantine War Ideology between Roman Imperial Concept and Christian Religion*. Vienna: Verlag der Österreichischen Akademie der Wissenschaften, 2012.

Kosiński, Rafał. "Leo II: Some Chronological Issues." *Palamedes* 3 (2008): 209–14.

—. *The Emperor Zeno: Religion and Politics.* Kraków: TYNIEC, 2010.

Kouroumali, Maria. "The Justinianic Reconquest of Italy: Imperial Campaigns and Local Responses." *In War and Warfare in Late Antiquity,* edited by Alexander Sarantis and Neil Christie, vol. 2, 969–1000. 2 vols. Brill: Leiden, 2013.

—. "Procopius and the Gothic War." PhD thesis, Oxford University, 2005.

Krakauer, Jon. *Where Men Win Glory: The Odyssey of Pat Tillman.* New York: Doubleday, 2009.

Krueger, Derek. "Christian Piety and Practice in the Sixth Century." In *CCAJ,* edited by Michael Maas, 291–315. Cambridge: Cambridge University Press, 2005.

—. *Writing and Holiness: The Practice of Authorship in the Early Christian East.* Philadelphia, PA: University of Pennsylvania Press, 2004.

Kruse, Marion. "The Speech of the Armenians in Procopius: Justinian's Foreign Policy and the Transition between Books 1 and 2 of the *Wars.*" *Classical Quarterly* 63 (2013): 868–93.

Kuefler, Mathew, ed. *The Boswell Thesis: Essays on Christianity, Social Tolerance, and Homosexuality.* Chicago: University of Chicago Press, 2005.

—. ed. *The Manly Eunuch: Masculinity, Gender Ambiguity, and Christian Ideology in Late Antiquity.* Chicago: University of Chicago Press, 2001.

Kulikowski, Michael. "Marcellinus of Dalmatia and the Dissolution of the Fifth-Century Empire." *Byzantion* 72.1 (2002): 177–91.

—. "Review of Christopher Kelly, *Attila the Hun: Barbarian Terror and the Fall of the Roman Empire.*" *London Review of Books* 31.3 (12 February 2009), 22–23.

Kusz, Kyle W. "From NASCAR Nation to Pat Tillman: Notes on Sport and the Politics of White Cultural Nationalism in Post-9/11 America." *Journal of Sport and Social Issues* 31.1 (2007): 77–88.

Langlands, Rebecca. *Sexual Morality in Ancient Rome*. Cambridge: Cambridge University Press, 2006.

La Rocca, Cristina. "*Consors regni*: A Problem of Gender? The *consortium* between Amalasuntha and Theodahad in 534." In *Studies in the Earlier Middle Ages of Pauline Stafford*, edited by Janet L. Nelson, Susan Reynolds, and Susan M. Johns, 127–43. London: Institute of Historical Research, 2012.

Larson, Jennifer. "Paul's Masculinity." *Journal of Biblical Literature* 123 (2004): 85–97.

Leader, Ruth E. "The David Plates Revisited: Transforming the Secular in Byzantium." *The Art Bulletin* 82.3 (2000): 407–27.

Lee, A. Doug. "The Eastern Empire: Theodosius to Anastasius." In *CAH*. Vol. 14, *Late Antiquity: Empire and Successors A.D. 425-600*, edited by Averil Cameron, Bryan Ward-Perkins, and Michael Whitby, 33–62. Cambridge: Cambridge University Press, 2000.

—. "The Empire at War." In *CCAJ*, edited by Michael Maas, 113–33. Cambridge: Cambridge University Press, 2005.

—. *From Rome to Byzantium, AD 363 to 565: The Transformation of the Ancient Roman World*. Edinburgh: Edinburgh University Press, 2013.

—. "Theodosius and His Generals." In *Theodosius II: Rethinking the Roman Empire in Late Antiquity*, edited by Christopher Kelly, 90–108. Cambridge: Cambridge University Press, 2013.

—. *War in Late Antiquity: A Social History*. Oxford: Blackwell, 2007.

Lefkowitz, Mary R. "Influential Women." In *Images of Women in Late Antiquity*, edited by Averil Cameron and Amélie Kuhrt, 49–64. Detroit: Wayne State University Press, 1983.

Lenski, Noel. "Assimilation and Revolt in the Territory of Isauria from the 1st Century BC to the 6th Century AD." *Journal of the Economic and Social History of the Orient* 42.4 (1999), 413–65.

—. "*Intium mal Romano imperio*: Contemporary Reactions to the Battle of Adrianople." *Transactions of the American Philological Association* 127 (1997), 129–66.

Leppin, Hartmut. *Justinian: Das christliche Experiment*. Stuttgart, Klett-Cotta, 2011.

Leyser, Conrad. "Introduction: Making Medieval Societies." In *Making Early Medieval Societies: Conflict and Belonging in the Latin West, 300-1200*, edited by Kate Cooper and Conrad Leyser, 181–201. Cambridge: Cambridge University Press, 2016.

Liebeschuetz, Wolfgang. *Ambrose and John Chrysostom: Clerics between Desert and Empire*. Oxford: Oxford University Press, 2011.

—. *Barbarians and Bishops: Army, Church, and State in the Age of Arcadius and Chrysostom*. Oxford: Clarendon, 1990.

—. "The End of the Roman Army in the Western Empire." In *War and Society in the Roman World*, edited by John Rich and Graham Shipley, 265–76. New York: Routledge, 1993.

—. "The Romans Demilitarised: The Evidence of Procopius." *Scripta Classica Israelica* 15 (1996): 230–39.

Lilie, Ralph-Johannes. "Die zweihundertjährige Reform: zu den Anfängen der Themenorganisation im 7. Und 8. Jahrhundert." *BS* 45 (1984): 27–39, 190–201.

Limberis, Vasiliki, *Divine Heiress: The Virgin Mary and the Creation of Christian Constantinople*. London: Routledge, 1994.

Ljubarskij, Jakov. "Quellenforschung and/or Literary Criticism: Narrative Structures in Byzantine Historical Writings." *Symbolae Osloenses: Norwegian Journal of Greek and Latin Studies* 73 (1998): 5–73.

Long, Jacqueline. *Claudian's In Eutropium or, How, When and Why to Slander a Eunuch*. Chapel Hill, NC: University of North Carolina Press, 1996.

Louth, Andrew. "Review of Peter Brown's *The Body and Society*." *JTS* 41 (1990): 231–35.

Maas, Michael. *John Lydus and the Roman Past: Antiquarianism and Politics in the Age of Justinian.* London: Routledge, 1992.

—. "Strabo and Procopius: Classical Geography for a Christian Empire." In *From Rome to Constantinople: Studies in Honour of Averil Cameron,* edited by Hagit Amirav and Bas Ter Haar Romeny, 67–84. Leuven: Peeters, 2007.

MacCormack, Sabine. "Latin Prose Panegyrics." In *Empire and Aftermath: Silver Latin II,* edited by Thomas A. Dorey, 143–205. London: Routledge, 1975.

—. "The World of the Panegyrists." In *Art and Ceremony in Late Antiquity. Art and Ceremony in Late Antiquity,* edited by Sabine MacCormack, 1–14. Berkeley, CA: University of California Press, 1981.

MacGeorge, Penny. *Late Roman Warlords.* Oxford: Oxford University Press, 2002.

MacIsaac, John D. "The Hand of God: A Numismatic Study." *Traditio* 31 (1975): 322–28.

MacMullen, Ramsay. *Corruption and the Decline of Rome.* New Haven, CT: Yale University Press, 1988.

Madden, Thomas F. "Triumph Re-Imagined: The Golden Gate and Popular Memory in Byzantine and Ottoman Constantinople." In *Shipping, Trade and Crusade in the Medieval Mediterranean,* edited by Ruthy Gertwagen and Elizabeth Jeffreys, 317–28. Brookfield, VT: Ashgate, 2012.

Markus, Robert A. *Saeculum: History and Society in the Theology of St. Augustine.* Cambridge: Cambridge University Press, 1989.

Martin, Dale B. "Heterosexism and the Interpretation of Romans 1:18-32." In *The Boswell Thesis: Essays on Christianity, Social Tolerance, and Homosexuality,* edited by Mathew Kuefler, 130–51. Chicago: University of Chicago Press, 2005.

Masterson, Mark. *Man to Man: Desire, Homosociality, and Authority in Late-Roman Manhood.* Columbus, OH: Ohio State University Press, 2014.

—. "Studies of Ancient Masculinities." In *A Companion to Greek and Roman Masculinities,* edited by Thomas K. Hubbard, 17–31. London: Wiley Blackwell, 2013.

Mathisen, Ralph W. *"Natio, Gens, Provincialis,* and *Civis*: Geographical Terminology and Personal Identity in Late Antiquity." In *Shifting Genres in Late Antiquity,* edited by Geoffrey Greatrex and Hugh Elton, 277–86. Burlington, VT: Ashgate, 2015.

—. *"Peregrini, Barbari,* and *Cives Romani*: Concepts of Citizenship and the Legal Identity of Barbarians in the Later Roman Empire." *American Historical Review* 3 (2006): 1011–40.

—. "Ricimer's Church in Rome: How an Arian Barbarian Prospered in a Nicene World." In *The Power of Religion in Late Antiquity,* edited by Andrew Cain and Noel Lenski, 307–25. Burlington, VT: Ashgate, 2009.

Matthews, John. *The Roman Empire of Ammianus.* London: Duckworth, 1989.

—. *Western Aristocracies and Imperial Court, A.D. 364-425.* Oxford: Clarendon, 1975.

Mattox, John M. *St. Augustine and the Theory of Just War.* New York: Continuum, 2006.

Mazzo-Karras, Ruth. *From Boys to Men: Formations of Masculinity in Late Medieval Europe.* Philadelphia, PA: University of Pennsylvania Press, 2002.

McCormick, Michael. *Eternal Victory: Triumphal Rulership in Late Antiquity, Byzantium and the Early Medieval West.* Cambridge: Cambridge University Press, 1986.

McDonnell, Myles A. "McDonnell on Kaster on M. McDonnell, *Roman Manliness: Virtus and the Roman Republic*." *Bryn Mawr Classical Review* 2007.03.38.

—. *Roman Manliness: Virtus and the Roman Republic.* Cambridge: Cambridge University Press, 2006.

—. "Roman Men and Greek Virtue." In *Andreia: Studies in Manliness and Courage in Classical Antiquity,* edited by Ralph M. Rosen and Ineke Sluiter, 235–61. Leiden: Brill, 2003.

McEvoy, Meaghan. "Between the Old Rome and the New: Imperial Co-Operation ca. 400-500 CE." In *Byzantium, Its Neighbours and Its Cultures*, edited by Danijel Dzino and Kenneth Parry, 245–68. Brisbane: Australian Association for Byzantine Studies, 2014.

—. *Child Emperor Rule in the Late Roman West, AD 367-455*. Oxford: Oxford University Press, 2013.

McInerney, Jeremy. "Plutarch's Manly Women." In *Andreia: Studies in Manliness and Courage in Classical Antiquity*, edited by Ralph M. Rosen and Ineke Sluiter, 319–44. Leiden: Brill, 2003.

McKechnie, Paul. "Tertullian's De Pallio and Life in Roman Carthage." *Prudentia* 24.2 (1992): 44–66.

McLaughlin, Jonathan J. "Bridging the Cultural Divide: Libanius, Ellebichus, and Letters to Barbarian Generals." *JLA* 7.2 (2014): 253–79.

McLynn, Neil B. *Ambrose of Milan: Church and Court in a Christian Capital*. Berkeley, CA: University of California Press, 1994.

McMahon, Lucas. "The *Foederati*, the *Phoideratoi*, and the *Symmachoi* of the Late Antique East ca. A.D. 400-600." Master's thesis, University of Ottawa, 2014.

Meier, Mischa. *Anastasios I. Die Entstehung des Byzantinischen Reiches*. Stuttgart: Klett-Cotta, 2009.

—. *Das andere Zeitalter Justinians. Kontingenzerfahrung und Kontingenzbewaltigung im 6. Jahrhundert n. Ch.* Goettingen: Vandenhoeck & Ruprecht, 2003.

Merrills, Andrew H., and Richard Miles. *The Vandals*. Oxford: Wiley-Blackwell, 2010.

Messis, Charálambos. "La Construction Sociale, les 'Réalités' Rhétoriques et les Représentations de l'Identité Masculine à Byzance." PhD thesis, École des hautes études en sciences sociales (Paris), 2006.

Millar, Fergus. *A Greek Roman Empire: Power and Belief under Theodosius II, 408-450*. Berkeley, CA: University of California Press, 2006.

Mitchell, Stephen. *A History of the Later Roman Empire AD 284-641: The Transformation of the Ancient World*. Oxford: Blackwell, 2007.

—. "Ethnicity, Acculturation and Empire in Roman and Late Roman Asia Minor." In *Ethnicity and Culture in Late Antiquity*, edited by Stephen Mitchell and Geoffrey Greatrex, 117–50. London: Duckworth, 2000.

Montserrat, Dominic. "Reading Gender in the Roman World." In *Experiencing Rome: Culture, Identity and Power in the Roman World*, edited by Janet Huskinson, 153–82. London: Routledge, 2000.

Moore, Robert I. *The Formation of a Persecuting Society*. 2nd ed. Oxford: Blackwell, 2007.

Moorhead, John. "Italian Loyalties during Justinian's Gothic War." *Byzantion* 53 (1983): 575–96.

—. *Justinian*. London: Longman, 1994.

—. *The Roman Empire Divided, 400-700*. Harlow: Longman, 2001.

—. *Theoderic in Italy*. Oxford: Clarendon, 1992.

—. "Totila the Revolutionary." *Historia* 49 (2000): 382–86.

Morris, Colin. *The Discovery of the Individual*. New York: Harper & Row, 1972.

Moss, Candida R. *The Myth of the Persecution: How Christians Invented a Story of Martyrdom*. New York: HarperOne, 2013.

Muhlberger, Steven. "War, Warlords, and Christian Historians from the Fifth to the Seventh Centuries." In *After Rome's Fall: Narrators and Sources on Early Medieval History, Essays Presented to Walter Goffart*, edited by Alexander C. Murray, 83–98. Toronto: University of Toronto Press, 1998.

Neville, Leonora A. *Heroes and Romans in Twelfth-Century Byzantium*. Cambridge: Cambridge University Press, 2012.

Noble, Thomas F. X., and Thomas Head. "Introduction." In *Soldiers of Christ: Saints and Saints' Lives from Late Antiquity and the Early Middle Ages*, ed. by Thomas F. X. Noble and Thomas Head, xiii–xliv. University Park, PA: Pennsylvania State University Press, 1995.

—, eds. *Soldiers of Christ: Saints and Saints' Lives from Late Antiquity and the Early Middle Ages*. University Park, PA: Pennsylvania State University Press, 1995.

Noreña, Carlos F. "The Ethics of Autocracy in the Roman World." In *A Companion to Greek and Roman Thought*, edited by Ryan K. Balot, 266–79. Oxford: Wiley-Blackwell, 2009.

O'Brian, Bruce. "R. W. Southern, John Boswell and the Sexuality of Anselm." In *The Boswell Thesis: Essays on Christianity, Social Tolerance, and Homosexuality*, edited by Mathew Kuefler, 167–78. Chicago: University of Chicago Press, 2005.

Odahl, Charles M. "The Christian Basilicas of Constantinian Rome." *The Ancient World* 26.1 (1995): 3–28.

O'Flynn, John M. *Generalissimos of the Western Roman Empire*. Edmonton: University of Alberta Press, 1983.

Parnell, David A. "Barbarians and Brothers-in-Arms: Byzantines on Barbarian Soldiers in the Sixth Century." *BZ* 108.2 (2015): 809–26.

—. "The Origins of Justinian's Generals." *Journal of Medieval Military History* 10 (2012): 1–16.

Partner, Nancy F. "No Sex, No Gender." *Speculum* 68 (1993): 419–43.

Paschoud, François. *Eunape, Olympiodore, Zosime: Scripta Minora*. Bari: Edipuglia, 2006.

Pawlak, Marcin. "L'usurpation De Jean (423-425)." *Eos* 90 (2003): 123–45.

Pazdernik, Charles F. "Belisarius' Second Occupation of Rome and Pericles' Last Speech." In *Shifting Genres in Late Antiquity*, edited by Geoffrey Greatrex and Hugh Elton, 207–18. Burlington, VT: Ashgate, 2015.

—. "Procopius and Thucydides on the Labors of War: Belisarius and Brasidas in the Field." *Transactions of the American Philological Association* 130 (2000): 149–87.

—. "The Quaestor Proclus." *GRBS* 55 (2015): 221–49.

Pohl, Walter. "Gender and Ethnicity in the Early Middle Ages." In *Gender in the Early Medieval World: East and West, 300-900*, edited by Leslie Brubaker and Julia M. H. Smith, 23–43. Cambridge: Cambridge University Press, 2004.

—. "Introduction: Ethnicity, Religion, and Empire." In *Visions of Community in the Post-Roman World: The West, Byzantium, and the Islamic World, 300-1100*, edited by Walter Pohl, Clemens Gantner, and Richard E. Payne, 1–23. Farnham: Ashgate, 2012.

Rabieh, Linda R. *Plato and the Virtue of Courage*. Baltimore: Johns Hopkins University Press, 2006.

Rance, Philip. "Narses and the Battle of Taginae (Busta Gallorum) 552: Procopius and Sixth-Century Warfare." *Historia* 54 (2005): 424–72.

Rankov, Boris. "Military Forces." In *The Cambridge History of Greek and Roman Warfare*, edited by Philip Sabin, Hans van Wees, and Michael Whitby, 30–75. Cambridge: Cambridge University Press, 2007.

Rapp, Claudia. "Hellenic Identity, *Romanitas*, and Christianity." In *Hellenisms: Culture, Identity, and Ethnicity from Antiquity to Modernity*, edited by Katerina Zacharia, 127–48. Burlington, VT: Ashgate, 2008.

—. *Holy Bishops in Late Antiquity: The Nature of Leadership in an Age of Transition*. Berkeley, CA: University of California Press, 2005.

—. "Literary Culture under Justinian." In *CCAJ*, edited by Michael Maas, 376–98. Cambridge: Cambridge University Press, 2005.

Reinink, Gerrit Jan. "Pseudo-Methodius: A Concept of History in Response to the Rise of Islam." In *The Byzantine and Early Islamic Near East*, edited by Averil Cameron and Lawrence Conrad, 149–87. Princeton, NJ: Darwin Press, 1992.

Reynolds, Susan. "Our Forefathers? Tribes, Peoples, and Nations in the Historiography in the Age of Migrations." In *Narrators and Sources of Early Medieval History: Essays Presented to Walter Goffart*, edited by Alexander C. Murray, 17–36. Toronto: University of Toronto Press, 1998.

Reydam-Schils, Gretchen J. *The Roman Stoics: Self, Responsibility and Affection*. Chicago: University of Chicago Press, 2005.

Rich, John. "Roman Rituals of War." In *The Oxford Handbook of Classical Warfare*, edited by Brian Campbell and Lawrence Tritle, 542–68. Oxford: Oxford University Press, 2013.

Richlin, Amy. "Not before Homosexuality: The Materiality of the *Cinaedus* and the Roman Law Against the Love Between Men." *JHS* 3 (1993): 523–73.

Ringrose, Kathryn M. *The Perfect Servant: Eunuchs and the Social Construction of Gender in Byzantium*. Chicago: University of Chicago Press, 2003.

Rohrbacher, David. *The Historians of Late Antiquity*. London: Routledge, 2002.

Roisman, Joseph. "The Rhetoric of Courage in the Athenian Orators." In *Andreia: Studies in Manliness and Courage in Classical Antiquity*, edited by Ralph M. Rosen and Ineke Sluiter, 127–43. Leiden: Brill, 2003.

Roques, Denis. *Synésios de Cyrène et la Cyrénaïque du Bas-Empire*. Paris: Editions du Centre national de la recherche scientifique, 1987.

Rosen, Ralph M., and Ineke Sluiter, eds. *Andreia: Studies in Manliness and Courage in Classical Antiquity*. Leiden: Brill, 2003.

—. "General Introduction." In *Andreia: Studies in Manliness and Courage in Classical Antiquity*, edited by Ralph M. Rosen and Ineke Sluiter, 1–24. Leiden: Brill, 2003.

Rousseau, Philip. "Antony as Teacher in the Greek Life." In *Greek Biography and Panegyric in Late Antiquity*, edited by Tomas Hägg and Philip Rousseau, 89–109. Berkeley: University of California Press, 2000.

—. "Bishops." In *Late Antiquity: A Guide to the Postclassical World*, edited by Glenn W. Bowersock, Peter Brown, and Oleg Grabar, 341–43. Cambridge, MA: Belknap Press of Harvard University Press, 1999.

—. "Monasticism." In *CAH*. Vol. 14, *Late Antiquity: Empire and Successors A.D. 425-600*, edited by Averil Cameron, Bryan

Ward-Perkins, and Michael Whitby, 745–80. Cambridge: Cambridge University Press, 2000.

—. "Sidonius and Majorian: The Censure in 'Carmen' V." *Historia: Zeitschrift für Alte Geschichte* 49.2 (2000), 251–57.

Ruse, Michael. *Homosexuality: A Philosophical Inquiry*. Oxford: Blackwell, 1988.

Sacks, Kenneth S. "The Meaning of Eunapius' History." *History and Theory* 25 (1986): 52–67.

Salzman, Michele R. *The Making of a Christian Aristocracy: Social and Religious Change in Western Roman Empire*. Cambridge, MA: Harvard University Press, 2002.

Sandwell, Isabella. *Religious Identity in Late Antiquity: Greeks, Jews, and Christians in Antioch*. Cambridge: Cambridge University Press, 2007.

Sarti, Laury. *Perceiving War and the Military in Early Christian Gaul, A.D. 400-700*. Leiden: Brill, 2013.

Schulenburg, Jane T., *Forgetful of Their Sex: Female Sanctity and Society, ca. 500-1100*. Chicago: University of Chicago Press, 1998.

Scott, Roger. "Chronicles versus Classicizing History: Justinian's West and East." In *Byzantine Chronicles and the Sixth Century*, edited by Roger Scott, 1–25. Burlington, VT: Ashgate, 2012.

Searle, John R. *The Construction of Social Reality*. New York: Free Press, 1997.

Shaw, Brent D. *Sacred Violence: African Christians and Sectarian Hatred in the Age of Augustine*. Cambridge: Cambridge University Press, 2011.

Shean, John F. *Soldiering for God: Christianity and the Roman Army*. Leiden: Brill, 2010.

Sidéris, Georges. "La comédie des castrats, Ammien Marcellin et les eunuques, entre eunocophobie et admiration." *Revue Belge de Philogie et d' Histoire* 78 (2000): 681–717.

Siebigs, Gereon. *Kaiser Leo I. Das oströmische Reich in den ersten drei Jahren seiner Regierung, 457–460*. 2 vols. Berlin: De Gruyter, 2010.

Sivan, Hagith. *Galla Placidia: The Last Roman Empress*. Oxford: Oxford University Press, 2011.

Sizgorich, Thomas. *Violence and Belief in Late Antiquity: Militant Devotion in Christianity and Islam*. Philadelphia, PA: University of Pennsylvania Press, 2009.

Smarnakis, Ioannis. "Rethinking Roman Identity after the Fall (1453)." *Byzantina Symmeikta* 25 (2015).

Smith, Julia M. H. "Introduction: Gendering in the Early Medieval World." In *Gender in the Early Medieval World: East and West, 300-900*, edited by Leslie Brubaker and Julia M. H. Smith, 1–22. Cambridge: Cambridge University Press, 2004.

Smith, Rowland. *Julian's Gods: Religion and Philosophy in the Thought and Action of Julian the Apostate*. London: Routledge, 1995.

Sorachi, Rosario. *Ricerche sui conubia tra Romani e Germani nei secoli IV-VI*. Cantania: Muglia, 1974.

Southern, Pat, and Karen R. Dixon. *The Late Roman Army*. New Haven, CT: Yale University Press, 1996.

Speck, Paul. "Wie dumm darf Zosimos sein?" *BS* 52 (1991): 1–14.

Stein, Edward. *The Mismeasure of Desire: The Science, Theory, and Ethics of Sexual Orientation*. Oxford: Oxford University Press, 1999.

Stein, Ernest. *Histoire du Bas-Empire*. Translated by Jean-Rémy Palanque. Amsterdam: Hakkert, 1968.

Stewart, Michael E. "The *Andreios* Eunuch-Commander Narses: Sign of a Decoupling of Martial Virtues and Hegemonic Masculinity in the Early Byzantine Empire?" *Cerae* 2 (2015): 1–25.

—. "Contests of *Andreia* in Procopius' *Gothic Wars*." Παρεκβολαι 4 (2014): 21–54.

—. "The Dangers of the Soft Life: Manly and Unmanly Romans in Procopius' *Gothic Wars*." *JLA* 10. 2 (2017).

—. "The First Byzantine Emperor? Leo I, Aspar and Challenges of Power and *Romanitas* in Fifth-century Byzantium." *Porphyra* 22 (2014): 4–17.

—. "The Soldier's Life: Early Byzantine Masculinity and the Manliness of War." *Byzantina Symmeikta* 26 (2016): 11–44.

—. "Some Disputes Surrounding Masculinity as a Legitimate Category of Historical Inquiry in the Study of Late Antiquity." *Masculinities: A Journal of Identity and Culture* 1 (2014): 77–91.

Stock, Brian. *The Implications of Literacy: Written Language and Models of Interpretation in the Eleventh and Twelfth Centuries.* Princeton, NJ: Princeton University Press, 1983.

Stoyanov, Yuri. *Defenders and Enemies of the True Cross, The Sasanian Conquest of Jerusalem in 614 and Byzantine Ideology of Anti-Persian Warfare.* Vienna: Verlag der Österreichischen Akademie der Wissenschaften, 2011.

Stouraitis, Ioannis. "Roman Identity in Byzantium: A Critical Approach." *BZ* 107 (2014): 175–220.

Syme, Ronald. *Ammianus and the "Historia Augusta."* Oxford: Clarendon, 1968.

—. "The Composition of the *Historia Augusta*: Recent Theories." *JRS* 62 (1972): 123–33.

Taylor, Rabun. "Two Pathic Subcultures in Ancient Rome." *JHS* 7 (1997): 319–71.

Teale, John. "The Barbarians in Justinian's Armies." *Speculum* 40 (1965): 294–322.

Testa, Rita L. *Senatori, popolo, papi: il governo di Roma al tempo dei Valentiniani.* Bari: Edipuglia, 2004.

Thompson, Edward A. *A History of Attila and the Huns.* Oxford: Clarendon, 1948.

Tinnefeld, Franz. "Prokopios [3]." *Der Neue Pauly* 10 (2001): 391–92.

Tougher, Shaun. "Ammianus and the Eunuchs." In *The Late Roman World and Its Historian: Interpreting Ammianus Marcellinus*, edited by Jan Willem Drijvers and David Hunt, 64–73. London: Routledge, 1999.

—. *The Eunuch in Byzantine History and Society.* New York: Routledge, 2008.

—. "Social Transformation, Gender Transformation? The Court Eunuch, 300–900." In *Gender in the Early Medieval World: East and West, 300-900,* edited by Leslie Brubaker and Julia M. H. Smith, 70–82. Cambridge: Cambridge University Press, 2004.

Treadgold, Warren T. *Byzantium and Its Army, 284-1081.* Stanford CA, 1995.

—. "The Diplomatic Career and Historical Work of Olympiodorus of Thebes." *The International Historical Review* 26 (2004): 709–33.

—. *The Early Byzantine Historians.* New York: Palgrave Macmillan, 2007.

—. *A History of the Byzantine State and Society.* Stanford, CA: Stanford University Press, 1997.

—. "Review of Kathryn Ringrose, The Perfect Servant: Eunuchs and the Social Construction of Gender." *International Journal of the Classical Tradition* 12.3 (2006): 466–69.

Urbainczyk, Theresa. "Observations on the Differences between the Church Histories of Socrates and Sozomen." *Historia* 46 (1997): 355–73.

—. *Socrates of Constantinople.* Ann Arbor, MI: University of Michigan Press, 1997.

—. *Theodoret of Cyrrhus: The Bishop and the Holy Man.* Ann Arbor, MI: University of Michigan Press, 2002.

—. "Vice and Advice in Socrates and Sozomen." In *The Propaganda of Power: The Role of the Panegyric in Late Antiquity,* edited by Mary Whitby, 299–310. Leiden: Brill, 1998.

Van Meter, David. *Handbook of Roman Imperial Coins: A Complete Guide to the History, Types and Values of Roman Imperial Coinage.* Utica, NY: Laurion Press, 1991.

Van Nijf, Onno. "Athletics, *Andreia* and the *Askesis*-Culture in the Roman East." In *Andreia: Studies in Manliness and Courage in Classical Antiquity,* edited by Ralph M. Rosen and Ineke Sluiter, 263–86. Leiden: Brill, 2003.

Viladesau, Richard. *The Beauty of the Cross: The Passion of Christ in Theology and the Arts from the Catacombs to the Eve of the Renaissance*. Oxford: Oxford University Press, 2006.

Vitiello, Massimiliano. *Theodahad: A Platonic King at the Collapse of Ostrogothic Italy*. Toronto: University of Toronto Press, 2014.

Ward-Perkins, Bryan. *The Fall of Rome and the End of Civilisation*. Oxford: Oxford University Press, 2005.

Whately, Conor. *Battles and Generals: Combat, Culture, and Didacticism in Procopius' Wars*. Leiden: Brill, 2016.

—. "Descriptions of Battle in the Wars of Procopius." PhD thesis, University of Warwick, 2009.

—. "The Genre and Purpose of Military Manuals in Late Antiquity." In *Shifting Genres in Late Antiquity*, edited by Geoffrey Greatrex and Hugh Elton, 249–61. Burlington, VT: Ashgate, 2015.

—. "Militarization or Rise of a Distinct Military Culture? The East Roman Ruling Elite in the Sixth Century." In *Warfare and Society in the Ancient Eastern Mediterranean*, edited by Daniel Boatright and Stephen O'Brien, 49–57. Oxford: Archaeopress, 2013.

Whitby, Mary. "Defender of the Cross: George of Pisidia on the Emperor Heraclius and his Deputies." In *The Propaganda of Power: The Role of the Panegyric in Late Antiquity*, edited by Mary Whitby, 247–73. Leiden: Brill, 1998.

Whitby, Michael. "Armies and Society in the Later Roman World." In *CAH*. Vol. 14, *Late Antiquity: Empire and Successors A.D. 425-600*, edited by Averil Cameron, Bryan Ward-Perkins, and Michael Whitby, 469–96. Cambridge: Cambridge University Press, 2000.

—. "*Deus Nobiscum*: Christianity, Warfare and Morale in Late Antiquity." In *Modus Operandi: Essays in Honour of Geoffrey Rickman*, edited by Michel M. Austin, Jill Harries, and Christopher John Smith, 191–208. London: Institute of Classical Studies, University of London, 1998.

—. "Emperors and Armies." In *Approaching Late Antiquity: The Transformation from Early to Late Empire*, edited by Simon Swain and Mark Edwards, 156–86. Oxford: Oxford University Press, 2004.

—. *The Emperor Maurice and His Historian: Theophylact Simocatta on Persian and Balkan Warfare*. Oxford: Oxford University Press, 1988.

—. "Greek Historical Writing after Procopius: Variety and Vitality." In *The Byzantine and Early Islamic Near East: Problems in the Literary Source Material*, edited by Avril Cameron and Lawrence I. Conrad 25–80. Princeton, NJ: Darwin Press, 1992.

—. "Images of Constantius." In *The Late Roman World and Its Historian: Interpreting Ammianus Marcellinus*, edited by Jan Willem Drijvers and David Hunt, 77–88. London: Routledge, 1999.

—. "Recruitment in Roman Armies from Justinian to Heraclius (ca. 565-615)." In *The Byzantine and Early Islamic Near East III: States, Resources, and Armies*, edited by Averil Cameron, 61–124. Princeton, NJ: Darwin Press, 1995.

—. "Religious Views of Procopius and Agathias." *Electrum* 13 (2007): 73–93.

Whittow, Mark. "Early Medieval Byzantium and the End of the Ancient World." *Journal of Agrarian Change* 9.1 (2009): 134–53.

Wildberg, Christian. "Philosophy in the Age of Justinian." In *CCAJ*, edited by Michael Maas, 316–40. Cambridge: Cambridge University Press, 2005.

Wijnendaele, Jeroen W. P. *The Last of the Romans: Bonifatius—Warlord and Comes Africae*. London: Bloomsbury Academic, 2014.

—. "Stilicho, Radagaisus, and the So-Called 'Battle of Faesulae' (406 CE)." *JLA* 9.1 (2016): 267–84.

Williams, Craig A. "The Meanings of Softness: Some Remarks on the Semantics of mollitia." *Eugesta* 3 (2013): 240–63.

—. *Roman Homosexuality: Ideologies of Masculinity in Classical Antiquity.* Oxford: Oxford University Press, 1999.

—. *Roman Homosexuality*, 2nd ed. Oxford: Oxford University Press, 2010.

Williams, Stephen. *Diocletian and the Roman Recovery.* London: Batsford, 1985.

Williams, Stephen, and Gerard Friell. *The Rome That Did Not Fall: The Survival of the East in the Fifth Century.* New York: Routledge, 1999.

—. *Theodosius: The Empire at Bay.* New Haven, CT: Yale University Press, 1994.

Wilson, Brittany E. *Unmanly Men: Refigurations of Masculinity in Luke-Acts.* Oxford: Oxford University Press, 2015.

Wolfram, Herwig. *History of the Goths.* Translated by Thomas J. Dunlap. Berkeley, CA: University of California Press, 1988.

—. *The Roman Empire and Its Germanic Peoples.* Translated by Thomas J. Dunlap. Berkeley, CA: University of California Press, 1990.

Wood, Ian N. *The Merovingian Kingdoms, 450-751.* London: Longman, 1994.

Wood, Philip. "Multiple Voices in Chronicle Sources: The Reign of Leo I (457-474) in Book Fourteen of Malalas." *JLA* 4.2 (2011): 298–314.

Zaccagnino, Cristiana, George Bevan, and Alexander Gabov. "The *Missorium* of Ardaburius Aspar: New Considerations on its Archaeological and Historical Contexts." *Archeologia Classica* 63 (2012): 419–54.

Zuckerman, Constantin. "L 'Empire d' Orient et les Huns: notes sur Priscus." *Travaux et Mémoires* 12 (1994): 160–82.

CREDITS

All images edited by Kismet Press LLP. All images in public domain unless otherwise stated. Those using Creative Commons licenses are republished under their original Creative Commons licenses, with due attribution:

Index

This monograph examines the various ways martial virtues and images of the soldier's life shaped early Byzantine cultural ideals of masculinity. It contends that in many of the visual and literary sources from the fourth to the seventh centuries CE, conceptualisations of the soldier's life and the ideal manly life were often the same. By taking this stance, the book challenges the view found in many recent studies on Late Roman and early Byzantine masculinity that suggest a Christian ideal of manliness based on extreme ascetic virtues and pacifism had superseded militarism and courage as the dominant component of hegemonic masculine ideology. Though the monograph does not reject the relevance of Christian constructions of masculinity for helping one understand early Byzantine society and its diverse representations of masculinity, it seeks to balance these modern studies' often heavy emphasis on "rigorist" Christian sources with the more customary attitudes we find in the secular, and indeed some Christian texts, praising military virtues as an essential aspect of Byzantine manliness. The connection between martial virtues and "true" manliness remained a powerful cultural force in the period covered in this study. Indeed, the reader of this work will find that the "manliness of war" is on display in much of the surviving early Byzantine literature, secular and Christian.

Michael Edward Stewart is an Honorary Fellow in the School of History and Philosophical Inquiry at the University of Queensland. His research focuses on issues of culture, gender, and identity in Late Antiquity. He has published a number of articles on these themes. His most recent paper, "The Danger of the Soft Life: Manly and Unmanly Romans in Procopius' Gothic Wars" will appear in the *Journal of Late Antiquity* in 2017.